REFORMATION STUDIES

ROLAND H. BAINTON

REFORMATION STUDIES

Essays in Honor of

ROLAND H. BAINTON

edited by

FRANKLIN H. LITTELL

✠

JOHN KNOX PRESS
RICHMOND, VIRGINIA

Library of Congress Catalog Card Number: 62-16259

PREFACE

The idea of a *Festschrift* is slowly gaining ground in the American scene. The present volume is written by students peculiarly indebted to Roland H. Bainton of Yale, and its intention is to memorialize that sense of personal and professional obligation. At the same time, it is the rising interest in Reformation studies—Professor Bainton's area of particular concentration—which gives rise to the hope that the studies here published may add to the body of knowledge in a field of Church History as well as give honor to one of its most distinguished practitioners.

The volume is so planned as to give attention both to the classical Reformation and to the often-neglected "Left Wing"—whose personalities, movements, and general significance Dr. Bainton has done so much to rescue from obscurity.

The writers include clergymen, college professors, and seminary faculty members. This too is appropriate, for he to whom we pay tribute has blessed both the people of God and the republic of learning in his ministry.

Special thanks are due to Ruth Woodruff Bainton, for both giving and keeping counsel; to Dr. Raymond P. Morris, for once again giving timely bibliographical assistance to a colleague's students; to the *Historische Kommission für Hessen und Waldeck,* for permission to publish the translation from the Marburg Disputation (pp. 147-167); to members of the editorial staff of John Knox Press, for enthusiasm and meticulous attention to detail. The editor wants to express his gratitude also to Dr. Charles T. Lester, Dean of the Graduate School of Emory University, for direct encouragement to this project, and to Dorothy Anderson and Dorothy Laughbaum for gifted and painstaking secretarial services.

F. H. L.

CONTENTS

Essays on the Left Wing of the Reformation

A BIOGRAPHICAL APPRECIATION

ROLAND H. BAINTON
A Biographical Appreciation

Georgia Harkness

"The history of the world," said Thomas Carlyle, "is but the biography of great men."[1] This volume of essays is dedicated to the honoring of a man who knows the biographies of the great men of the Reformation, and, indeed, of the entire sweep of ecclesiastical history, as few men do. Much of his genius lies in the capacity to make these men of the past—whether the famous great or the little known but significantly contributory figures of the Reformation—come to life for the man of today.

Other essays in this volume will carry forward the knowledge of these great men of the Reformation—Luther, Calvin, Melanchthon, and others—and of the movements they initiated and furthered. The scholarly methods of investigation and presentation stimulated by the study of church history under the man to whom this volume is dedicated will be apparent in these essays. Mine is the less exacting but perhaps no less important task of reminiscing about a great man of the recent past and the living present—Roland Bainton himself.

Already I seem to hear him in his modesty protest. Great? Well, perhaps he will not go down in history alongside of Luther and Calvin. Yet there is more than one kind of greatness. His own careful attention to Reformation figures like Castellio, Butzer, and Hans Denck gives evidence that one does not need to stand at the apex of fame to be worthy of high tribute. And if one accepts Matthew Arnold's definition of greatness as "a spiritual condition worthy to excite love, interest and admiration,"[2] then there can be no question that Roland Bainton is a great man.

It is not my purpose to give a "Who's Who" statement of our friend's *curriculum vitae*. After all, he appears in that eminent and expansive volume; the volume appears in almost every library; the reader can seek it out for himself. History does not consist in the chronological sequence of names and dates, important though it is that these be ac-

curate. (Who has studied under Roland Bainton's direction and not
learned promptly the importance of accuracy as the foundation of
living understanding?) Some events, however, need to be set down
with dates and places as a framework for whatever else will be said.
That they need not be numerous is itself significant, for the fact that
he has spent forty years teaching in one school is a basic reason why
his influence has gone so deep and why this volume of essays is now
being dedicated to him.

Roland Bainton was born in Ilkeston, Derbyshire, England on
March 30, 1894. His father, the Reverend Herbert Bainton, was a
Congregational minister, and the life story of this modest, winsome,
deeply Christian man is delightfully told in Bainton's recent book,
Pilgrim Parson. Roland's stay in England was of short duration, however, for on May 19, 1898, "the day when Gladstone died"[3] (note the
historian speaking!), the family left Ilkeston for Vancouver, B. C. where
his father was to serve another Congregational church. Herbert Bainton was not a man to keep silent on a moral issue, and when the Boer
War broke out he did not hesitate to say publicly that he deplored it.
As a result a faction of superpatriots seceded from his church. When
the war was over, thinking that the dissidents might return if he left,
Herbert Bainton began to look around for another church. This move
brought the family in 1902 to Colfax, Washington, where Roland
grew up.

The relation between Roland and his father was unusually close,
and as one reads the story of the elder Bainton one sees the roots of
Roland's pacifist convictions, his intellectual and personal integrity,
and his outgoing friendliness. But to return to the sequence of events,
Roland attended Whitman College, receiving his A.B. in 1914; went
to Yale Divinity School for his seminary training; received his B.D. in
1917 and his Ph.D. in 1921. This sojourn at Yale was to be of life-long
duration, for since 1920 he has been teaching church history there,
first as an instructor, then in the usual sequence of promotions as as-
sistant and associate professor, and since 1936 as the Titus Street Professor of Ecclesiastical History.

When the first World War broke out, he was faced with the critical
decision which every young man of military age confronts. His decision, based on an even more clear-cut pacifism than his father's, was
to become a member of a Quaker Unit of the American Red Cross.
Since that time he has maintained a close relationship with the Quakers and is both an ordained Congregational minister and an affiliated
member of the Society of Friends. This witness against war and for

constructive measures of international friendship has led him to be a life-long member of the Fellowship of Reconciliation, writing and speaking from this standpoint as occasion required. He and Mrs. Bainton have served as representatives of the American Friends Service Committee, and during the second World War his witness brought reassurance to not a few men in the Civilian Public Service camps.

In 1921 Roland Bainton married Ruth Woodruff. They have five children, Olive, Herbert, Joyce, Cedric, and Ruth. Both Roland and Ruth have a strong sense of the integrity of the Christian family, and Roland with all his busyness about matters of historical scholarship has always had time for his children.

This, in outline, is his life story, save for the fifteen books and scores of articles he has written. His influence as scholar and teacher has brought him a number of honorary degrees, of which perhaps the most rewarding was the one in 1948 from the University of Marburg which has the oldest Protestant seminary in Europe. This catalogue of events is relatively brief, as the lives of great men go, but it reflects a life rich in service and unique in its achievements.

I first became acquainted with Roland Bainton in the fall of 1928. In applying for a Sterling Fellowship at Yale I needed to have a subject. More for this prudential reason than because of any consuming initial interest, I set myself the task of probing the ethics of John Calvin to test the validity of Max Weher's thesis as to the bearing of Calvinism on the spirit of capitalism. In retrospect I realize how presumptuous was this attempt, for I knew too little about church history and less about Calvin. That it finally eventuated in the book *John Calvin: the Man and His Ethics*—my one excursion into Reformation history—was due more to Bainton's encouragement and discipline than to anything else.

Encouragement and discipline I link together advisedly, as I believe anyone must who has ever studied with Professor Bainton. In spite of my having been awarded the fellowship, which committed me to the project, he would have been justified in casting me out the first week. Perhaps he wanted to! But he did not. He showed me patiently, and without any visible martyr's complex, where to begin and how to go at it. He enrolled me in his seminar in Reformation history, and I have memories that few if any of the other contributors to this volume have, for it met then in his office in the old building in downtown New Haven. I may confess in retrospect to a few qualms as to the propriety of a woman's going up to the second floor of a man's dormitory to get to class! But there seemed no alternative, and since nobody else seemed to make any fuss about it, I decided I had better not raise the issue.

I do not remember all that I heard in that small, darkish, book-lined room. Yet I recall vividly the scholarly information, marvelously detailed and enlivened with humor and the touch of down-to-earthness, that poured forth from the teacher's lips. It came faster than I could write it down, but enough "stuck" for Calvin, Farel, Beza, Castellio, Servetus, and other figures of those dramatic days to come alive for me. From then on, the long hours and many weeks spent with the dusty folios of the *Calvini Opera* in the semidarkness of the dungeon-like stacks of the old library had a purpose. I cannot say there was no drudgery about it, but the drudgery was redeemed by an interest that made it worthful.

When I began writing up my findings, I was soon to discover the scholar's rigor. Nothing was to be affirmed on the basis of memory or of general impressions. Every reference must not only be stated but must be checked and double-checked. The relevant contemporary sources must be consulted. Calvin's French was easy reading for me, but if I needed to read German, in which I was much lamer, then I must read it. Universally the students of Bainton's whom I have known have witnessed to this rigorous scholarship. If one did not wish to work, and to work long and carefully, sometimes in foreign languages, then one had better not elect his seminars.

This discipline the professor required not only of his students but of himself. At the time I studied with him he had published nothing except some articles and historical monographs, but was working on the heretics of the Reformation. When I protested that the great wisdom he had already amassed ought to be put into a book, he said he had not yet had time to read all the sources. I well recall (I wonder if he does!) his reply when I tried as gently as possible to suggest that this wisdom might never get into print, "I have resolved not to go up in an airplane or to go swimming alone until this is finished." One of his colleagues, who like myself was inclined to publish without waiting to read everything, deplored Bainton's "passion for perfection" as depriving the world of knowledge it ought to be getting. I cannot say whether the resolution above stated has been maintained to the present in regard to other projects, but the material I wanted him to publish in 1929 did appear in 1951 in *The Travail of Religious Liberty*.

It is evidence both of Bainton's self-discipline and of his facility in learning that he is an accomplished linguist. I was astonished to discover that whenever there seemed to be important material to be delved into in any language not familiar to him, he proceeded to learn it. I cannot say how many he now reads and speaks, for he has kept on acquiring more. This linguistic ability has been a great asset not only in historical research but also in his contacts with foreign students, who again and again have been made to feel befriended and welcome through his ability to speak their native tongue.

Probably the best known of Bainton's books are his Abingdon award-winning life of Martin Luther, *Here I Stand,* and *The Church of Our Fathers,* written originally for children and young people but widely read by adults. Others which indicate the range of his interests are a life of George Lincoln Burr; *Hunted Heretic,* a life of Michael Servetus, who was burned for heresy in Geneva in 1553; *The Martin Luther Christmas Book,* consisting of excerpts from Luther's sermons on the nativity; *The Reformation of the Sixteenth Century; The Age of the Reformation; Yale and the Ministry;* and as evidence of a deep concern for Christian family life, *What Christianity Says About Sex, Love and Marriage.* His most recent volume is *Christian Attitudes Toward War and Peace.* In each of these, whatever its theme, the historian and the Christian in Bainton speak with clarity. Almost as if in reciprocity for his own wide familiarity with other languages than English, several of these works have been translated. Publications abroad are in a number of languages—German, French, Italian, Spanish, Japanese, and modern Greek.

A quality which appears in both the teaching and the writing of Roland Bainton is his unusual skill in phrasing. With a rare facility for finding just the right word or image or turn of the sentence, he makes what some would regard as the dead past come to life, the most technical material readable. When others popularize it is often to oversimplify and to sacrifice substance if not truth for the sake of journalistic clarity and liveliness. This Bainton never does. Yet anyone with no previous knowledge of Luther can read *Here I Stand* and come away from it with much more knowledge than before, not only of Luther but of the crosscurrents of the Reformation. For the same reason it is not strange that *The Church of Our Fathers* is one of the most widely used of Bainton's books.

Opening this at random for an illustrative sample I find an item not hitherto known to me, and possibly not to some readers of this volume. I shall quote it at some length to indicate the author's sly humor and lightness of touch alongside of his historical knowledge. In explaining the provisions of the Benedictine rule and the characteristic requirements of monastic life he tells how noon came to be so called:

The hour of noon used to be at 3:00 in the afternoon. "Noon" comes from the Latin word *nona* which means the ninth hour. Counting from 6:00 that would be 3:00 in the afternoon. The monks were required to wait until "noon" for dinner. They could not change the rule, but they did move up the hour. That is why noon is now at 12:00. The monks ate in perfect silence while one of their number, who had already eaten, read to them from some good book. If a monk desired anything at the table, he was directed to ask for it by signs, as, for example: for an apple, "put thy thumb in thy fist, and close thy hand and move afore thee to and fro"; for milk, "draw thy left little finger in the manner of milking"; for mustard, "hold thy nose in the upper part of thy right fist, and rub it"; for salt, "flip with thy right thumb and thy forefinger over the left thumb." After dinner came naps; then work again in the fields; at sundown, evensong and bed, with the young monks sandwiched between the old to prevent any scuffle.[4]

It is not alone the author's skill in phrasing, touches of humor, or an eye for pungent detail that makes these books interesting. They are illustrated with a marvelous collection of early and often contemporary woodcuts which over the years he has gathered from various sources. Some are humorous; others are simply illustrative of characteristic activities. Some are intricate and show high artistry; others are meaningful in their plainness. A few of them attempt to make graphic the intricacies of theology, as, for example, one which portrays the Godhead and the four evangelists in the attempt to make clear what the Trinity is and is not. A fair sample is those which accompany the passage quoted above: a monk cutting down a tree while another figure is perched precariously at the top of it hacking out the upper branches; a friar out with his net catching blackbirds for the monastery table; another devoutly reading at the lectern. Turn the page, and one sees a tonsured monk teaching equally tonsured children. Illuminated initials demonstrate how the letter Q is made into an artistic design showing the monks occupied in log splitting or in harvesting.

Most of these illustrations are woodcuts. But not all; some are line drawings made by the author. And this brings us to another of Roland Bainton's remarkable talents—his ability to draw and sketch, even to the making of cartoons and caricatures. Though I studied with him only one year, I have long known him as a colleague in a theological discussion group meeting twice a year, first at New Haven and then at Washington. (This group used to be known as "the younger theologians" until with the advance of the years this term became highly anachronistic!) Many a time I have seen him busy with his pen or pencil while a more loquacious brother went on at length defending the truth. Taking notes? Doubtless he was taking note of all that was going on, for his subsequent observations so indicated. But what his fingers were doing was drawing a picture, accenting the most salient and not always the most complimentary features of the speaker.

This talent was put to rich use in his happy relations with his children. Anyone who has visited the former Bainton home at Woodbridge will recall the lovely Heidi murals, painted by him all over the walls of the basement as the children were growing up. I do not recall their details—only the impression that any child would be fortunate to have this kind of locus of activities provided by this kind of father. One who has had even a marginal contact with this active, merry, wholesome family has recognized the close-knit nature of its bonds.

This skill in line drawing is evident also in *Pilgrim Parson*. Not only are the Bainton ministerial forebears—six of them in two generations —sketched in pen and ink, but one sees "the Americanization of Herbert Bainton" as he learns to peel apples for canning and run the old style washing machine, Father reading poetry as in successive stages he falls asleep in his chair, Father weeding and digging and thus maintaining his deep-seated British love of a garden.

What is lacking in this book, though whether it is extant elsewhere I have no knowledge, is a picture of Roland Bainton himself on his bicycle! Encased in an enveloping tarpaulin to shield both man and bicycle from the rain, he rides to and from his classes in scorn of weather. The dust jacket of *Pilgrim Parson* says of its author, "He is an incorrigible individualist who persists in riding a bicycle twenty miles a day (he insists that he likes it); a water-colorist and caricaturist; and a do-it-yourselfer 'who enjoys fixing everything in the home with the exception of major plumbing.'"

One of his devoted former students has given me a word picture not only of the tarpaulin-clad bicycle but of Professor Bainton transporting a mattress on the same bicycle with equipoise. The do-it-yourself item gains concreteness from another who has told me of calling at his home in the country and finding him alternating between the labors of cleaning the septic tank and preparing the index for *Here I Stand*. And as for individualism, the class arrived in the seminar room one day to find him lying on the floor with a handkerchief over his eyes. Dead? A stroke, or some other serious illness? By no means. Just an early arrival with a little leisure for an extra bit of rest!

Such items may indicate that Bainton is "a character." He is a lovable, scholarly, deeply Christian character. For forty years he has poured himself not only into historical research and writing but into his students. Few if any have ever studied closely with him without feeling themselves not only better informed and better instructed but better men and women for his outgoing friendliness and the warmth of his personality. Had he written nothing at all in his "passion for perfection," his would still have been a great life, worthy of the tribute being paid to him by the contributions to scholarship appearing in this volume.

Roland Bainton has taught, and written, and lived in a crucial epoch of the twentieth century, and in so doing he has touched the lives and quickened the minds of an innumerable host of persons. Because of him large segments of human life—in the family, in the church, in the nation, and around the world—have been stirred to greater wisdom and to finer living. Such a contribution is indisputable evidence that one need not thrust himself into the limelight in order to shed the light of Christian truth and love toward ever widening horizons.

ESSAYS ON LUTHER

Faith and Knowledge in Luther's Theology

N. Arne Bendtz

Luther's theologizing is not without its presupposition. It is tied to the Christian doctrines and the traditions of the Church. Now, if this doctrinal substance should be at variance with the premises he had reached through the inference of reason and experience, where should the highest authority be placed? Has faith priority over knowledge or knowledge over faith? Or are they related to each other in such a way that a conflict between them is only an expression of man's beclouded creatureliness? These questions are crucial to a true understanding of Luther's theology. In spite of the fact that Luther often has been called an "anti-intellectualist," it is the aim of this paper to show that Luther operates in his thinking both as a philosophical realist and as a religious fideist. Is this radical contrariness of the realist and the fideist elements actually resolved in Luther? *No.* But it is continually being mediated. It is mediated by Christ. In him the human realm and the divine realm coexist. Christ affirms both realms as God and man. God, as the creative word, is of the same fabric with man, and our experience is identical with the reality of God's being; the difference here is one of degree alone. But Christ is also transcendent, of one substance with the Father, the redemptive word. God is here totally different from the structure of the life of man and man's own understanding of it. Thus, in Christ both realism and fideism are to be affirmed as valid.

I. Luther—the Realist

Often Luther asserts that man has a certain knowledge of God. This knowledge of God has a certain ontological basis. He does not object to an investigation of reason in this field. On a few occasions he gives a rational demonstration of the existence of God. From the beauty and order of the universe man can by inferences know of the existence of the Creator.[1] His eternal power and Godhead are known by the benefits bestowed by him. The law of mutual assistance rules in creation. Men as well as animals mutually assist each other. But the opposite is also true. The stronger oppresses the weaker. But "there exists in the world the highest being who is exalted over all and assists all."[2]

This affirmation of man's knowledge of God is an eclipsed heritage from the ancestors.[3] A pious father must have taught his children to pray to God at the rising of the sun and to return thanks for such a marvelous and miraculous light, illuminating and sustaining everything. But the idolatrous children must have addressed their prayers to the sun itself.[4]

The idea that the reality of God can be understood by his works is repeated over and over again. He elaborates greatly on this subject in his commentary on the Epistle of Paul to the Romans. God's invisible qualities, the Godhead, the eternal power, have been made visible to all men. This is evident from the worship of all men through the ages. Man by making himself idols acknowledges that he believes in an immortal power who is able to help him. "They have the idea of God in their hearts."[5] If man has no substantial knowledge of who God is, he would not be able to have a consciousness of a divine reality. Man knows that the Deity is powerful, wise, righteous, good, and merciful towards those who invoke him. Consequently, this knowledge must have been given man by God.

In Luther's exposition of the prophet Jonah, he stresses the fact that the world knows and reason perceives that God is exalted and superior to all. This is demonstrated by the invocation of God by all pagan religions. So when Epicurus and Plinus deny the existence of God, they behave like fools by plugging their ears and covering their eyes to escape from hearing and seeing. They forcibly darken their understanding, but in spite of it they cannot escape the light in their troubled consciences. Man knows that God can save him from all evil. "This natural light of reason extends so far that it perceives God as good, gracious, and merciful. It is a great light."[6]

Not much weight is attached to the stringency of the demonstration of this natural knowledge of God. Luther reckons with an inherent God-consciousness in the nature of man in line with the general ideas of Scholasticism.[7] Man knows by analogical inferences that God exists, that he has created the world, rules man's destiny, and bestows all good gifts.[8] Because of this knowledge of God, man also knows that it is his duty to worship God. Thus the commandments of the decalogue and the commandment of worship have both been inscribed in man's soul.

It is indeed interesting to observe how far Luther sometimes can go in recognizing man's knowledge of God unaided by revelation. It is raised above all doubts that man's knowledge leads him to the acceptance of the existence of God. Man's knowledge is in principle a true knowledge and a true idea of God. Man knows that God is gracious and merciful and that all good things come from him. All pagan religions have basically a true conception of God.[9]

Man's knowledge of God goes so far that man knows what God is in himself. The meaning of this formulation is that man perceives God's eternal power and his metaphysical properties.[10] Man, unaided by faith, has a true metaphysical knowledge of God. The philosophers are right in their rational development of God as the Lord of all things. They discuss and treat God and Providence very skillfully.[11]

Man's knowledge of God includes the awareness of the will of God. To this moral awareness, God presents himself as a relentless demanding Will who recompenses according to deserts. This knowledge is applied in temporal things. It leads to the best in political and civil affairs. It possesses great discernment in all temporal things.[12] This knowledge is based upon experience. Here truth consists in the agreement and conformity of the fact of God with man's intellectual perception. Man's soul receives impression by the senses of the outward and visible facts of God. The intellect through abstraction creates the concepts. These concepts are the substantial forms, or beings, that dwell in the particular thing. Consequently, Luther is here a typical realist, i.e., the universal is according to its nature before the particular. But his process of knowledge is reversed, i.e., from the particular to the universal.

II. Luther—the Fideist

According to Harnack,[13] Luther asserted no antagonism between faith and knowledge in the realm of revelation. His attack was not directed against the operation of reason as an aid to knowledge but against reason in the sense of work righteousness. But the antagonism between faith and knowledge in Luther is not limited to a dismissal of knowledge insofar as it revolts against the doctrine of salvation through faith. Luther, during his whole career, asserted a radical antagonism between faith and knowledge. More than once he expresses himself in the sense that faith would lose its unique quality in proportion to the degree in which it was based upon knowledge. It belongs to the concept of faith that it is contrary to human knowledge. Faith is not needed if knowledge has been attained.[14] Faith is never based upon knowledge, but upon obedience to God's Word.

There are all conceivable degrees of contrast between faith and knowledge. The contrast can be formulated thus: Man never knows God's will toward him.[15] Man cannot know the love which made God send his Son to the world for its salvation. Nor can human knowledge vanquish the anxiety of conscience and fear of death.[16] Therefore, knowledge must be mortified, its eyes pricked out. Knowledge must be beaten down by acts wrought by faith to overcome the contempt of God, to purge unbelief and grumbling over his wrath.[17] Faith yields to God's Word, even though human knowledge considers it foolish and absurd. Faith receives the message that he who wants to appease God must believe in the Son who suffered on the cross. But human knowledge, in terms of a moral sense, objects: Have I then labored to no profit? Here the radical antagonism and enmity between faith and knowledge is expressed.

The antagonism of knowledge to faith in terms of the incapacity of man to enter into the mind of God and to conceive how God could humble himself and suffer is also asserted in other contexts. Human knowledge cannot perceive the reason for the existence of sin. Nor can it comprehend why death is to be inflicted as punishment of sin. It is absurd and preposterous that sentence should be passed over acts and deeds which men are driven to by an inescapable necessity. Human knowledge blames the potter for the bad result and not the earthen vessels.[18]

Human knowledge is unable to enter into the mind of God and find salvation. In spite of this fact it is "very presumptuous and dashes along like a blind horse." It takes cobwebs to weave garments, sand to bake bread. It measures air with spoons and transports light in cups. It sows the wind and reaps the whirlwind.[19]

Human knowledge cannot concretely assimilate the truth of faith. It has not the ability to draw the practical consequences. It cannot trust in God's care. For faith receives everything from God's hand— adversity, prosperity, life, death, heaven, and hell.[20] Here the antagonism between faith and knowledge is of a practical sort. Human knowledge cannot digest the thoughts of faith in a living way. It faces a stone wall in God's mysterious dealings in life. It cannot comprehend why the Son of God should be victorious by suffering and dying or why and how man is to be brought to God through the inferno of tribulations and humiliation of spirit.[21]

From a rational point of view, many of the Christian doctrines are preposterous. They contain contradictions and proclaim things over and above human knowledge. At this point Luther, the fideist, is in open conflict with Luther, the realist. He asserts that the attempts of the higher schools to arrive at an understanding of the concepts have led to miserable results in the field of religion. The learned concepts do not make man wiser. The efforts of Scholasticism to comprehend the mystery of the person of Christ have not brought the church closer to the truth, nor have they given added clarity to the subject. In spite of these ideas, Luther, on other occasions, makes use of the whole learned apparatus of Scholasticism.

There are articles of faith in Holy Writ that have been placed above human knowledge by God. They are the doctrines of the Trinity, the Incarnation, the sacraments, regeneration through baptism, resurrection of the body.[22] Believers are not "such ducks and geese" that they are not aware of the contradiction involved in the doctrine of the three separate persons in the divine Being. "God is One . . . and yet there exists with God, the Son and the Holy Spirit. We must let God himself answer how his unity can be preserved under these circumstances."[23]

Furthermore, the contradiction between faith and knowledge is obvious regarding the doctrine of the person of Christ. God is eternal, yet he is dead. "It must be the Devil and his Mama." A man, Jesus, created heaven and earth. These are the logical consequences of the doctrine of the two natures of Christ. They lead to inescapable contradictions which nonetheless must be accepted.[24]

The skill of logic employed by human knowledge leads to wrong results when applied to faith. A conclusion drawn upon two true premises may be wrong. All of the Divine essence is in the Father. The Son is of the Divine essence. Consequently, the Son is the Father. But this conclusion would not be dogmatically correct. The majesty of the subject renders it impossible to master the dogmatic questions with the skill of logic. Luther does not elaborate in detail concerning the use of logic in the field of theology. But logic must be rejected if it leads to statements that are contrary to the doctrines of Holy Scripture. By pursuing the path of human knowledge, Karlstadt has laid waste the whole realm of faith. By drawing the conclusion that man receives only bread in Holy Communion, and that Christ's body is now located in heaven, he dashes into the Scriptures with unwashed feet.[25]

It is absolutely necessary in the divine-human relationship that a Word should be given that surpasses human knowledge. Adam and Eve had a true knowledge of God in Paradise, but in spite of it God gave them a divine Word above human knowledge "which it was necessary to embrace in faith," i.e., the Word concerning the tree of knowledge.[26] This Word also became the source of temptation. All temptations begin by the attempt of human knowledge "without the Word to interpret God and the Word of God." It is as fruitless to comprehend God by sheer human knowledge as it is to overarch the heavens with one's fingers. Regarding the articles of faith, human knowledge is unable to handle the subject and only the appropriation of faith is fitting.[27]

Man must submit himself under the revealed and spoken Word. He must act in faith that God's Word is true although it may seem foolish. By following his own knowledge he cannot hear God's speech, but only his own muttering. Critical knowledge admits that God is too high for man. Thus it is foolish to strive after knowledge of God, apart from God's speech to men in Christ.[28] It is fruitless to torment oneself with morbid broodings and speculations to reach the divine realm. Human knowledge cannot encompass it. But the articles of faith have been given in Holy Writ. And they must be received as they have been written. The articles of faith are true and real although they cannot be handled by human knowledge.

The antagonism between faith and knowledge cannot be overcome by another kind of knowledge of faith. The conflict between faith and knowledge concerning the doctrine of incarnation is not mitigated by the growth of faith. To be sure, the growth of faith can strengthen the trust on God's promise. But the absurdity of faith remains antagonistic to human knowledge.[29]

Luther, indeed, refutes the use of human knowledge in his affirmation about God and his will toward men. God is totally different from the structure of the life of man and man's own understanding of it. Therefore human knowledge is incapable of entering into the mind of God and of conceiving how God could humble himself and suffer. Hence, God is beyond and above anything that man can experience. He is the totally Other.

III. How Are Faith and Knowledge Co-ordinated in Luther?

The relationship between faith and knowledge was intensely discussed during the Middle Ages. To a large extent Luther seems to move within the framework of Scholasticism. Like Thomas Aquinas he assigns the highest authority to faith. A proposition contrary to revelation is false. God's metaphysical properties are accessible to human knowledge. But there are mysteries which human knowledge cannot fathom. "It is impossible to attain to the knowledge of the

Trinity by natural reason. . . . By natural reason we can know of God only that which of necessity belongs to Him as the cause of all things, and we have used this as a fundamental principle in treating of God. Now, the creative power of God is common to the whole Trinity; and hence it belongs to the unity of the essence, and not to the distinction of persons. Therefore, by natural reason we can know what belongs to the unity of the essence, but not what belongs to the distinction of the persons."[30]

Luther, on one occasion, mentions that the Trinity is mirrored in the nature of things.[31] Generally speaking, he is in agreement with Thomas Aquinas regarding faith and knowledge. However, there is an important difference. In Thomas, faith and reason are co-ordinated through a rational synthesis based upon the doctrine of *analogia entis*. There is no conflict between faith and knowledge but the latter must be subordinated to the former. Human knowledge is an implement in the service of faith, showing the groundlessness of objections to revealed doctrines. Luther is more cautious, and would tend to say that human knowledge is not capable of clarifying what is meant by analogy. The problem is whether the likeness of God is a matter of degree or a matter of quality. Because of the qualitative difference, Luther is forced to either one or the other of the extremes, either faith or knowledge. Thus to Luther, radical analysis shows that faith and knowledge are the two basic categories of predication. Can this radical contrariness of faith and knowledge be resolved? Thomas attempted to resolve it by a rational synthesis. This is not possible for Luther. Luther resolves the problem by mediation. It is mediated by Christ. In him the human realm and the divine realm coexist. Christ affirms both realms as true God and true man. Both faith and knowledge are to be affirmed as valid.

They are held together by the form of Christ. This form is a sacrificial-sacramental structure and it shows Luther where and in what respect he can use faith and where human knowledge must be the controlling factor. But faith and knowledge coexist and can be separated only by an abstraction. They intermingle in the elements of every event in the life of the believer. Thus Luther operates with a new type of analogical method which is enlightened to the fact that it is in reality a coexistence of faith and knowledge—not an analogy of being but an analogy of existence.

To Luther it is obvious that human nature has an inherent consciousness of God, and he is of the conviction that the order and beauty of creation point to the Creator. But he also continually emphasizes that human knowledge cannot acknowledge the way of salvation by faith. It is the moral consciousness of man that rebels against the idea of a salvation by faith without meritoriousness and worthiness. Even though, from a logical point of view, it could be shown that the doctrine of forgiveness does not contain objectionable elements, it is still over and above human knowledge. No one can find the divine forgiveness for Christ's sake without a sure word from God himself. Nature, history, man's inner being, testify to something quite different than to divine grace. Nothing in experience lends support to faith in God's mercy. No skill of logic is able to disclose it. Only through the Word is it unveiled.

Faith employs theoretical judgment. But these theoretical judgments are procured independently of analogical inferences and human experience. However, the notion of God is a part of human experience. In spite of this right notion of God, man localizes God's revelation incorrectly. Human knowledge cannot by itself find or appropriate it. Therefore a knowledge of another dimension must be laid bare. For this reason, human knowledge, without the clear Word of God regarding the need of a mediator, is sheer darkness. The new knowledge comes through the gospel. This is a new light. This is not a new logic but new thoughts. Man must accept what God in his gospel communicates about himself. Human knowledge provides information about the visible life, the earthly life. But man is directed to God's Word for true knowledge of God and the eternal life. This opens a new field of knowledge which does not correspond to the domains of human knowledge.

However, this religious knowledge is in a certain sense co-ordinated with other branches of knowledge. Faith is not an atheoretical act. Luther does not separate faith and knowledge and place them on different levels in the sense that faith should just be a practical act. All truths mutually harmonize, although the same proposition might not be true in all the various branches of science. That the Word became flesh cannot possibly be true in the field of human knowledge. But it is true in the science of theology. The knowledge of faith enters into conflict with the rules of human knowledge. And human knowledge collides with the valid rules of faith. Even in the other branches of science examples can be found that what is true in one science is not necessarily valid in the other. That moisture is moist is true in the science of meteorology, but it is obviously not true in the science of fire. This exhibition of parallels regarding the contradiction between the knowledge of faith and human knowledge would be senseless if

Luther did not hold that the articles of faith were a kind of knowledge as well as the propositions of human knowledge.[32]

The truth communicated by Holy Writ is a kind of knowledge like the other branches of science. But Luther *only indirectly* discusses the nature and the co-ordination of this knowledge to other branches of knowledge. Although it is not directly based upon experience and cannot be logically demonstrated, and although it is only uncovered through the divine self-disclosure, the two kinds of knowledge are mediated in terms of the form of Christ. The form of Christ is related to wholeness of the believer's existence who lives at the same time in the realms of human knowledge and faith knowledge. This form is a *sacrificial-sacramental structure*. This structure is the God-engendered means whereby the tension of the full reality in man's existence between the abiding power of *hybris* and faith knowledge, concerning the forgiveness of sin, is maintained. Grace, therefore, is both God's knowledge of man's desperate situation and also his power to help. In this process the believer is forced into the form of Christ, a life in continual conflict with the desperate situation of *hybris*. God permits *hybris* to remain in the world as a fire that never goes out to keep the believer dependent upon God's mercy through which God's mighty actions are revealed. Therefore the form of Christ is God's medium through which he forces the believer into experiences of *intellectual,* physical, spiritual insufficiency for which there is absolutely no provision or help to be had from man-made resources in terms of human knowledge, but only from God, which necessitates faith knowledge.

Finally, we raise the question again. Is the radical contrariness of faith knowledge and human knowledge resolved in Luther? *No.* But it is being mediated. It is mediated by Christ. In him the human realm and the divine realm coexist. Christ affirms both realms as God and man. Christ is both immanent, of one substance with men in terms of the creative Word, and transcendent, of one substance with the Father in terms of the redemptive Word. Both faith knowledge and human knowledge are to be affirmed as valid. They coexist in every element of every event in the existence of the believer. And so a new type of analogical method is actually practiced by Luther which is enlightened to the fact that it is in reality a coexistence of faith knowledge and human knowledge, not an analogy of being but an analogy of existence.

A Reasonable Luther

Robert H. Fischer

As is very well known, Luther called reason a nasty, nasty word. Forthwith the friends of reason have taken counsel together. Some have determined never to speak to the cad again. Some would wash out his mouth with soap and demand an apology. Some would institute a libel suit. Others sigh at Luther's one-sidedness, but urge that a reconciliation be worked out, feeling that the two would make such a handsome couple.

Perhaps if we understood Luther better, we might find that he is not an irrationalist, not even irrational, not even particularly unreasonable.

There are a number of reasons why it is often difficult for Luther's theology to get a reasonable hearing in the Anglo-Saxon world. The most elemental rebuff comes from what we may call the "What-else-can-you-expect?" school. What reasonable theology can you expect from a German peasant so uncouth as to say, "If God commanded me to eat dung, I would do it"?[1] Or so superstitious as to fling ink bottles at devil apparitions? Or so bullheadedly dogmatic as to refuse Zwingli's gentlemanly handclasp at Marburg, or to assert that if God should declare two and five are eight, "then I would believe it against my reason"? What can you expect from a man who, as Lord Vansittart, Dean Inge, and Thomas Mann assure us, is the ancestor of Nazism?

Secondly there is the "Anybody-knows" school. Why take this man's theology seriously? Anybody knows that man has a genuine free will, and that if sin is the diametrical opposite of goodness, it is nonsense to say that the best men sin in their best works. Anybody knows that a body can't be in two places at the same time. The law can't be both the holy, good gift of God, and the tyrannical enemy of God, at the same time. Why take this man seriously, moreover, when one can prove *anything* from him? We may tolerate paradoxes, if necessary, but must we put up with provoking contradictions and pathetic inconsistencies? The late Anglican scholar, H. Maynard Smith, used to quip that it is not difficult to understand any one of Luther's writings,

unless one compares it with any of his other writings! A sparkling epi-
gram, no doubt, but a sophomoric judgment.

If all one needs is an excuse to ignore Luther's theology, these
will do. Of course, these reasons are beneath the dignity of scholarship. But one can find scholarly reasons for quickly disposing of
Luther's theology. To a modern epistemologist, Luther is irrational.
To a practical churchman, he is irrelevant. To a systematician, he is
irresponsible.

The late Douglas Clyde Macintosh was an extreme spokesman for
the epistemological dismissal of Luther. Satisfied of the "impartiality
and reasonableness of God," Macintosh needs to waste no words on
Luther, nor for that matter on Calvin. He does waste many words on
their sons Kierkegaard, Barth, Tillich, and others, but in the end he
uses a convenient Dispos-all for the whole plate of garbage: "Reac-
tionary Irrationalism."[2]

How does one account for the complacent way in which Anglo-
Saxon scholars dismiss Luther in the realm of practical churchman-
ship? Well, he is German: irrelevant for *us*. Secondly, once Ernst
Troeltsch has convinced us that Luther's theology and ethic are essentially medieval, it is unreasonable for us to take them seriously.
Again, earnest moralists often fear that Luther (like St. Paul) ignores
or undermines morality. Wesley, you recall, accused Luther of "a total
ignorance with regard to sanctification."[3] In the same way, strenuous
empiricists fear that Luther was too dogmatic or mystical to respect
common sense. The net effect of these charges, in solo or in concert,
is that Luther's thought is quite irrelevant for our modern church
and public life.

From the systematician's point of view, we often hear it said con-
descendingly: Luther just wasn't much of a thinker. This was the
implication of A. C. McGiffert's *Protestant Thought Before Kant*.[4]
Today students read in Norman Sykes' *The Crisis of the Reformation*
that defective education and limited learning made Luther ill-
equipped to frame a new system of sound doctrine, nor did his polem-
ics with the radicals "produce a state of intellectual calm suitable to
the careful pondering of fundamental theological questions."(!)[5]

Here then we have three scholarly methods, to name no more, for
bringing Luther to trial for his attitude toward reason. Three methods,
with a common result: the easy disposal of Luther's theology.

A funny thing, though. Luther's theology has a way of not staying
disposed of. This the historian can prove from recent books by the
Protestant Heinrich Bornkamm and the Roman Catholics Adolf Herte

and Ernst Zeeden, who have traced the compulsion of age upon age to wrestle with this Luther's thought. This the theologian can corroborate, for example, if he is alive to present-day ecumenical thinking, especially Faith and Order discussions. For the churchman and the social thinker, too, signs are emerging that Luther's practical thought may yet yield some surprisingly creative insights.

Suppose we ask ourselves, then: How reasonable is Luther?

In a sense, this is a very unreasonable way to state the question. It may imply that reason is the maiden and Luther the suitor. But convinced as he is that the damsel is no Lily Maid, Luther no doubt would hardly thank anyone for appointing himself to the role of go-between. Again, the question may imply that reason is the judge and Luther the defendant. But this is a part of the problem to be solved, not an axiom to be assumed at the beginning.

On the other hand, since my intentions here are modest, I shall allow the question to stand. I shall confine myself in this essay to an apologetic against the charge that Luther's theology is consciously irrational or unconsciously unreasonable and inconsistent, and an intimation that he is still very much worth listening to in his own terms.

II

Against the authority of Church and empire at Worms Luther took his stand. The significant thing there is not the assertion that he stood upon his conscience, but the question of what his conscience stood upon.

According to his well-known statement, it appealed to Scripture and reason: "Unless convinced by testimonies of the scriptures or by clear reason, I will not recant!"[6] Doesn't this show clearly that for Luther, as for the Middle Ages in general, Scriptures and reason are the twin sources of authority? The answer is no. Many years ago Hans Preuss subjected Luther's formula to critical scrutiny.[7] To summarize Preuss briefly and a little too simply, Luther viewed the term *ratio* in three ways: (1) Reason as logical method; this Luther unhesitatingly approved. He had to use it in the oftener-than-weekly disputations at the university. In his controversies with Erasmus and Zwingli, Luther frequently argued not that his opponents were too rational, but that they were not rational enough!—guilty of defective logic and even misunderstanding of grammar. In many instances he makes good his point; in others he is less convincing. But in any case, such a procedure belies the charge that Luther shrank from or flouted reason as a tool of argumentation. (2) Reason as the presupposition and the normative principle of all social and cultural life. Here the term includes what we would call "common sense." This too he approved, freely acknowledging the wisdom of Aristotle, and for that matter Aesop, in this realm.

> And it is certainly true that reason is the most important and the highest in rank among all things and, in comparison with other things of this life, the best and something divine. It is the inventor and mentor of all the arts, medicine, law, and of whatever wisdom, power, virtue, and glory men possess in this life. By virtue of this fact it ought to be named the essential difference by which man is distinguished from the animals and other things. Holy Scripture also makes it lord over the earth, birds, fish, and cattle, saying, "Have dominion." That is, that it is a sun and a kind of god appointed to administer these things in this life. Nor did God after the fall of Adam take away this majesty of reason, but rather confirmed it.[8]

Luther urged that abler people are needed in the professions of law and political administration than are needed in the office of preaching!—"For in the preaching office Christ does the whole thing, by His Spirit, but in worldly government one must use reason. . . . Therefore governing is harder. . . . "[9] Indeed, in so far as the church is an empirical institution, it too operates in the realm and under the norms of law and reason, not of some alleged revelation or esoteric principles.[10] (3) Reason as the basic principle and norm in the sphere of salvation: here reason is *a whore!*[11] Why?

Luther's attack upon reason in religion came partly from Occamism. He agreed with the Occamists that philosophy and theology are separate realms, and that the causality principle cannot automatically penetrate the latter. But Luther's attack differed fundamentally from Occamism's. Occamism approached theology by way of epistemology; Luther criticized epistemology, as we shall see, by means of the "theology of the cross." Faith for Occamism is a natural human achievement; its activity is a blind assent to prescribed dogma. Faith for Luther is a wondrous, supernatural gift of God; its activity is a personal, responsible life of trust in the God who has come to us in Jesus Christ. Occamism did not consider reason in the realm of salvation a wicked woman, but simply a trespasser in a sphere beyond her competence. Luther considered reason in the realm of salvation a harlot who seduces men away from trust in the true God.

> Our reason knows that God is. But who and what He is, who actually is God, that reason does not know. . . . The Jews . . . knew that Christ was among them and walked with the people. But who He was, they

did not know. . . . So reason plays blind man's buff with God and makes always mistakes, and misses every time, calling that God which is not God and again not calling Him God who really is God. Reason would not do either if it did not know that God is, or if on the other hand it knew who or what He is. . . . Therefore in trying so hard, reason gives God's name an honor to whatever it considers is God, but never finds him who is really God, but always the devil or its own vanity which is ruled by the devil.[12]

Luther, I said, did not come to this theological view by way of philosophical epistemology. Rather, he criticized epistemology by means of his *theology of the cross*. This expression does not signify a special topic in Luther's theology, viz., an aspect of his Christology; it is a particular approach to theology, standing in diametrical contrast to what he calls "theology of glory." The titles refer to the window through which the theologian chooses to look in understanding his God. Theology of the cross means that we find God by his gracious coming down to us, disclosing himself to us especially in the cross of Christ; theology of glory is the human ascent of rational or mystical speculation or ethical idealism, which sets theologians to prattling about God's essence and his formal attributes "as a cobbler prattles about his leather."[13] Theology of the cross finds God's self-revelation in concrete historical events; theology of glory looks for it by abstracting "pure," timeless, "spiritual" knowledge from all taint of material and historical contingency. Theology of the cross does "see" or "know" God, in the biblical sense, but what it *sees* is not God's face but God's *posteriora* (Exodus 33:18-23). "Show us the Father," said Philip, asking for a theology of glory. "He who has seen me has seen the Father," replied Jesus with a theology of the cross—an answer, by the way, which Philip could not grasp with his reason (in the time of John's chapter 14) but only with his faith (in the light of chapter 20).[14]

Theology of the cross "sees" or "knows" God, then, in faith, not in reason, for when God has come into history definitively in Jesus Christ, he has come veiled—i.e., contrary to all reasonable expectation and comprehension—in infirmity and lowliness and suffering. He came *to* the lowly and suffering—to people where they need him. So, too, Christ deals with his followers as his Father dealt with him; he redeems them by "leading them down into hell and bringing them back" (see I Sam. 2:6), and he sends them forth into a ministry of reconciliation like his own, which reconciles by means of a "lost love" —a love that carries the burden which evil causes but refuses to carry, all the while never ceasing to be love.[15]

It was this theology that shaped Luther's conception of reason. His attack was directed against reason's efforts to storm the citadel of God. It was also a keen defense against the redeemed Christian's temptation to let his reason infiltrate the citadel of faith, producing out of "revealed" materials a "theological system" which automatically preserves and reproduces faith or promises us something more certain than faith. But this attitude toward reason can hardly be called "irrationalism." Luther thinks it is what St. Paul meant by "the wisdom of God." "Scripture and clear reason," then, means the incomprehensible good news in Jesus Christ, plus whatever consequences can be reasonably drawn therefrom, directly and necessarily, without the intrusion of alien principles—especially of would-be autonomous reason.

In this light we can test Luther's reasonableness at the points where he has been accused of being most unreasonable: (1) his alleged contempt for mathematics, (2) his doctrine of the enslaved will and predestination, (3) his doctrine of the Lord's Supper. In view of persistent misunderstandings of his social ethics, it would also be useful to examine the "practical reason" in Luther, but we shall forego this inasmuch as the charge of unreasonableness is less frequently encountered in this realm.[16]

III

First the famous "two and five are eight" passage. It stands in a sermon on the Second Article of the Creed. The wondrous person of Jesus Christ holds Luther transfixed, and permanently baffles his reason. Notice the context and the accent of this argument over numbers. Luther is speaking about what God hypothetically *may do,* but it is clear that his interest is consumingly centered upon what God actually *has done.* God has commanded men to use their reason to the utmost in subduing nature and bringing order into the common life. But it is different in "matters which I cannot control with my wisdom":

> I hear that Christ has one divine essence with the Father. And yet it is true that there is no more than one God. Where shall I grope or grasp, start or finish? It sounds ridiculous in my ears, and does not penetrate my reason. Yes, and it should not penetrate it! Rather, I should reply: if I hear the Word coming down from above, I believe it even though I cannot grasp it and cannot understand it. Nor do I wish to get it into my head, in the same way that I can grasp with my reason that *two and five are seven,*—and nobody can show me otherwise. But if *He* spoke from above and said, 'No, but they are *eight,*' I should believe it against my reason, and feel: All right!—if *I* want to be the judge, I won't believe! As for myself, though, I shall believe him who is the judge and arbiter. This you should do here also, even

though reason cannot bear it that two persons are one God. That
sounds as if I said: two are not two, but two are one. Here you have
the Word and reason in direct opposition. Reason should not assume
the position of master, nor act like a judge or doctor, but should doff
its cap and say: two are one; I do not see it or understand it, but I
believe it. Why? For the sake of him who has spoken it to us from
above. If it came from me, or if reason tried to say it, no man would
make me believe it. I would shove mathematics under his nose and
show him that he should accept it, that he must yield to me. But
when it comes down from heaven, I will believe what he tells me, that
two—yes, that all three persons are just one true God, not two or
three Gods.[17]

IV

The same Christological motif determines Luther's use of reason
in his fight with Erasmus. Contrary to a common impression that he
deduced the bondage of man's will from the metaphysical principle
that God causes all things, Luther's views about both the enslaved
will and God's providence and predestination were derived from—
and to be limited by—God's revelation in Jesus Christ.[18] This controversy over free will, then, concerned salvation, not information;
it was no exaggeration of an obscure and unimportant doctrine, but
a matter of life and death.[19] Luther's treatise, moreover, was no extreme or immature retort; the views of Luther that Erasmus chose
to attack had been developed and tested in open discussion for almost
a decade. Nor was Luther's rejoinder colored by personal animosity
or temperamental excitability.[20] He knew exactly what he wanted to
say, and he felt confident of his superiority in the argument as long
as the agreed premise was the scriptural doctrine of the will.

Erasmus had accused Luther of all sorts of *absurdities*. If God causes
all things including evil, then God is not just. If God is as incomprehensible as Luther's doctrine of predestination purports him to be,
then Luther has no right to make so many dogmatic statements about
him. If man is under necessity to sin, if he is a driven beast, then man
cannot be said to sin, for he is not responsible. Or if man's will is
"nothing," then it can *do* nothing, even evil. If the will is not free,
then the scriptural commandments, exhortations, and promises of reward are absurd.

Erasmus' critique neither caught Luther off guard nor drove him
to irrational extremes. The critique would have been devastating if
Erasmus' humanistic premises had been sound. He assumed, for example, that (1) man's soul naturally aspires to good; (2) man's will

must be free, else it is not will; (3) God is essentially comprehensible; no statement about him that is basically unreasonable can be true; (4) Scripture is essentially reasonable, and where it appears otherwise it requires reinterpretation.[21] But these premises are not axioms of reason; they are metaphysical and religious affirmations!—dogmatic "assertions" from a man who disparaged dogmatizing![22] If these premises proved vulnerable, the critique drawn from them would simply fall apart; at best, Erasmus' attack could convict Luther of errors, but not dismiss his argumentation as absurd.

Luther's reply constitutes no retreat from reason. He scorns the suspicion that he flouts the laws of identity and contradiction; "what is more impossible," he asks, "than that the same number may be both nine and ten at the same time"?[23] Moreover, he does not doubt that man has and always retains a psychological power of choice, and that even the worst man remains man, with a very active will. When Luther speaks of the will as a "nothing" or as a ridden "beast," however, the issue is not whether man has a choice, but what determines his choices and how far man has this *will* in his own power "before God," i.e., confronted by God's judgment or grace. Commenting on John 15:5, I Corinthians 13:2, etc., Luther says, with considerable psychological sensitivity:

> I am aware that an ungodly will is a *something,* and not a mere non-entity! . . . [But] he who is without charity is 'nothing' in grace.[24]
>
> A man without the Spirit of God does not do evil against his will, under pressure, as though he were taken by the scruff of the neck and dragged into it . . . but he does it spontaneously and voluntarily. And this willingness or volition is something which he cannot in his own strength eliminate, restrain, or alter. He goes on willing and desiring to do evil; and if external pressure forces him to act otherwise, nevertheless his will within remains averse to so doing and chafes under such constraint and opposition. . . . Ask *experience* how impervious to dissuasion are those whose hearts are set on anything! . . .
>
> On the other hand: when God works in us, the will is changed under the sweet influence of the Spirit of God. Once more it desires and acts, not of compulsion, but of its own desire and spontaneous inclination. Its bent still cannot be altered by any opposition; it cannot be mastered or prevailed upon even by the gates of hell; but it goes on willing, desiring, and loving good, just as once it willed, desired, and loved evil. *Experience* proves this too. How firm and invincible are holy men, who, when forcibly constrained to sin, are the more provoked thereby to desire good—even as flames are fanned, rather than quenched, by the wind. Here, too, there is no freedom, no 'free-will', to turn elsewhere, or to desire anything else, as long as the Spirit and grace of God remain in a man.

Thus, when we are captives of Satan,

> We acquiesce in his rule willingly and readily, according to the *nature of willingness, which, if constrained, is not 'willingness'*; for constraint means rather, as one would say, 'unwillingness' *(noluntas)*. But if a stronger appears, and overcomes Satan, we are once more servants and captives, but now desiring and willingly doing what *He* wills—*which is royal freedom.*
>
> So man's will is like a beast standing between two riders. If God rides, it wills and goes where God wills. . . . If Satan rides, it wills and goes where Satan wills. Nor may it choose to which rider it will run, or which it will seek; but the riders themselves fight to decide who shall have and hold it.[25]

Actually, man thereby becomes no block or stone; "God does not work in us without us," but precisely works in us that we co-operate with him.[26]

If anyone is an obscurantist here, refusing to apply his mind to ultimate problems, it is not Luther but Erasmus. On page after page, often with telling effect, Luther spotlights Erasmus' dilettantism in regard to Scripture and his fuzziness about God's justice and comprehensibility and man's powers. Erasmus is caught not only in evasions but also in self-contradictions,[27] e.g., when he asserts both that "the human will is wholly ineffective without grace" and that it "can apply itself to those things that lead to salvation."[28] In the debate over Scripture, Luther often argues, Erasmus' advice "should have been given to Moses and Paul before they wrote, and also to God himself."[29]

Luther at least applies his mind to the hilt and realistically wrestles with the ultimate mystery of God and evil. He is driven to acknowledge, as Augustine and Aquinas also were, that the God of creation and providence works all things, even evil, in the sense that all beings exist and move only by his power. On the other hand, Luther is sure that God is not the author of evil, and that God does not *make* sin but rather makes use of evil instruments.[30] Far from applying his reason too little, it may be argued that he takes it too far: After distinguishing between the *revealed* God and God *hidden* "in his own nature and majesty," with whom we have nothing to do, Luther seems to know more about the latter than he has any right to know:

> God hidden in Majesty neither deplores nor takes away death, but works life, and death, and all in all; nor has He set bounds to Himself by His Word, but has kept Himself free over all things.[31]

It might have been clearer if he had said, as he often does in similar circumstances, that it *appears to our minds* that God neither deplores nor takes away death, etc. To claim to know what is true *coram deo*—

"before God," or "in God's sight"—does not mean claiming to see with God's eyes, *except* in the sense of apprehending what God has clearly revealed to the man who knows he stands *coram deo*. Otherwise one would be guilty of the "theology of glory" which Luther so vehemently attacks. We may notice, then, (1) that "death" in this context is not identical with sin or evil; the discussion concerns Ezekiel 18:23, "God does not desire the death of a sinner";[32] and (2) concerning the limits of our knowledge of God, Luther offers the proper corrective even to Luther!—viz., we must hold closely to what God has clearly revealed to us.[33]

Luther, meanwhile, felt impelled not only to assert the limits of reason's competence in matters of salvation but also to examine why reason forever tries to cross them. Why do the "wise" err in understanding this realm?, Erasmus asks.[34] Luther acknowledges that reason is the highest faculty of man, and maintains that it can understand many things about God and nature and human nature. Time after time he calls upon reason, experience, common sense, the common man, nature, the world, the flesh—even "free will!"—to illustrate and corroborate his assertions, sometimes remarking that these assertions would have to be acknowledged even apart from Scripture.[35] But such insights operate in what would later be called the phenomenal realm; they do not penetrate the noumenal. The human reason and will naturally seek happiness, but they never seek "life and salvation" in the realistic and abiding sense that God intends. To no one, Jews or great philosophers, did it ever occur that the way to righteousness and salvation was simply to believe on Jesus Christ.[36] For human reason has an inveterate drive to set itself up as the norm of man's relation to God, and to define according to its own principles how God must act; it *measures* God, and refuses to acknowledge his works unless it can comprehend *how* and *why* God does what he does.[37] In the last analysis, then,

> Man's failure to grasp God's words does not spring from weakness of understanding . . . No, the cause is the wickedness of Satan, who is enthroned and reigns over us in our weakness, and who himself resists the Word of God.[38]

Here emerges the sharp contrast between Luther's and Erasmus' views of reason. For Erasmus reason is a supratemporal thing, by definition good; man becomes good by conforming to it, and to this eternal reason man's mind has free access. Since reason is itself from the eternal realm, Erasmus felt no worry that he might be placing reason above God. Thus in speaking of reason, Erasmus passed with ease back and forth among logical discernment, human conception and judgment, the orderliness of the world, and the mind of God. For Luther this was an astonishing and, in view of the Scriptures, arrogant dogmatism. He was keenly aware that our faculty of reason, though undoubtedly divinely given, is humanly operated. The more genuinely personal the subject matter, the more fragmentary and fallible are the results of reason. When we touch the realm of salvation, reason not only is fallible but persistently tends to become imperialistic and dictatorial. Erasmus had a correct and important intuition in discerning that Christianity is a way of life, not a dogmatic system, and in desiring a psychologically comprehensible theology. But he committed a fateful blunder in assuming that he could establish a Christianity free of dogma, propagated by rational instruction—*eruditio*—and arbitrated by sovereign reason. Luther was convinced that Christian faith is a crucially different matter from erudition even at its most "spiritual." Faith involves the whole being of man in the presence of God, not just his mind; moreover, faith is a supernatural, gracious gift to one whose impotence to obtain it by himself can only be described as bondage and blindness. This faith has a cognitive core: a knowledge of what God has done and promises to do. Therefore faith involves "confession," doctrinal "assertions"; "take away assertions, and you take away Christianity."[39]

Would-be autonomous reason cannot even comprehend the necessary assertions of the Christian faith *after* they have been declared. It cannot make sense of the assertion that God and man have become one being.

> So one of the main reasons why the words of Moses and Paul are not taken in their plain sense (by Erasmus) is their 'absurdity'. But against what article of faith does that 'absurdity' transgress? And who is offended by it? It is human reason that is offended; which, though it is blind, deaf, senseless, godless, and sacrilegious, in its dealing with all God's words and works, is at this point brought in as judge of God's words and works! On these same grounds you will deny all the articles of the faith, for it is the highest absurdity by far—foolishness to the Gentiles and a stumbling-block to the Jews, as Paul says—that God should be man, a virgin's son, crucified, sitting at the Father's right hand. It is, I repeat, *absurd* to believe such things![40]

This is why Luther lays such emphasis on God's revelation in the Scriptures as our one sure seat of authority, and why he insists on a literal, historical interpretation of Scripture, freed from all artificialities and alien norms.[41] But even here Luther is not trading reason for a crass fideism, an obscurantist dogmatism. Throughout his treatise, but especially in two remarkable discussions of the clarity of Scripture,[42] he offers a number of correctives and curbs to the Christian's tendency to claim to know more than he ought.

(1) Our faith knowledge is limited because our rational power to understand the *words* of God's revelation is limited.

> I certainly grant that many *passages* in the Scriptures are obscure and hard to elucidate, but that is due, not to the exalted nature of their subject, but to our own linguistic and grammatical ignorance; and it does not in any way prevent our knowing all the *contents* of Scripture . . . (namely, that Christ, God's Son, became man, that God is Three in One, that Christ suffered for us, and will reign for ever). . . . Take Christ from the Scriptures—and what more will you find in them?[43]

The words used in Scripture and the assertions they convey are plain, but do we understand them in their native intention? Our understanding needs to be corrected and clarified by the best linguistic and historical scholarship available. Luther's own painstaking and persistent labors in expounding and translating the Scriptures prove that he took this principle seriously.

(2) The *scope* of our knowledge of God—and even of our own essence—is limited. This insight relates first to the *character* of God's revelation. We may understand the words accurately, but do we understand the *message* conveyed in the assertions? Only if we accept the message as applying to ourselves personally; *our* life is at stake! This is existential knowledge—commitment—not spectator knowledge —philosophy—and for it we need the gracious work of the Holy Spirit in our hearts.

> Nobody who has not the Spirit of God sees a jot of what is in the Scriptures. All men have their hearts darkened, so that, even when they can discuss and quote all that is in Scripture, they do not understand or really know any of it. . . .The Spirit is needed for the understanding of all Scripture and every part of Scripture.[44]

Precisely so, what we may know about God is limited by what he has chosen to reveal about himself. Speaking of the problem of election Luther declares:

> Where God hides Himself, and wills to be unknown to us, there we have no concern. . . . This will is not to be pried into, but to be reverently adored. . . . God in His own nature and majesty is to be left alone; in this regard, we have nothing to do with Him, nor does He wish us to deal with Him. We have to do with Him as clothed and displayed in His Word, by which He presents Himself to us.[45]

This is the Word centered in Christ. Beyond its clear message we have no right to dogmatize. Consequently, Luther distinguishes between God and our knowledge of God, God and his Word, God and his works, the hidden God and the preached God.[46] We do not grasp God himself in his inner essence and majesty, as speculative theologians and mystics may purport to do; our comprehension has to do with listening to what God has said to us and tracing what God has concretely done and still does. Here we need the faith to accept and be satisfied with what God has revealed.

(3) *Our experiential apprehension* of God's message is limited. We may assent to God's message with our heads, but do we accept it in our lives? What God *reveals* comes to us *hidden* in experiences which utterly upset our rational judgments and expectations.[47] To receive God's revelation in experience we need a faith which through lowliness and suffering discerns God's presence and his address to us beneath what reason regards as only a stumbling block and foolishness. Here it is precisely the greatest saints who exercise the greatest humility in their claims to divine knowledge.

(4) Even when our faith knowledge is true, it bears not only a fragmentary but also a *provisional* character, in view of the coming consummation. In the "light of grace" we have many unanswered questions. But "do you not think that the light of glory will be able with the greatest ease to solve problems that are insoluble in the light of the word and grace . . . ?"[48]

V

Though he rejected transubstantiation, Luther insisted that the body of Christ is literally, substantially present in the Lord's Supper. This view embarrassed the Elizabethan translators of his *Galatians Commentary,* but they pleaded that we should not "for one little wart cast away the whole bodie" of his work,[49] and many people to this day denounce his Eucharistic theology as either mystical or gross and irrational.

The best source for examining this doctrine is the *Great Confession concerning Christ's Supper,* 1528,[50] the real theological climax of a carefully pondered, long-drawn-out polemic against the Zwinglians. Note that Zwingli did not consider Luther's views of God's election and man's unreasonable; unlike Erasmus, Luther's new adversary was a strict predestinarian and by intention a rigorous biblicist. But it was different in regard to the Lord's Supper. Zwingli's two main

arguments are, first, that to interpret the words of institution literally
is *impossible* in view of Christ's ascension, for a body by definition
occupies space, and thus Christ's body, being now in heaven, cannot
be bodily present in the sacrament; secondly, even if it were possible,
it would be *useless* in view of John 6:63, "The flesh is of no avail":
nothing material can actually bestow a spiritual benefit. For these
reasons Luther's contention for the Real Presence is absurd.[51] It is
important that Zwingli meant: "absurd" not so much to reason as to
"scripture and the creed."[52] Nevertheless, against an adversary who
made a principle of the assertion that in the Scriptures God does not
"put before us many incomprehensible things" to believe,[53] Luther
suspected that Zwingli's real ground was that doctrines like the Real
Presence are "burdensome to the people" and "difficult to believe."[54]
Such a faith, Luther argued, would destroy the doctrine of the Incarnation and would reduce the Savior to a "mere saint."

This Christological issue which we have encountered as the key
signature in the previous subjects also dominates Luther's thought
here. We shall therefore confine ourselves to three aspects of his comprehensive argument which indicate his use of reason. (1) Luther's
insistence on a literal interpretation of the words of institution represents neither mysticism nor irrationalism. If God spoke the words,
they can be neither impossible nor useless, but must be true whether
we understand them or not. It is best, therefore, simply to cling to
God's own words. But this does not imply that God's words in themselves are alien to the realm of reason. Just the opposite! The *words*
are plain and familiar. Language belongs to the realm of bodily
things over which reason presides. Even the Word, in the sense of
the words themselves, belongs in this realm along with "water, Christ's
body, and his saints on earth,"[55] which are the vehicles through which
the Spirit comes to us. "Seven-year-old boys" can understand them.[56]
"A heathen, a Jew or a Turk," on hearing Christ's words,

> must acknowledge that they speak of the body of Christ which is in
> the bread. How otherwise could the heathen and the Jews mock us,
> saying that the Christians eat their God, if they did not understand
> this text clearly and distinctly? When the believer grasps and the
> unbeliever despises that which is said, however, this is due not to
> the obscurity or clarity of the words but to the hearts that hear it.[57]

Luther will not grant, then, that when Christ spoke of his *body* he
really meant his *divinity*, as Zwingli urged! If Zwingli may do anything he wants with the text, what can stop him?[58] Luther, incidentally, rejects the suggestion of some Occamists that we must speak

of a "double truth," or a special "logic of faith" applying in the realm of revelation. He opposed the Sorbonne assertion that "Truth is the same in philosophy and theology," by citing the doctrines of the Incarnation and the Trinity. By a perfectly good syllogism one could "prove" that the Son is the Father,—but it would not be true! But

> This arises not from a defect of the syllogistic form, but from the power and majesty of the material, which cannot be confined in the narrowness of reason or syllogisms. This material indeed is not contrary to, but rather outside, inside, above, beneath, this side of and beyond all dialectical truth.[59]

(2) Luther constantly maintains that the Swiss do not use reason enough. He charges Zwingli with ignorance of grammar. For example, "I am the true vine" cannot mean "I represent the true vine"; rather, the vine represents Christ.[60] Also of elementary logic: for example, Zwingli argues that "Christ is not in the Supper in the same form in which he was crucified, therefore he is not in the Supper."[61] Again, says Luther, when Christ declares of the bread, "This is my body," reason "shakes its head and exclaims, 'Oh, it is quite impossible!' " Luther retorts:[62] (a) reason must not presume to judge God; (b) to assert an impossibility here on the basis that a body necessarily is confined to space is to commit the fallacy of trying to prove an uncertain proposition by another still more uncertain; (c) for two diverse substances to be one substance "is not contrary to scripture, indeed, it is not even contrary to reason or true logic." His proofs from Scripture are the doctrines of the Trinity and the Incarnation, but he goes on to argue that there are other kinds of union of beings in human experience, such as angel and flame of fire, Holy Spirit and dove—hence a unity of bread and Christ's body is not necessarily absurd. Indeed, logic "should first seek the aid of grammar," which often embraces two beings in a single expression by the figure *synecdoche*. This recourse to synecdoche does not contradict a literal interpretation of Christ's words, for synecdoche acknowledges the real presence of both "beings" referred to, whereas Zwingli's *alloeosis*—reference to one being while actually meaning the other—precisely does not.

(3) Most offensive of all to many people has been Luther's doctrine of the ubiquity of Christ's body.[63] But this too is no retreat from reason. One reason why the words *may* be literally true, Luther holds, is that "body" may have other modes of presence than the local or spatial one measured by our senses. For Christ's body to pass "through the gravestone and the locked door" is one illocal mode (i.e., not bound by ordinary laws of space and place), which he shares with

spirits and with the saints triumphant. Another, attributable to Christ alone by virtue of his unique union with the Godhead, enables Christ's humanity to share in God's omnipresence. Reason grasps the local mode; faith is needed to perceive the second and third.

> Must a text be unclear if a thing is invisible and none but the believer perceives it? . . . If everything that faith teaches is invisible, then this text cannot be clear: 'God created heaven and earth', for God and his creativity are invisible.[64]

Regardless of whether Luther's theory is found convincing or not, at least it cannot be dismissed as irrational. The ubiquity *theory* depends on the acknowledgment of various modes of presence, just as Zwingli's argument depends on the strictly spatial definition of "body." Luther was clear that such philosophizing could indicate *how* Christ's words *may* be literally true, but also that his Eucharistic *faith* by no means depended on this philosophical support. Luther's theology depended much less on the *how* than Zwingli's on the *how not;* significantly, Luther's Large and Small Catechisms utterly bypass such theorizing and simply build on the faith that Christ is truly present in the sacrament. It is much more debatable whether Zwingli realized the danger of rationalism in the way he argued from the necessarily spatial character of "body" and from the inability of the material to convey the spiritual. When Luther attacked those two principles, he did so not on the basis of a metaphysical position, but neither did he speak from an antimetaphysical position or a contempt for reason. His attack arose from his insight into the way God acts in Jesus Christ and in Scripture and in all of history.

The adequacy and permanence of Luther's theology, of course, remain subject to dispute, but one must acknowledge a massive consistency and clarity and even power in his use of reason. On the basis of his theological principles Luther applied his reason faithfully, and his principles gave an important though carefully limited place to reason.

Anfechtung in Luther's Biblical Exegesis

C. Warren Hovland

Perhaps few theologians were ever better qualified to speak about the nature of doubt, temptation, anxiety, and the dark night of the soul than Martin Luther. His theology was hammered out in the workshop of his own soul. Sometime after 1530 he wrote:

> If I should live a little while longer, I would like to write a book about *Anfechtung*. Without it no man can rightly understand the Holy Scriptures or know what the fear and love of God is all about. In fact, without *Anfechtung* one does not really know what the spiritual life is.[1]

The word *Anfechtung* has no real equivalent in English. Professor Bainton, who first introduced me to the centrality of the term in Luther's thought, says the word has as much right to be carried into English as *Blitzkrieg*. He defines it simply as "all the doubt, turmoil, pang, tremor, panic, despair, desolation, and desperation which invade the spirit of man."[2] Jacob Grimm in the *Deutsches Wörterbuch* explains that the word comes from the middle-high German word for "bodily-struggle."[3] The base of the word, *fechten,* means "combat," "struggle," or "attack." In theological usage the word is often translated "temptation." However, it is interesting to note that Luther prefers the word *Anfechtung* to *Versuchung* even in his translation and explanation of the sixth petition of the Lord's Prayer.[4]

Two types of *Anfechtung* beset Luther: one was the whole matter of faith *(Glaubensanfechtung),* the other was the matter of his vocation *(Berufsanfechtung).* Much attention has been given to the struggle for faith of the young Luther and the spiritual depressions he encountered before the evangelical awakening of 1513.[5] It is the intent of this essay to show that both the struggle for faith and the questions about his vocation continued to plague Luther throughout his life and did, in fact, continue until the very last year of his life. "I did not learn my theology all at once," he wrote, "but I had to search deeper for it where my temptations took me."[6] The author of "A Mighty Fortress Is Our God" could also have periods when he would say, "Love God? I hate him."[7] The year 1527 was one of the most severe periods of doubt and suffering. In August of that year he wrote to Melanchthon:

> For the last week I have been thrown into death and the pit, my whole body so bruised that I still tremble in all my members. I had almost lost Christ and was thrown to the billows and buffeted by storms of despair so that I was tempted to blaspheme against God.[8]

Some attempts have been made to explain Luther's *Anfechtungen* on a psychological basis. Professor Reiter, a Danish psychiatrist, has attempted to plot the cycle of Luther's manic and depressive phases. He finds Luther had depressive phases in 1505, 1507-1519, 1521, 1523-1524, 1527-1528, 1529, 1532, 1535-1536, 1539, 1541, 1543-1546, and that he had periods of exaltation from 1519-1521 and from 1522-1526. This treatment is open to question on many counts.[9] It rests on an assumed diagnosis of "manic-depressive" without adequate evidence. There is abundant evidence in his literary works alone that even during his depressive periods Luther was able to produce a prodigious number of sermons, commentaries, letters, hymns, poems, etc. The years 1519-1521 are also far from manifesting uniform exhilaration since they include periods of severe anxiety about his vocation. Luther's physical health does not always correlate with his mental health either.[10]

Others have sought an explanation in terms of psychoanalytic theory. One of the most recent of these is the work of Erik Erikson entitled *Young Man Luther: A Study in Psychoanalysis and History*.[11] Using a basically Freudian orientation Erikson sees the relationship between Luther's father and the young Luther as determinative for the whole course of his spiritual development. His thesis is that Luther, once a sorely frightened child, recovered through the study of Christ's passion the central meaning of the Nativity. He shows how his depressions and anxieties were essentially a search for a self image. Beginning with the problem which all adolescents face, namely the identity crisis, Luther had to work through the problems of intimacy, generativity, and integrity. Although Erikson is highly dependent on fragments of Luther's recollections of childhood, he has grasped some of the essential psychological dynamics of his soul struggle. He is conscious of the tremendous cost to Luther and the significance of his spiritual struggle for human history. He says that both Luther and Freud came to realize that "the child is in the midst." Both men perfected introspective techniques permitting an isolated man to recognize his patienthood.[12] However, Erikson's study deals only with the young Luther and he is content to show that Luther's concept of a "gracious

God" was able to replace the stern father of his youth. His thesis does not account for the continuing *Anfechtung* which Luther suffered after the evangelical awakening.

The attempt to explain Luther's soul struggles on the basis of a *Zeitgeist* also seems inadequate. It is sometimes said that Albrecht Dürer was one of the few people who could understand Luther. His portrait of "Knight, Death, and Devil" may be taken as typical of medieval mentality. It portrays an armored knight riding off to meet the foe, with death and the devil stealthily stealing behind him. Now it is true that Luther, like all medieval men, lived in a thought world peopled with demonic spirits. He could be frightened almost to death by the sound of a rustling leaf or flee in terror from a devil who might be lurking in the murky shadows. Luther was very fond of quoting the passage in Leviticus 26:36 which speaks of the fear which may be generated in a person by a rustling leaf. There are at least five passages where the sound of the rustling leaf is coupled with lightning.[13] This may be accounted for by recalling the moment of terror he felt in the thunderstorm just preceding his entry into the monastery. Undoubtedly the two phenomena were tied together in his mind. Yet Luther's *Anfechtungen* were, as we shall see, more than the fear of evil spirits which was shared by his contemporaries.

"In all *Anfechtung* we are dealing directly with God." *(In aller Anfechtung geht es unmittelbar um Gott.)* This was Luther's basic thesis. While many moderns may seek psychological, sociological, historical, and psychoanalytic interpretations,[14] for Luther the problem is the religious problem *par excellence:* How do I stand before God? *Anfechtung* is a life and death matter for him since man's whole destiny is at stake: "The soul hangs precariously on a thin thread dangling between eternal life and eternal damnation."[15] Since Luther's thought is both biblical and experiential it may be said to be characterized by an emphasis on the I-Thou relationship. *"Gott begegnet uns offt wer ihn kunde grussen."*[16] Truth, for Luther, always emerges as a result of a personal meeting with God in the Word. This is the essence of the divine-human encounter. But this encounter often engenders feelings of anxiety, dread, uncertainty—in short, *Anfechtung*. Therefore we may tentatively define *Anfechtung* as *the terror the individual feels in the moment he is confronted with some dark aspect of God.* God may confront man as judge, as enemy, as tempter, as the hidden one, and as the arbitrary one.

In seeking an understanding of his own spiritual problems Luther came to see the Bible as a collection of biographies of those who were

suffering *Anfechtung* and a record of how God permitted the pious
to fall into this state and how he helped them out again. He wrote:
"I find in the Scriptures that Christ, Abraham, Jacob, Moses, Job,
David and countless others have tasted of hell even in this life."[17]
Thus Luther came to read the Bible in the light of his own experience
and grew in the conviction that God continued to tempt his chosen
ones. This was supremely true in the case of Christ who knew these
dark hours during his ministry.[18] Luther grasped the heart of Paul,
Abraham, and Jonah as few other men have because in part, at least,
he projected into their spiritual struggles the memory of his own. He
thus came to feel that he was a part of the fellowship of those who bear
the marks of pain—men like Job, Jeremiah, and David who could proclaim their faith only in the midst of continuing struggles. Luther
may well have said with Dostoievski, "My Hosannas have gone through
the deep purgatory of doubt and despair."[19]

We turn now to an examination of some of the aspects of God
which the biblical figures encountered in their *Anfechtung* situation.
First we deal with *God as judge*. One of the most frequent types of confrontation with God recorded in the Bible is that of the individual who
has broken the moral law or who is in disobedience to God's will. When
confronted with the just and holy God, man's conscience is troubled
and he sees God as a stern judge before whom he stands accused. It is
clear that the Reformer's rediscovery of the gospel was also fraught
with terrible consequences for the individual. He realized that the God
with whom man has to deal is the holy and perfect God, and that the
demands he makes on man are complete perfection and submission.
This means that every ladder to heaven, every treasury of merit, was
of no avail—was in fact sin. Luther's thought started with God, whose
honor demanded that man uncompromisingly do his will. The implication of this "new conscience" means that Luther had transferred all the
dilemmas and dualism of the Catholic system of morality to the heart
of the individual. Professor Ritter has characterized Luther's religion
as "the religion of the heroic *Willensmensch* who bears about in his
own breast the contradictions of good and evil which rend the world
asunder."[20]

In his exegesis of the *Anfechtungen* of Adam, Cain, Jonah, Joseph's
brothers, Moses, David, and the Psalmist, Luther described this experience of meeting with God as judge. In each case communion
with a loving Father has been broken and the realization of the separation is made manifest in an uneasy conscience. While it is true
that this aspect of God, the God with "the strange face" seems to be

found more in the Old Testament than in the New Testament, Luther
felt that this was an abiding and necessary attribute of God's nature. It
is to be noted that his treatment of all these instances occurs long after
the period of his evangelical experience; he was working on the Genesis lectures up until a year before his death.

In his rich and emotionally charged language, Luther describes the
first *Anfechtung* situation in one of his sermons preached in 1523.

> When the heat of the day had passed and it was cool, they heard the
> voice of the Lord. Then the garden suddenly became too narrow—
> that is, in their conscience they knew that they had sinned. But there
> was no room to flee and the Lord was already too close to them. The
> conscience experiences the greatest damnation when we know that
> we have sinned. When conscience comes there is no comfort any-
> where, one must either despair or God must return. In the hour that
> the Lord spoke saying, "Adam, where are you?" both Adam and Eve
> were in death's hour. This question sounded hard and foreign to
> them, for the Most High had previously treated them as his beloved
> children and now he acts as if he didn't know them. Therefore, Adam
> thought: God is hostile toward you. Heaven and earth pressed in
> upon him, everything became too tight for him, and he was unable
> to flee.[21]

We see in this description some of the classic elements of *Anfechtung*. If one recognizes the symbolism involved in this myth one can
also see the tremendous relevance for our own modern *Anfechtungen*.
Note the element of metaphysical insecurity when "the garden becomes too narrow" and the feeling of the hostility of the created
order so that even the sound of a rustling leaf strikes terror in Adam's
heart.[22] The cool of the garden at vesper time suddenly becomes a
scene of "judgment, terror, and fright."[23] The tormented conscience
now sees God in the form of a stern judge before whose tribunal it
must appear.[24] The existential categories are sharpened; the unique
ambivalence of the relationship makes the individual more conscious
of the severity of the ultimate separation. The normal response to this
situation is the attempt to flee from one's responsibility, yet "the more
we try to flee the closer God comes to us." The act of independence,
the refusal to have any Lord to whom he would be responsible, mani-
fests Adam's basic sin of pride. Yet now he knows he *is* responsible.
One might coin the word *"Verantwortlichkeitsanfechtung"* (responsi-
bility-*Anfechtung*) for this situation. When Adam cannot flee he becomes self-defensive—this is symbolized by the fig leaves. Luther has
no patience with Adam's attempt to transfer responsibility to Eve.
This is the highest affront to the divine majesty: "The fool is going

to punish God for sending him the Temptress."[25] Finally, Luther points out that the Fall involves the loss of the *imago dei*. One of the prime factors in *Anfechtung* is that man has a distorted and incomplete picture of God. As Luther had come to know experientially, the search for a gracious God is made more difficult because the original *imago* is so blurred that man easily forms a wrong concept of God. The tragic element in this meeting with God is that Adam refuses to recognize that his judge is also his gracious God. *Anfechtung* continues until one is able to confess one's sin and throw himself on God's mercy.

Cain also experienced this confrontation with God the judge.[26] Luther suggests that Cain's problem was that he doubted even the existence of God and thus sinned against the First Commandment.[27] Luther felt that if in the most severe temptations one could hold to the promise implied in the command, "I am the LORD *your* God," there was hope. Yet in the case of Cain it seemed as if this hope were denied. One might call this state the ultimate rejection of meaning and hope.

For Luther the whole Jonah narrative is a description of the tormented conscience. The sea trip is made into an allegory of the hardening, awakening, and doubting conscience. The confrontation with God the judge, or with the law, is a necessary experience for the Christian; without this one cannot come to true faith. "All honest and pious Christians are just like Jonah; they also are thrown into the sea, yes, into the depths of hell . . . All saints must also descend with their Lord into the inferno."[28] The story is also to remind us of what death—*Anfechtung* can be like, for in the belly of the whale Jonah "looked death in the face . . . Here are drawn all the hellish aspects of eternal damnation, eternal anxiety, distress, eternal death, fear and despair."[29] Jonah's attempt to flee to the heathens and away from God's demands is interpreted as the attempt to save oneself by the law. The helplessness of the ship's company represents the failure of all work-righteousness. But the real miracle of the book of Jonah is that just when everything is called into doubt and nothing seems possible, God gives us grace and faith. When Jonah was able to say: "Thy waves have come over me," he was on the way to being released from *Anfechtung*. In a strikingly autobiographic note in the 1526 commentary on Jonah, Luther observes:

> Just when I was in death's deepest throes and had the least hope, and there seemed the least possibility of life, the Lord came with his power and by a miracle led my life out of death and destruction. So when a string holds the strongest it breaks.[30]

A second aspect of God that is revealed in *Anfechtung* is that of *the enemy*. This in a sense is a development of the idea of God as judge. Man must not only appear before the tribunal of God but he must face the angry One, his prosecutor is also his enemy. Luther treats this theme in his study of Job, and in Psalms 6 and 118.

Luther called Job "a unique book of theological rhetoric." One theme runs throughout the book: God is hostile toward me and I toward him.[31] Interestingly enough his translation of the Old Testament was held up chiefly because of the difficulties he encountered with the book of Job. He wrote, "Job is as little willing to endure our translations as to hear the comfort of his friends. We work on the book of Job so that in four days we are scarcely able to complete three lines."[32] The Hebrew poet who is the author of the book is compared to Vergil and the hero to Aeneas. "The author is a man who has seen and experienced a great many temptations and *Anfechtungen*. Only a man who has lived through such an experience can understand this."[33] This raises the problem of the relation of Luther's own experience of *Anfechtung* to his work as translator and interpreter of Scripture. We may well ask whether the *Anfechtung* he finds in Job is a projection of his own difficulties and whether his own problems sometimes interfered with his work as translator as well.

"When death stared Job in the face and God deprived him of everything, then his words give testimony to what kind of thoughts a man can have against God. Then Job thinks that God is not God but a vain judge and an angry tyrant, who deals only with force and without concern for man's good."[34] At first Job had suffered only physical *Anfechtung* but when he questioned God's wisdom and purposes he was thrown into the depths of spiritual turmoil. Part of Job's problem was that he did not know how long or how far God would tempt him. Yet he had faith enough to see that God was only concealing his love, so that he could finally say, "Even though it appears that you have turned your face from me, yet I will not believe that you are my Enemy."[35]

Luther turned to Job as a book of comfort during his own sufferings. In July 1536, while suffering a severe attack of constipation and palpitations of the heart he was reminded of Job. He marvelled at the sensitivity of the human heart and what it was able to endure. He notes that it is the most frequent member to be attacked and it is stormed "as if it were a wall three feet thick." Out of his own sufferings, both physical and spiritual, Luther claimed that he was really able to understand Job while a writer like Hieronymus was only able "to write some thoughts about the book" because he had never really had severe *Anfechtung*.[36]

In the period from 1513 to 1532, Luther dealt with the Sixth Psalm in six different works.[37] In both the 1517 and 1525 exposition Luther states that the main theme of the Psalm is that God often appears as our enemy. This kind of experience does not happen to many people. In the Gospels this happened to the Canaanite woman; David, Job, and the German theologian Tauler are mentioned by Luther as among the "experienced" who have tasted of this most difficult kind of spiritual suffering.[38] The common notes in the various treatments of the Sixth Psalm are these: First, *Anfechtung* is regarded as a punishment from God who appears as man's enemy. Second, the experience of judgment is so strong that it is compared to a foretaste of hell, and it often weakens the body as well as the spirit. Third, it attacks the saints especially, since it is connected with the question of predestination, an outgrowth of spiritual pride. Fourth, release comes only when one confesses his own inability to save himself and puts his trust in God alone.

In his exegesis and commentary on the 118th Psalm in 1529, Luther wrote, "This is my Psalm and I love it. Although I love the whole Psalter, I am especially fond of this Psalm as it has helped me and served me in great need. It is more precious than all wealth, power and glory."[39] It was during the year 1529 that Luther had a wound in his tibia, and so in commenting on verse 13 ("I was pushed hard, so that I was falling") he says, "We are such weaklings and are so easily agonized that if we have a little pain in the leg or hear the rustle of a leaf we cry to heaven with complaints. But what a tiny evil this is compared with the great goodness we receive from God."[40] Then Luther proceeds with some practical counsel. Noting that the Psalmist says, "I cry to the Lord," he advises: "Don't just sit there by yourself or lie on your belly with your head hanging down and let these thoughts bite into you, and don't get eaten up worrying over them. Get up, you lazy fellow, and then get down on your knees and hold up your hands to heaven and pray a Psalm or the Lord's Prayer and bring your complaints to God."[41]

The Psalmist is also much concerned with the anguish of death. Is it the devil or is it God who then "beleaguers a heart and storms the conscience with dread, doubt and despair"? The devil is indeed active in death's hour in bringing forth such petty sins as taking one too many drinks, or sleeping too long in the morning, or laughing in church. Luther suggests that it is good perhaps that man does not have to face his *real* sins: unbelief, despising God, and the basic fact that we do not really fear, trust, and love God with all our heart. He says, "I don't think there is any faith on earth that could stand face to face with this fact without falling and despairing utterly." The anxiety about death is created by persecution, pestilence, sickness, and all the dangers of life. These were all very real to Luther. When faced with this kind of threat to one's existence, in which the whole cosmic drama of redemption and salvation is enacted, Luther advises us to address the Tempter with these words: "What are you looking for, my good works or my righteousness? I haven't any, my power is not my power; the Lord is my strength. I know nothing of either sin or holiness in me, nothing except the power of God."[42] This was the secret of the faith of the Psalmist and of Luther.

Luther also deals with the *Anfechtung* experiences of biblical characters when they are confronted with *God the tempter*. This he finds to be the case with Eve, Judas, Peter, and Paul. The classic illustration is the temptation of Eve.[43] While the narrative pictures her as being tempted by the devil, Luther indicates that this temptation was sent by God to test her faith. For in Luther's faith it must be remembered that God is almighty and the devil is always subordinate to him, therefore in every situation man must respond directly to God. Luther indicates that one of the basic temptations which God sends man is the temptation to devise a picture of God which is more in harmony with reason or with nature than the God of the Bible. This is the temptation to a false faith, to accept an inadequate view of God and to be committed to it. Judas was tempted by a few pieces of silver, but underlying this was the real temptation—betrayal of his Lord.[44] On the other hand God tempted Peter with presumption. He was overconfident in his faith and did not realize how faith must be a continuing struggle. When the darts of Satan attacked Peter through the mouth of the servant girl, "his faith toppled and he fell into the depths of despair."[45]

Paul's "thorn in the flesh" is interpreted by Luther as high, spiritual suffering and he claims that the papists have never understood this. "These clumsy, awkward, unexperienced people have never known about any other *Anfechtung* than the evil tendencies and desires of the flesh, and so they interpret Paul in this light."[46] Both medieval and modern Catholic polemic against Luther probably misunderstand him on this point. It is not a question of erotic desire or a contest between the lower and the higher capacities of the soul. Luther makes this distinction clear.[47] He knew the struggles against the flesh which even Augustine, Hieronymus, Francis, Benedict, and Bernard had also suffered, "but the devil just laughs up his sleeve at all these things."[48] All of this is temptation at the pure level of physical temptation. It does not touch the vital point of faith. One may indeed succumb to these temptations and not be lost. The danger of these temptations is rather the negative one, i.e., in overcoming them one may feel righteous and fall prey to spiritual pride.

But the matter goes further. The chief objection to the Catholic understanding at this point is that "temptation," as they use it, refers to a relationship between the individual and a moral code or an ethical *habitus,* while *Anfechtung* deals with a direct relationship to God, the Absolute. This difference has been well stated by Søren Kierkegaard:

> *Anfechtung* is in the sphere of the God-relationship what temptation is in the ethical sphere. When the ethical relationship to reality is the maximum for the individual, then temptation is his greatest danger. Hence it is quite in order that *Anfechtung* is left out, and it is only an instance of slovenliness that it is identified with temptation. But it is not only in the manner just described that *Anfechtung* differs from temptation, but the orientation of the individual is also different in the two cases. In temptation, it is the lower that tempts, in *Anfechtung* it is the higher; in temptation, it is the lower that allures the individual, in *Anfechtung* it is the higher that, as if jealous of the individual, tries to frighten him back.[49]

In other words, if the individual should be able to conquer simple "temptations," he might never confront the dark aspects of God or learn the lessons that this experience might teach him. In *Anfechtung*, on the other hand, one has to do with God alone, and the purposes of God alone are good, but he may use various methods and mediums ("strange faces") in order to incite the individual to a faith relationship.

We turn now to an examination of those instances where God appears to hide or conceal his true nature. *God the Hidden One* is the basis of the *Anfechtungen* of Jacob, Joseph in the Old Testament, and Mary the mother of Jesus.

"God is He that is hidden; that is his property."[50] This is a part of Luther's classic description of God as *Deus Absconditus* and man is confused and anxious when he encounters it. There seems to be a kind of masquerade by God, "for he often conceals himself under his armour."[51] His purpose for thus concealing himself is indeed not always clear. Sometimes it indeed seems arbitrary: "God gave us this mask and so it must be."[52] Even the creator God is a hidden God. Why? Luther answers that God's will to save can only be acknowledged and confessed when the possibility of falling also exists. Therefore God's concealment is a prerequisite for revelation and also for faith.

In his study of Jacob, the man who wrestled with God, we see personified the existential struggle of one who has a terrifying meeting with the Wholly Other. Jacob's struggle, like Luther's, is for a right understanding of God. Jacob at Jabbok became a favorite theme in Luther's sermons; we find it in sermons in 1524, 1527, 1528, and in the Lectures on Genesis, 1535-1545. Jacob is a child of promise and in his encounter with God he tries to hold fast to his faith, but God first drives him into anxiety. Jacob does not know who he is fighting with at Jabbok, whether it is a spirit or a man. Luther uses a variety of phrases to describe Jacob's opponent: In one passage it is "the devil," in another it is "God," in another, "the Lord," twice he uses the phrase, "an angry God," in another it is "the Son of God," and in still others it is "Christ himself."[53] In vivid language he describes the struggle which ensues. It is night and "the night is no one's friend." (It was the time when Luther had his worst bouts with melancholy.) Jacob is alone. He must leave wife and children and stand naked and alone to do battle. Note the close relationship between the physical and spiritual suffering described here:

> When courage remains and the heart does not despair, then a strength and power flow to the body. But when fortitude fails, then all strength vanishes and the body cannot stand on its own feet . . . When God attacks a man he does not seize him by the skin, but within, so that the marrow wastes away and the bones become weak as the flesh. This is also what Christ experienced in the Garden of Olives.[54]

Jacob is praised for his persistence in wrestling with God, even the God "with the strange face." Grasping him where he was most pliant he said, "Now Lord, you have promised us grace and mercy and that you will help us and make us holy. Help us now, Lord, it is high time!"[55] This kind of prayer is holding God to his word; it is finding the soft (weich) spot where God may be grasped. Jacob was thus even able to overcome the predestination anxiety. When he seemed to hear the terrible voice: "You will be lost, Jacob!", he answered, "I will not be lost because God does not want that to happen . . . Besides, I will hold fast to his first promises."[56]

Anxiety must have marked many moments in Joseph's life, especially when he was cast into the pit or when he sat loitering in Potiphar's prison. Both "pit" and "prison" are powerful Anfechtung symbols. In a sermon preached in 1534, Luther suggests that the tentatio Joseph suffered most from was unanswered prayer.[57] He cried for twelve years before he was heard. The more he cried the more it seemed that God concealed himself from him. It is compared with the prayer in Gethsemane where the longer he prayed the less help seemed forthcoming. In Joseph's case the purpose of the concealment by God was to strengthen his faith and to weaken his self-confidence. God often thus appears to be hidden under a "no" but faith must find the "yes."

Mary suffered severe anguish when her son was lost in the Temple at Jerusalem. In this experience she could not hold on to the Christ who could alone save her. "She sunk into the abyss of hell and endured great *Anfechtungen* so that she despaired utterly and would have died of anguish."[58] This led Mary into both questions of predestination and of her responsibility. No other mother can quite understand this for Mary had lost not just a human son but the Saviour of the world. She must have thought, "O God in heaven, help me if I have lost him. What will be required of me? What if God now decides that he does not want me?" To this Luther adds: "All other suffering is like a fox's tail compared to this."[59] But it was not only the three days he was lost but during the whole thirty years of his life Mary must have suffered, for during much of this time God was hidden from her and she was not aware of what the purpose of all this was. But all suffering fades into insignificance when we stand at the foot of the cross and watch this young, innocent man at the full height of his powers mocked and spat upon, and see him hanging there with hands and feet nailed to the shameful cross.[60]

For the Christian not only the Word but the sacraments can also be an aid when God seems to hide himself. In one of the *Table Talk* references Luther is reported to have said:

> To think God's thoughts as opposed to Satan's thoughts is to say, 'I am a believer in the Son of God'. Secondly, I am baptized and called to a belief in the Church. Since I am baptized and believe in Christ, it certainly follows that God hears me. Even though he conceals his love from me, one must realize that this is a part of his wisdom and God is accustomed to deal with us in this manner. For Moses said that God desires to dwell in darkness. Therefore since he has set his residence in darkness we must often see only his back side.[61]

One should also remember, that all the saints who have ever lived are a part of the great cloud of witnesses and that they exercised their faith by wrestling with these same spiritual struggles. By means of this the faith of the whole church is exercised. In fact, this is one of the marks of the true church according to the Reformer: "The Church is a small band of very miserable men, very abject and full of despair in the face of the world."[62]

Finally we turn to examples of the meeting with *God the Arbitrary One*. Two examples of the *Anfechtung* arising out of this encounter are Abraham in the Old Testament and the Canaanite woman in the New Testament. In both cases God appears to be undependable, arbitrary, and even capricious. For example, God who had given the commandment not to kill now seems to order Abraham to slay his own son. God who had previously promised his seed would be given to Isaac and that he would be the father of many generations now orders Isaac killed. "God was now as unpredictable as the weather (*wetterwendisch*) and contradicts himself."[63] This is a riddle which no one can solve "except the Holy Ghost." The rational facilities seem to be at a loss. "What can reason say to this? It is completely frustrated, there seems to be no avenue of escape and we can only say that the game is up." In his picturesque way he describes it thus: "God plays with him as with an apple. Abraham has to hold still and let it go with him however it will. Thus does God seem to play with his saints a very enjoyable play, but they see something very different in it." Two additional factors make the *Anfechtung* more severe. First, the time interval of three days, and secondly, the fact that Abraham cannot tell anybody. It is no wonder that Abraham "roasted in his thoughts and was devoured with anxiety," so that each new thought caused his heart to pound within him. He must have thought: "Why does God act so strangely *(narrisch)*? What have I done to deserve this?"[64] For when it appears that God is capricious and undependable the heart is likely to fall into murmuring against God and be subject to the highest temptation, i.e., hatred of God (*odium dei*). The alternatives with which Abraham was faced were, either God is lying, which for a man to say is blasphemy, or God hates me, which is an occasion of despair.

For Kathie, Luther's wife, this picture of a capricious God who would command a father to slay his son was too difficult to understand. Luther confessed his own doubts about how he would react to such a demand. Kathie said, "You can't persuade me that God would require such an atrocity from anyone. The very idea of murdering one's own son!" Luther's retort was typical, "But are you able to believe that God was willing to let his only-begotten Son be crucified when nothing was more dear to him in heaven or on earth?"[65]

As our last illustration we turn to the *Anfechtungen* of the Canaanite woman described in Matthew 15:21ff. Luther was very fond of this story. Between 1523 and 1544 he preached on this text thirteen times, most frequently on Sunday *Reminiscere*. His most complete treatment is in the Postils and since they were prepared for use by others, he seems to have been willing to have even preachers who had not experienced his personal struggles of soul use this material. We may well ask why this particular text intrigued him so. Perhaps because the predestination question which continued to be a source of anxiety for him was so well treated here. Perhaps because he, too, felt "outside the fold" after the break with Rome. Undoubtedly the picture of this lone woman fighting her way through to faith against such overwhelming obstacles challenged the Reformer. But perhaps more than anything else, Luther saw this story as a source of comfort for "poor, miserable, needy, sinful and despised mankind, so that in all their need they should know to whom they can flee and where they can find help and comfort."[66]

In three hard blows (*Schläge*) Jesus tested the faith of the Canaanite woman. The first is when he appears undependable, strange, and arbitrary, concealing his grace from her. With the second blow she is driven into the predestination anxiety. In answering that he was not sent except to the Jews, it is as if Jesus were saying, "It is true that men say of me that I am kind and friendly, but I am not this way toward everyman. This woman does not belong and she is not worthy of this grace."[67] In the third and final blow, Christ implies that she is a dog when he says that it is not good to give the children's food to the dogs. This is a *tentationes de indignitate* of the most severe kind. Luther admits, "If this had been said to me, I would have run off. This is the hardest text of all, to be called a dog."[68]

The person in uncertainty wants above all an assurance of the dependability of God. How can one explain why God then so often appears strange, foreign, and hidden from man? Are these dark aspects of God real or are they only the products of our consciousness? At times, Luther suggests, God does not really mean to appear this way and this is only a kind of game (*Spiel*). So Christ did not mean it in earnest when he called the Canaanite woman a dog.[69] But to the woman it seems a real battle, a life and death struggle for faith. It even appears that the disciples have more mercy than Christ himself. But the hope of finding a gracious God by means of someone else interceding and turning the heart of God toward mercy also fails. Luther had tried this way and found it was of no avail. Therefore one can only stand as "a naked bride," trusting in nothing in the universe to support one. The Canaanite was brought to a state where she was left "swaying between the Yes and the No." This is the true description of doubt. (*Verzwei-*

flung is literally "torn in two.") Only the deepest kind of faith can find the Yes which lies buried under the No. It is the ability to endure these periods of *Anfechtung* which Luther finds most remarkable. It is the ability to see the positive character of God, the love for his creatures behind the dark face. "God is like the sun which conceals its rays under the clouds, but after not too long it shines forth again." [70] This is the great miracle, the miracle of faith.

"It is living—no rather dying and facing damnation, not thinking, reading and speculating that makes a theologian." [71] Thus Luther, through his own experience and through his study of the Bible, came to see that for all the great figures of the Bible, all the saints of the church, and in his own life *Anfechtung* is to be thought of as a blessing, a means of strengthening one's faith. In these hours of spiritual struggle we "learn to see how Christ drives and pursues our faith so that it will become strong and firm." Only for this reason does God thrust "sin, death, hell, God's anger and judgment before our eyes—to drive us to depend on his Word with all our heart." Luther points out that in death's hour our own unworthiness and the predestination questions loom largest.[72] In death's hour all comfort seems to leave us and we stand completely naked; when we are deserted by all creatures our conscience trembles and we can see no way out of the situation. Then, as the final act of the cosmic drama takes place for us, we must stand before God and say, "Away with all my goods, my cattle and my wife, away with all my goodness. Thou alone, O God, art my hope and my consolation." [73]

Medieval Consolation
and the Young Luther's Despair

John von Rohr

The despair which Luther experienced during his early monastic years was poignant, though not unconsoled. And yet this very consolation was of such a nature as ultimately to contribute to the despair's further poignancy. Thus there would seem to be a strange inversion in which the remedy provided for spiritual disease by the medieval church actually became occasion, in Luther's experience, for the intensification of the disease itself. As long as the helps offered remained within the context of an essentially legalistic theology, they actually served less as help than as hindrance, and effective consolation for his soul's agony was therefore delayed for Luther until it could find basis in an evangelical understanding.

The disease of despair was precipitated in his monastic experience largely by his struggles with the law. Caught up in the requirements of a system which placed major emphasis upon meritorious obedience as an avenue to the divine favor, Luther gave his most intensive energies to the task of the law's fulfillment. The system, of course, was not a simple Pelagianism, for according to the patterns of scholastic theology the process of salvation involved an intricate interweaving of merit and grace. This was true even of the late scholasticism, for though it departed from its Thomistic predecessor through a heightened emphasis upon the independent power of the human will, this *via moderna* still maintained the necessity of God's gift of sanctifying grace for the obtaining of salvation. The gift was the divine *habitus* without which men would be unacceptable before God and without which their good works would not be sufficiently meritorious to be worthy of eternal reward. In his wisdom God had so decreed, and the "stamp" of his grace was required if one's works were to stand most fully in the divine favor. It is not enough to fulfill the law simply "according to its substance," for the fulfillment must also be "according to the purpose of the lawgiver," that is, in the state of infused grace.

And yet, though salvation is not apart from grace, it also is not apart from merit, and indeed the greater burden of emphasis in the late medieval scholastic theology seems to have been placed here and particularly upon the powers of the human will in merit's attainment. Repudiating Thomas Aquinas at this point, these late scholastics saw no need for prevenient grace or any special divine help, for by simply working under the general concurrence of God which is present in all things the human will in its freedom can fulfill the law's requirements, including the loving of God above all else. This would mean that through his natural powers a man can perform those acts which will properly dispose his soul for the reception of the divine *habitus,* for grace comes when God looks with favorable consideration on these merits and stamps them with the ornament of divine acceptance. And when the most perfect of natural acts is accomplished, namely, the loving of God above all else, one can expect without question that grace will be immediately infused. Moreover, the bestowal of the supernatural *habitus* may even be expected by one who has failed to fulfill the requirements of the divine law, provided that he has accomplished all that he possibly can in an attempt to meet their demands. Out of his liberality God will accept the works of one who has been able "to do all that lies within him" (*facere quod in se est*) and thus will infuse the gift of grace. So the practical effect of this point of view, as in the case of Luther himself, was to send men out to achieve those merits which would be beneficial for their salvation, preliminary *merita de congruo* as preparation for God's gift, and then, when stamped with grace, the further *merita de condigno* to which reward could be given. Therefore, despite the inclusion of grace, the major emphasis fell upon the law and one's responsibility to fulfill it.[1]

It is this struggle with the law that lay then at the heart of Luther's monastic despair, for his agony was in large measure that of one who knew his efforts to be inadequate and thus of one who stood not meritorious but guilty before the judgments of God. These were experiences which he called his *tentationes de indignitate,*[2] and so by the very designation may be seen to rest upon his sense of unworthiness. He later recalled that when in the monastery he tried to live as the "Sophists" urged, namely, in sinless fashion, but such an attempt only drives one to despair.[3] Even when he was most diligent, he could not feel that he had wholly succeeded,[4] and even when he did appear to have succeeded in the eyes of others, he still was unable to pass that judgment upon himself.[5] In fact, increased holiness brought only greater uncertainty,[6] and though he lived as an irreprehensible monk, he felt compelled to recognize himself as "a sinner of troubled conscience."[7]

His conscience was troubled, of course, because of its unusual sensitiveness and by observations that had to do much more with the character of the inner life than with the realm of external action. Luther's earnest introspection compelled him to find sin in the realm of attitude as well as of act. He knew that God desired not only "righteous deeds, prayers, studying, reading, devotions, meditations, and other works," but also a "quiet, kindly, and obedient spirit,"[8] and his failure was in the latter as well as in the former. More than an obedient spirit, he found within a self-seeking spirit, and this became the major basis for his unrest. So beyond his concern over actual sins, his conscience also brought forth an intense concern over the root of those sins, and it is here in one respect, as he himself noted, that he differed from his contemporaries.[9] More than they, he sensed the power and the danger of man's egocentrism[10] and thus could say later, in reflecting upon his monastic years, that even when he was most diligent in following the monastic requirements, self-seeking always returned, making it impossible for him to find peace.[11] Technically, according to his inherited theology, the mere presence of such "concupiscence" did not constitute sin, for there could be guiltiness only if the will gave its consent to these promptings of selfish desire. But for Luther, so deeply conscious of the presence and power of egocentrism, this distinction in theory could have little meaning in reality. He knew self-seeking to be a "raging, unrestrained, disobedience of the flesh against the spirit," like a horse with a broken bridle which rears up and rebels against its rider.[12] In this state of awareness the ambiguous matter of consent lost much of its meaning, and conscience itself was troubled by the presence of such an overpowering foe.

So Luther knew himself to be "a sinner of troubled conscience," and this meant despair before the judgment of God. Then the words, "the righteousness of God," became a "thunderbolt" in his heart,[13] and twenty years later he said that he once hated so strongly this description of the divine that even yet he trembled out of habit whenever he heard mention made of it.[14] The experience of despair was thus the fear of God's righteous judgment. He knew Satan to hold before him the syllogism: God hates sinners; you are a sinner; therefore, God also hates you.[15] And similarly, this despair involved terror before Christ who would be the instrument of the divine punishment on the final day of judgment.[16] So he feared Christ more than he feared the devil himself,[17] and he was terrified even when he simply heard the name of

Jesus spoken.[18] He knew the Son of God to be a condemning tyrant,[19] and would have fled his presence, only to find such escape impossible.[20] Thus the judgment of God, both present and future, struck terror into his heart. It is, he said later in describing one of these experiences, to be in such distress that there is not even any secret place which is not filled up with the most bitter sadness, horror, trembling, and grief, so that one's spirit senses and drinks in nothing but eternal pain.[21] Luther's struggle with the law led to a guilt-laden conscience and to the accompanying fears of divine condemnation.

But the church was accustomed to the problem of guilt, and there were available for Luther all the helps of medieval consolation. Standing in fear of the judgment of God was not the innovation of an obscure monk in the sixteenth century. Luther's perceptions of sin may have been more intense than was customary, but they were far from new. The experience of all sensitive men involves floundering in the face of the law, and the ministrations of the church, whether by ordinary channels of mediation or by special recommendations of consolation, were therefore prepared to cope with this distress. But for Luther these helps were strikingly unsuccessful and indeed even became occasion for the further intensification of his despair.

The major consolation for the guilt-laden conscience was presented to Luther through the sacrament of penance. This was the church's most significant sacrament for the sinner, that channel of grace through which forgiveness could be bestowed and man re-established as acceptable in God's sight. Here the burden of guilt could be removed, the eternal punishment due for sin remitted, and the sinner granted once again the divine *habitus* of grace. And so Luther knew that when his struggle for holiness failed he could always turn to this sacrament for aid, for through the fulfillment of its conditions the divine wrath could be appeased and God once more be reconciled to men.[22] And yet, though he gave himself with diligence to the practice of confession,[23] he could not find peace.[24] He continued to doubt in spite of his penance[25] and was unable to quiet his troubled spirit.[26] He could not be certain as to whether his sins were really forgiven,[27] and he remained in fear and terror before the wrath of Christ.[28] In short, he found the sacrament of penance to be not a source of confidence but a source of such despair that he could later reflect upon it by designating it a "penance of the devil."[29]

The plain fact seems to be that, despite its offer of grace to the sinner, penance itself was so conceived as still to be within a legalistic framework and thus really of no lasting avail to the sensitive conscience struggling in the grips of the law. It is true that the *habitus* of grace granted through the channel of penance was adjudged, strictly speaking, not to be earned. One did not actually merit forgiveness of sins, for that was God's gracious bestowal upon the unworthy. And yet, the efficacious working of the sacrament was dependent upon the satisfactory fulfillment of prior conditions by the penitent himself, and it is in the problem of these prerequisites that Luther's grave difficulties with penance seem to have occurred. He later noted that in the sacrament he could find no forgiveness of sins, for it threw him back into the fruitless struggle for righteous works.[30]

Some of this frustration undoubtedly was attached to the prerequisite condition of oral confession. In this early monastic period Luther apparently believed in the necessity of a complete confession as the basis for a complete absolution, and thus he later recalled being disturbed over the possibility of omissions from his recital of sins.[31] He likewise remembered that his attempts to reach the goal of thoroughness were so intensive that the very act of confessing made him into a "sorry wretch"[32] and from his later perspective he maintained that his spirit had always been troubled in those early confessions because one's conscience can never find in one's works a basis for firm consolation.[33]

But the problem of penance also involved a more profound dimension than simply the recollection and cataloging of sins, and Luther's major difficulty in this sacrament seems thus to have been with the still prior condition of contrition. He knew no confession to be valid unless it were contrite, that is, motivated by a genuine and selfless sorrow for one's sin. God does not pardon the unrepentant sinner, and repentance itself must be of that high order which draws upon this purest sense of sorrow. The confession books of the Middle Ages were largely agreed that more than attrition is needed by the penitent if the sacrament is to be efficacious. This lesser remorse for sin, arising out of fear of punishment, is insufficient in itself as basis for pardon. A worthy and adequate penitence must come from higher motivation, the sense of regret at having offended God himself in sin's violation of the divine law. Therefore contrition is necessary—the sorrow which arises not out of love of self but out of love of God. And it is here that Luther was thrown back especially by the sacrament of penance into his fruitless struggle for righteousness under the law.

Principal among the requirements of the law was a supreme love for God, and so the *dilectio dei super omnia* became a major goal to which Luther's efforts in the monastery were directed. This was indeed the final and determinative end of his monastic endeavors, for as

poverty, chastity, and obedience were means to the overcoming of self-
will and self-assertiveness, they were the very channels through which
a higher love than that for self or for the things of the world could be
developed and expressed. So Luther later recalled that in his monastic
years he devoted both his body and his life to this purpose, putting
from his mind all thoughts of women, wealth, and honor in order that
he might manifest a love for God with his whole heart.[34] But the
struggle for this love was as fruitless as it was intense, for the total
legalistic complex in which this was cast rendered it impossible for
Luther to feel that the desired end had really been attained. The
legalism, of course, pictured God as retributor, rewarding the worthy
and punishing the unworthy. And for one who knew himself to be unworthy the problem of a love for God was thus great indeed. Luther
reasoned in this manner: To love God fully and above all other things
is to desire that he truly be God. It is to desire that he exercise his
power and his justice completely and that his purpose of righteous
retribution become unqualifiedly manifested in his relationship to men.
But how then, he would ask, could he love God? Such a love would
really be a yearning that God punish him for all eternity for his sins!
Indeed, who can love the God who rages, judges, and condemns?[35]
Nor did it help to read in Gabriel Biel the consoling word which advised banishing from one's mind thoughts of God's power and justice
and finding solace in reflections upon the divine mercy.[36] Luther knew
full well that the sensitive conscience fearing divine judgment simply
does not think out of existence the basis for that fear[37] and, further,
that mercy itself was understood within the context of justice as the
mercy which rewards those who are worthy.[38] So it was really not possible to love the judging God above all else. As a matter of fact, he
later recalled that during these monastic years he not only did not
love, but also actually hated "the righteous God who punishes sinners."[39] He could love God only if he knew that God first loved him,
but this love he did not know. And his problem was thus insoluble in
view of the very nature of his understanding of God.

But the sacrament of penance called for contrition, and the sorrow
which was contrition could arise only out of a love for God. So Luther
was thrown back by the sacrament into a renewal of his fruitless struggle with the law and led into a vicious circle of despair. In order to be
absolved from his sin he needed to love God above all else, but in order
to love God in this way he first needed to know that his sin had been
forgiven. Holiness was a condition for pardon, but for Luther pardon
was a necessary condition for holiness. Thus he struggled here for that

which he could not attain and was led by the sacrament itself to deeper unrest. His conscience continually exclaimed to him: "You have not been satisfactorily contrite!",[40] and he was then driven to doubt, hatred, and despair.[41] He later recalled that because of this doctrine of contrition his life in the monastery was one of great sadness,[42] for the certainty of absolution rests upon the certainty of contrition, but the latter is always in doubt.[43] Luther could not believe that his sins had been forgiven because he could not believe that he had been fully contrite.

It should be noted further, however, that consolation utilizing the doctrine of attrition was offered at this point, for it was held that if full contrition were found impossible then one could come to his confession in attrition and the sacrament itself could transform this imperfect sorrow into one of perfection.[44] Johann Paltz, teacher in the Augustinian Order in Erfurt, had advanced this view in Luther's own time, combining attrition with prayer to the saints and "doing all that lies within one" as the basis for the sacramental transformation of this lesser sorrow into one of selfless love. Indeed, he added that the sacramental transformation is possible even for those who do less than that which lies within them if they only make some movement toward the good, for if it were not, then the passions of Christ would be largely lost inasmuch as there are so many Christians who do not utilize their powers to the full.[45] But again, Luther could find no help here. It may be, as Boehmer has suggested, that the failure was in the contradiction of the theory to Luther's own experience, that is, in his recognition of the continuing selfish character of his sorrow unchanged by any sacramental transformation.[46] But it is more likely, as Holl has insisted, that Luther simply had nothing whatsoever to do with attrition in this early period.[47] The demands for the perfections of the law lay very heavily upon him, and the *dilectio dei super omnia* undergirding contrition was chief among those obligations. In fact, it is then likely that attrition itself became for him a sin which needed to be confessed along with the rest, for that imperfect sorrow rested basically upon a love for himself rather than upon a love for God. And so he struggled on, confessing his sin, being uncertain about his contrition, and then confessing anew.[48] Thus again, because he could not believe he was fully contrite,[49] the sacrament of penance became not a means of consolation but a cause for despair.

Yet even this greater unrest was not wholly unknown to the theological writers of the late Middle Ages,[50] and one finds still further helps for distressed spirits frequently suggested in the literature of consolation. It was maintained, for example, that if one continues to be disturbed by his sin and cannot believe that he has done all that is necessary in order to receive full absolution, he can turn to God in hope, remembering that in the Scripture God had frequently commanded men to hope, and believing that through his obedience to this command the promises of divine mercy would be fulfilled. One must place his faith in God's goodness and find his consolation in the confidence that God will save those who put their trust in him.[51]

That Luther was confronted by this "command to hope," apart from any knowledge that he may have had of it through the literature of consolation, appears not to be unlikely. He later recalled that while he was in the monastery he was reminded of it on one occasion by his preceptor,[52] on another occasion by a monastic brother,[53] and on a still further occasion by a priest.[54] Yet even this consolation, with its seemingly evangelical character, was of little avail.[55] The fact of the matter seems to be that, in spite of its emphasis upon a need for confidence in his faithfulness as one who will fulfill his promises, this call to hope was still not emancipated from the whole idea of merit and reward which dominated the thought of Luther's day. One must indeed hope for God's mercy, for God had so commanded, but the ultimate basis for one's faith must still be the conviction that one's own accomplishments were adequate for the receiving of the gifts of God's graciousness.[56] The consolatory writings emphasized that one must "do all that lies within him" as basis for confidence of the reception of grace, and then even the very humility which is recommended in laying oneself in trust before God takes on the character of meritoriousness.[57]

And so Luther was again thrown back into the struggle for work-righteousness even by this command to hope. Applied to the question of absolution, where he seemed particularly to have been faced by this matter, it meant that his hope for forgiveness must still rest on an adequate fulfillment of the conditions which the sacrament of penance imposed. That it really had no more extended meaning for him than this is strongly suggested in his later recollection of that occasion on which he was reminded of this "command to hope" by the priest to whom he was confessing. There, he recalled, he was told to hope in God's mercy and go in peace. But the result, he added, was that he continued to be extremely disturbed over the conditional nature of absolution.[58]

Recognizing, however, the distress that can continue to come to a person of sensitive conscience as he views the nature of his own works in the light of the judgment of God, the authors of the medieval literature of consolation sought to provide a still further means for the tempering of despair. It was their added suggestion that the laws which one attempts to fulfill as he endeavors to attain to holiness need not be affirmed in all of their seeming severity. Their requirements can be modified and the seriousness of violations against them be lessened, thus providing to even the person of unusually sensitive conscience a basis for consolation in his effort to bring them to fulfillment. Certainly, it was held, this is true of the laws of the church in the sense that violation of ecclesiastical ordinances need not be construed as mortal sins. But, it was added, this modification of severity could also be applied to the law of God—and in a twofold sense. A first application had to do with the distinction between precepts and counsels. Though a fulfillment of the counsels of the law is salutary, still it is never really required for salvation. It is enough to follow the precepts, even though they are a lesser good, for they are still good by virtue of the fact that they are the commands of God.[59] Though more could have been required, God is content with adherence to the precepts which he has given.[60] And second, it was further held that the precepts themselves are never to be thought of as beyond the power of human fulfillment. Violation of the precepts can indeed be mortal sin, but one must remember that God does not require anything which man cannot accomplish.[61] Thus, when one "does all that lies within him," he can be confident of the acceptability of his life before God.

Probably the modification of ecclesiastical law, especially as it applied to liturgical and devotional requirements, was not particularly relevant to Luther's situation, for his despair was of a nature more profound than the type of scrupulosity which worried over penalties for carelessness in the use of one's ecclesiastical vestments or for negligence in the saying of one's canonical hours. It is true, of course, that Luther had been taught the seriousness of offense involved in violation of the monastic Rule and of the ecclesiastical requirements in general, and he was unquestionably concerned over the matter of correct fulfillment. Even allowing for the polemic element which colored his later recollections, one must recognize the kind of factuality that undoubtedly lay behind his remembrances pertaining to this matter. For instance, it was undoubtedly an expression of later exaggeration when he said that under the papacy he had learned that fornication, adultery, murder, and theft could be annulled through indulgences, whereas if one did not have a candle in the Mass he was guilty of an unforgivable sin for which no indulgence was furnished,[62] and yet he knew this latter to be a very serious offense. Similarly, that the prayers of the liturgies were a "torture" to him in the monastery undoubtedly rested in some real measure on his knowledge that neglect or error of even a most minute nature in the reading of the responses of the choir was deemed sufficient to place him in danger of a very serious judgment.[63] Thus there is also reason to recognize the personal basis for Luther's later praise of Gerson as one who does assist the conscience by showing that these ecclesiastical offenses are not really mortal sins.[64] Yet, again, this aspect of the matter would not have touched Luther's deepest problem. In the last analysis he was not simply a monastic *Skrupulant*. Deeper than the problem of the Rule was the problem of righteousness. More profound than concern over the liturgy was concern over love. The modification of the ecclesiastical law may have provided some consolation at one level, but by no means did this relieve the more troubling element in Luther's despair. That had to do with his relationship to the requirements for love and righteousness in the divine law itself.

It is at this crucial point, however, that the consolations offered through modification of the law failed to speak effectively to Luther's problem. On the one hand, his primary difficulty was not with the counsels but with precepts. The requirements of poverty, chastity, and obedience were not the principal cause of his trouble, but rather the underlying command to love God with his whole heart, of which the fulfillment of the evangelical counsels was but a higher expression. He knew himself to be a sinner not because he could not live in poverty, but because his actual self-denial was motivated by self-love; not because he could not be chaste, but because his actual chastity lacked the motivations of spontaneity out of love for God which it should possess; not because he could not bow his will in humility to that of his monastic superior, but because that very humility became occasion for self-congratulation and pride. Thus Luther's chief difficulty with the law lay in his seeming inability to fulfill even that minimum requirement of love for God which was laid upon all, and it would then be of little help to be reminded that a fulfillment of the evangelical counsels is not actually necessary for salvation.

But even more important, the further suggestion of modifying the precepts themselves could have little meaning for one in Luther's state of mind. Luther's primary point of reference in understanding the content of the law was not anthropocentric, but theocentric. It is God's law which is laid upon men. That is the basic consideration, and the law's content is to be determined, therefore, not in terms of man's power for fulfillment, but solely in terms of God's desires in requirement. God may actually require more than one can accomplish, but one's responsibility is by no means lessened thereby.[65] And so Luther knew himself to be confronted by a supreme obligation. The very voice of God spoke to him, demanding perfection. He could not modify in any way these requirements, but only seek to obey. The great peril of a false security was in fact present in any attempt to believe that God's demands are not as strict as they really are.[66] So the modification of the divine law could bring no consolation, for Luther began his thinking not with man, but with God.

There is also a further dimension of Luther's agony and the consolation offered to it which needs to be noted, however, for the time came in his monastic struggle when his despair moved beyond despair of self to be likewise a despair of God. To his *tentationes de indignitate* there were added *tentationes de praedestinatione*.[67] In specifying the character of this latter distress, it needs to be observed that this involved genuine fear of predestination to punishment by arbitrary divine action. The stress of the *via moderna* upon the freedom of the human will in the process of salvation did not mean that the theological system was completely and unalterably tied to the rationalism of a pattern of merit and reward. Had that been true, there could be no fear of predestination as divine arbitrariness, for God himself would be bound by the requirements of his justice, and predestination would simply be based upon foreknowledge of one's merits or sins. But actually, the voluntarism of the *via moderna* stressed the freedom of the divine will, as well as the human, and thus the possibility of a shattering of the rationalism of the system of merit and reward through the irrationalism of the free actions of an arbitrary God. It would seem to be this additional element of the potential divine caprice that became basis for the further intensity of Luther's anguished experience.[68]

It was as one who, while seeking to earn his salvation through the meritoriousness of his works, could not be certain that even the best of those works would be accepted by God as meritorious, that Luther experienced his deepest despair in this monastic period. Thus he later recalled that though he followed faithfully the requirements for prayer set forth by his Order, he could not have the assurance that God was pleased thereby.[69] The same uncertainty of acceptability accompanied the saying of the Mass,[70] and when he had devoted himself most fully to the ascetic works of his calling, mortifying his flesh almost to point of death, he was still troubled by the question, "Who knows if these are pleasing to God?"[71] And then uncertainty gave rise to fear, the terrible fear that God had arbitrarily chosen not to be for him but to be against him. Now it mattered not, so he believed, even if he made full atonement for his sins, for God's judgment would still rest upon him.[72] God was his antagonist, and there was no escape. He faced the terrible question, "Who knows if I am one to whom God has chosen to be merciful?",[73] and with it the haunting fear that God had indeed chosen to reject him and to consign him to the everlasting pains of hell.[74] This was the abyss of deepest despair, the sense of being forsaken through an arbitrary act of divine predestination.[75]

But even such agony, of course, was not unknown to the writers of medieval consolation. And yet once again, the consolation offered was not only unavailing, but actually failed by virtue of the fact that it, too, led Luther back into his fruitless struggle with the law. The dominant emphasis found in the consolation for predestination-distress urged that one recognize these experiences as sent by God for redemptive purposes. By bringing intense doubt and despair they can assist in the elimination of pride and false security. Indeed they can then also lead conversely to the development of saving virtue, for as one endures the sufferings patiently, his presumption can be changed into that humility which will make him more worthy of eternal favor. And then the further word is also added that this is, actually, the highest manner in which a conformity to Christ can be expressed. Christ himself knew despair—and most intensely through a sense of being divinely forsaken. Even he was not spared a spiritual descent into hell and all the fear of God's willful abandonment. And so as the nature of meritoriousness is to be found in a conformity to the life of Christ, the highest type of merit lies in a following of this aspect of Christ's experience, entering with him into the pit of its suffering and enduring with him the intensity of its pain. The experiences of predestination-despair can be viewed as God's instruments leading one on the path to salvation.[76]

With such thoughts as these Luther was likewise most assuredly familiar. Not only were they in the literature of consolation, but also they would have come to him from Staupitz, who frequently consoled Luther in this despair.[77] To some extent, of course, they must have influenced him positively. He later found consolation for this type of agony by seeing in it a conformity to Christ, though the meaning of that conformity came to be interpreted by him in a radically different fashion. It is not that one finds in Christ even at this point an example to be followed for the achievement of merit, but rather that one can look at the fact of Christ in the faith that what God worked in him by way of victory over predestination-despair can also be worked by God in us. The conformity is thus envisaged as a triumphant act not of human, but of divine, power.[78]

In the light of this, however, it is not too much to presume that in the monastic years, and thus before the development of this evangelical interpretation, the consolation of *conformitas Christi* was not fundamentally helpful and perhaps even led to an intensification of Luther's basic problem. The underlying presupposition was still that of work-righteousness as the way to salvation, and the proclamation of the divine purpose of these predestination-terrors was still a call to merit. Thus Luther would have been confronted once again with the obligation resting upon him for the development of the humility worthy of salvation and led anew into the despair which any such effort inevitably brought forth. Even the consolation for fear of predestination threw him back into the struggle with the law.

One final word of general consolation, however, was offered to despairing spirits by the medieval church, for it was held that in the last analysis no one could be absolutely certain about his salvation unless that certainty were given to him by a special revelation. A certain amount of doubt was a normal part of the life both of the world-Christian and of the monk. Thomas Aquinas had laid down this principle centuries earlier,[79] and Johann Paltz has enunciated it again in Luther's own day.[80] The Christian must find a middle ground between absolute certainty and despair, and that meant that a measure of doubt would be natural in his religious outlook. The best for which one could hope would be a moral or probable certainty that his life is acceptable to God.[81]

So Luther knew that even though a man was righteous he could not be absolutely confident of his salvation until the Day of Judgment.[82] He learned that though one lived righteously, he still could not be certain that he was in the state of grace.[83] Indeed, he even knew that when one had fulfilled all of the requirements of the law, he ought then to pray that God guard him from being so presumptuous as actually to believe that he now possessed the Holy Ghost.[84] Thus the medieval tradition taught Luther that absolute certainty was impossible and that doubt was a normal part of the religious life.[85] If all else failed, could not this become a means of consolation for him in his despair?

The key to the answer would seem to lie in the final word of the question itself, for the fact is that Luther was not in the state of simple doubt, but in that of utter despair. His basic problem was not that of one who seemingly fulfilled the law and then remained uncertain as to whether or not his work would really be accepted, but rather that of one who could not believe that the law had been fulfilled in the first place in the actions of his life. The consolation of the normality of doubt presupposed the presence of a certain amount of confidence; namely, the probable certainty that one is in the state of grace. But for Luther not even this degree of certainty was possible, for he was far too conscious of his sin. Thus, though doubt was normal, Luther knew his doubts to be abnormal, and he could find no help here. His problem struck deeper than the level of necessary uncertainty of grace, for his struggle was with the law, which he could not fulfill, and then with the angry God who would condemn him eternally for his failure to fulfill it. Consolation couched in the patterns of legalism could not provide real help. Such help could come only with the advent of evangelical understanding.

Luther's Frontier in Hungary

William Toth

On August 1, 1533 the Hungarian bishop at Szerem, Stephen Brodarics, dispatched a lengthy letter to Pope Clement VII (1523-1534) in
which he reported the alarming spread of "Lutheranism" in Hungary.[1] The teachings of Luther and his followers, he wrote, have
penetrated the entire kingdom, the areas under the jurisdiction of
Ferdinand as well as Transylvania ruled by John Zápolya, and are
assiduously striking deeper and deeper roots. Everything is coming
under the sway of Lutheran teachings, which are widely preached.
The priests are marrying, indulgences and dispensations are despised,
and the representatives of the Holy See are lost for counsel against
such things. To their defense of indulgences comes the inevitable reply
from every mouth: freely you have received, freely give.[2] Everywhere
there is preaching in criticism of the Roman See and it seems advis-
able to omit the complaints against excessive taxation, the neglect of
spiritual things and concern for merely the material things of life.
There is need for a council and the restoration of many things, he ad-
monishes. No reasonable arguments can be marshalled in defense of
the old verities which the followers of Luther, Brodarics continues in
another letter,[3] counter with quotations from the Gospels and the letters of Paul. The report of Paul Szondi, the apostolic penitentiary,
will confirm these observations, he adds.

The intelligence of this advance of the Lutheran heresy brought a
quick reply from the Pope,[4] whose anxiety is understandable not only
in light of the political developments in the home base of this religious deviation but also because from the beginning of his pontificate
Clement had been designated as "Protector of Hungary," an honor he
took seriously. Now even in his protectorate a new frontier of the Lutheran heresy was developing to plague the Roman curia.

This enormous success on the eastern periphery of the Roman
church is a historical phenomenon taking place somewhere in the
middle of Luther's career as a reformer.[5] Before his death in 1546 his
movement will have arrived at a peak point of achievement in Hun-

gary. Then it will yield to the predominating influence of Calvinism. How the adoption of the "new faith" occurred and what factors in Hungarian history and Luther's movement interplayed to bring about this religious reorientation during Luther's lifetime will be the burden of this essay.

The ready acceptance of the "new" tenets in Hungary cannot be accounted for merely as the result of historical circumstances at the turn of the sixteenth century, often regarded as transitional by Catholic historians of this age. A full understanding will come by asking whether there was a disposition in the inherent character of the Hungarian church to respond favorably to such a program as that which challenged the age from Wittenberg. A complete answer to this question would lead us too far afield. Nevertheless, several considerations are in order.

Hungarians, having been Christianized,[6] had developed their political, social, economic, and intellectual life on the patterns dominant in the West during the Middle Ages. The kingdom of St. Stephen, in its institutions and customs, generally came to reflect the powerful influences that were already established in the Romano-Germanic west. For instance, the first Hungarian university at Veszprém, founded during the reign of Béla III (d. 1196)[7] was copied in every respect after Paris. Another profound effect of the West upon Hungary was the nature of feudalism as it was inherited. To this day Hungary has not outgrown the agricultural economy that its mentor, the church, with its scholastic philosophy and its system of latifundia, cultivated so zealously. By and large, the nomadic Hungarians adopted western culture and grew up in identification with it. Yet, a resistance to this universalism in favor of national individuality is a recurrent theme of these first five hundred years. The Hungarian clergy always provided leadership to such opposition.[8] Although basically loyal to the religious institution and culture which in the heyday of Cluniac influence brought it into being, the Hungarian church, in its unique constitutional role, generally looked upon itself as a ward of the nation against hostile designs either of the nobility or the Roman curia.[9] Moreover, both clergy and nobility, maintaining lively contacts with western culture, were well acquainted with western efforts in the thirteenth and fourteenth centuries to assert nationalism over against the universal claims of the church. Their king, Sigismund, played a key role in one of the most notable encounters between universalism and nationalism at Constance, to which Hungarian prelates and nobles, representatives of towns, professors, and students of the University at Buda, were witnesses.[10] From this and succeeding reform councils they took back to their country knowledge of contemporary critical thought in support of their own interests, if these were jeopardized by Rome.

While the Hungarian church was initiated and developed integrally with the Roman organization, political circles again and again assumed skeptical, if not hostile, attitudes toward the political aims and alliances of the Roman curia.[11] A common front with universal western Christianity might ensure the survival of the nation, but in the process of state-building it was also interpreted to mean jeopardizing its national independence. As universalism was breaking down in favor of particularism represented by national interests, the Hungarian nation clearly was part of the tug-of-war. Paradoxically, the nation became aware of Luther's movement both because it shared in the tradition of universalism and because of the rising force of particularism. Isolation from the cultural climate was unthinkable.

The nation could, of course, have turned to the church in the East, with which it was contiguous along its Transylvanian border. Perhaps the only influence emanating from this direction was the confirmation of a concept already well established in the West, namely, that Christianity can exist without a Roman pontiff to whom Christ demands obedience from all. Adherents of Constantinople and Rome had for centuries constituted a legal problem in Transylvania. Coexistence triumphed, and with the increasing influx of Eastern Orthodox—Rumanians, Ruthenians and Serbs—these schismatics were ultimately even given exemption from the payment of tithes. Fraternization among peoples led to mutual appreciation as well as reciprocal conversions.[12] By the sixteenth century one fourth of Transylvania was made up of Rumanians;[13] their physical existence alone tended to minimize the idea of unchangeableness and subtly to fortify the concept of a possible alternative interpretation of Christianity.[14]

The most virile contact with the West immediately prior to the Reformation movement was, of course, Humanism. The Renaissance ruler, Matthias Corvinus, opened the floodgates which the inept rule of his Jagelloan successors could not close.[16] Critical thinking, as elsewhere on the continent, found a place in the numerous houses of the monastic orders and their schools. Pelbart Temesvári achieved such eminence as preacher, for instance, that between 1498 and 1521 his sermons reached fifty-two editions.[17] Young men from the upper social group and from the prosperous cities went abroad to study at Paris, Prague, Vienna, Cracow, and the Italian universities. Statistics for the years 1458-1490 show 1263 students at Cracow, 951 at Vienna, and

66 at Padua in addition to those enrolled in the native university at Pozsony where Humanism thrived.[18] The membership of the Danubian Sodality included several outstanding Hungarian humanists.[19] The influence of Erasmus, however, appears to have been limited, for by the time his writings found their way into Hungary they were confronted with the more acceptable Lutheran views. Nevertheless, the tide of Erasmian piety seems to be reflected, at least partially, in the endeavors of urban communities to expand their autonomous privileges by selecting qualified clergy for their pulpits, controlling ecclesiastical benefices, and directing religious and moral life without respect to episcopal legalities.[20] Separation from Roman officialdom could not have been contemplated even if the laws of Matthias against heretics had not equated it with treason,[21] but an alienation of spirit involving critical thought and a sensitivity to change was definitely cultivated.[22] Traditional ideals and institutions were being subjected to re-examination and a climate of liberality favored new forces of thought.

The strong, centralized rule of Matthias ended in 1490 with his death and the succession of two weak foreign kings, Wladislas II (1490-1516) and Louis II (1516-1526), ushered in an era of reckless confusion throughout the nation on all levels. The feudal lords were bent upon re-establishing a medieval order based upon private agreements. Their eagerness to enlarge their power and their landholdings was only partially checked by an embryonic middle class, the lesser nobility, which was just emerging politically and struggling hard for its independence, influence, and rights[23] and demanded its share of the national wealth. In the scramble for power, position, and prestige, the politically immature and socially insecure representatives of the lesser nobility were tempted to make deals with the old families, as Stephen Werböczi, the author of the *Tripartitum* or the codification of laws, and, if unsuccessful, to rally the true nationalists and the disgruntled elements under the banner of the opposition, like John Zápolya, wealthy governor of Transylvania. The authority of the crown and constitutionalism were openly flaunted by islands of oligarchies in pursuit of self-aggrandizement. Not only was the country exposed by these circumstances to possible attack from the threatening Turkish menace on the outside but, internally, the confusion fomented dissatisfactions. Most symptomatic of this condition was the Peasants' Revolt of 1514, headed by George Dózsa, a nobleman who was supported by the leaders and priests of the privileged agricultural towns. But equally reflecting the dissatisfactions of the times was the growing strength of the nationalist party in the Diet, which, attributing the deplorable state of things to the presence of a foreigner on the throne, succeeded in 1505 in forcing through a law that forbade the future election of anyone but a native son. The connivance of Wladislaw with the emperor, Maximilian I, successfully frustrated this nationalistic aim in the election of Louis II but did not allay the fears of nationalists, for the king, though well-meaning, was too inexperienced to cope with corruption in high places, economic deterioration, and the nervous confusion occasioned by the military proximity of the Turks. "In state and church alike there emerged rifts, disintegration, parties, bent upon mutual annihilation," concludes a historian.[24]

The moral leadership of the church in the midst of chaos and confusion had ample opportunity to assert itself, as it so often did in the past, but it did not. Along with the authority of the king, ecclesiastical influence was on the downgrade. A Catholic historian provides us with the following description of conditions in the Hungarian church at the turn of the century: "Even more devastating upon the church were its own sins and deficiencies, prevailing disorders in government, the breakdown of discipline, and the immorality of the priesthood. . . . The bishops vied with secular lords in pomp, excesses and worldly pleasures and, to pay for them, preoccupied themselves in amassing wealth.[25] Some engaged in trade; others joined up with Jews to lend money on interest . . . Others exploited the lower clergy to such an extent that they had to seek the protection of the nobles . . . The lower clergy were no better than their superiors. The decrees of councils testify that the morals of the clergy taken as a whole were not such as to set an example of Christian life to the people. Ignorant in the main,[26] many of them engaged in worldly pursuits and neglected the people who, for lack of schools,[27] depended solely upon the church for instruction. The natural consequence of this was that the minds of the people were not enlightened by sacred instruction . . . religion lost its power over the people through ignorant and indolent priests, its true significance was not comprehended and it degenerated into sensual, outward mechanical ceremonies."[28]

Patently, the Hungarian church at the end of the Middle Ages had lost its capacity to give direction and example to national life. Paralyzed to a greater degree by its inward deterioration than by the catastrophe at Mohács later in 1526, it stood in sore need of spiritual quickening. Many sensed this need not only among the people at the grassroots but also among those who assumed their reform position on the basis of a clear knowledge of reformist activities prevailing in

other parts of the universal western church. The hammer blows of
Luther on the castle church door at Wittenberg in 1517 could readily
attract favorable attention in the kingdom of St. Stephen lying athwart
both sides of the Southern stretches of the Danube.

Several factors must be considered which at the time militated
strongly against Luther's success among Hungarians.

One of these was the predominance of foreign advisors at the court,
which caused the nationalist party to strive toward closing its ranks.
The proponents of nationalism despised everything foreign—king,
priests, nobility, but especially everything that was German. The
papal nuncio perceptively reported to Rome: "Hungary and Germany are natural enemies, on account of which whatever is favored
by one is certainly to be rejected by the other."[29] The queen, Maria,
sister of Ferdinand the Hapsburg ruler of Austria, was German;
George of Brandenburg,[30] having become ward of the infant king,
was all the more unpopular in the higher nationalist circles as he
married the widow of John Corvinus, inherited the vast possessions
of the Hunyadys, and blocked the ambitions of certain Hungarian
nobles to obtain this influential office. The councils of the nation appear to have fallen prey to foreign domination, a circumstance all the
more perilous to nationalists as the court entertained and encouraged
the heretical *pestis* and, in a tight spot, threatened more than once to
embrace Lutheranism in case the Pope allied himself with Francis
against the Hapsburg Charles. This strong opposition of the nationalists lulled even the clear-headed papal nuncio, Burgio, into a sense
of false security *vis-à-vis* the growing influence of Lutheranism, when
as late as August 17, 1524 he transmitted this intelligence to Rome:
"Since Hungarians are great enemies of the Germans, I suspect that
one of these days they will be involved in a great scandal on the pre-
text that they do not wish to tolerate Lutherans."[31] The nationalists,
however, were soon to rise above this antipathy and reverse their position toward the new movement.

Closely allied with this deterrent factor was the Turkish threat,
which like the sword of Damocles hung over the nation. Where to
obtain aid in this national peril? Nationalists felt that security could
not be based on the foreign influences ensconced in the court. The
head of Christendom had again and again failed central-European
peoples in the previous century. Singlehanded, Hungarian leaders
like John Hunyady and his son, Matthias Corvinus, had effectively
held back the tide of Ottoman invasion, a feat accomplished only by
dint of the unified effort of the nation itself, it was felt by national-

ists. Lack of confidence in the ability of the leading group to hold the reins of government competently and with moral responsibility was confirmed in the minds of nationalists, beyond a shadow of doubt, when, in 1521, a powerful Turkish thrust reached the Southern lines of fortifications and the government was in no position to render assistance to the outposts. The moral bankruptcy of the court was exceeded only by the financial muddle into which the country had gotten.[32] Nationalists shared the views of the Venetian envoy who reported concerning the vast national potentials of Hungary: "If the King of Hungary were in a position to dispose freely of his country's natural resources and manpower, he could easily vie with any other ruler."[33] The king could be in this position of strength to defend the nation, provided the person of the king were one which represented the will of the nation. To the nationalists of the lesser nobility the foreign kings at Buda constituted the chief obstacle to national security. As a political weapon, therefore, the presence of a foreigner at the head of the nation explained to them why the Turkish thrust continued unabated, why the treasury was empty, why no effective strategy of self-defense emerged, and why the taxes and the precious possessions of the church were being dissipated. Meanwhile, however, to bolster its position the court, nobles and high priests alike, had not only professed its undying adherence to the old faith, still persuaded to secure its power and position through whatever strength was inherent in the old order, but it also went so far as to enact stringent laws against "heresy," in order to demonstrate its unswerving loyalty. At this point, many among the lesser nobility of native Hungarians began to look with greater favor upon the new religious views and, in this change of heart, affected of course by a complex of elements, national feeling particularly after the catastrophe of Mohács saw the future of the nation in the radical changes advocated by Luther. The Saxons in Transylvania joined the Hungarian lords. Nationalism and Reformation merged.

At first, the Peasants' Revolt in Germany, generally believed to have been caused by Lutheranism, tended to offset the shift. But, a question gradually dawned upon the minds of many: Had not the revolt of the Hungarian lower classes preceded that? There was no Luther then. The causes of social and economic dissatisfaction, then, are more basic. Moreover, what redress of grievances came about as a result of the national rebellion under Dózsa? None, but the further depression of social and economic conditions by the court and its adherents in its pursuit of wanton self-aggrandizement. It became evident that national improvement depended upon an intellectual, social, and economic program that found its basis in something else—in the liberating ideals of the German Reformer.

Concerning the swift circulation of the ninety-five theses throughout Europe a contemporary wrote that within four weeks these propositions went into all of Christendom.[34] Tetzel noted in a letter to Miltitz before the end of this notable year, "Since Martin Luther the Augustinian aroused and set the nobility against me—not only throughout Germany but also in the kingdoms of Bohemia, Hungary and Poland, I am safe nowhere."[35]

How did they get into Hungary? General agreement prevails among Hungarian scholars, in spite of the lack of evidences, that the first carriers were the traders and monastic priests, both foreign and native.[36] By 1521 Stephen Werböczi, one of the notable delegates to Worms, claims to be fully informed of Luther's views from personal reading of his works.[37] One John Korb writes to the priest of Selmecbánya, Gregory Soravus, in August 1521 that he has sent him several Luther books of great interest.[38] That the writings of Luther were being read is confirmed by the testimony of a citizen of Sopron who during the search for heretics in 1524 affirmed that he could not rightfully be blamed for reading books that were being sold in the open market.[39] The popularity of the Luther writings must have mounted considerably, since the king felt constrained to dispatch a letter of warning to the citizens of Nagyszeben at the beginning of 1524 in which he said, "We have been informed and shocked that the sacrilegious teachings of a certain Martin Luther, long ago excommunicated along with his followers from the church by the apostolic Holy See, should have so beclouded the reason of many everywhere that, disregarding the evangelical truth and the teachings of the fathers, all of you should possess, read and observe the books written by him."[40] In February of 1525 an even stronger edict, sent to the citizens of Bártfa, imposed the penalty of death and the confiscation of goods upon those holding Lutheran views and books.[41] The first martyr to the cause was a humble servant of the brother of Conrad Cordatus, who in 1524 sent some Luther books to friends in Buda, where the purveyor of the forbidden literature was burned,[42] while around the same time a similar fate overtook a German merchant on the Western boundaries of the country at the hands of a nobleman.[43] The proscribed books of Luther were penetrating into all corners of the land.[44] On the estates of certain lesser nobles, like Peter Perényi and Thomas Nádasdy, who achieved independent political power as nationalists, protection was not wanting by 1525;[45] on the estates of others, many evidences of persecution were likewise noted.

Although the archbishop of Esztergom, George Szathmári, as primate of Hungary ordered (1521) the reading of the papal bull against Luther,[46] outstanding preachers like Paul Speratus (1484-1551), who went to Hungary from Würzburg in 1522, and Simon Grynaeus, who had found a safe haven at Buda after a checkered career as a liberal in Vienna, introduced Luther in the pulpit. The royal court at Buda became a center of reform ideas, Queen Mary and George of Brandenburg, the king's ward, being very sympathetic listeners of Conrad Cordatus until his banishment in 1524. Other preachers followed suit,[47] presumably preaching in the vernacular.[48] These sermons went far in their advocacy of reform ideas. They demanded freedom in the practice of religious beliefs and changes in the mass,[49] particularly with respect to the possibility of omitting auricular confession.[50] The procession was declared to be useless[51] and the building of churches and altars not a necessary evidence of piety.[52] The primary duty of the preacher, the citizens of Selmeczbánya observed, was to preach the word of God.[53]

Particularly odious in the eyes of preachers of the liberal persuasion was the sale of indulgences, the concrete evidence for which is to be seen in the failure of the special fund-raising campaign of 1525.[54] Burgio reported that at Buda only 300 florins were received, disillusioning to say the least, all the more since when the collection box was opened there were found chips of glass and ceramic, counterfeit coins, and a note reading, "Take your holy year to Rome and leave us our money." The papal nuncio was moved to inform Sadoleto: "From these you may see how the religious situation has deteriorated in this country in the last twenty-five years." A quarter century earlier the collection amounted to 125,000 florins, while now, he lamented, it will be fortunate to get three to four thousand—a sad deterioration for which he held Luther responsible.[55]

Luther's attack upon the Roman doctrine of excommunication, likewise, found its supporters.[56] The right of depriving people from salvation, they declared, lay within the jurisdiction of God not man, particularly not men who used this disciplinary instrument to force the collection of moneys. Wherever Luther became known, fasting also was abandoned. In 1524 the regions of Szeben and Brassó flaunted the regulations by consuming proscribed foods on fast days.[57]

The power of the clergy came under attack first of all among the citizens of towns. Priests were ridiculed in songs,[58] a practice becoming so annoyingly widespread that the bishop of Gyulafehérvár issued an extensive pastoral letter in which he threatened the perpetrators with excommunication.[59] Sermons were demanding that canonical law in general, since it had originated in the mind of the devil not the Holy Spirit, be declared invalid. Even the spiritual authority of the priesthood was questioned in a sermon (1524) at Sopron by one who claimed that the Pope and the bishop have no more authority than a simple priest,[60] while two years later a "Lutheran" priest was charged with teaching that everyone is a priest and may baptize.[61] Clerical celibacy also was condemned as a device of the hierarchy to bolster its power position[62] and, more often violated than observed, constituted a source of scandalous behavior so that, while formerly adulterers were barred from attendance at mass, now adulterers and fornicators were permitted to recite it[63] before the altar. The effects of such preaching were soon visible in the number of those who forsook the religious orders, took wives to themselves, and achieved peace of mind in the resolution of former inner conflicts.

That these ideas were having their effect upon the young men of the nation is borne out by the fact that an increasing number of students were being attracted to Wittenberg. The rectors of the university noted thirteen of them between 1522 and 1526 and nine more by 1530 in spite of the confusion regnant throughout Hungary after the battle of Mohács.[64] No records exist to tell of reform activities by them upon their return except in the case of Matthias Biró Déváy, of whom more later, but it is noteworthy that, from the twenties on, the trend among Hungarian students going abroad was to seek out and study at the centers of the Reformation movement.[65]

Let us look next at the attitudes manifested at the court prior to the Mohács catastrophe.

The spread of Luther's doctrines was definitely affected by the character of Louis II's court. A mere child at his enthronement in 1516, Louis was regarded as a "talented youth" but "too inexperienced, too young, and too much under the influence of his courtiers."[66] The fulcrum of political power lay in the hands of George of Brandenburg, the king's ward, and Stephen Werböczi, the palatine, who constitutionally stood next in legal authority to the king. After Louis' marriage in 1521, the young queen, Maria, granddaughter of Maximilian I, exerted considerable influence in setting a cultural tone that appealed alike to the German retinue of the Brandenburgian prince and the liberal-minded Germans whom the queen brought with her from Vienna. An Erasmian, she favored the critical preaching of Conrad Cordatus and John Henckel, protected them, and at once stood in the cross fires of party strife in religious matters. Luther fully appreciated her services to the cause as witnessed by the comforting words expressed in the dedicatory preface to his *Vier tröstliche Psalmen an die Königen zu Ungarn.*[67] Werböczi remained a confirmed adherent of the old faith.[68] The Brandenburgian prince was not above providing a stiff defense of his controversial compatriot in after dinner conferees but his sympathies merely served, in the beginning, to alienate nationalists toward the court. The hierarchy was ably represented—the papal curia by Cardinal Thomas Vio and Antonio Giovanni barone del Burgio, sent as nuncio in the middle of 1523 with 60,000 gold pieces in his strongbox for the use of the king.[70] Wielding great influence, especially in view of his control over the papal funds deposited in the Fugger bank of Buda, Burgio considered his most urgent function the collection of funds for defense against the Turks and the maintenance of a strong state organization that could be depended upon by the Pope. "If this country were in agreement and had a good government," he asserted, "this country would be most effective in deterring the Turks."[71] At the head of the hierarchy and occupying the third position of power in the nation was László Szalkay, archbishop of Esztergom, competent, a consummate orator, a cobbler's son skyrocketed into prominence, thus hungry for property and for the cardinal's hat promised him. One of his first acts after his elevation to the highest ecclesiastical post of the land was to have Grynaeus, Cordatus, Kreisling, and other liberal preachers displaced and driven from the country; yet eager to express his loyalty to the royalty surrounded by liberal Germans, he could scarcely exert himself fully in behalf of the old faith. We cannot know the real sentiments of the young king. As ruler his behavior toward the church was in every respect correct, no doubt due to the presence of the papal dignitaries and his dependence upon their financial assistance. Such pressure, presumably, lay behind his letter to Frederick of Saxony in 1524 protesting his protection of Lutheran heresies and, thereby, being the cause of disorders in other countries. Frederick in the same year assured Louis that the faults attributed to Luther by the king, namely that he spreads doctrines contrary to Christianity, that he insults Christian princes and praises the Turks, are malicious fabrications.[72] This intriguing bit of royal correspondence ends on this note.

The attitude of the government found most apt expression in the legal enactment of the Diet of 1523 at Buda and in another for which the Diet of Rákos was responsible in 1525. The law of 1523 revived the medieval penalty concerning the loss of head and the confiscation of goods for heresy and in Article 54 called upon the ruler "as a Catholic prince to punish every Lutheran, their supporters and followers as open heretics and the enemies of the most holy virgin Mary."[73] Two years later the penalty was increased to burning at the stake. The law clearly stated that "all Lutherans must be rooted from the country and wherever they may be found, they must be freely apprehended by ecclesiastical as well as secular authorities and burned."[74] That secular authorities should be extended such wide powers, contrary to the *ius canonicum,* indicates without a shadow of doubt the extent to which Lutheran reform ideas had penetrated the country by now.

The consequences of this law, reluctantly confirmed by the signature of the king, are noteworthy. The representative of the emperor, the Lutheran Schnaidpeck, left the country; so did the Brandenburgian prince; likewise, a large percentage of the queen's German retinue.[75] A German bookseller was burned and other burnings followed. Werbőczi was reported to have miserably tortured eight Lutherans on his estates.[76] Other lords acted similarly, and news of their martyrdom reached even Luther.[77] A campaign against suspects in Buda during the summer of 1525 yielded one Lutheran who under severe torture confessed the names of other fellow travelers. So many of the most prominent citizens were involved that, on the advice of certain sober members of the government, among them the queen, the case against them was dropped on the ground that the city would become depopulated through the executions and reduced to a village.[78] Fortunately for the harassed, protection was amply available by this time on estates scattered in various parts of the land,[79] but the queen's position excited the nuncio's suspicions of her liberal flirtations.

Louis, prevailed upon partly by the nationalists and by the orthodox ecclesiastics, dispatched officials to ferret out the heretics and edicts to supplement the law in towns where defections had been reported. To Sáros County, where, according to reliable sources, "many, especially ecclesiastics, profess the Lutheran sect and diffuse it openly and everywhere," he wrote that defectors should be mercilessly punished lest the common people be led astray.[80] To the city council of Bártfa a much firmer tone characterized the royal edict: "In as much as we have been shocked to learn that among you is a master from Cracow but who was born in your city, as well as others, who profess the Lutheran heresy and sect, in open contempt of our published orders, we thereby enjoin upon you, under penalty of the loss of head and goods, immediately to search out the aforementioned master and others such as profess the Lutheran sect and, if they are of the secular order, to punish them by means of every instrument of torture and, if they are of the spiritual order, to consider it your duty to surrender them to the vicar of Eger, because, if we learn that you give aid and comfort to these heretics and leave them unpunished, or favor them in spreading the pernicious Lutheran contagion among Christians, know that the aforementioned penalties will be inflicted upon all of you without mercy."[81] Due to the meager response to such efforts the government went so far in encouraging the enforcement of its inquisitorial decrees as to grant all confiscated properties to the royal agent and the landlords.[82] The decree sent to Count Mark Pemfflinger, wealthy Transylvanian governor of the Saxon "nation" long suspected of his Lutheran leanings,[83] like many other such decrees, went on the rocks of both irrepressible enthusiasm for reform measures in Transylvania and the menacing encampment of Sulemein's forces along the borders of Hungary.

The battle of Mohács on August 29, 1526 represents a turning point in the destiny of the reform movement[84] not only for Hungary but also in general respects. But the agitation to drive back the Turkish hordes occupied the attention of Europeans primarily as "the third great menace" of the age[85] and only in a secondary way out of sympathy for the distraught Hungarian Christians. Luther's interest, likewise, centers predominantly upon the relationship of the Turkish threat to the general imperial problem, included in which, of course, was the fate of his reform movement, and not specifically to the loss sustained by Hungary either in 1526 or 1529 or 1541 and thereafter. When Luther dedicated his work *Vier tröstliche Psalmen* to the widowed queen, he made it clear, however, that he was not unmindful of the deeper meaning behind Hungary's disaster. If the Hungarian bishops had not obstructed the path of the gospel, Luther wrote, the whole world would have shouted that the Lutheran heresy was responsible, but now it is incontestible that the punitive hand of God has descended upon the people because of the obdurate opposition to the gospel by unregenerate leaders. He blames the bishops of the church, whose conduct had been brought to his attention by Hungarian students at the university as well as the exiled Cordatus.[86] The Hungarian experience supports what he has been saying all along. To Luther the Turkish menace spelled the judgment of God; it could be removed only by a true reformation, a *sine qua non* of a successful crusade under united secular (never papal) leadership. Luther's thesis on the Turkish question had been misconstrued in Hungary before Mohács, as it had been elsewhere, but afterwards, it is significant, reforming preachers and secular lords stood in universal agreement that the whip of God was lashing against the backs of his people because there still were many who had not turned from the Roman error.[87] Hungarian literature after the Mohács disaster nowhere refers to the opinions of Luther on the Turkish question as an argument against the advancement of religious reforms.[88] In fact, the opposite is true.

One of the sources of Luther's views on the Turkish problem appears to be linked to the Hungarian experiences with the Turks even prior to Mohács. In 1530 Luther republished a small book entitled *Libellus de ritu et moribus Turcorum* with a preface in which he explained that the work had so fascinated him that he deemed its reprinting worthwhile.[89] He regarded the book as a true mirror of facts. This book was written by a Hungarian—anonymously referred to as Sebesi—who had been imprisoned by the Turks in 1438 during the storming of Nagy Szebes in southern Hungary and who escaped to Rome, where sometime between 1475 and 1481 he recounted his observations on the Turks in writing. His work was reprinted anonymously again and again and seems to have helped to focus Luther's interest in the religious aspects of the Turkish problem.[90]

Luther continued to have contacts with Hungarians to the end of his life. He corresponded with noblemen, town councillors, clergymen, and teachers. In 1539, for example, a high government official, whose son was being instructed by preachers of Lutheran persuasion, inquired about Zwinglianism and Luther courteously replied, expressing amazement at his thorough acquaintance with Zwingli's opinions and urging that he remain steadfastly opposed to the Swiss errors. As a follow-up, he subsequently sent the official the manuscript of one of his works.[91] To the citizens of Eperjes Luther wrote in 1544, "It was with heartfelt pain that I read your sad letter, seeing God's wrath, as well as the weighty burden of our sins, which has constrained God to send the furious horde of Turks against us. God grant that we may come to ourselves and by our repentance obtain reconciliation."[92] During the wars against the Turks Luther frequently received news of events in Hungary and printed them.[93] Moreover, he entertained Hungarian students in his home, one of them Matthias Biró of Déva, shortly to be called "the Hungarian Luther" in tribute to his services to the cause, receiving free board and room and another, John Stockel, like so many other students enjoying Luther's hospitality, remaining in debt.[94] More grateful was the Hungarian student who presented him with some seeds, which Luther planted in his garden, believing them to be mandrakes such as Rachel had given to Leah (Genesis 30:14).

Of the two kings, the Hapsburg Ferdinand, brother of the emperor, and the nationalist, John Zápolya, who succeeded to the divided throne after Mohács, Luther had nothing but contempt for the former. Both began their rule by instituting inquisitorial measures against the followers of Luther, believing them to be responsible for the great disaster, but, shortly, for political reasons in the midst of the twelve-year-long civil war, relaxed their attitude. Luther, nevertheless, kept up his blasts of criticism against Ferdinand in his letters and table talks. While he once recognized Ferdinand as much more competent than his brother, he had no respect for him, chiefly because, as he said, he destroys the evangelical churches, persecutes its pastors and, with the blood of martyrs on his hands already, he plans to extirpate Lutherans as soon as the Turks are taken care of.[95] As a matter of fact, political conditions throughout Ferdinand's reign prevented such a course. Indeed, some of his prominent military leaders, like William Rogendirf and Leonard Felsz, were left undisturbed in their Lutheran views. Against Hungarian magnates favoring reform ideals he could not take effective punitive action, since if he did so they would defect to the party of the nationalist king, Zápolya. Such defections he endeavored to hold to the minimum by making munificent gifts from the secularized ecclesiastical properties. Laws enacted toward the end of his rule in defense of Roman Catholicism aimed, at best, to curb the Anabaptist and Sacramentarian heresies, not the Lutheran sentiments of his nobility. It is also true that his hostile decrees were generally disregarded even by his Hungarian loyalist nobles.[96]

With the advantage of greater perspective derived from observation of a comprehensive report, Luther might have formed a truer, more optimistic picture of the Hungarian trends. Held back by the chaos and confusion of the war, reform activities shortly picked up speed and developed a momentum in terms of results justifying the conclusion that by 1545 "the separation of the majority of churches in Hungary from the Roman Catholic church had taken place."[97] Events transpiring in Hungary during the last two decades of Luther's life had brought triumph to his cause on the central-Danubian frontier.

How may we explain this transformation? In the complexity of the responsible factors the most decisive was the disillusionment of the nobility in the emperor and the Pope. The emperor had turned a deaf ear upon the plea for aid against the Turk. Clement had sent a slim purse but through the League of Cognac diverted military assistance from the West, clearly showing that his Christian interests were overshadowed by selfish political considerations. Reforming preachers as well as nationalist noblemen did not fail to read the signs of the times and exploit them. The nationalists of Transylvania and elsewhere[98] were not deterred from making an alliance even with the Turkish invaders in order to obtain their political objective of independence,[99] according to a previous determination at the Diet of 1505, and, even if they might otherwise have entertained scruples regarding this alliance, the excommunication by Clement of John Zápolya, upon whose head had been placed the sacred crown of St. Stephen, tipped the scales. World politics also convinced many that their future lay with the ideology that opposed both Pope and emperor, together with their supporters. The Turkish alliance proved to be an excellent tool for political maneuvers re-enforced by genuine conversions, and in the Turkish-occupied territories the presence of "the scourge of God," the Turks, from whom neither Hapsburg nor papal power could free the people, moved them to look for aid and comfort in a renewal of religion. The unfortunate politics of Clement severed the bonds that had bound the Hungarian nation in loyal relations to Rome and played into the hands of Luther.

Another decisive factor aiding the advancement of the reform movement lay in the secularization of church property. This occurred primarily for reasons of national security. This progressive deprivation was made possible because prelates had fled from their estates and, by default of circumstances, ambitious landowners had fallen heir to them. Because the law of 1521 empowered the ruler to alienate ecclesiastical holdings on a temporary basis for the sake of national defense, both Ferdinand and Zápolya seized vacant benefices and kept or distributed them liberally among their supporters. In 1539 Aleander, the papal nuncio, reported, for example, that Ferdinand had sold one third of the church's secular possessions.[100] Compounding the resultant demoralization was the failure to fill ecclesiastical vacancies with a personnel that might have defended the interests of the church. Thus, vast ecclesiastical latifundia were transferred to the lesser and upper nobility, among which the contending parties desired to ensure their power position. The loss of control over lands in the world that still operated pretty largely in the pattern of feudal concepts signified a corresponding loss in authority directing the religious sentiments of the people working the lands. Even before the principle of *cuius regio, eius religio* was incorporated into law, its practical application obtained. It is not to be supposed that conversion occurred because of these land transfers, but rather the point is that re-establishment of ecclesiastical control was frustrated by the new religious climate that found its inner sources in the soul of the nation.

The period of twenty years after Mohács reveals all the characteristics of a nation in a state of religious transition. What was called Lutheranism often amounted to purely a desire to reform without systematic and sharp doctrinal focus. Around the time of Luther's death this sharpening of the focus began to occur. In northern Hungary, for example, it is represented by the confessional formulation, *Confessio Pentapolitana*,[101] of the five free royal towns of Kassa, Löcse, Bártfa, Eperjes, and Kisszeben, all of them Ferdinand ruled.

The Diet of 1548 had taken stringent action against heretics, mentioning the Anabaptists and Sacramentarians by name.[102] Omission of Lutherans from the proscribed list indicated tacit toleration, particularly in view of the large number of delegates in agreement with the German Reformer's position. When the officials proceeded to carry out the law, the citizens of these towns became apprehensive and a meeting of the ministers was convoked at Eperjes on August 14, 1549. The religious formulation was presented to the assembled ministers and citizens by Leonard Stoeckel, rector of the school at Bártfa, a former student of Luther and Melanchthon.

In content this document stands in agreement with the famous statement of faith presented over a decade and a half earlier to the imperial Diet at Augsburg. To its irenic tone as well as its unequivocal rejection of Anabaptism and Sacramentarianism may be attributed the approval with which it met both in ecclesiastical circles and at court. It accepts the orthodox Lutheran view of the Holy Eucharist[103] and predestination[104] and makes baptism indispensable to salvation. With respect to religious ceremonies, order of worship, and the dress of the clergy, the retention of old forms are recommended.

The intent of this confession was not to distinguish the new faith from Roman Catholicism but rather to protect what was considered the true faith from the innovations then penetrating into the land. Unity in the reformed church without a schism was the objective, but reformation was understood in the spirit of Luther. This endeavor succeeded admirably, for, adjusting to the unique political circumstances, Luther's followers in northern Hungary produced a confession on the basis of which the reform of the Christian faith could move forward and be strengthened in the central-Danubian frontiers.

ESSAYS ON CALVIN

The Relation of God's Grace to His Glory in John Calvin

Henry Kuizenga

The bifurcation of his system by the twin decrees of election and reprobation must, Calvin realized, close somewhere in the oneness of God. The system so tidily branched and nicely balanced must be rooted and established in some trunk-principle of the divine economy.

This principle in Calvin is the glory of God. Both of the decrees express and serve God's sovereign glory. The end and purpose of all existence is the realization of the glory of God. This idea is consistent with the theocentricity of Calvin's thought. All things have their existence from God and are real in that they testify of his excellence. Likewise, all men come to themselves and are most truly men as they exemplify God's sovereignty.

As sovereign over his creation, God is "jealous" of his glory; that is, he is concerned that creation shall not fail to realize itself in the fulfillment of that glory. To that end he governs creation by his providence. Since man is the crown of creation, the highest concern of God in providence is that his glory shall come to expression in the destinies of men. By his eternal decrees God not only realizes his glory in the lives of men and in all creation but also, in that very realization, lifts all of creation to the pinnacle of self-realization.

The study of how God realizes his glory by the decrees will reveal the relation of grace to glory and something of the nature of grace since it will reveal the nature of God, the giver of grace. What, then, is the glory of God in the decree of election?

God's glory in election is the demonstration of his grace in providence. In his absolute freeness God chooses his people and carefully brings them to his own blessedness. In this God takes delight. Calvin says, ". . . there is nothing that is more peculiarly his own [i.e., God's], or in which he desires more to be glorified, than goodness."[1] With goodness, Calvin in this connection means specifically graciousness or mercy; the goodness of redeeming lost men is God's glory.

In a commentary on Romans 9:22, Calvin says that Paul in his use of the term "glory" equates glory with mercy. "The word *glory*, which is here twice mentioned, I consider to have been used for God's mercy, a metonymy of effect for the cause; for his chief praise or glory is in acts of kindness."[2]

This interpretation of God's glory in election is consistent with Calvin's entire explication of God's grace, especially as he explains God's graciousness in the Incarnation. The principle of *agapé* involves God's giving himself in Christ for the benefit of his elect. God's condescension in Christ, with all the human ignominy it brought him, together with God's further condescension in the Holy Spirit to redeem men, is the revelation and realization of God's glory. Once God in his love has, by his gracious operation in men's lives, led men to their glorification, men become "illustrations of the glory of God."[3] God's glory lies in his self-giving because by giving himself he engenders self-giving in men. For once men have been won to God's own love, the excellencies of God are fanned out in their lives.

God in his absolute freeness to realize the purposes of his eternal will decrees that some shall come to salvation and others to destruction. What is the glory of God in reprobation? Or, how does reprobation serve God's glory?

It is immediately obvious, salvation and damnation being two different destinies, that God's glory must be differently derived from them. To be sure, the two decrees share a common feature with respect to God's activity in relation to men: They both manifest God's sovereign freeness. Calvin emphasizes that God is free to deal as he chooses with men. The simple fact is, Calvin says, that in the exercise of this absolute freeness, God chooses (as both the Scriptures and human experience seem to Calvin to testify) to destine the majority of men for destruction. So both the decrees show God's glory because they both show that God is free. But Calvin's interpretation of God's disposition of his freeness in election clearly teaches, too, that God's glory does not consist of a mere neutrality of freeness, but that God, being God, in his freeness purposes the realization in men of his goodness. His highest glory in his relations with men lies in his liberation of men from sin for the accomplishment of his own goodness. By the strength of his goodness God is free.

If then, as Calvin himself teaches, God's glory lies not primarily in his arbitrary freeness but in a freeness to realize the good purposes of his love, then how does God glory in reprobation; that is, in the eternal condemnation of the majority of mankind to unfreeness? To this question Calvin first answers with a pious counsel of silence. ". . . for the everlasting scheme of the divine purpose is beyond our reach."[4] ". . . but the cause of this depends on the secret will of God."[5] "Yet the cause of eternal reprobation is so hidden from us that nothing remains for us but to wonder at the incomprehensible purpose of God."[6]

But it is already too late for Calvin to be that silent on the nature of the glory which God derives from reprobation. Calvin teaches that God has revealed his righteousness in Jesus Christ. In his elaborate doctrine of God's gracious dealings with his people, Calvin unequivocally teaches that God's greatest pleasure lies in showing his mercy and in accomplishing salvation. The whole history of God's dealings with men is the history of his revelation of himself as the king of love. No wonder, then, if Calvin himself feels it necessary to explain God's decree of reprobation by something other than the appeal to the mystery of God. To refuse to say anything else than that reprobation lies hidden in the mystery of God's "good pleasure" is to invite the conclusion that God's glory, after all, is his arbitrariness more than it is his goodness. For if God's good pleasure can lie in the destruction of men, then what are men to think of God's goodness on the one hand or of his freeness on the other? These two, which God unites by his condescension in grace, would once more fall apart. But Calvin is firm in his teaching that God's might and his goodness are indissoluble. "Nothing can be more preposterous than to imagine that there is in God a power so supreme and absolute . . . as to deprive him of his righteousness."[7]

How, then, does Calvin reconcile reprobation with God's freeness to realize his righteousness? After his injunction upon others to be silent on the subject of God's motives for the decree of reprobation, Calvin goes on to say that God's glory in reprobation lies in the vindication of his justice and holiness. It pleases God to show his glory in the salvation of some and in the damnation of many more. In this way God realizes both sides of his righteousness: his mercy in the salvation of the elect; his justice in the damnation of the reprobate. So Calvin can say of Matthew 26:24 on the subject of Judas, "God . . . appointing the reprobate to the day of destruction, illustrates also in this way his own glory."[8] In a commentary on II Thessalonians 1:8, Calvin says, ". . . it is necessary that God should inflict vengeance . . . for the sake of his own glory."[9] God cannot show his mercy to all men because his righteousness demands vindication in punishment as well as in salvation. "Justice requires that he [God] should likewise show himself to be a just judge in the infliction of punishment."[10] "His unblamable justice shines forth no less in the perdition of the reprobate than in the salvation of the elect."[11] Speaking elsewhere in the *Institutes* of the decree of reprobation, Calvin says, "Yet it is certain that he [God] determined thus, only because he foresaw it would tend to the just illustration of the glory of his name."[12]

So Calvin's answer to the question, "What is God's glory in reprobation?", is more than an awed silence, more even than to say that it lies simply in the freeness it shows God to have in choosing as he wills. Calvin presses on to say that God's glory in reprobation lies in the satisfaction of his justice.

From the protest of men that it is unfair of God from eternity to decree the destruction of the reprobate, Calvin appeals to man's own sense of moral responsibility to justify the decree. In the passages in which he makes this appeal, he sometimes speaks as though the fate of the reprobate were not determined from eternity, but as though it depended upon man's own free decision. "No man, therefore, is condemned on account of having despised the Gospel, except he who, disdaining the lovely message of salvation, has chosen of his own accord to draw down destruction on himself."[13] And in a passage from Calvin's commentaries on Isaiah we find, ". . . the cause of all the evils which we endure is our rebellion against God. When we repent, he is reconciled to us, and the rods with which he chastised us are no longer employed."[14] Calvin's explanation for what appears on the surface at least to be a self-contradiction of what he elsewhere maintains concerning man's relation to God's decrees would be, in his own words: "Neither was Judas excusable because that which befell him was foretold, seeing that he fell away, not being compelled by the prophecy, but only by the malice of his own heart."[15]

In this connection Calvin sometimes speaks the language of congruism and prescience as distingushed from his own doctrine of strict predestination by absolute decree. In a passage on the book of Nahum we find: ". . . God is hard and severe toward refractory men . . . and he is merciful and kind to the teachable and the obedient—not that God changes his nature . . . but because he treats men according to their disposition."[16]

Calvin is not unaware of the logical dilemma in which he thus involves himself. In fact, he fearlessly mixes the appeal to moral responsibility with his insistence upon the decrees.

> The reprobate wish to be thought excusable in sinning, because they cannot avoid a necessity of sinning; especially since this necessity is laid upon them by the ordination of God. But we deny this to be a

just excuse; because the ordination of God, by which they complain that they are destined to destruction, is guided by equity, unknown indeed to us, but indubitably certain. Whence we conclude, that they sustain no misery that is not inflicted upon them by the most righteous judgment of God. In the next place, we maintain that they act preposterously, who, in seeking for the origin of their condemnation, direct their views to the secret recesses of the Divine counsel, and overlook the corruption of nature, which is its real source.[17]

We may say then that according to Calvin man's reprobation has its source in his own corruption, but its cause in God's decree and ordination. This is all the more confusing when Calvin in the same paragraph avers that the source of man's corruption is God's decree by which he "was created to that misery to which he is subject."

In another passage, one from his commentaries on the Psalms, Calvin even more sharply points out the logical dilemma into which his own position leads him.

If it is objected, that God in vain and without ground utters this complaint (that man does not repent), since it was in His power to bend the stiff necks of the people, and that, when He was not pleased to do this, He had no reason to compare Himself to a man deeply grieved; I answer, that He very properly makes use of this style of speaking on our account, that we may seek for the procuring cause of our misery nowhere but in ourselves. We must here beware of mingling together things which are totally different—as widely different from each other as heaven is distant from the earth. God, in coming down to us by His Word, and addressing His invitations to all men without exception, disappoints nobody. All who sincerely come to Him are received, and find from actual experience that they were not called in vain. At the same time, we are to trace to the fountain of the secret electing purpose of God this difference, that the word enters into the heart of some, while others only hear the sound of it. And yet there is no inconsistency in His complaining, as it were with tears, of our folly when we do not obey Him. In the invitations He addresses to us by the external word, He shows Himself to be a father; and why may he not also be understood as still representing Himself under the image of a father in using this form of complaint? In Ezekiel xviii.32, He declares with the strictest regard to truth, 'I have no pleasure in the death of him that dieth,' provided in the interpretation of the passage we candidly and dispassionately take into view the whole scope of it. God has no pleasure in the death of a sinner: How? Because He would have all men turned to Himself. But it is abundantly evident, that men by their own free-will cannot turn to God, until He first change their stony hearts into flesh: yea, this renovation, as Augustine judiciously observes, is a work surpassing that of the creation itself. Now what hinders God from bending and framing the hearts of all men equally in submission to Him?

Here modesty and sobriety must be observed, that instead of presuming to intrude into His incomprehensible decrees, we may rest contented with the revelation which He has made of His will in His word. There is the justest ground for saying that He wills the salvation of those to whom that language is addressed, (Isaiah xxi.12) 'Come unto me, and be ye converted.' In the second part of the verse before us, we have defined what it is to hear God. To assent to what He speaks would not be enough: for hypocrites will grant at once that whatever proceeds from His mouth is true, and will affect to listen just as if an ass should bend its ears. But the clause is intended to teach us that we can only be said to hear God, when we submit ourselves to His authority.[18]

Confusing as this language is, yet it is clear that with it Calvin appeals to man's moral responsibility in order to justify God's seeking his glory in the punishment of the reprobate. But if this appeal to the human sense of justice is valid, then the objections raised by this sense of justice to Calvin's idea of God's economy with men are also valid. There are two such objections: (1) If God's justice required the eternal punishment of the reprobate to establish his glory, then the elect should suffer the same penalty for their sins in order to make that vindication complete. (2) Anselm used to teach that the reason the Saviour had to be both God and man was in order that the penalty for man's sin against God's infinite majesty might be infinitely paid. And Calvin himself says, commenting on Colossians 1:14, ". . . for by the sacrifice of his death all the sins of the world have been expiated."[19] If the sins of the world were *all* expiated by Christ's death, and according to Anselm, the forgiveness won by Christ is infinite because Christ is infinite, then does not Calvin by his argument in defense of reprobation place God in the position of requiring that the penalty for the sins of the reprobate be paid twice, once by Christ upon the cross and again through all eternity by the wretched sinner himself?

But whether God's glory in reprobation can be justified before the bar of human justice and moral responsibility or not, the appeal to human justice is really, with reference to Calvin's own teaching, not a valid appeal to begin with. For the decrees of God, by Calvin's own vehement insistence, cannot be brought into judgment by reference to mere human understanding. The only basis in human judgment for understanding and appraisal of God's works is the basis God provides by his Spirit in transforming human judgment so that it can judge on the basis of divine wisdom. We should then be always careful to introduce divine wisdom as the standard for our judgments.

But on the basis of divine wisdom as revealed in the New Testament by Jesus and as explicated by Calvin himself in his doctrine of election, the glory which God derives from reprobation, whether justified or not justified in the appeal of justice as man understands it by reference to his own sense of moral responsibility, is altogether of an inferior quality to the glory of election as understood by reference to God's own revelation of himself in the Incarnation.

For the glory in election is based on the *agapé* principle. Jesus pronounces as a universal principle and therefore as expressive of God's own love for men, these words: "For whosoever will save his life shall lose it: and whosoever will lose his life for my sake shall find it."[20] So we may interpret, ". . . joy shall be in heaven over one sinner that repenteth . . ."[21] Calvin himself so understood the way of God's love in contrast to man's way (paraphrasing what Isaiah says for God in 55:8): "I am not a mortal man that I should show myself harsh and irreconcilable to you. My thoughts are very different from yours. If you are implacable, and can with difficulty be brought back to a state of friendship with those from whom you have received injury, I am not like you that I should treat you so cruelly."[22]

But the glory of reprobation, Calvin says, consists in God's exacting eternal satisfaction for the transgressions of men whom he by eternal decree has foreordained to destruction. For the understanding and approval of this decree and this glory, Calvin refers us, as noted earlier, to our own sense of justice, and beyond that he enjoins silence and the praise of God's mysterious ways. "Whenever you hear the glory of God mentioned, think of his justice. For what deserves praise must be just."[23] But the praiseworthiness of God's glory is established in men's lives by Jesus' interpretations of God's justice and by God's entire revelation of his righteousness. Calvin in the above quotation is appealing to the praiseworthiness established by his exposition of God's love in election to inspire our praise of God's punishment in reprobation.

There are then two kinds of glory. The principle of *gloria dei* which Calvin introduces to bind the decrees back into the oneness of God is itself split by the decrees. Calvin is left with a God who seems to have a dual personality, a schizophrenic God.

This is seen most clearly as a trinitarian problem. Christ as the eternal, pre-existent Son of God should be coauthor with the Father of the eternal decrees of God. Calvin, though he speaks of Christ as the mirror of our salvation and often says that we are elected in Christ,[24] yet does not make Christ simply the author of the decree of election. Paul

Jacobs in "Prädestination und Verantwortlichkeit" wishes to anchor Calvin's doctrine of election in the Trinity in order to show that election is not a mechanistic determinism but the loving eternal purpose of God to bring his people to salvation. He tries to put Christ as close as possible to the decree in Calvin in order to answer the accusations of Kampschulte and C. Ritschl that in election God decrees an end result for the accomplishment of which Christ is the mere medium. Christ, says Ritschl, e.g., is actually shut out of the actual act of making the decree.[25] It is interesting to notice that, however closely Jacobs can find Calvin associating Christ with the actual decree, yet he never says that in Calvin Christ is anywhere the author of it. Christ is the mediator from eternity; the Saviour of all the Old Testament saints; Christ is the eternal Word of God: Christ is the gauge of our election; Christ is the election itself; Christ, as the way of salvation, is the result of the eternal decree of election; Christ is the example of our election.[26] All these—but Christ for Calvin is not himself the author of the decree.

May it not be that Calvin kept Christ free from actual authorship of the decree of election in order to keep him free from authorship of reprobation? But once shut out of actual authorship of the decree, it is impossible to get Christ convincingly back into the plan of salvation except as the functionary who carries out a decree made by the Father. Jacobs is disappointed that the religious interpreters of Calvin's theology (Schneckenburger, Gasz, Dorner, Ahnlich, Köstlin, R. F. K. Müller) do not more radically correct the mistakes of the speculative school of Calvin researchers (Alex. Schweitzer, Baur, Heppe, Frank, O. Ritschl). But the speculative interpretations take their rise on the wedge Calvin himself drove between Christ and the decree. Then the religious interpreters in their effort to interpret Calvin religiously could only say that for Calvin there is no salvation outside of faith in Christ. Müller could say that, at last, despite his obvious determinism, Calvin in the doctrine of election gave his heart the rule over his head. Their work does not satisfy Jacobs. "The religious interpreters of Calvin," he says, "though they were obviously aware of the difficulty, yet did not clear it away. Instead of beginning with Christ in their thinking about predestination, they saw the Christocentric elements of that doctrine only as religious adjuncts decisive in its development."[27] Jacobs rightly diagnoses the problem in Calvin to be a trinitarian one. But Jacobs himself seems not to see that, unless Christ is author of the decree of election, he cannot be used to absolve Calvin's system from its mechanistic determinism.

Jacobs says of reprobation, "The concept of mechanistic causality remains in use in the negative doctrine of the bondage of the human will to sin because it cannot be dislodged by the witness of the foundation and body of Christ."[28] But neither is the ground of the mechanistic causality in Calvin's doctrine of election removed until Christ is author of the decree. Jacobs is right in making the problem a trinitarian one. Does he fail to see that the trinitarian problem concerns not only election but also reprobation? The decrees involve Christ as author, or Christ is not the Son coeternal with the Father. But if Christ is to be the author of election, then so he must be of reprobation. Calvin shied at this. He chose rather to make God the author of both decrees and Christ the executor of that of election. Thus Christ is not the revelation of the whole mind of God, but only the obedient administrator of one side of that mind. The problem of mechanistic causality remains. Moreover, the greater problem of the duality of God's personality presents itself.

Karl Barth states the problem thus: "The old Reformers really were not right when they were ready to see in the reconciliation and revelation which happened in Jesus Christ the medium but not the foundation of election, and when they were willing, rather, to misplace the eternal election in a decree of God which happened before the actuality of the Cross and the Resurrection."[29] He goes on to say that the doctrine of the decrees may open the door to the interpretation of predestination as a philosophy of determinism or of empiricism. Shut Christ out, in other words, and then, if Christ be the Son of God, you are well on the way to shutting God out of the decrees too.

The right view, Barth says, is to see in Christ the whole revelation of God and count him author of election and reprobation both. Why, he says, do the theologians not include rejection (*Verwerfung*) in their Christology? "Does Jesus Christ, then, come to men only as the Bearer of God's 'yes'? Does He come so, and not at the same time as the Bearer of God's 'no'?"[30] Then Barth asks whether, for these theologians who so divide reprobation and election in the theology of the decrees, rejection is any more the expression of God's justice than election. Elsewhere he points out that Christ is the whole revelation of God. Exactly in Christ is all God's majesty, holiness, and love most brilliantly revealed and understood.

> But the oneness of God within Himself, the oneness of the Father with the Son, cannot be shattered; His sovereignty cannot be subverted, and neither by the fact that the Son, nay that the true God is now become even more truly man ... How should God's sovereignty thereby not become even greater not in itself, that is, but greater for us and to us as a revealed and reconciling sovereignty.[31]

The glory and majesty, the righteousness and justice of God are of a piece and are all revealed in Christ. So Christ is not separated from God nor the Father from the Son by the decrees, and the mind of God is not split into compartments one of which operates on the level of vengeful justice and the other on the level of selfless love. Justice and mercy together serve the same supreme value of God's righteous love. When God comes in Christ, he comes in mercy and in judgment. But mercy and judgment are the expression at all times of the same righteous love at work.

Calvin's theology, then, and in spite of his introduction of the principle of God's glory, remains divided along the line separating the decrees. This is true unless we should follow the interpretation of God's grace sometimes suggested by Calvin that it is a means by which God seeks and realizes his selfish aggrandizement for its own sake. In this sense God would be gracious in order to serve his own glory. In his first edition of the *Institutes* Calvin says that God pours out his grace upon new converts in order that in them his glory may be seen.[32] Elsewhere he says, "the glory of God is the highest end, to which our sanctification is subordinate."[33] The interpretation of the glory of God as a principle apart from and superior to God's grace makes that glory a principle under which both decrees can be understood as serving God's glory in a similar fashion. This is the interpretation of Arthur Savary:

> The decree of God, by which the elect are predestined to eternal glory, has the glory of God as its purpose. The God of Calvin, in His relation to predestination, is a God who is alike indifferent to the damnation of the reprobate and the salvation of the elect; He has no concern except for His glory. It is for His glory that He decrees the eternal misery of some and the endless blessedness of others.[34]

With this interpretation of God's glory and of his grace, the principle of glory would unite the decrees and save the unity of God for Calvin's system. Then God would receive a positive vindication of his supremacy from salvation and a negative from reprobation. Then Calvin would be subordinating grace to glory in order to subordinate both salvation and reprobation under the heading of sovereignty and make God one again. But then the quality of both God's grace and his glory would be adversely affected by the decree of reprobation; adversely, that is, in the light of the biblical idea of God's graciousness to his people, an idea which is everywhere present in Calvin's own explication of the grace of God toward his elect. In short, then, Calvin's God would not be the God of the Scriptures.

Even with this interpretation of God's glory, however, Calvin would be involving himself in a glaring contradiction. For he has honestly admitted, when explaining the biblical idea of God's grace to his elect, that God realizes his greatest glory in showing the mercy of his salvation.[35]

But Calvin teaches that God operates on two levels to accomplish his glory. On the first level he operates to redeem men and glories in their redemption. On the second level hè operates to condemn men and glories in the righteous vengeance with which he punishes them. This position is strikingly illustrated in this passage from the *Institutes:*

> Therefore, as God regenerates for ever the elect alone with incorruptible seed, so that the seed of life planted in their hearts never perishes, so he firmly seals within them the grace of his adoption, that it may be confirmed and ratified to their minds. But this by no means prevents that inferior operation of the Spirit from exerting itself even in the reprobate.[36]

Why should God who is absolutely free to realize the glory he desires content himself with the inferior glory of vindicating his justice with the eternal punishment of the reprobate? Does it not imply God's defeat first to say that he best serves his glory in the redemption of some men, and then to say that he ekes out some satisfaction also from the damnation of other men?

This is the more forcibly argued when we consider how Calvin restricts the number of the elect to a small fragment of mankind. For thus Calvin seems to teach that the glory accruing to God from humankind must come, for the most part, from their reprobation. Calvin could argue that God receives more glory from the salvation of one elect than from the reprobation of a hundred sinners. And for that very reason it is vain to propose that God seek his glory in reprobation. Why should Calvin, of all people, teach that God must do with less than the greatest glory?

The introduction of the interpretation of God's glory as his self-seeking does not, in other words, serve the purpose of unifying Calvin's theology. It does not because Calvin's main teaching on the nature of God and his grace makes it impossible. If this interpretation of God and his glory is to serve the purpose for which it was suggested, Calvin must do one of two things: (1) repudiate his main teaching on the nature of God and his grace, or (2) repudiate his teaching on the decree of reprobation. They cannot stand together. But once give up the decree of reprobation, and the need for explaining God's glory as self-seeking no longer exists, and the New Testament conception of grace as Calvin himself taught it can again come into its own. Christ is once more the true and full revelation of the only true God.

Calvin's Theological Method and the Ambiguity in His Theology

John H. Leith

In 1909 William Adams Brown, one of the most competent of recent American theologians, undertook to speak on Calvin's influence
upon theology and was embarrassed for lack of anything original to
say. He found it impossible to approach Calvin's theology in the spirit
of an explorer, for the latter's teachings were already commonplace
knowledge. Further study of the Reformer's theology, he felt, offered
no chance of new discovery.[1]

It is now apparent that Calvin research has not reached any simple
agreement as to the content or nature of his theology. Actually the
disagreements are both numerous and important. There are conflicts
between the strict Barthians and the students of Brunner,[2] between
the traditional Calvinists and the Crisis Theologians,[3] between the
French and the Germans,[4] between the historian of dogma, Reinhold
Seeberg, and the Calvin scholar, Peter Barth.[5] In contrast to the Calvin scholars who have taken the Reformer seriously as a teacher of
this generation, the liberals have labeled him a fundamentalist.[6]

The very diversity in interpretation on the part of students of Calvin has become itself a problem of Calvin study. In 1922 Herman
Bauke asked the question: What is the peculiar character of the theology which makes all of these contradictory opinions possible?[7] He
was convinced that the experience of the preceding century had proved
the inadequacy of every attempt to solve these problems by the study
of any one doctrine or even of the content of the whole theology. The
solution of the problem, he felt, lay in the study of the *Formgestaltung*
and not of the content of the theology. Three characteristics of the
Formgestaltung provide an explanation of the contradictory conclusions of Calvin research and offer a key for a true interpretation of
his theology.

The first is a formal, dialectical rationalism. This does not mean
that Calvin's theology is rationalistic in the Stoic or eighteenth-cen-

tury sense. It is not a rationalism of material but of form in which the dogmatic materials appear, by which they are bound together, and in which they are expressed and systematized. This fact accounts for the difference between the theologies of Calvin and Luther, which, in regard to content, are very much the same. It also accounts for the fact that the German who thinks in terms of content rather than form has difficulty understanding Calvin's theology.

The second characteristic of the form of Calvin's theology, according to Bauke, is the *complexio oppositorum*. Calvin's theological method is not the deduction of a system from one or two central doctrines. He does not seek to find some *Diagonale* or *Stammlehre* or central doctrine or material principle from which individual dogmatic teachings can be deduced and developed. On the contrary, he seeks to bind existing individual dogmatic teachings which are even in logical and metaphysical contradiction into a systematic coherence. This characteristic explains the existence of many contradictory interpretations, for interpreters have concentrated on one doctrine and neglected others which are equally important. Martin Schulze's studies are a good example of this fallacy.[8]

The third characteristic is biblicism, by which Bauke meant a law which governed the pattern of Calvin's thought. The Reformer sought not merely to take the materials of his theology out of the Bible but also to make his theology a complete and consistent representation of the Bible.

Bauke's study was a genuine step forward, for it made plain that every attempt to interpret the *Institutes* must consider the form as well as the content. He dealt a devastating blow to the notion that Calvin was a speculative systematizer who deduced a system of theology from one or two principles. Most of the recent Calvin scholars are in agreement with Bauke's conclusion in this regard; however, his study did not put an end to contradictory interpretations.

While Bauke's study has much to contribute to the understanding of Calvin's thought, at least three objections must be raised to his conclusions. In the first place, his emphasis on the paradoxical character of Calvin's theology obscures its inner unity. It gives the impression that his theology is merely a collection of individual teachings formally and dialectically thrown together. In the second place, the question must be raised whether it is possible to separate fully form and content. For example, is the content of the definitions of predestination and reprobation completely free from their rationalistic form? Finally, the question must be asked as to whether the formal character of

Calvin's thought is consistently the same. If the formal character varies, then Bauke's thesis is inadequate.

Unquestionably, the diversity in the interpretation of Calvin has multiple sources and explanations. Surely one source of the diversity is the theological perspective of the commentator. Barthians read Calvin in the light of Barth and fundamentalists in the light of scholastic Calvinism. This is especially apparent when Calvin is made to answer contemporary theological questions. These radically partisan studies produce divergent interpretations and leave the actual historic development of Calvinism unintelligible.

Another source of diverse interpretations is Calvin's deliberate use of paradox. In a study published in 1868, Köstlin maintained that Calvin's theology can be regarded as a system only if the word is duly qualified. While the *Institutes* reveal a tendency toward systematization, there is an increasing hesitancy in the various editions to draw the conclusions which the systematic approach demands.[9] The failure of Calvin study to discover any central dogma from which the system is deduced supports this judgment. Émile Doumergue described Calvin's procedure as the "méthode des contrariétés."[10] Calvin was ready to sacrifice logical consistency in order to do justice to the complexity of Christian revelation and experience.

Calvin's use of paradox has been the occasion of contradictory interpretations, as the interpreter has laid hold of one doctrine to the neglect of another. A notable instance is the attempt to interpret Calvin in an otherworldly fashion to the neglect of his very significant emphasis on the importance of history and enjoyment of this created world.

A further explanation of diversity in the interpretation of Calvin's theology is found in the failure of Calvin to integrate the various strands of thought which went into his theological development. An example can be found in the confusion between the Hebraic and Platonic interpretations of the relationship of the soul and the body which is apparent in Calvin's writings.[11]

There is, however, still another source of diversity of interpretation of Calvin's theology. It lies behind the conflict between those scholars who conclude that Calvin's theology is dominated by its emphasis on the personal and living claim of God on every man, and other scholars, equally competent, who find that Calvin substitutes a code book for the living claim of God and a legal institution for the body of Christ. It is the source of the radical disagreement between those who discover that Calvin's theology is Christocentric and those who find it to be a denial of the spirit of Jesus Christ. This problem in Calvin interpretation roots in ambiguities in Calvin's theological methodology.

An illustration of this type of problem can be found in Calvin's discussion of the glory of God, which is a fundamental concept in his whole theology. God's glory, Calvin writes, is made known in the structure of the world.

> . . . God hath not darkly shadowed his glory in the creation of the world, but he hath everywhere engraven such manifest marks, that even blind men may know them by groping.[12]

God's glory consists partly in his wisdom and his power.[13] It also consists in his authority[14] and his righteousness.[15] It is manifested in the many proofs of his fatherly love which one finds in the world.[16]

The glory of God, however, principally shines forth in Christ and in the gospel which he proclaimed. In him God's perfect glory and majesty are revealed.[17]

> . . . The glory of God principally shines in this,—that he is reconcilable and that he forgives our sins. God indeed manifests his glory both by his power and his wisdom, and by all the judgments which he daily executes; his glory, at the same time, shines forth chiefly in this,—that he is propitious to sinners, and suffers himself to be pacified; yea, that he not only allows miserable sinners to be reconciled to him, but that he also of his own will invites and anticipates them.[18]

The glory of God is revealed in the cross of Christ,

> for in the cross of Christ, as in a magnificent theatre, the inestimable goodness of God is displayed before the whole world. In all the creatures, indeed, both high and low, the glory of God shines, but nowhere has it shone more brightly than in the cross, in which there has been an astonishing change of things, the condemnation of all men has been manifested, sin has been blotted out, salvation has been restored to men; and, in short, the whole world has been renewed, and everything restored to good order.[19]

Calvin, however, did not stop with the assertion that God's glory is principally revealed in his forgiving love. He introduces the analogy of an earthly king's glory as a means of impressing upon his readers and hearers the significance of the glory of God.[20] If a prince is injured, death is not considered too much to exact in revenge. If we avenge the injuries done to men, how much more should we avenge any outrage against the majesty of him who made heaven and earth. Consequently, when the honor of God is at stake, we must suppress all natural affection and prefer the glory of God to all human considerations. Thus Calvin writes:

> Why is such implacable severity demanded unless to show us that . . .
> as often as his glory is involved our mutual humanity is erased almost
> from memory?[21]

> For in that you show that you are truly zealots in the service of God
> if you kill your own brothers and stop at nothing, scorning the order
> of nature, in order to show that God rules above all and that his de-
> cree is sovereign.[22]

These may be overstatements of the fact that God is the Creator and that man in himself is not significant, but they are certainly dangerous overstatements. However high Calvin's motives may have been in such statements, they were the justification of deeds which have the appearance of brutality and inhumanity. They explain how Calvin could desire the death penalty for Servetus without any apparent emotional disturbance,[23] though he was fully capable of feeling the poignancy of death.[24]

Calvin himself was unaware of any inconsistency between the foregoing statements and his assertion that the glory of God was principally revealed in his redemptive love. This very fact makes these aberrations all the more dangerous for those who seek to learn from Calvin today. While it is difficult to isolate the source of his inconsistency, it seems to be at least in part due to Calvin's theological method. While he avows the greatest loyalty to Scripture, he actually goes beyond Scripture as a result of an almost irresistible tendency to extrapolate rationally the scriptural data. It was Calvin's intention to bring men into the living presence of the King of Glory; and his theology, as far as we can judge, was the context in which men did come into that presence. However, it must also be said that he sometimes substituted an abstract rationalization of an earthly king's glory for that living presence.

The same problem which is here illustrated in Calvin's discussion of the glory of God is also found in Calvin's doctrine of predestination. Calvin's insistence that election is in Christ,[25] that Christ is the "gaige,"[26] the register,[27] and the source[28] of election is very difficult to harmonize with the more formal definitions of predestination such as:

> Predestination we call the eternal decree of God, by which he has
> determined in himself, what he would have to become of every indi-
> vidual of mankind. For they are not all created with a similar des-
> tiny; but eternal life is foreordained for some, and eternal damnation

for others. Every man, therefore, being created for one or the other
of these ends, we say, he is predestinated either to life or to death.[29]

How can a Christological understanding of predestination fit with
Calvin's assertion on one occasion "that God would suffer only those
infants to be destroyed whom he had already damned and destined to
eternal death?"[30]

Another illustration of the same problem can be found in Calvin's
doctrine of the law. It is not without reason that some Calvin scholars
find that Calvin's doctrine of the law is very personal and existential
while others accuse Calvin of being a legalist and of establishing a
theocracy in Geneva.[31] There is a basis for each interpretation.

The problem which these contradictions raise cannot be solved by
adding up the available data and then concluding that the side which
has the greater weight of evidence represents Calvin's true opinion.
While this may be true in certain cases, such a procedure would be
based upon the assumption that these inconsistencies are occasional
aberrations which do not occupy a serious place in Calvin's thought.
This is basically what Wilhelm Niesel does in his study, *The Theology
of Calvin*.[32] In developing the thesis that Calvin's theology in form
and content is Christocentric, he ignores the considerable evidence
which points in the opposite direction. The frequency with which
these inconsistencies occur and the thorough way in which they penetrate Calvin's thought indicate that another approach must be taken.

The evidence seems to point to a breakdown in Calvin's theological
methodology as at least a very important factor in this problem of his
theology. Calvin's theological method was basically commentary on
Scripture and creed, but free from the scholastic pattern of propositions in logically deductive order and from the later desire of a Schleier-
macher to systematize, bringing each theological proposition into a definite relation with all others. It was Calvin's intention that his theology
should reflect his conviction that God personally confronts men in the
Bible, where his living image is revealed.[33]

> It [the Bible] is the mirror in which we contemplate the face of
> God in order to be transfigured in his glory. It is the royal sceptre
> with which he governs us as his people, and the staff which he gives
> us to teach us that he wishes to be our Shepherd. It is the instrument
> of his alliance which he has made with us . . . in order to be joined
> with us in a perpetual bond. It is the witness of his good will through
> which we have repose in our consciences, knowing where our salva-
> tion lies. It is the only pasture of our souls, to nourish them into
> eternal life.[34]

It was also Calvin's intention that his theology should reflect his conviction that the one thing which we must search for in all the Bible is
Jesus Christ.[35] Yet it cannot be said that Calvin's theology consistently
maintains the living presence of God without objectifying it or the
Lordship of Jesus Christ without distorting it.

Certainly one reason why Calvin did not consistently fulfill his theological intention, thus giving rise to diversities of interpretation, is
that his theological intention was continually threatened by certain
developments of his basic theological methodology. These developments, while never dominating Calvin's theology, became increasingly
influential in later Calvinism, making it all the more necessary that
they should be recognized in Calvin himself.

One factor which entered into the development of Calvin's theological
methodology was a formal biblicism. Calvin set out to make his theology and polity a consistent and complete representation of the biblical
materials. This procedure was predicated upon three ideas about the
Bible: (1) "Everything that relates to the guidance of our life is contained in [the Scriptures] abundantly";[36] (2) "There is nothing revealed in the Scriptures, that is not profitable to be known";[37] (3) the
essence of Scripture is very clear so that every Christian can profit
therein.[38] Calvin did not have the benefit of modern historical criticism, and he did not always make use of his own avowed principles of
interpretation. In theory he distinguished between the Old and New
Testaments and asserted that God's full disclosure of himself has taken
place in Jesus Christ. In actual practice, however, these distinctions
were frequently forgotten in his expositions of the Scripture. Moreover,
Calvin felt a compulsion to incorporate the whole Bible in an un-
differentiated sense into his theology, though the fact that he uses portions of the Bible much more frequently than others indicates that this
inclination did not dominate his theology.[39]

The second factor which entered into this scholastic methodology
was implicit confidence in the competence of reason to theologize on
the basis of the biblical materials. In the second book of the *Institutes*
Calvin left no doubt about the sinful corruption of reason, and everywhere he rejected reason as an avowed source of theology. However,
reason did become a source of his theology through speculation about
and organization of the biblical materials. Calvin betrays little doubt
as to the full competence of reason in the systematization and rational
elaboration of the biblical materials. A factor which may have contributed to this confidence in reason was his doctrine of providence.
Whether this doctrine led to the practical reversal of his opinion

about the sinful corruption of reason is not of too great significance, for the results are the same in any case.

On the basis of the presupposition that the Bible supplies infallible material for theology and that reason is competent to manipulate and theologize about those materials, Calvin was convinced that he possessed the truth. When he was involved with Trolliet about the doctrine of predestination, he told the Council at Geneva: "So far as I am concerned, my masters, I am quite certain in my conscience that that which I have taught and written did not arise out of my own head, but that I have received it from God, and I must stand firmly by it, if I am not to be a traitor to the truth."[40] Calvin was convinced that he had the right to punish heretics because he possessed the "infallible truth." He objected to punishment of heretics by Roman Catholics on the ground that they did not have the truth and would therefore punish innocent persons.[41] Beza's judgment that Calvin's theology never changed may be relevant here.[42] These facts are indicative of a notion of truth which is rigid and absolute and of a failure to see that the dialectical tension of opposing views may be nearer the truth than dogmatic pronouncements. This static and impersonal notion of truth has not only led to acrimony among theologians who believed that truth could be absolutely possessed in precise formulas and argued about who possessed it, but it has also obscured Calvin's own emphasis upon the personal and deeply mutual relationship of man to God, which expresses itself in the Christian life.

Furthermore, this understanding of Christian truth tends to eliminate all mystery from faith and to destroy religious paradox as a means of expressing the content of faith. While formal paradoxes may be retained, all mystery is taken from them; and they become a logically satisfying and speculative unraveling of man's relationship to God.[43]

The biblicism and the rationalism which entered into Calvin's theological methodology continually threatened his theological intentions, but they never dominated his theology as they did later Calvinism. Yet they are present in Calvin's work. Hence to overlook them in emphasizing the existential and Christocentric character of Calvin's theology is just as serious as the dismissal of Calvin as a legalist or a fundamentalist.

The inner unity of the Christian life and of Calvin's theology is not some abstract principle but the vital fact that man has to do with the living God every moment of his life. His theology represents a magnificent effort to give expression to what it means to have to do with the living God every moment of one's life. No interpretation of the *sola gloria Dei* has been more vivid and dynamic than Calvin's. For this reason Calvin speaks to the needs of this generation. And for this reason it is crucial that the interpreters of Calvin concentrate neither upon the failures nor the successes of his theology but upon his theology as a whole. On the basis of Calvin's own principles, no human achievement in theology can ever be final or complete. Every statement of doctrine must be continually reformed by the Christian community's apprehension of the word of God as revealed in Jesus Christ. When Calvin is accepted as no more and no less than he is, then he becomes a teacher to this generation.

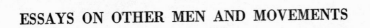

ESSAYS ON OTHER MEN AND MOVEMENTS

Lefèvre d'Étaples:
Three Phases of His Life and Work

John Woolman Brush

About the year Columbus was setting foot on the islands of the new hemisphere and the unholy Alexander VI was taking the papal throne, a little man from Picardy was beginning to make an impact on the scholar's world of Paris. Specifically, this man was lecturing on Aristotle. Before a decade and a half had passed, this Lefèvre d'Étaples, with the capable help of his students, had effected a large-scale publication of the Greek thinker, in an improved Latin text, adorned with commentary.

Just before the new century was born, this same man, Faber Stapulensis if you like, had published mystical writings of Pseudo-Dionysius and of Ramon Lull. He was also becoming enamored of the writings of Nicholas of Cusa, church statesman, subtle and profound thinker, his thought brilliantly lighted by mystical insight and vision, who has been lauded as one of the truly great men of his century, the Fifteenth. It was a long and decisive love affair that Lefèvre carried on with these and other mystical writers.

Early in the second decade of the Reformation century, Martin Luther, monk and teacher engaged in a do-or-die combat over his soul's salvation, was eagerly marking up the margins of two works from Paris, one a Fivefold Psalter, the other a Commentary on Paul's Epistles. These were fruits of the scholarship and the spiritual experience of our same scholar. We must add that these two significant works had not by any means exhausted Lefèvre's vital and enthusiastic relationship to the Book of Books.

Our aim is to observe briefly these three phases of the life and work of this French scholar and man of faith, with the hope of linking them, or at least of relating them: the Aristotelian, the mystical, and the biblical. Writing on Lefèvre in 1914, G. V. Jourdan expressed himself to this effect: "It appears vain to expect that a satisfactory biography will ever be written."[1] As recently as 1955, the king of living students of the subject has said at least that Lefèvre's widespread achievements "have not yet found their historian."[2] The only man who ever essayed the task was Karl Heinrich Graf, over a century ago.[3] Every student in the field, however, owes an incalculable debt to Augustin Renaudet, especially for his master-work of 1916.[4] It is generally held that one strong reason Lefèvre has never been completely put together is that historical scholarship has as yet failed to explain Lefèvre's true place in Aristotelian and philosophical studies. One scholar has asked if Lefèvre might not have contributed to the mind-set in which Galileo worked.[5] One may venture some credence in this as we read A. N. Whitehead's opinion to the effect that Aristotle faded out as far as philosophical development was concerned, but lived on in power to undergird modern science.[6]

Let us open up at once an enlargement of the Aristotelian phase, which belongs first in Lefèvre's interests and development. Before he embarked on an important visit to Italy, this scholar and teacher from Picardy had already, in 1491 or so, expounded Aristotle to his Paris students. These were the sunrise days of the French Renaissance. French education and thought were pathetically shackled in the rusty chains of scholasticism. Lefèvre was appalled, as Erasmus and Luther were to be, by the futile logic-chopping which absorbed the energies of the universities. Erasmus and Luther, of course, were to turn decisively away from Aristotle. Lefèvre d'Étaples, however, assumed the mission of rescuing the true Aristotle from the bad texts and the tedious tradition-bound commentaries.[7]

In Italy he made contact with the Aristotelian teaching of the Venetian Ermalao Barbaro, then at Rome. He also visited the Platonic school at Florence under those priestly men of speculation, Ficino, and Pico of Mirandola. He may have been fired up by the ambition of Pico to reconcile Plato and Aristotle. Later on, Lefèvre was to reveal himself in his mystical interests and his mystic spirit as a child of the Platonic tradition, or, to stand on safer ground, of the Neoplatonic. It is clear from the beginning, then, that our three phases will interpenetrate. There never was, we mean to say, a pure Aristotelian phase of Lefèvre's life and work.

Lefèvre's exhaustive work in presenting Aristotle afresh, in wide range, to the men of the awakening French Renaissance, was a heroic and self-effacing achievement. Their due meed of credit must go to his pupils and co-workers, such as Charles de Bouelles and Clichtowe, and we doff our hat to the printing house of Estienne. Always about the master is a swarm of busy bees. A new start in French philosophic study and reflection is inaugurated. Lefèvre's goal reminds us a little of Descartes' subsequent aim to foster clear, logical thought, mathematically clear. Admirers of the French tradition of rational clarity take note of Lefèvre's contribution, even though its specific impact, as we have said, is not yet sufficiently understood. Renaudet says of the Paraphrases on Aristotle's Physics (1492) that it is a work of pedagogy rather than of doctrine.[8] Imbart de la Tour, joining it to the edition of the Metaphysics which followed it, calls the ensemble "the first book of French philosophy."[9]

Though we are separating the Frenchman's life and work into three phases, we need to see, as far as we can, the whole man all the way through. The early Lefèvre is not simply an editor and interpreter of Aristotle; and the later Lefèvre, to the end, never lets his Aristotelian studies collect dust. The very thesis we are advancing is that the second phase, the mystical, colors not only his Aristotelian work, but that it deeply affects the final or biblical chapter in his life. We cannot expect that he learned from Barbaro a pure Aristotle, whatever that is. It was certainly a different Stagirite from him of the "waning" Middle Ages. Barbaro's quest was the Christian one of answering "the anti-Christian interpretation of the Averroists of Padua."[10] We need at once to see in Lefèvre not only the Aristotelian interest and the love of the mystics, but a man devoutly and earnestly Christian. In Rome he was shocked by the mores of the religious men, and sought out some monks from the north with whom he might celebrate a sober Christmas. Perhaps the future reformer was born of that shock, and the biblical phase of his interests foreshadowed.

Before observing directly the mystical phase of Lefèvre's work, we may do well to stress the breadth of the Paris scholar's interests and deliverances. Mathematics in the academic sense, and numerology, or what we may loosely name number-mysticism, belonged to his repertory, as well as astronomy and what we might call today its half-witted stepsister, astrology. Lefèvre and his students edited texts in this broad area. Boethius on Arithmetic is an example, coming from Henri Estienne's press in 1503. Here is another item, on music! What an educator he was! Patristics are within his range: Polycarp's Letter, Ignatius (eleven letters!), Hermas, Rufinus' Latin translation of the Recognitions, and the Homilies of Pseudo-Clement. Also he edited Ficino's translation of Mercurius Trismegistus. A recent biographer of Guillaume Postel (1510-1581) reveals how many of these interests and even of attitudes of Lefèvre are echoed in the younger man, who never seems, however, to acknowledge any debt to the renowned elder. Postel and Lefèvre both owe something great, as we shall see, to Cusa, in a certain passion to comprehend and harmonize all faiths and all knowledge.[11]

This breadth of Lefèvre's thought and aspiration may mark him as an eclectic, but the ability to live in such breadth with any degree of integrity may possibly indicate the irenicist and the mystic of the Cusa school. The Florentines cultivated this urge to harmonize diversities and varieties. Between the rational meadows of Aristotle and the deep woods of biblical and Pauline faith, I see Faber Stapulensis walking this broad road. He was not systematic enough in theological construction, and possibly not profound enough, to work out a summa of his three phases. As we observe, however, his lifelong engagement with Aristotle's rational thought, and his erudite and fervent love of the Bible, we would name his mystical spirit, fuelled by his studies in the outstanding men of the unitive way, as the middle or harmonizing factor. We shall observe this more closely later as we relate him to Luther and Calvin.

Though we shall turn only to Luther and Calvin for relation and comparison, we find we can garner some views and utterances of Lefèvre that remind us somewhat of certain extreme phases of the "Left Wing of the Reformation." We only mention this for its possible reflection of the temperament of the mystic in him. I refer particularly to a certain afflatus of prophecy as evident, for example, in his much-quoted words to William Farel, concerning the imminent renewal of the world by God. His discovery of the Bible's wealth of divine wisdom and saving grace, during the years at St. Germain-des-Prés, kindled within him a lively hope for the human race. The Word of God seemed about to be reborn with outreaching and saving power. There is an ecstatic optimism that almost reflects the Joachimite vision of history.[12] His eloquent expression of this has been culled by Editors Ross and McLaughlin for an entry in their Renaissance reader. The paragraphs belong in the important Meaux work of 1522, and glow with the age that is seeing "a greater knowledge of languages, more extensive discovery of new lands, and wider diffusion of the name of Christ," than ever.[13] Lefèvre held that after the time of the apostles the church had fallen, a very common view of the Left Wing, but that now, "Why may we not aspire to see our age restored to the likeness of the primitive Church?"[14] In his further faith in an eternal gospel which makes a written gospel unnecessary, and in an age when all shall be spirit-sighted, we are reminded of some of his contemporaries who bypassed church organization and sought to live above any bondage to the letter of Scripture. These ideas, to be sure, may simply belong in the humanism of the time.

To pick up Lefèvre's engagement with the mystics, let us mention Ramon Lull. This man of Mallorca, two centuries earlier, had united in himself the clear mind of the rational philosopher with the burning heart of the poet, the mystic, and the missionary. The plain truth about Lefèvre is that he needed much more than the Aristotelian corpus to feed upon. Aristotle offered the perfect pathway, the consummate preparation, the necessary discipline of the mind, but to what goal? The way of mathematics and logic must lead to the mount of vision. Man's metaphysical longings beg for something like union with God.

Nicholas of Cusa, like Lull, had found the way through mathematics to infinite reality. The German cardinal, wrestling with the infinite in mathematics, came to contemplate the infinity of God. Charles de Bouelles, Lefèvre's co-worker, edits Cusa, expounds his "Art of Opposites," and points up Aristotle as the necessary guide on the way to a higher degree of knowledge. Where the great Greek must leave us is where Pythagoras and Paul and Cusa enter, to lead us into the silence, which is life-in-death.[15]

The mystics love the concept of silence. One may find hints of it in Ignatius of Antioch, an edition of whose letters Lefèvre gave to the world.[16] The Pseudo-Dionysius, who had a great influence on Lefèvre, had much on silence.[17] We see here the love of paradox or apparent contradiction: life-in-death, the silence which is eloquent with the power of truth, the "Divine Darkness," and the ignorance which is the highest and holiest wisdom. We must remember that Lefèvre believed this wisdom came from the true Dionysius, friend of Paul the Apostle, and that therefore it bore apostolic credentials. This fact must be called to mind when we observe later Faber's engagement with the teachings of Paul. There is in Paul a mysticism of the indwelling Christ, and the Apostle can meditate on that wisdom of God which is foolishness to men. He, too, could be caught up into the rapture of a higher vision.[18] But we cannot imagine Paul writing as the unknown named Dionysius wrote: "The soul, leaving all things and forgetting herself, is immersed in the ocean of Divine Splendor, and illuminated by the Sublime Abyss of the Unfathomable Wisdom."[19]

The mysticism of holy ignorance leads back to Cusa's striking work, "Of Learned Ignorance."[20] Hahn finds in Lefèvre a reference to the "ignorance which is superior to knowledge" and also to the sacra ignorantia.[21] We read in him, Lefèvre, of that mystical blindness that is more blessed than all seeing.[22]

Most of the familiar mystical figures are common in Lefèvre's biblical commentaries. In poverty of spirit, in penitence, in holy apathy, we become as nothing and are rapt in ecstasy within the greatness of God. The drop of water is lost in the boundless sea, and the spark in the great fire.[23]

Let us look into the development and significance of the biblical phase of Lefèvre's work.

Lefèvre's main concern with the Bible, as is well known, begins with his settlement in the Abbey of St. Germain-des-Prés and his joyful discovery of its manuscript riches. In the year of his starting there, he and Clichtowe translated four books of John of Damascus' *De Orthodoxa Fide*. A purpose of this work was to supplant Peter Lombard's *Sentences,* which had reigned so long as a theological guide, and which had by this time been the occasion of utterly fruitless discussion. To revive the Damascene was to present a theologian who had professed to build all on the Bible.

Then came in 1509 the *Psalterium Quincuplex,* representing not a completely original step in biblical scholarship, but certainly a bold landmark in its time. We are not specifically weighing Lefèvre's abilities as linguist and scholar, so we shall not analyze this work, save to say that its introductory letter and its commentary reveal his almost breathless enthusiasm for the riches he has discovered. We shall mention the work again. He had found Christ all through the book of Psalms, but he would find him more directly in the Apostle Paul, whose Epistles with commentary he published in 1512. His championship here of justification by faith alone, five years before Luther's Theses, makes this a marked book, and other bold challenges to Catholic tradition seemed to point also to its importance in the drive for a reformation of the Christian church of the West. These works for scholars led him into sharp controversy. Here was a doughty champion who entered the lists on behalf of the *hébraisant* Reuchlin in 1514. It was a courageous man who challenged the ancient tradition that the three Gospel Marys were really one and the same person, and who crossed swords with Erasmus over a verse in Hebrews.

Called to assist his patron, Bishop William Briçonnet, in a religious renewal in the diocese of Meaux which aimed at a restoration of primitive Christianity, Lefèvre entered upon the boldest and most brilliant period of his career.[24] Margaret Mann sees definite influence of Erasmus upon him in a new critical verve, and a shedding of some of the credulous traditional elements in his mind. "Under Lefèvre's pen," she writes, "flow phrases more and more Erasmian."[25] The New Testament commentaries and meditations that he sends forth now reveal him as nearer the powerful Lutheran stream in evangelical thought and conviction, and it seems fair to affirm that the Luther he had earlier influenced now exerts a clear influence in reverse. Mann sees him as becoming more and more *biblien,* and less and less credulous, though she also reminds us that he never gave up his mysticism.[26] June of 1522 brought forth his *Commentarii initiatorii in IV Evangelia,* which not only reveals strong Lutheran influence in its bolder utterances, but again reveals most clearly the strong mystical bent of his mind, as if Luther had not the power to break the Dionysian tradition to which he had been so firmly tethered. The New Testament in the French language marks a new and exciting stage in his career, appearing in 1523 and so relating itself irresistibly to Luther's German version and Tyndale's English. The hortatory epistles to the Gospels (June 1523) and to the Epistles (September) reverberate with his trumpet calls to a revival of true religion among all the people.[27] Near the beginning of 1525, Lefèvre put out his *Epîtres et Evangiles des cinquante-deux dimanches, avec briefve et tres utile exposition discelle,* popular homilies on the New Testament.

The candle of official patience, however, had about burned out. Four years previous, a hundred propositions of Luther had been condemned by the Sorbonne (April 15, 1521). The royal protection for the reformers of Meaux, encouraged by the redoubtable Marguerite of Navarre, could not hold up against the threats of heresy indefinitely, especially when the king himself plunged into military defeat and captivity. Berquin, spiritual son of Erasmus and Luther, had been condemned in 1523, and Bishop Briçonnet, thoroughly frightened, put bits on his more uncompromising preachers or effected their removal. After the Pavia defeat of 1525, Meaux was finished, or at least this *fabriste* chapter, and Lefèvre with Roussel, one of the more forthright preachers, fled toward Strasbourg in order to escape the summons to the Parlement of Paris.

King Francis I subsequently recalled the aging scholar to a safe berth under royal patronage, but the only final security for him now was under the motherly shawl of Marguerite of Navarre in her castle at Nérac. Lefèvre's translation of the Bible into French, a fresh work with which Rely's version of 1487 was not to be compared, was his last great achievement. Impossible to publish in France, it saw the light of day in Antwerp, 1528-1530. This became the basis for the standard Bible of French Protestantism, that is, Olivétan's (1534-1535), as also for many revisions made at Louvain.[28]

Protestantism owes this man much. I asked a venerable French Reformed leader the hackneyed question: "Was Lefèvre a Protestant?" He responded unequivocally: "Yes, we claim him because he believed in the sole authority of Scripture, justification by faith, and he rejected the Catholic conception of sacrament." To press the question here is not my aim. We can certainly understand the pride with which French Protestant scholars date the Reformation in Europe from 1512, with the publications of Lefèvre's Commentary on the Pauline Epistles. If I were asked the question myself, however, I should return a very equivocal answer, the main reason being by this time more than obvious, namely, that I find the tracks of the medieval mystic everywhere in his work. It is not hard to show that a clear-cut Protestantism involved a decisive break with the main directions of the Catholic mystical tradition.

A closer look at the very works that superficially suggest Lefèvre as the John the Baptist of Protestantism reveals that most of his bolder utterances are qualified in other spots by his distinctively Catholic and mystical views. The work of the Meaux period would seem to open up an almost-Protestant reformer, save that these writings are still and always heavily loaded with his mystical presuppositions.

We propose now to stand Faber Stapulensis briefly alongside of Luther and Calvin, with the purpose of showing in clearer light how his mystical thinking seals him off by himself. Our purpose, we affirm, is not to stand at the gate of the Protestant temple and deny entrance to the scholar from Picardy. We merely hope to advance our thesis that the Dionysian mystical is the dominant component in Lefèvre's theology, despite his vital engagement with the Scriptures and his hearty and sincere commitment to church reform. With Renaudet, we see him too faithful to "the study of a philosophy and a mysticism totally foreign to the genius of classic antiquity"[29] to be reckoned a true humanist. And by the very same token we see his position on the edge of the biblical revival a heavily qualified one. The mystical rules him ever.

It is very revealing that all through his earlier years at St. Germain-des-Prés, Lefèvre was interchanging Bible study with further adventures with the mystics. To observe the chronology of his publications makes this quite clear. Between his publication of the Quincuplex Psalterium and the Commentaries on Paul, for example, appeared his edition of Ruysbroek (August 3, 1512). And, after the Paul, was issued his *Liber trium vivorum et trium spiritualium virginium* (June 1513).[30] What wonder then that those two striking manifestoes of the dawning biblical revival should be so revelatory also of Lefèvre the mystic, the spiritual son of Cusa and Pseudo-Dionysius? Cusa he published in 1514. As an aging man by the time Luther posted his ninety-five theses, Lefèvre could hardly be expected to change the mystical bases of his theism and his spiritual culture. Such a concept as that of the hierarchy of being was part of his mental fiber. Furthermore, justification by faith will not capture his allegiance in a fully Lutheran sense, because he has gone to school too long to those for whom "love is the hierophant of all the mysteries."[31]

Lefèvre thinks magnificently of God, as do Luther and Calvin. Lefèvre's theism, however, is dyed with the mysticism of the immeasurable and the infinite, built on the kind of metaphysics that runs to diagrams. The sort of diagrams we find on Lefèvre's pages, not only in his book on Pseudo-Dionysius, but even in his Quincuplex Psalterium, are very far from Luther's mind, and Calvin's.[32]

I should refer my reader to Hahn's closely written article, *Faber Stapulensis and Luther,* for an extended discussion of the very significant differences between the two. He brings us into the Quincuplex Psalterium, for example, to see the neoplatonic feeling in such words as these:

> O God most exalted, God transcending all things, and rising very high above all things.[33]

> O God . . . Who art uncomprehended because Thou art according to Thyself incomprehensible, hast portrayed Thyself through all things so Thou mayest be comprehended.[34]

Then he insists on the great difference between the hidden God of Lefèvre and the hiding God of Luther. Luther's conception is of the "revealed crucified God who works in opposition to human reason."[35]

The "natural" mysticism that led to ecstasy of "intoxication"[36] was far from Luther, whose deepest cry to God is perhaps the "Abba Father," the child's cry that is answered in the assurance of forgiveness and of a peaceful conscience. Luther, in his spiritual quest, had been influenced by the Rhineland mystics, but what he took from them finally was not their metaphysics.

Salvation for Lefèvre is tied up with the traditional three-step mystical ascent. In him there is a strong infusion of what would later be called Quietism: The Allness of God stands over against the nothingness of man, and here is the sense of man as the purely passive instrument in the hands of the One who will play the music. And even here is the ἀπάθεια, that utter detachment that has a long history in the Greek, Stoic, and mystical traditions.

Other familiar mystical concepts are recognized, as the Original-Image relation of God and Man, and the ethic of the imitation of God and of Christ.[37] Lefèvre's imitation theme, however, is pursued on very different lines from Erasmus' "Philosophy of Christ," and it is doubtful if we can speak soundly of an imitation of Christ in Luther at all. For Lefèvre, for example, we imitate God in our love for our neighbor, who bears God's image. Our imitation of Christ is marked by our humility, our ἀπάθεια, our self-naughting, our suffering, our ascetic severity, our poverty. Following Christ into the mountain to pray is a call to contemplation.[38] This is the Lefèvre who, reading Lull in the very early days of our recorded knowledge of the former, is strongly drawn to the monastic life, where there is the quiet seclusion and every inducement to mortify oneself in the direction of the mystic vision.

It is well known that Luther was significantly influenced in his expository principles by his reading of Lefèvre's Psalterium and the Commentary on Paul's Epistles. His twofold interpretation, supplanting the classic fourfold of long tradition, was essentially Lefèvre's, and from the Paris scholar also he took his concept of the work of the Spirit in giving the right spiritual meaning.[39] Lefèvre's spiritual guidance, however, is conceived in distinctly mystical terms, as illumination. This gift of the Spirit is purely of God's grace, but without it no man can read the Scriptures aright.

As to Lefèvre's relationship to Calvin, we first remind ourselves, of course, of their only recorded meeting, when the young humanist, author of a work on Seneca's "On Clemency," met the older man at Marguerite's castle at Nérac. The year was 1534, after Calvin's flight from Paris because of the alleged relationship he bore to Nicholas Cop's heretical address and his association with luthériens. It would seem a propitious moment for the old warrior, licking his wounds and preparing for death, to make an indelible impression on the younger man, so shortly afterward to startle the learned world with his first sketch of the Institutes. Lefèvre recognized Calvin's personal gifts, and said of him after the visit: "Calvin will be a distinguished instrument in restoring the kingdom of God in France."[40]

Hard pressed to fix a point for Calvin's "conversion," John T. McNeill suggests Nérac and Lefèvre as the occasion and instrument.[41] This is an interesting conjecture, and it is not improbable. To allege a clear intellectual influence, however, is another thing. François Wendel sees "no common measure between the religious aspirations of Lefèvre and reformed dogmatics."[42] If one sees any common measure between that great antithesis which Lefèvre shared with Marguerite, of "God who is All and man who is nothing," and Calvin's sense of our creaturely dependence on the will of the Sovereign God, one must surely read further and deeper. The exalted theism of Lefèvre and Marguerite is derivative rather from Hermes Trismegistus, Pseudo-Dionysius, and Cusa.[43] Calvin clearly never spent much time in the house of the traditional masters of Western Catholic mysticism, Augustine excepted, and from the Bishop of Hippo he plucked from a different branch of that widespreading tree. In his discussion of the angels, Calvin in the *Institutes* speaks his mind bluntly on Pseudo-Dionysius. The passage seems too significant for us to omit quoting it in this connection. He is discussing the angels.

> No man can deny that great subtlety and acuteness is discovered by Dionysius, whoever he was, in many parts of his treatise on the Celestial Hierarchy; but, if any one enters into a critical examination of it, he will find the greatest part of it to be mere babbling. But the duty of a theologian is, not to please the ear with empty sounds, but to confirm the conscience by teaching things which are true, certain, and profitable. A reader of that book would suppose that the author was a man descended from heaven, giving an account of things that he had not learned from the information of others, but had seen with his own eyes, but Paul, who was "caught up to the third heaven" (II Cor. 12:1ff.), not only has told us no such things, but has even declared, that it is not lawful for men to utter the secret things which he had seen. Taking our leave, therefore, of this nugatory wisdom, let us consider, from the simple doctrine of the Scripture, what the Lord has been pleased for us to know concerning his angels.[44]

Consider, moreover, Calvin's exalted sense of the authority of Scripture with this judgment on that mysterious author's mind: "For Dionysius, the Scripture is hardly more than a part of tradition and without doubt the least valuable because the most material."[45]

It is possible that we have made too much of Pseudo-Dionysius in this short essay. Yet his repute remained great in the early decades of the 16th century. Imbart de la Tour reminds us of this repute in the face of Luther's and Erasmus' attacks on that mystical author. "The Sorbonne," he writes, "had affirmed, almost as a dogma, the authenticity of the treatises of the Areopagite . . . and Clichtowe had borrowed from the Celestial Hierarchy some of his weapons against Luther."[46] It is worthy of note that Grocyn and Colet across the channel both worked on Dionysius. We are reminded that Colet and Lefèvre shared not only their historical approach to the Bible but their inclination to this specific mystic author.

Faber Stapulensis begins his amazing career, when first we meet him, thinking and teaching in a Greek temple, foursquare and symmetrical, symbol of reason and logic and clarity. Aristotle is his priest. Faber's irrepressible longings, however, and his reach for the infinite, change the temple's lines, and the right angles bend out into Gothic arches and soaring vaults. The one he calls Dionysius is now reading the office, with Lull and Cusa and others of the charmed order of mystics chanting the responses. Aristotle has not retired, but continues to serve as chief usher and master custodian. King David and Paul the Apostle join the choir as soloists, and the heart of the humble worshiper is set afire when the music of the Psalms and Epistles is lifted, telling of the Word made flesh. Yet the chant of the mystic choir is resumed, and the eyes of Lefèvre d'Étaples continue to turn toward the lofty pointed windows through which peer ranks of shining angels.

Continental Protestantism
and Elizabethan Anglicanism (1570–1595)

John M. Krumm

How did Anglicanism in the later years of the reign of Elizabeth I regard the churches of Continental Protestantism? In the exciting early days of the Elizabethan Settlement there had been no question as to the closeness and cordiality of the relationships between the Anglican leaders and their counterparts on the Continent, especially the Swiss Reformers. John Jewel, Bishop of Salisbury from 1560 to 1571, wrote to Henry Bullinger of his nostalgia for Zurich in the warmest and most extravagant terms: "O Zurich! Zurich! how much oftener do I now think of thee than ever I thought of England when I was at Zurich!"[1]

Most of the Elizabethan appointees to the Episcopal bench in the early years of the reign were drawn from refugees who had fled abroad during the reign of Queen Mary. Richard Cox of Ely had been at Frankfort, James Pilkington of Durham had been at Frankfort, John Jewel of Salisbury had been at Zurich and in Frankfort, Edmund Grindal of London had been at Strassburg, Edwin Sandys of Worcester had been at Strassburg, Robert Horn of Winchester had been at Zurich and Frankfort—almost all of the earlier Elizabethan bishops knew the leaders of the Reformation abroad from personal contacts established in the time of their extremity as refugees from the Marian reaction. Their feelings for Continental Protestantism were not only those of kinship and alliance based upon theological congeniality but the warmer and more intimate sense of friendship and deep sympathy which would grow up among fellow workers in the same church and community. The most notable exception to this rule was the Archbishop of Canterbury, Matthew Parker. It is obvious that as a consequence of Parker's having had no direct contact with Continental Protestantism, he having remained in England throughout Mary's reign, his comments upon the unsolicited advice that sometimes came from abroad about English church affairs were a little less than entirely cordial.[2] Despite this lingering irritation, however, Parker acknowledged the theological indebtedness of the Church of England to the Continental Reformers and conceived the relationship of Angelicanism to Protestantism abroad in close and co-operative terms.

In what ways was this early sense of sympathy and kinship affected by the course of events in the middle and later periods of the Elizabethan reign? In the natural course of events, of course, death removed the earlier leaders, and a generation of English bishops—and also, of course, of leaders of Continental Protestantism—arose who knew nothing of the personal friendships and contacts of an earlier time. By 1581 Jewel, Pilkington, Parkhurst, Horn, Cox, and Bullinger were all dead, but even earlier than that the temperature of Anglican-Continental Protestant relationships had cooled decidedly under the impact of English theological controversy.

In this connection the spotlight must turn on Thomas Cartwright, who in 1569 had become Lady Margaret Professor of Divinity at Cambridge and at once undertook a series of lectures on the first chapters of the book of the Acts of the Apostles. These lectures, in which he developed a theory of ecclesiastical polity based, as he claimed, on the Scriptures as well as "the example of foreign churches,"[3] were destined to "turn Puritanism into a new channel."[4] Suddenly the Puritan movement in the Church of England had come to maturity. No longer were its leaders to be content with occasional forays against incidental outrages in ceremonial, vestments, and church usage. Here in the Cartwright lectures was a frontal attack upon the whole basis of the Anglican establishment. Inevitably, a new chapter in the relationships between Anglicanism and Continental Protestantism had been opened.

The earlier tactics of Puritanism, of course, had also strained somewhat even the friendly ties which linked an Anglican like John Jewel to a Swiss Protestant like Henry Bullinger. Bullinger writes to Theodore Beza that he cannot be made to believe that men whom he knows as well as he knows the English bishops could be the tyrannical monsters which the English Puritans are describing.[5] The Puritan strategy both before and after Cartwright's change of front was to appeal consistently to the example of Continental Protestantism in support of their own proposals for Anglican Church reform. In the Puritan document, *An Admonition to the Parliament* (1572), the authors had included "a letter of Beza, and another of Gualter, wrote as it seemed in their behalf: intending thereby to show, that they had the approbation of two famous foreign reformed churches, namely of Geneva and Zurich."[6] Cartwright himself frankly admitted the influence that the foreign reformed churches had on his views. In his controversy with John Whitgift, Cartwright asked, "Is a Reformation that is good in France not also good in England? Would the discipline which is proposed for Scotland be detrimental for this Kingdom here? Surely God hath set these examples before your eyes to encourage you to procede to a complete and prompt Reformation."[7] Indeed, Cartwright turned as naturally to Beza and Geneva for support as the earlier Anglicans had turned to their friends at Zurich, Basle, and Strassburg, for Cartwright like them had been an "exile" too. After his expulsion from Cambridge as a result of his novel views on polity, he spent a year in Geneva in closest association with Beza, and a firm and lasting friendship developed.[8] Although Cartwright was willing enough to criticize foreign reformers and to differ with them—sometimes an overwhelming majority of them[9]—nevertheless it was natural and inevitable that he should draw them into his debate with the Anglican authorities on his side.

It cannot be denied that a new sort of independence and sharpness of resentment begins to creep into Anglican writings about Continental Protestantism in general and Geneva in particular in the controversy with Cartwright and the later Elizabethan Puritans. It is reminiscent of Parker's annoyance at those who would make the continental Reformation a pattern for other churches to follow, and it contrasts sharply with the subservience and mildness which characterized the Marian exile bishops. In his examination of Cartwright before the High Commissioners in 1591, Richard Bancroft, then Bishop of London, detailed some of the "inconveniences" that came about in some reformed churches that followed the "discipline," to which Cartwright was so devoted. "Do not we know from whom you draw your discipline and Church government? Do not we know their judgments and their practice? Which is to bring in the further reformation, against the Prince's will, by force and arms? It is well known how one of the English Church at Geneva wrote a book, to move to take arms against Queen Mary; and Mr. Whittingham's Preface before it: and who knoweth not that the Church of Geneva allowed it? Also, we have seen the practice in France. Likewise it is written in the Scottish story, how Mr. Knocks [sic] moved the nobility of Scotland to bring in the Gospel with force, against the Queen there. And likewise well known, that Mr. Calvin was banished from Geneva, for that he would have brought in the Discipline against the will of the magistrate."[10] In his *A Survey of the Pretended Holy Discipline,* Bancroft goes to new lengths in criticizing the methods of reformation used by Calvin: ". . . nothing will content them [such men as Calvin], but that they build themselves; and therein also they are very inconstant. Now this must down, now that must up; now this must be changed and that must be enlarged: here the workmen mistook me; this is not in good proportion, away with it; I will have this square changed into a round, and this round altered into a square. A fitter metaphor could not well have been found, to have showed the unstayed minds of such manner of reformers."[11] What is more, Calvin's authority was as absolute and unquestioned as that accorded the ancient Bishop of the city of Geneva "that they should all be constrained, all the sort of them, to dance after his pipe."[12] Indeed, the major part of Chapter II of Bancroft's *Survey* is given over to a critical and sometimes sneering review of the history of Calvin's dealings in Geneva, intended, according to Bancroft, to correct the general impression "as though that form of Discipline had come lately from heaven, with an Embassage from God, that all the Churches in the world must frame and conform themselves to the fashion of Geneva."[13]

In the publication of Calvin's letters, done by Beza, was discovered the former's comment on the Second Prayer Book of Edward VI: "Multas video fuisse tolerabiles ineptias." This phrase, to be echoed again and again in the critical estimates of Calvin among Seventeenth Century Anglicans, led Bancroft to say scornfully that there was "not one point of substance in it, for to persuade a child" and he wondered that Beza saw fit to include it in the edition of Calvin's letters.[14]

Bancroft's bitterness extends also to the position which Calvin and later Beza held in Reformation circles. Referring to the Reformation in Scotland he observes sarcastically that "all must be done as it was at Geneva. As any doubts did arise among them . . . yet no man but Mr. Calvin for his time, and afterwards Mr. Beza, (as though they had been such Peters for the Protestants, as the Bishop of Rome pretended himself to be for all Papists) was accounted of sufficiency or able to dissolve them."[15] Indeed, says Bancroft, Beza is to be compared in his arrogance with Pope Leo: "I wish a man would read the Epistles of Leo, sometime Bishop of Rome, and confer them with this of Beza's, to consider whether took more upon him, Leo where he might command, or Beza where there was no reason he should at all have intermeddled."[16] Here is, of course, a note entirely new in Elizabethan Anglicanism, a note of resentment and annoyance and bitterness that would have been inconceivable on the lips of Parker or any other of the earlier Elizabethan divines. Adrian Saravia expressed it more mildly and yet with unmistakable emphasis—"That the opinion of Mr. Beza was not the rule of reforming the Church."[17]

This new independent spirit in Anglicanism began to manifest itself also in matters of doctrine as well as of discipline. It first finds expression in the relatively minor matter of some sermons by the Dean of Lincoln in 1590 in which some of Luther's strong language about Christ's bearing of the sins of man gave considerable offense. Strype says the trouble was not really doctrinal but arose from the Dean "reading some foreign Divines of great name, and confiding over much to their theology and writings."[18] John Whitgift, Archbishop of Canterbury, after a careful examination, assured the Chapter of Lincoln that "we find the Dean in substance of doctrine to differ from us in no point . . ." He explained that the offensive words had been found in Luther and Calvin "whom we in our judgments therefore do mislike . . . And because you shall not doubt of my opinion in this matter, I would have you to understand, that I think Luther, in saying, Christ was *omnium maximus latro, homicida, adulter, fur, sacrilegus, blasphemus,* etc., and whosoever followeth him therein, or any other, writing or speaking so intemperatly [sic] and unadvisedly, do write and speak contrary to the phrase of Scripture and to the truth, and indeed blasphemously."[19]

A more important matter, full of significance for the future course of theological thinking in Anglicanism, was the controversy over Calvin's teachings on predestination, indefectible grace, and other fundamental issues. The controversy headed up in a struggle between Baro and Whitaker, both public professors of divinity at Cambridge, representing respectively the more modified and the more rigid type of Calvinism. Whitaker reported to Whitgift on June 13th, 1595, that he had listened to a most distressing "determination," namely "That justifying grace and faith might not only be lost, in some *finally,* but even in the elect, for a time *totaliter.* And that this was proved by the example of David. And P. Martyr and Calvin were alleged as teaching the same: whom all men . . . knew to be of a clean contrary judgment. And there was an insinuation given that we . . . who teach and have always taught otherwise, are Anabaptists. I was present . . . and heard it with mine ears, to my great grief."[20] That the undisputed sway of Calvin at Cambridge was facing a formidable challenge was obvious when William Barret, a Fellow of Gonvil and Caius College, in the course of a sermon *ad clerum* in St. Mary's in April 1595, "did venture to declare his mind, with some sharp and unbecoming speeches of that reverend man [Calvin] and other learned foreign Protestant writers,

(exhorting the auditors not to read them)."[21] Although forced to make
a retraction, Barret was obviously unrepentant and appealed to Whitgift when the University sought to punish him. The frankness and
openness of his attack were quite unheard of, and the University officials told Whitgift that "such impudent challenging of Calvin, Beza,
P. Martyr, Zanchy, and others, of error in doctrines of faith . . . they
never knew in our Church heretofore."[22]

The Heads must have known that in Whitgift they were dealing with
a representative of the newly self-conscious Anglicanism. The Archbishop had won his spurs in the Cartwright controversy at which time
as Master of Trinity and after November 1570, Vice-Chancellor, he had
led the campaign which eventuated in Cartwright's dismissal from
Cambridge. It is therefore not surprising to learn that in the controversy surrounding Barret's sermon the Calvinist party seemed to have
bypassed Whitgift and sought to deal with the more pliable Chancellor
of the University, Lord Burleigh.[23]

Whitgift took a decidedly moderate position in the Barret controversy. He was not entirely satisfied that the University officials had
not gone beyond the requirements of the Anglican formularies in the
language of the retraction which had been demanded of Barret. The
Archbishop confessed, for his part, that he thought ". . . the Scriptures
were plain, that God by his absolute will did not hate and reject any
man, without an eye to his sin."[24] As for Barret's attack upon the
foreign divines, Whitgift admitted that "to traduce Calvin and other
learned men in pulpits, he could by no means like: neither did he
allow the same toward Augustine, Jerome, and other learned Fathers.
Which nevertheless had often and many times been abused in the University without control. And yet if a man would have occasion to control Calvin for his bad and unchristian censure of King Henry VIII,
or him and others, in that peremptory and false reproof of this Church
of England, in divers points, and likewise in some singularities; he
knew no article of religion against it. Much less did he know any cause
why men should be so violently dealt withal for it; or termed ungodly,
popish, impudent. For the doctrine of the Church of England did in
no respect depend upon them."[25]

The controversy was a prolonged one, and Barret made two appear-
ances before the Archbishop to defend himself against the charges of
the Heads of the University. In his second he was asked, "Whether he
doth not acknowledge it a fault, in that he inveighed so bitterly and
contumeliously against those excellent men, Peter Martyr, John Calvin,
Theodore Beza, Hierom, Zanchius." Barret's answer was, "I acknowl-

edge the learning of these men; and therefore I said nothing personally of them: but because they brought in some errors into the Church of God, and defended them, being brought in; therefore I, a student of true and catholic doctrine, and doing the office of a Preacher, the reason of my office required that I should confute them. And therefore I produced some things against John Calvin and Theodore Beza, and touched them by name: but against the rest nothing at all. If those things which I said seemed too bitter, and were an occasion of scandal to any pious and truly religious, I repent me that I traduced them."[26]

The Heads declared these answers unsatisfactory and further investigation was conducted. Finally the Archbishop himself gave his judgment upon Barret's explanation, and referring to his statement about the foreign reformers, Whitgift declared, "Indeed I mislike . . . that he should once name them to their reproach. That errors might be confuted without naming of the persons to their discredit; especially such as had laboured in the Church, and that did concur with us in the chief and principal points of religion. Notwithstanding, we had been little beholden to some of them, who rashly and uncharitably had believed some reports of this government, and took upon them to censure us in books printed . . . But we must take heed . . . that their bare names and authorities carried not men too far, as to believe their errors, or to yield unto them that honour of forbearance of reproof, which was not yielded unto any of the ancient Fathers."[27]

The Archbishop throughout the controversy maintained a sort of middle-of-the-road position, on the one hand plainly manifesting many sympathies with the Continental Protestant position, and on the other hand insisting that some of their more extreme statements, especially those recently sharpened at the hands of the more dogmatic Continental Calvinists, could not legitimately be pressed as necessary interpretations of the Anglican formularies. Although he clearly expressed agreement with the Heads at several points in the Barret controversy[28] Whitgift stood stubbornly in a middle-of-the-road position, necessitated by the facts of theological history, and was the despair of the extremists of his own time as well as of some modern scholars.[29]

Further light is thrown upon Whitgift's attitude by the much more widely known controversy between Peter Baro and Whitaker on these very points. Whitaker, obviously genuinely alarmed at the breach being made in the Calvinistic front at Cambridge,[30] conferred with Whitgift and, assisted by Tyndal of Queens, drew up the famous Lambeth Articles, finishing them November 20, 1595. As Pearson has said of them, they "defended the doctrines of Calvin as forcibly and

dogmatically as the Puritan body could wish."[31] They were intended
to settle the controversies which had been distracting Cambridge, and
perhaps represented a slight modification of the extreme language desired by Whitaker.[32] It must be confessed, however, that on the main
points they represented the general line that the Heads had been insisting upon as sound and orthodox. They asserted an eternal double
predestination to life or to death, the efficient cause of which was not
a foreknowledge of the individual's faith, or perseverance, or good
works "or anything which dwells in the person predestinated" but only
the will of God. The number of the elect was fixed and could be neither
augmented nor diminished. Those who are not elected to life are necessarily for their sins condemned to damnation. "True, lively, justifying
faith and the sanctifying Spirit of God are not in the case of the elect
extinguished, are not lost, do not disappear either finally or totally."
In setting them forth for the use of the University Heads, Whitgift
added some words of warning: ". . . in teaching them, discretion and
moderation should be used . . . And that the propositions nevertheless
must so be taken and used as their private judgements, thinking them
to be true and correspondent to the doctrine professed in the Church
of England, and established by the laws of the land: and not as laws
and decrees."[33] Even though they were commended thus moderately,
the Articles did not receive a cordial welcome at Court. Robert Cecil
informed Whitgift that the Queen "had commanded him to send unto
his grace, to acquaint him, that she misliked much that any allowance
had been given by his Grace and the rest, if any such points be dis-
puted; being a matter tender and dangerous to weak ignorant minds."[34]
Burghley made a similar comment when Whitaker showed him the
Articles. As Strype tells us, "And concerning the proposition of Predestination, he seemed to mislike of it . . . and drew by a similitude,
a reason from an earthly prince. Inferring thereby, that they charged
God with cruelty, and might cause man to be desperate in their wickedness.[35]

Peter Baro, Lady Margaret Professor of Divinity from 1574, was soon
the focal point of the struggle by reason of a sermon *ad clerum* on
January 12, 1596, in which he set forth three propositions: (1) That
God created all men according to his own likeness, i.e., to eternal life
"from which he chased no man unless because of sin; (2) That Christ
died sufficiently for all; (3) That the promises of God made to us, as
they are generally propounded to us, are to be generally understood."[36]
Whitaker instantly took action against him, claiming he had denied
the Lambeth Articles. It is interesting to notice in the controversy that

followed that Baro was occasionally censured for stirring up these troubles in view of the fact that he was a foreigner. He had been born near Paris and had received his ordination from Calvin himself at Geneva in 1560. There is no evidence that he ever received episcopal ordination but neither is it clear that he officiated in any priestly functions in the Church of England. He was at Cambridge by 1573. The Queen told Whitgift that Baro ". . . being an alien . . . ought to have carried himself quietly and peaceably in a country where he was so humanely harboured and infranchised, both himself and his family."[37] The Archbishop repeated this point in his letter to the Vice-Chancellor "how unfit it was that he, being a stranger, and receiving such courtesy and friendship here of good will, and not for any need we had of him (God be thanked) should be so busy in another commonwealth, and make himself as it were author of new stirs and contentions in this church."[38] The Archbishop of York declared that he "wished he were in his own country, and not to disturb the peace of our Church."[39] Baro indeed found allies for his point of view from among continental divines. A letter to Niels Hemmingsen, a former pupil of Melanchthon, refers to the fact "that we have hitherto been permitted to hold the same sentiments as yours on grace." With the letter Baro enclosed a manuscript of his own on the subject of Predestination in which he distinguished three possible views on the subject which had been held among the Protestant theologians and ventured to criticize Calvin, Beza, Luther, and Zanchius and to affirm his own adherence to views which he asserts are those of Melanchthon, of Hemmingsen himself, as well as of the overwhelming majority of the Fathers of the early church.[40] Nevertheless Whitgift determined not to proceed further against Baro, urging him in the future to avoid such troublesome subjects; and so the whole matter was passed over for the time being, leaving only the unmistakable impression that the Cambridge strongholds of Calvinism could be breached on occasion. The election of Overal, who had supported Baro in the controversy, to replace Whitaker as Public Professor of Divinity showed the way the wind could be expected to blow in the future.

Anglicanism, of course, despite these contentions about the details of Calvin's theology remained in close relationship with the whole Protestant movement, and continued to think of herself as maintaining the general cause of Reformation religion. In a sermon before the Queen in 1574 Whitgift had enumerated the Protestant notes in Anglicanism: "We have taught you the true doctrine of justification, the true and right use of the Sacraments. We have confuted the erroneous and damnable points of Papistical doctrine, as transubstantiation, the sacrifice of the Mass, purgatory, worshipping of images, praying to saints, the Pope's supremacy, and such like."[41] Whitgift would never have conceded that any of these fundamental matters was to be questioned by a loyal Anglican. In the Parliament of 1586, Sir Christopher Hatton, prompted by Whitgift, spoke earnestly of the excellence of the English Reformation and "how many letters had been written hither by strangers, to congratulate the sincerity and happiness thereof."[42] Indeed so high was the esteem of such a Reformation leader as Henry Bullinger in England at this time that his *Decades* was published in 1584 and ordered to be read by every candidate for the ministry. It must not be supposed that the debates about Calvin and Beza and their doctrines represent any Anglican declaration of independence from the main stream of Continental Protestantism. This was a serious family quarrel in which the representatives of Geneva were thought to be pushing themselves upon the others, but Whitgift assures Beza that he seeks the prayers of the church at Geneva ". . . to help us and the whole Church of England: which we do dilligently for you and your Church settled there with you, and will do hereafter, by the grace of God."[43]

This attitude becomes clear in the whole discussion upon the main point of Cartwright's attack—the polity of the church. The Anglicans were well aware that, despite the almost overpowering example of Geneva, episcopacy was not without sympathizers among the leaders of Continental Protestantism. One of the chief sources of ammunition against the Puritans was the fact that episcopal government had received at least tolerant acquiescence if not enthusiastic approval at the hands of a very impressive number of foreign divines. It is apparent that the defenders of the Anglican episcopacy were well versed in the writings of the Reformers, and made use of their knowledge to trap their Puritan opponents on a multitude of small points as well as to establish the general position that no continental divine was to be found in a dogmatic denunciation of "prelacy."

This theme runs through all the Anglican controversial material of this period. Even Bancroft, who may well represent the extreme of anti-continental feeling, fortifies his argument against Cartwright with generous references to Zanchius, for example, and quotes Calvin as against Beza and Beza against Cartwright. Zanchius's allowance of episcopacy is based, according to Bancroft, on "true and religious humility" which recognizes that one must "have regard to those Reformed Churches which retain both Bishops and Archbishops" and which says therefore ". . . who am I that should presume to reprove that which the whole Church hath approved."[44] Bancroft shows also that the Geneva school of thought has become increasingly dogmatic and that Beza is now insisting upon discovering the basis of ecclesiastical polity in Moses, a point which Calvin had not mentioned. "See how they carry us from post to pillar, Mr. Calvin is no body with Beza."[45] Finally even Beza is cited to the effect that ". . . if the Church of England, being underpropped with the authority of Bishops and Archbishops do firmly abide, as this hath happened in our memory, that she hath had men of that order, not only worthy Martyrs of God; but most singular Pastors and Doctors . . . Let her enjoy this singular goodness of God, which I pray she may do so for ever . . . Geneva [does] not prescribe to any Church to follow their peculiar example, like unto ignorant men, who think nothing well but that they do themselves."[46]

Thomas Bilson in his *The Perpetual Government of Christ's Church*, largely an attack upon the idea of lay elders, pointed out that Calvin himself had occasionally expressed a generous and tolerant view of episcopacy which his avowed followers in England might well emulate. ". . . you do Calvin wrong; who though in some things he dissented from the Fathers of the Primitive Church in expounding some places that are alleged for this new discipline, yet gravely and wisely he giveth them that honour and witness which is due unto them. His words treating of this point are these . . . [Bilson then quotes a portion of the *Institutes*, IV, iv, 1 concluding with the words] 'For though the Bishops of those times made many Canons, in which they seem to decree more than is expressed in the sacred Scriptures: yet with such wariness did they proportion their whole regiment to that only rule of God's word, that you may easily see they had almost nothing in their discipline different from the word of God.' I could wish that such as seem to reverence so much his name, would in this behalf follow his steps. He declared himself to bear a right Christian regard to the Church of Christ before him; and therefore is worthy with all posterity to be had in like reverend account, though he were deceived in some things, even as Augustine and other Fathers before him were."[47] Whitgift also cites Calvin's statement about the selection of a leader in the first apostolic fellowship: Therefore well saith M. Calvin in his *Institutions*, cap. viii: "That the 12 apostles had one among them to govern the rest, it was no marvel; for nature requireth it, and the disposition of man will so have it, that in every company (although they be all equal in power) yet that there be one as governor, by whom the rest may be directed."[48] Obviously this was a telling bit of strategy

—to accuse the Puritans of disloyalty to Calvin and to contend that Anglicanism would have been acceptable to him if he had known a little more about it. So Elizabeth could answer a petition for the new discipline which came to her from the Parliament of 1586 that she had ". . . fully resolved . . . upon the truth of the Reformation, which we have already . . . Her Majesty hath been confirmed in her said judgment of the present reformation, by the letters and writings of the most famous men in Christendom, as well of her own dominions as of other countries."[49]

The main Anglican argument against the Puritans began by asserting nothing but the propriety of the episcopal polity in the English situation, the fact that it did not contradict Scripture (wherein no particular polity was prescribed), and the fact that because of antiquity and for other reasons it was a better sort of polity than the discipline of Geneva. There was no attempt initially to suggest that the lack of the episcopal government was a serious defect. Whitgift assured Beza specifically that he and the other English bishops ". . . minded nothing more than to vindicate the form of the government of the English Church, and of the Liturgy . . . in the mean time, no where opposing the discipline of any other Church, or in the least reflecting thereon."[50] He defended Adrian Saravia, who had aroused Beza's wrath by publishing *In Response to the Tracts on the Orders of the Ministers of the Gospel,* by assuring the Genevan divine that Saravia's only purpose was ". . . to assert *degrees* among the Ministers of the Gospel" and that the book ". . . was wholly undertaken, without the injury or prejudice of any particular Church."[51] Bilson says that Geneva and England ought to have different sorts of ecclesiastical polity because they have different political situations in respect of civil affairs. "They live in a popular state; we in a kingdom. The people there bear the chiefest rule; here the Prince . . ."[52] Similar sentiments found expression in a semi-official statement made by the Bishop of Winchester in 1584, in reply to petitions for ecclesiastical reform along Puritan lines made by the Commons to the Lords. "It is also written by divers learned men, that one state of discipline and government of the Church is convenient under heathen princes and magistrates, and another under such princes as favour the Gospel; yea, and that the form of government and discipline, that may very well stand in a particular city, and the territories thereof, cannot possibly be practised in the state of a whole country and kingdom, without great inconveniences; and therefore, that the example of particular states cannot be brought into this realm without some danger in altering the whole laws and state thereof."[53]

One of the retractions demanded from a Calvinist don at Cambridge in the theological controversies at that University has been cited as an example of "Anglican apologetic." It is noteworthy that it makes no claim whatever for any kind of divine sanction for episcopacy, being content to rest the case wholly on the grounds of history and expediency.

> I do not think that there is set down by the word of God any precise form of eternal regiment of the Church which must of necessity be observed in all times and places without exception; but am persuaded that for the better government of particular congregations, her Majesty may establish such orders, as by her godly wisdom with the advice of her godly and learned prelates she shall find to be most expedient for the state of her country, according to her Majesty's pre-eminence in church government established by the laws of this realm, and expressed in her most just title, which is both agreeable to the word of God, and conformable to the example of most ancient churches, which have been ruled by Christian magistrates.[54]

This was all that Anglicanism was prepared to claim at this juncture of the controversy, and it proved precisely to be too much for the full-fledged Calvinists for whom the divine right of presbyteries was an essential article of belief.

It must be confessed that Whitgift, at least, was not always consistent in this matter. At times he seemed to agree with the sentiments of his colleagues, Cooper of Winchester, and Bilson cited above. "I am persuaded," he wrote, "that the external sort of government of a Church under a Christian magistrate must be according to the kind and form of government used in the commonwealth; else how can you make the prince supreme governor of all states and causes ecclesiastical? Will you so divide the government of the Church from the government of the commonwealth that, the one being a monarchy, the other must be a democraty or aristocraty?"[55] And again ". . . notwithstanding government or some kind of government may be a part of the Church, touching the outward form and perfection of it, yet is it not such a part of the essence and being, but that it may be the church of Christ without this or that kind of government; and therefore the 'kind of government' of the church is not 'necessary unto salvation.' "[56] On the other hand Whitgift sometimes confesses that he thinks all churches ought to have retained the episcopacy, as when he declares in the *Defense of the Response to the Admonition,* "I would wish that those two countries [France and Scotland] as far as religion goes were in the same state and condition as England."[57] It is also possible that he was prepared to question the validity of orders conferred by a presbytery, although this is doubtful. In the famous Travers case, he replied to Travers' contention that "Ministers lawfully made in any Church of sound profession in faith were acknowledged such in any other; and this to be the universal and perpetual practice" by making a significant caveat "always excepting such Churches as allowed of presbytery, and executed it."[58] At the same time, as if ordination by a regularly constituted presbytery were not in itself proof of a defective ordination, Whitgift points out that Travers' case is further weakened by the fact that he ". . . gadded into other countries, to be ordained by such as had no authority" and that the reason for this was to avoid having to subscribe to the Articles before the proper authorities. Whitgift's statement on episcopal ordination is restrained and modest, confining itself to the single question of the legality of nonepiscopal ordinations *in the Church of England*. On this one point, he simply declared "That the laws of this realm required, that such as were to be allowed as Ministers in this Church of England should be ordained by a Bishop."[59]

A new line of approach, which inevitably carried with it tremendous implications for the attitude of Anglicans toward Continental Protestantism, was first broached by Richard Bancroft in a sermon at Paul's Cross, February 9, 1589, in which he maintained the divine obligation of episcopacy. This was indeed, as Gwatkin calls it, "a short and easy method with the Puritans."[60] Strype believes that it was upon instruction of Whitgift himself that Bancroft took the line that *the Bishops of England had superiority over their inferior brethren,* jure divino, and directly from God."[61] The Puritan sympathizer, Knollys, of the Privy Council, at once sought to show that such a doctrine derogated the Royal Supremacy, and it was on this point that the heat of controversy centered. More far-reaching in its effect was the work of Adrian Saravia, who in 1594 wrote a treatise on the ministry, in which he pointed out the antiquity of the episcopacy and his conviction that it had fallen into ill repute chiefly because of the pretensions of the Bishop of Rome. His opinion of the Geneva system was outspoken and plain: "Therefore of this new manner of governing the Church, he was, he said, of the same opinion that others held of the government of bishops, namely that it was *human,* and to be borne with, till another that was better could be obtained: and on the other hand that which was disallowed of, as *human,* seemed to him to be *divine;* as being that which, as well in the Old as New Testament, was instituted by God."[62] In a later summary of his position, Saravia declared ". . . that he had defended the episcopal authority to be of Divine institution and apostolical tradition; and that it was taught, as well by the word of

God, as by the universal consent of all the churches." [63] This testimony gained impressiveness in the eyes of many Anglicans because it was set forth so confidently by one who had been himself a minister of the reformed Church in Holland and, as Strype says, ". . . then lived and conversed among such as followed the Geneva form . . ." [64]

It is important to observe that to say that the episcopacy was of divine institution did not carry with it the implication that the lack of it invalidated the ministry and sacraments of any church. Just as the Puritans of Cartwright's type regarded the Geneva discipline as ordained of God and therefore necessary to the well-being of the Church, so now the Anglicans of the Bancroft school could make the same claims for episcopacy. Similarly just as Puritans resisted the Separatist movement and stedfastly remained in the Church of England, admitting that its corruption and lack of lay elders did not invalidate its ministry of Word and Sacraments, so Anglicans of the extreme Bancroft school would not go so far as to disown their sister churches of the continental Reformation because episcopacy was lacking. There is no suggestion in Bancroft, Whitgift, or Bilson that Anglicanism is different in essence from any of the other churches of the Reformation. We have here no conception of a "bridge church," which is distinct from Continental Protestantism on the one hand as it is distinct from Rome on the other. The position of Bancroft and Saravia, however, certainly makes possible a further extension of the argument to the point where Anglicanism can claim to be a branch of the Catholic church in a way that those who lack episcopal orders cannot do. In this sense, we may say that Bancroft laid the ground for a sort of Anglican "separatist" movement that finds its culmination later in the thought of Laud and even later in the Restoration divines. Whitgift, at least, would surely have resisted such an interpretation as earnestly as Cartwright denounced the Separatists.

The dates in the title of this essay are intended to leave out of discussion the impact of the work of Richard Hooker, in whom Anglicanism achieved a new kind of philosophical and in some ways theological independence of Continental Protestantism. Even before his classic *Laws of Ecclesiastical Polity,* however, some of the distinctive marks of what becomes identifiable later as Anglicanism emerged into view. There was a disinclination to wade too deeply into theological controversy especially with reference to the favorite themes of the Calvinist theologians. There was an impatience with foreign interference in English Church affairs. The first hints that the Anglican arrangements for church polity were not only to be tolerated in the Christian church at large but had the claim to be *jure divino* began to be heard. But in all this there was a refusal, as Archbishop Brilioth says of Richard Hooker, "to disinherit his church from the treasures of the Reformation any more than from those of the early Church."[65] Elizabethan Anglicanism is proudly and gratefully Protestant, not only, as Brilioth says, in the sense of "the negation of Rome" but also "in the appropriation of the new orientation of religion produced by the Reformation."[66]

New Light on Butzer's Significance

Franklin H. Littell

Revival of interest in Martin Butzer (1491-1551), Reformer, has been marked in the last thirty years. Always appreciated as a leading personality of the sixteenth-century Reformation Butzer has only lately begun to come into focus as a formative factor in the history of Protestantism. The delay is in good part due to the lack of a full, critical edition of his writings—a labor finally begun by the Protestant theological faculty at the University of Strassburg, but still far from completion. Another reason for lack of balanced appraisal is the fact that many of the documents on his extraordinary service to the Church of Hesse, in the encounter with the Anabaptists and in the establishment of a territorial church with discipline, only became available ten years ago.

Indeed, although his influence as a distinguished exile upon the order and liturgy of the Church of England has long been alternately asserted and denied, it was as late as 1934 that a definitive study established his virtual authorship of the Anglican Ordinal.[1] Finally, to indicate yet another area of major importance, it was only in 1957 that a book was published which began to do justice to Butzer's contribution to the "ecumenical" disputations and negotiations of the sixteenth century.[2] As the picture comes into focus we begin to see the great Strassburg Reformer as a man of stature and originality. In his willingness to discuss with leaders of the most various opinions and to incorporate into the practice of the established church the lessons learned (e.g., Confirmation, Church Discipline, small group work in the "Gemeinschaften"), Butzer contrasts very favorably with the Protestant scholastics and persecutors. His relations with Anabaptism, Anglicanism, and Calvinism were substantial and creative. His emigration during the Interim and death in exile have diverted attention from his great statesmanship in Strassburg, Hesse, and the Rhine Valley. It is not only his influence on Anglicanism that entitles him to rank among the foremost forces of the sixteenth century.

Butzer's great strength was expressed in his doctrine of the Holy Spirit. Both Lutheranism and Calvinism speedily fell into legalism, the piling of precept upon precept, the savage persecution of those who read the script differently, the brutal wars of religion which destroyed 80% of the people and reduced the German lands to poverty and disease for generations. Neither the Lutheran Formula of Concord (1577) nor the Calvinist Canons of the Synod of Dort (1618-1619) satisfactorily expressed a *consensus fidelium*. Both signified a willingness to settle for particularity long after the ability to discuss charitably had atrophied. Both required abandonment of universal perspectives, the canonization of particular formulas, the eclipse of eschatology. Both, in their lack of hope in things to come, lack of confidence in God's continuing purposes, derived from a scholastic mind-set which was insufficiently chastened and governed by a vital doctrine of the Holy Spirit. Butzer could have instructed the brethren, but even in his own time he was accused of "enthusiasm," of sympathy with the "Anabaptists of Münster," of spiritualizing tendencies. Because he remained open to discussion and was willing to learn even from those with whom he had little in common, he was condemned by the dogmatic and inflexible for supposed instability and uncertainty of stance. Actually, he believed that the ultimate decision rested neither with hierarchy nor professional theologians but with the whole body of believers.

Even ordination of the church's servants rested in the midst of the church; the corruptions which had entered the church after the early times were to be overcome by a scriptural restoration of the ministries as functions of the calling of the whole church. The bishop is a "supreme presbyter," representing the college of presbyters. The presbyter represents the congregation of the faithful. True decision is reached in council, with the Holy Spirit in the midst.[3] His greatest difficulty with the leaders of the Anglican "Reformation" was precisely because of his insistence that final authority and decision must rest with the church and not with King, Prince, or Town Council.[4] Butzer's view of the sacraments, too, emphasized the whole church as the locus of the Holy Spirit. The church order of 1534, written after the dispute with the separatists, emphasized the work of the Holy Spirit. The various aspects of church order are determined, to be sure, by reference to Holy Bible and the experience of the early church. But even the assurance that the Bible is God's word comes to us as a gift of the Holy Spirit.[5]

We have now concrete evidence of Butzer's willingness to discuss issues and seek a genuine *consensus fidelium* in the documents of the Marburg Disputation (1538). Here, as advisor to Philipp of Hesse, he demonstrated his willingness to learn as well as teach. As a result of his acceptance of church discipline, in dispute with the Anabaptist leaders, this phase of Christian discipleship was introduced into the Church of Hesse at the Ziegenhain Synod (1539). In the only case of the sixteenth century, over 200 Anabaptists rejoined the established Church of Hesse. Beyond that, there is evidence that Butzer's striking success with the Anabaptists influenced John Calvin's thinking about the nature of Christian discipleship. During this same period Calvin was an exile in Strassburg; when he returned to Geneva he introduced church discipline as the "third mark" of the true church with (1) Word and (2) Sacrament, and from that time "the ban" became a permanent part of Reformed—as well as Anabaptist—teaching and practice.

The translation which follows makes available for the first time in English one of the most important exchanges between state church Reformation and pioneer free churchmen. It is a major section of the Marburg Disputation, a turning point in Reformation ecclesiology.

1538 Oct. 30-Nov. 3. *What Butzer debated with the Anabaptists at Marburg.* The Report of the secretary, Valentin Breul.

I. Jorg Schnabel: Church Discipline (*Bann*). The Church. Usury (*Wucher*).* Baptism. Government. The Humanity of Christ. Absolution. II. Leonard Fälber of Maastricht: the Ministry. Separation. III. Hermann Bastian: Church Discipline. Government. Baptism. His Recantation. Peter Losse.

Done Wednesday after Sts. Simon and Jude the apostles (Oct. 30) in the year 1538. In the presence of Crafft Rauen, Dr. Eisermann (Montanus) Hartman Schlern, the Rector, Master Adam, Dr. Trachen, the Pastor, and other learned men, also the Mayor, Town Council, and others among the most important citizens of Marburg.

In the beginning Dr. Eisermann held up the Anabaptists to critical review, [describing] how they had been treated in various ways previously, that they might be brought back to a right understanding of the divine holy Scripture. But because that was fruitless, our gracious prince and lord had brought God-fearing strangers here who should discuss with them, with the hope that if they previously had acquired rancor or hard feelings these could be eliminated; and one of them should speak up—Jorg Schnabel or Leonhard—and the others keep still, so that the discussion could be carried through and completed in orderly fashion. And then Jorg Schnabel, after he had conferred with Leonhard and Peter Losse, said that one couldn't give the other his proxy; [he hoped] it wouldn't be held against them.

They were asked why they had separated themselves from our church [*gemein*]. His answer came back, that he was repelled by false doctrine. When he had first heard the Lutheran doctrine he had be-

* Under "Usury" the Anabaptists included both avarice in business and the church tax system.

come a servant of the cash box; he hadn't realized that [pursuing] much commerce was against the Bible. In the first chapter of Amos* it is written: "Therefore shall the land mourn, and every one that dwelleth therein shall languish; even the priests thereof shall fall." And in the New Testament it stands: "God will judge every man according to his work." Note: "He has not spared the angels in heaven." Now such is written for an example. Note that in Hebrews the same is written. Because of these he entered into discussion with his [stated] pastor, for he saw that it was worse with him than with the pope; and especially he explained to him two matters, usury and church discipline. Note: He had read about these matters in Luther, Melanchthon, and in Dr. Eisermann's book which he wrote on the common necessity, that they wrote perversely. And now he hoped that he should give honor to the gentlemen present; and his pastor conceded that things were ill in the church; he would do his duty and he, Jorg, was answerable before God that he also look to the matter. But the pastor lightly let the matter drop. When they were next together, he, Jorg, had said: "Pastor, here is money that I am to contribute, but such is forbidden in the Bible and in the city there are many poor people." The pastor said: "It is our Lord's command that the cash box be enlarged." And, in sum, he declared to pastor, mayor, and town council that he wished to separate from them. Note: He had spoken here in the Marburg church office of the same two articles, church discipline and usury—which they maintain improperly. Note: The Marburg pastor had cited him to the authorities, that he wanted to overthrow kings and punish all evil with the sword. In that he had done him an injustice.

Then Martin Butzer began by calling diligently on the Lord God and admonishing that all present should also earnestly beg for grace. Then he told how our honored prince and lord followed this matter with earnest care and therefore it was of the greatest import that those in error should be brought again to a right understanding, etc. Now the Anabaptists were being asked what was the reason they had separated themselves from the parish. Thereupon Jorg had pointed out two reasons, one, church discipline, and the other, that the pastor wouldn't face the issue of usury. Here Butzer asked if they didn't have other points. Said Jorg: "Yes, but these are the most important."

(Butzer) He hoped that a repentant life was preached here and that Christ had redeemed us. He hoped that the pastor and the preachers wouldn't have fellowship with anyone who didn't do that. But the way church discipline was exercised was plainly set in Matthew 18:17. And whoever now wasn't living in great sin and declared to the church as such and then publicly convicted, one couldn't ban according to the text. For Judas took communion, but was not yet convicted before the church. Now there cannot be a church without church discipline (ein ban). And wherever there are whoremongers, usurers, and other sinners among the brethren who after brotherly warning declared according to the gospel will not reform, they shall

* Actually a paraphrase of Hosea 4:3.

not be kept in fellowship. The preachers show this beyond all doubt in proclaiming the death of the old Adam and putting aside of all sins. And because Judas was not convicted before the church, Christ gave him communion like the others. He believed that the preachers gave no one the sacrament who would not stand aside from sins, whom one should let go as an enemy of God. No one can be banned unless he will not listen to the church or has been brought before the church. Christ preached his word; the one to whom it applies has to be held all the more urgently by the ban. And the Anabaptists have no justification from the Scriptures to separate from the church, for St. Paul refers to such in the churches as can be read about in I Corinthians 5:1, that they were puffed up, were immoral to a degree worse even than the heathen. Paul expelled the one who bedded with his stepmother; that was properly done, and one should cite first who is to be expelled.

Jorg: I spoke of usury. Although this church was to be better than the papist, I have evidence in my heart that led to my separation: for avarice is now double in the church.

Butzer: I spoke of church discipline. We intend to speak with you first about this and later about usury. You don't have cause enough to separate yourselves, for you shouldn't be more strict than Christ, who commanded to cut off only those who will not hear the church after adequate warning and conviction, even though they've been exposed thoroughly to the proper text, Matthew 18.

(Jorg) He had given answer on church discipline and discussed with his pastor the way Matthew 18 stands written. And that the preachers have withheld the sacrament from the open sinners was more of a warning than an improvement.

(Butzer) Jorg didn't deal with the pastor according to the text, Matthew 18, for he didn't take it to the fellowship and to the church. Thus even the believers didn't agree with him in condemning the pastor. The church must exercise the ban. If a mayor didn't use his office and the community suffered, it wasn't for a single citizen to unseat him. In the same way a solitary citizen in the kindom of Christ can expel no one. By his separation Jorg had offended the community and done no honor to the Word of God.

(Jorg) He had acted justly according to his understanding. For he had only shown the pastor that he should stand apart from those things which were wrong. Because he wouldn't stand apart, he had justly separated himself.

(Butzer) He would like to see the text: whether the pastor expelled the sinner or whether a single person might separate himself.

(Jorg) He hadn't separated himself from the parish or the people but only shunned the pastor along with his doctrine.

(Butzer) Said he had shunned the community for he had shunned the preaching [service]. For there one is to hear the Word, receive the sacrament, pray, and give alms. And according to the gospel (Matt. 23:2)—"they sit on Moses seat," etc.—they are not to pay attention to the person of the preacher. In short, no individual alone is to remove a mayor or pastor or because of them, where they are lazy in their offices, to sunder himself from the civic and Christian community with the other citizens and Christians. Those who belong to Judas have heard the Word of God. He desired again to have the ground and proof text for his separation; for he had not shunned the pastor but the office of pastor.

(Jorg) Repeated the words of Matthew 18; the church hasn't had the strength to live up to it. So he pointed it out to the mayor and town council; and if Butzer wouldn't give it adequate acceptance he would let it stand to his record. But he was certain of it in his heart.

(Butzer) The Lord gave the key to the church and not to any single individual.

(Jorg) Said the church had shown itself to be incapable of such discipline.

(Butzer) Nevertheless he hadn't acted properly in relation to the church; even if it had been foul in its leadership. Neither he nor any other individual is empowered to expel someone and especially not to appropriate the common service of the church. Expulsion was for two purposes, that the good be not corrupted by the bad and that those cut off may be shamed. He asked again as before, since the church had not expelled the pastor, that Jorg might show the text on the basis of which he had shunned pastor, pastoral office, and the whole fellowship before an official expulsion by the church [had taken place].

(Jorg) Said still: He had punished them according to the ordinance (even here in the church office his weakness was demonstrated, but he didn't abandon it). Note and watch him: he did it justly, in separating himself.

(Butzer) Among the Corinthians the church had managed the communion improperly, that is with prophesying by tongues and much more; but the apostles had not therefore expelled the church, and Jorg had no divine command, when he immediately punished the pastor, that he should separate himself.

(Jorg) Said: After Paul showed the Corinthians their crimes they improved themselves and expelled some.

(Butzer) Indeed they expelled those cited, but grew in much other wickedness, as Paul complained in the other Epistle to the Corinthians (12:20): "I feared, lest when I came to you . . . ," etc. But be that as it may, Jorg still hasn't brought a holy text forward which would justify his separation, even though the church may have been neglectful in exercising church discipline.

(Jorg) Repeated his previous argument, that [they] have acknowledged it to be wrong and have indicated as much to them here in the church office. And since they were all at ease in this practice, he hoped he had done justly and stopped with that.

(Butzer) Concluded from it that he had showed no text for his separation; for those only are to be shunned who will not hear the church.

(Jorg?) That's what the church says, but asked if then the one who had a better understanding of the matter shouldn't separate from them when they didn't do what was Christian?

(Butzer) To punish and warn whoever doesn't walk the right path, and to shun all evil, is not forbidden. But to separate one's self, that is wrong.

(Jorg) Paul says (Gal. 5:21): "The wicked shall not inherit the Kingdom of God." And now when they do evil shouldn't he go apart from them, that perhaps there may be some who would improve themselves?

(Butzer) The wicked who harden in it will not inherit, etc. But that all who are of Marburg are wicked, that he can't believe. Said again, he had no proof text.

(Jorg) He had authorization all through the Bible to shun evil.

(Butzer) Conceded, to avoid evil. But when he has admonished someone, he has no proof text that he should separate from him as long as the church doesn't expel them.

(Jorg) He was convinced from the very beginning that the preachers don't have the Word; he has shunned them and evil.

(Butzer) Repeated his request that he be shown the proof text for his shunning.

(Jorg) Said this church was presented to him as a Christian church. Asked if it was still a Christian church after it recognized one's sin and didn't expel them.

(Butzer) Should give proof text for his shunning. Wherever there is a church which gladly hears God's Word, that is a Christian church. And where it doesn't expel the sinner, he has no ground to shun them. Where there are believing people and they have a preacher and other leaders, even if they are found to be negligent to discipline a person for something disruptive, no other individual shall take it on himself to shun them or expel them whom such a church hasn't banned.

(Jorg) Believed [the discussion] should have been closed earlier and his answer remained: If it were the church of Christ then it would have gone ahead with such an understanding; since it hasn't done it, it is no believing church and he won't accept it unless he is convinced by the Bible itself.

(Butzer) Spoke to those standing about; they have heard this talk and he will also finish off and have the decision put to the church of Christ.

On The Church

(Butzer) Jorg said before that there was no Christian church here. Reason: it had not banned [anyone]. Believed there had never been a pure church on the earth, else we would not have to pray: "Forgive us our sins"; and asked if he didn't acknowledge the church, which Christ recognized and which yet had shortcomings (mangel), to be a Christian church.

(Jorg) Requested that each answer be heard separately.

Butzer: Yes.

Jorg: A church would not be condemned which is organized according to the true order of Holy Scripture, namely, with repentance, faith, baptism, doctrine, the laying on of hands, even if it has inadequacies.

Butzer: There would never be a church built which didn't acknowledge inadequacies and beg God's grace. The church at Corinth was also a congregation of God, which Paul rebuked for committing so much wrong; nevertheless he wrote them as belonging to the one church; and as long as the church retained the true doctrine and sacraments one should defer to the leaders when they are unrighteous. Christ let himself be circumcised, holding fast to [the ordinance] even though the main part of the people was in the wrong and the priests were thoroughly out of order. And he desired that Jorg should show if the teaching was wrong, if the sacrament was not rightly maintained. Paul recognized in all his Epistles the churches of Corinth, Thessalonica, Rome; but nevertheless in the same Epistles he rebuked many errors and inadequacies. And where there is such a church, even with no more than one or two who teach well, he should not turn away as long as the pure doctrine and sound sacraments are there.

(Jorg) Said to the last points that he wanted to hold fast to those who have rightly understood the Lord. Said Philipp Melanchthon visited and discovered that the teachers had forgotten repentance; that caused much wickedness. Our teachers do the same. Luther said: It is impossible for me to build a true Christian church because I don't have the people for it, etc. Now Luther wasn't clever enough to build such a church; since it was not to be interpreted as rebellion, he must have said it for a warning.

(Butzer) The communion of saints was in the Lord. But there was no church so perfect that it could act sturdily enough against wickedness, as Paul writes in all his Epistles, even though it be a church of God like to that at Jerusalem. And there Christ didn't pay attention to the whole mess nor to the perverted priests and yet kept all the ceremonies of the community with the few good people. It's not to be denied that both Melanchthon and Luther have complained that many pastors proclaim faith without repentance. The reason why Luther said he wasn't clever, he couldn't yet set up a church, he didn't have the people yet, is for this reason: there can't be expulsion without prior special admonition and correction. But he lacked people to commission with the special admonition and bringing before the church. If one acted in disorderly fashion, that was rebellious. One must admonish in love often and much, as a diligent mother scolds her children, even though she loves them very much. At the time of Christ and the apostles there was also no ban. Reason: they didn't have the people who could have exercised the warning and brought them before the church. Whoever is in Christ is in the church; whoever is not, doesn't belong in the church; yet he can't justly be expelled or be shunned by someone by any other means than according to the ordinance of Christ.

On the following Thursday Butzer first recapitulated the doings of the day before. And he asked Jorg if he conceded it to be a church where they believe in the Word of God. Answer: Those who commit themselves to the truth and stand obediently in Christ, them he respects as a church.

(Butzer) Here, too, they are agreed that there have always been easy livers and sinners in the church. But when they aren't cited they are not to be banned. Even after the sending of the Holy Spirit the eleven apostles had many shortcomings; yet their heart was loyal to God. And today, too, even among the most saintly, not to speak of the weak and stupid, much error and inadequacy are found in the midst of the true faith and fellowship of the church.

(Jorg) Asked if he thought the church from which he [Jorg] had separated himself was a Christian church.

(Butzer) He would let specific people answer what had to do with specific people; and the church at Aldendorf is to improve whatever is bad. Whoever won't hear the church shall be expelled. And in our church it is to be handled and preached as stated in the confession given the emperor. But if there is error and shortcoming in doctrine and sacraments, let Jorg point it out.

(Jorg) Would like to know if the church in Aldendorf is the church of which Matthew 18 was written.

(Butzer) Where teaching is Christian, there is a church—here in Marburg, in Aldendorf, and in the whole land of Hessen the same is built up. But if there are tares in the midst, they must be borne with until the harvest unless they become so prominent that they can be rooted out advantageously and without danger to the wheat; all of which must always be done according to the oft-cited ordinance of Christ.

(Jorg) Asked, when the Word is there and not the power, if he still held the church at Aldendorf to be such a church? He would convince them that they have behaved and acted against the Word.

Butzer: Let us hear that; go ahead and point out the deficiency.

(Jorg) He complained of the leaders, the teachers, as he had said yesterday, on usury and the ban. But what happened to him was like a master swordsman who finds another at his post, and his sword and authority are taken from him. Three and a half years ago they took their books away from them and threw them into darkness. But they still have comfort in their hearts. They desired that they be given a Bible, as they should be treated by the church.

(Butzer) Even if their books were taken away, they still didn't have sufficient cause, they have acted unwisely, to separate themselves; if they had cause enough then, then they must still have it and could give reasons. Requested that they point out the inadequacies in doctrine, sacraments, and life.

(Jorg) He found evidence in Scripture how the church should act; and he has come here to show the people when they have done wrong. Since they have been jailed, he would convince them from Scripture.

(Butzer) The honorable gentlemen and all of us desire to hear the ground of his separation. Now he brings forward nothing but the error of certain servants, which he has not yet established and proved to them; and even if he had proved it, he had heard yesterday that that wasn't sufficient basis for his separation; since he wanted to be judged in his own case he did an injustice to the church. Whoever follows the confession given to the emperor, him they would accept. But whoever had deficiencies, he should be improved.

(Jorg) Yesterday pointed out two articles; would also show their inadequacies. Under the papacy it didn't happen that the poor people were driven out of house and home. But they were driven now, and the authorities said in Wolkstorff that if he followed what he knew they wouldn't sit still but the law would be enforced more severely yet.

Master Adam answered him immediately, said the opposite, and referred to and cited the princely law on the matter.

(Butzer) Whatever church persecuted the innocent did wrong. If the church persecuted them and he wished to condemn it, then he was judging his own case.

(Jorg) Said still they weren't the church; Paul said (Rom. 14:17) the kingdom of God was peace and righteousness. They pursue unrighteousness and create disturbance among the citizens of Marburg, so that people flogged and drove them out; and when they asked the council and citizens of Marburg the very people who flogged them said they didn't deserve it and they were acknowledged to be pious people by them.

(Butzer) No injustice in the church was to be justified. He has not established that the church in Hessen was without righteousness, for he also hasn't established yet that injustice was done him and that he unfairly suffered for peace, etc. Said the church hadn't cited them and put them in the tower, but the government (oberkeit) did it; and it was justly done for they caused unrest; when the church desired to be at one with them, then they despise the whole church, draw away from it whenever they can and unsettle many simple consciences. They want to be pious, and they say they've been done injustice; but they have to demonstrate that they have separated themselves from us and set up serious division and trouble justly; thereby nobody was made pious, but considerably damaged in many ways; in this they are not yet justified by anything in our churches; and that which Jorg cited had no weight, for we approve the ban and disapprove of usury, which were the only two points yet brought forward.

(Jorg) Is satisfied that they intend to let the guilty remain until Christ come, and evidently they won't listen to what he has demonstrated; so he can only recommend it to him who will judge [the matter].

(Butzer) Let him point out what they do; that he hasn't proved!

(Jorg) Pointed it out in part today and yesterday.

(Butzer) Said to those present that they have heard that the ban wasn't thrown out and that usury wasn't wanted in the church.

(Jorg) Declared they have shortcomings in the sacrament. Luther and Zwingli have caused division, and our church misused the sacrament.

(Butzer) Any who want to be at peace can indeed be at peace in their unity. There were two things, in the supper the sign and that which it signified; and they have always heard that the fellowship of the body and blood of Christ is given in it.

(Jorg) Because they are not a Christian church, they also administer the sacrament improperly. That they misuse it, and that in disorderly manner, has been exposed to the light of day; for they use it with drunkards, usurers, and harlots.

(Butzer) The churches of Hessen maintain, according to the confession tendered the emperor at Augsburg, that the flesh and blood of Jesus Christ are received in the sacrament. In the sacrament we receive the flesh and blood, etc., that feeds and sustains us unto salvation. But when Jorg says drunkards, etc., are admitted, if he points one out who has been banned and convicted, who has been given the sacrament, then that will be altered for the better.

(Jorg) The reason this discussion takes place is that the ban remains unused. The papists have kept a better order than we.

(Butzer) The ban was not to be allowed to decline, Matthew 18; I Corinthians 5; II Thessalonians 3:14, say also, the elders shall watch over the church and a housefather over his household. The issue is to be handled with those who loan in sin; if they will not hear they are to be expelled; however hard the ban is felt, yet Christ drove the meeting even more energetically than banning. But there was no supervisory office that had brought a charge.

(Jorg) Has demonstrated his opinion where shortcomings were to be found. If Butzer wasn't content with it then it would just have to be that way.

(Butzer) Said to the audience, teaching was according to the confession. Whoever didn't do that, he could be cited [for it].

On Usury

(Jorg) He had demonstrated from Scripture that one should not practice usury, neither with gold nor with goods.

(Butzer) They say they wished to justify no usury; and he must give evidence and cite where usury exists. For they condemn usury as he does.

(Jorg) They practice usury, taking of twenty guilders one. But now for twenty guilders they required a measure of grain; that was two or three and a half guilders. Now in the first place the church took one guilder from twenty; this was forbidden in the Scripture.

(Butzer) Read to him from the 6th chapter of Luke (vss. 31, 34), where the Lord said, "whoever asks of you give to him," and "lend to those from whom you expect nothing in return," etc.; and demonstrated from it that the Lord himself had given this rule for all such cases: "Do unto others what you would have them do unto you." According to it, therefore, when the matter has to do with one's neighbor, whatever we justly would wish if we stood in his place, or that we ourselves would take as let or loan, which would mean to us not only no excessive profit but also gave no basis for hope to receive again the loaned amount, that we should do for our neighbor, as we would hope in such a case to happen to us. Where, however, the neighbor has a gain won from use of the gold of another, who in the meantime is not without a certain disadvantage, then love requires that he also share such profit with his neighbor, whose gold he used. Where now it is managed accordingly, be it with rents or other business, then it has been done in love and no one has a complaint. But wherever the neighbor has been injured, we condemn that also. But now when the common rule in the matter is five out of a hundred, those who use others' money can easily pay with their profit. If then the treasury at Aldendorf has managed according to this rule of justice, Jorg has no complaint against them; for those people have been put in charge of the treasury money, in order to earn more; and thus when one's own goods are sold to the treasury, from them the blessing of God may be expected for the poor people. All church money should be divided into three parts and used: the one part is to be assigned for the maintenance of schools and church personnel; the second for the care of all needs in the parish and of special persons; the third is for building churches and for maintenance. But because unfortunately many needs show up in it, and thereby the believers don't give so much to the treasury, it must be looked to that those who hold the treasury also serve the poor. Where now some one serves his own investments with the money of the poor, shouldn't he also share from it with the poor people? God forbade the Jews that they take usury which damaged the neighbor, and not such a just distribution of the profit to which the Lord sends his blessing— from the money of one and the trade or sales of another. Where such a tax is raised, with which the poor tax collector is criticized, injustice is done. But when five guilders are taken from a hundred according to the common rule, with it he can also make his own investments. But where the case is ambiguous, love shall be the master. Such business is a service and a work of love—no usury and also not forbidden by God.

(Jorg) How profitable love has been, has been demonstrated in fact.

(Butzer) The papists also desire to condemn our people, saying things get worse all the time. Our doctrine is this: Work repentance and also good. And it isn't the fault of the teaching that people don't do it. In the Old and New Testament it has always been the nature of God's Word that it always irritated those people who didn't accept it, just as is thoroughly demonstrated in Romans 1. "Many are called, but few are chosen" (Matt. 20:16). Those who don't accept the doctrine, after it has been thoroughly explained to them, they sink more deeply daily and give occasion for the saying: "Since the new doctrine has been preached, many people have become worse." Indeed, what has happened is what the prophets, Christ and the prophets have proclaimed—as indeed the histories and other writings show. The gospel washes us of all evil wherever it is rightly accepted. But now only the fourth seed brings forth fruit, as Christ says.

(Jorg) It has been spoken well, but he has not been rejoined; the actualities must be dealt with.

(Butzer) That we shall do.

On Baptism

(Butzer) Repeated what the argument was about and since Jorg claimed the sacraments were misused and specifically baptism, he said: We ask of you, since you blame us for abuse, that you point out the abuse to us.

Jorg: You misuse baptism, because the teaching of the gospel is that men are first to be convicted of their sin, afterwards they are incorporated in the fellowship of the holy church; which [ordinance] you let fall, when you baptize infants.

Butzer: We say, the ordinance is as he says when the adults are dealt with, but with the children there is another order. In the Old Testament, God had his covenant with Abraham and gave him thereby the seal, circumcision, and promised him thereby he would be a gracious God to him and his seed. Now Christ has wrought a covenant for us heathen who believe on him, and God will also be the God of our children and even so will have the sacrament of the rebirth, which baptism is for us, just as circumcision was in the old (covenant), confessed in his church.

Jorg: I hold to the text: "Go forth and preach." Now faith comes from hearing; the children can't hear, etc.

(Butzer) Asked if he believed that the children would be saved.

(Jorg) He had the text: "Let the children come unto me," etc. (Matt. 19:14). With that he would let it be settled.

(Butzer) When he acknowledged that the children were saved and yet said the children couldn't hear, he contradicted himself, for they also use the word at the end of Mark, how the Lord said (Mark 16: 15-16): "Preach the gospel to all creatures, whoever believes and is baptized, the same shall be saved." For there follows immediately: "Whoever doesn't believe," namely who have heard the gospel, "he will be damned"; because then the children don't hear, as Jorg says, they must then be damned, where this ordinance of the Lord also applies to the children . . .

Jorg: We find nothing in any apostolic act except that they have acted first in repentance. The children have no understanding; therefore they cannot repent.

Butzer: At the end of Mark, Christ established an ordinance, how the adults should be dealt with. But the Lord saves our children also, as Jorg himself acknowledges, and accordingly, as soon as the adults give themselves to him he takes up their children also in his covenant of grace. Like a prince, when he grants someone a patent of nobility, he takes up also the children and all the succession with it. Genesis 17:7: "I will be God to thee and thy seed"; thereby he is also the God of our children. For when the adults are accepted the children are also accepted. We must regard the Bible as to what baptism and

the covenant of the Lord may be. Now whoever would say there
shall be no woman at the sacrament because no woman was there
then when the Lord first held it, he would be doing wrong; yet one
couldn't display a single clear word by which the Lord declares it or
gives an example according to which women should also participate
in the holy sacrament. But since one understands the nature of the
sacrament, it is easy to see that this sacrament shall also be administered to the women, for they also belong to the community of
Christ as believers. Thus God now calls the children to salvation and
will have the same publicly demonstrated as by the adults in the
sacrament of rebirth; and Christ certainly affords all the gift and the
evidence of grace which the adults have had; whoever then understands the manner of the sacrament will not exclude the children;
even if one could dispute whether the apostles baptized whole households to the last detail and we had moreover no express command:
Baptize children!

Jorg: Since then the ordinance of the apostles isn't to be kept, baptize the children and let it stay that way, teach no repentance and
improvement.

Butzer: It was the ordinance of the apostles to baptize according
to the ordinance which Jorg cited, but the children according to the
ordinance of circumcision; and when the children are grown they
are to be catechized faithfully and taught to maintain everything
which the Lord has commanded.

Jorg: It is clearly written to circumcize the children, but not this.

(Butzer) [asked] if we should abandon what we have no express
command for, such as giving the sacrament to women.

Jorg answered: No; one would do wrong not to administer it to
them.

(Butzer) [asked] whether we did wrong to celebrate Sunday.

Jorg: No.

(Butzer) Then he shouldn't condemn the case of infant baptism
either, even if there is no clear command so that one had good basis
in Scriptures. The apostles proclaimed the services on the Sabbath
and sinned not even though there was a clear word against them:
"Thou shalt do no work on the Sabbath day." Thus Christ acknowledged the resurrection of the dead without an express word which
proclaimed the resurrection of the dead. When Christ enlarged his
covenant of grace with the heathen, how should we then exclude
the children? How do we surpass in that the Word of God, how do
we go beyond [the rule of] love?

Jorg: I will hold to that, where I'm certain that the apostles have
baptized the repentant, and let go where I'm uncertain.

Butzer: We'll show you our argument. At the end of Matthew
(28:18-20): "to me is given all power," etc. Thus "Go forth, and
make me disciples of all nations, baptize them and teach them to
observe." There we have sufficient command that we must accept
the children. If we are to accept the nations, then we must accept
them, as the people were added to the Israelites. How so? In this:
"He will be God to you and your children." Now I ask if the children

don't belong to the people. Then follows after baptism: "Teach them to observe all things their life long, what I have commanded you." According to this interpretation the teaching comes after baptism, although from it one can't tell what order the things follow each other as with some ordinance with a clear declaration. For we have Mark 1:4-5: John came, baptized and confessed their sins, and followed the preaching of John unto baptism; just as people also confessed their sins first, before they were baptized. We have the last of Matthew: "Make disciples of all nations," and therefore we shouldn't exclude the children. "Let the children come unto me, for they belong in my kingdom," in my church, and "whoever doesn't accept the kingdom of God as the children," etc. (Luke 18:16-17). And that is our foundation: As the Jews were accepted, so are we and our children accepted in the sacrament of rebirth.

Jorg: The first reason, which is from the apostles, pleases me more than yours; and even if it were the way it isn't and can't be proved, there would still be much misuse of it with use of sponsors, eating, and drinking.

(Butzer) Where is the commandment, where is the proof text, etc.? Note: As to the misuse of sponsorship, Abraham also held a celebration at the circumcision of his son. And in the Old Testament they ate and drank on festival days. Sponsorship was used by the time of Augustine and arose out of love. Specifically, as John was born the neighbors came together; there, too, men have eaten and drunken. But we condemn misuse.

(Jorg) His reason has been heard and he wanted to let it rest there; and the Bible gives no better than this.

Butzer: This dispute stands to the judgment of God and of the church.

On Civil Government (Von der Oberkeit)

(Butzer) Said that government had been challenged, that the Christians should have no civil government. Repeated then the confession which was given to the emperor at Augsburg.

(Jorg) Had nothing against it, for the Scripture instructs them that he should be obedient to the government. But when the government doesn't use the sword properly he will not obey it.

(Butzer) The subject is to be obedient to government in everything where it isn't obvious that the subject would act against God if he obeys. And where it isn't quite obvious, the subject is to obey the higher conscience and not set himself to judge the government and its commands. If, however, the subject knows that the government will order him to perform a public wrong, then he should not obey —like Saul's troops, when they were to murder the priests for they knew that they were publicly innocent (I Sam. 22:17).

On the Humanity of Christ

(Butzer) Explained this article from various texts and concluded that if Christ didn't acquire flesh from Mary, then he was no human, and asked if Jorg also saw shortcomings in that.

Jorg: I hold to the article of faith: He is conceived of the Holy
Ghost, born of Mary the virgin.

Butzer: Romans 1:3: "He is a son of David according to the flesh."

(Jorg) Held to the article of faith; what he hasn't understood God
will give him in good time. Could not deny that there was a basis [of
argument] there, in what Butzer said, but he couldn't speak much
against it.

(Butzer) Mary of the house of David was of child by the Holy
Ghost; thereby the Bible speaks of a son of David. Note: The Mün-
sterites have said: Christ received no flesh from Mary. Now Elizabeth
(Luke 1:42) said: "Blessed be the fruit of thy body"; that must be
understood according to the manner of Scripture, what fruit of the
body alone is meant; thus receiving from her body blood and flesh,
Christ became her natural son, yet the community of mankind was
added.

(Butzer) Asked if they had further reason to separate themselves
from us?

Absolution

(Jorg) His [list of] shortcomings have been heard in fact, but there
is a further deficiency, namely this: The following after was mentioned only in the community of sin, among whom were many unrepentant, etc. Specifically: When wrong doers have denied life,
then they were promised the Kingdom of God and that they should
not die as a murderer according to the Scriptures.

Butzer: When one says: I repent of my sins then he is given absolution; but they can't see into his heart. And although everyone
should watch that he doesn't escape suffering due to murder and
robbery, etc., even if that is the situation with him, he should carry
his pain like the thief on the cross and seek grace of the Lord, which
he will certainly find, as the thief found it. And Butzer asked Jorg
if he had something further.

Jorg: No, but if Master Adam and others found shortcomings in
them, they should cite them.

(Butzer) The defect they found in them was that they separated
themselves from us without cause. For we do not want to set church
discipline aside, nor justify usury; we proclaim a repentant life; we
maintain the sacraments according to the meaning of Scripture and
according to the confession delivered at Augsburg. Prayed that they
and Jorg should let it be known if they would again join us in all
Christian matters.

Jorg answered they would think it over.

There followed the process with Leonhard of Maastricht. And the
same Leonhard said that as his brethren had answered to the articles,
in them he saw other deficiencies and will demonstrate it as simply as
possible and with evidence from the Bible. First he asked Mr. Butzer
from whence came his calling to preach according to the rule of
Christ.

(Butzer) Whoever can serve the church, he serves as best he is able. Now the church has called those here who can preach; and Paul commanded Titus to occupy the city with capable people (Titus 1:5). And even so are our preachers provided.

(Leonhard) But he hasn't thereby sufficient evidence as to who sent them.

Butzer: No one can preach except he be sent, Romans 10:15. With whatever one has one should serve the church.

Leonhard: When I see you come with such signs as Christ commanded of them, namely that they should be born again, joined to Christ with the death of sins, then I will believe in you.

Butzer: Him whom they may convict, that he isn't at one with Christ, we will not allow to be a preacher.

Leonhard: Christ said, John 3:7, "Unless ye be born again," etc. Now I know none who has been resurrected in such a rebirth through falling away of the first life; I find that they take the opposite position, do not gather with Christ but rather scatter.

(Butzer) He should demonstrate in what particular.

(Leonhard) His complaint has been heard, that they won't have the abomination stopped and have become accomplices of the pope through infant baptism; in this [practice] they have abandoned the good in order to build up the abomination.

(Butzer) Infant baptism was given them by God's ordinance, by it the children of God are accepted. Hezekiah, Isaiah, etc., and others too renewed the covenant of God, but nevertheless did not circumcize the people again. In the Old Testament the covenant of the Lord was renewed with the paschal lamb. And our preachers have done the same with the Lord's Supper. And because they confess the faith we must recognize them as Christians even though they haven't renewed the baptism.

Leonhard: I feel that you don't have a living word for which God sent his beloved son to us; you have a dead word, as evidenced by your fellowship, else you would draw away from the evil.

Butzer: You complain because you aren't highly thought of.

Butzer asked Leonhard whether their elders had an act or a living word.

(Leonhard's answer) They have a living word that can bring the people from evil to good and totally renew them.

Butzer: Would God that Münster and all of them had a living word that could kill the old Adam in us all! Pour out your living word on all of us here and all men, that we might be pious indeed. And since now you can't do that and think nevertheless that you have a living word, then permit the word of Christ, of the apostles and that now preached, which is a word, a living word indeed, whether they are immediately improved in a special way who are called to life or not.

Leonhard: I find no one who has been converted from his previous stained life. And thereby he cannot see that they have a living word.

(Butzer) That is no logical sequence. The word has been preached for a long time; if there is no improvement there, then it is no word of God. At the end of the 4th book of Kings (II Chron. 36:15): "I have ever sent prophets and they worked among you." And when he says he has not yet found one, etc., then he should reflect that he should not judge; he has known without doubt many people, and many have sealed their confession with their blood, and he could not know what each does for good in another land. Therefore it is very frivolous of him when he says that he hasn't found one.

Leonhard: As to the charge that I let fall a judgment that I shouldn't. I say: What God's word judges, that we do not judge, yet we use the word according to his command. Therefore when one judges it is not a judicial sentence.

(Butzer) Asked if it is a good line of reasoning [to say] the people are not converted by the word, therefore it is not God's word.

(Leonhard) He wished to hold to the clear evidence. Christ doesn't let himself be found in the higher schools.

(Butzer) Said Leonhard won't give God the praise, that the line of reasoning wasn't sound. Then he turned to the audience and said, Christ did preach in the higher schools, for he was in the synagogues and preached to all creatures. But the little common folk have come to hold it against the word—[an attitude] one finds among princes and peasants and in other places; and they know within them and not from the Word of God—that the specialists, from them the teaching of Christ is hidden; to them, moreover, the lowest people are equal.

Leonhard: Christ says: "The tree is known by its fruit," Matthew 12:33-34. *The mouth flows over with what the heart is full;* that one can then judge. Therefore they cannot establish that they are sent, for they show no good fruit.

Butzer: How can such a logical line be sound: It is a bad tree for I have seen no good fruit from it! What then if the tree were in Calcutta and I am here and see no good fruit on the tree, does that mean therefore it doesn't have any? He, Leonhard, has not seen anyone. Therefore, he judges frivolously. He prayed that they should judge what they see and not then act as though they were equal to God. For it was for that that God cast the angels from heaven.

(Leonhard) They have heard from his brother that they wanted to do that good which they recognize and acknowledge. But the preachers were the first to cite his brother before the government and have claimed he was rebellious. He never read that of any apostles or prophets, for God was a God of peace.

(Butzer) He should have held his judgment that no fruit appears in our church, for he lied when he said that he had kept it a secret. We grant: Whatever preacher persecutes a good man doesn't do right. But now the Anabaptists are prosecuted not because they aren't pious but because they cause the church great mischief and damage. The one who damages his neighbor isn't pious; yet more impious is he who would withdraw from him the doctrine of God and the sacraments, as you and yours do, which causes the people the most severe damage, namely, in religion; these are the most impious of all, even if they even drink no wine, eat no flesh, love all austerity, always pray, and make use of everything that seems spiritual. This is also

Satan's style and usage, that he introduces false religion with pretended austerity of life, as also happened with the false prophets about whom Paul complained in Colossians 2:16 ff. This was also evidenced by the Manichees and others who ravaged the holy religion most severely. The preachers call no one unjustly to prosecution. But they preach, as Paul taught them (Rom. 13:4), that the government doesn't carry the sword for nothing, but brings fear to all who do evil and therefore the greatest fear to those who do the most grievous wrong, to damage holy religion. And if the Anabaptists suffer as wrong doers, God will have no wrong so severely punished as blasphemy. And they haven't yet given evidence that our church or preachers are a bad tree. Christ drove the people out of the Temple who damaged religion.

Leonhard: You must admit that from the beginning the pious have never persecuted the impious.

Butzer: That I deny, for who drove Lucifer from heaven except Piety in heaven. Note: Paul strongly drove the false apostles.

Leonhard asked: Did Paul persecute the others?

Butzer: Yes, and that with true Godly fervor, for the false apostles persecuted them with a false, devilish fervor.

(Leonhard) Where did Jacob prosecute his brother Esau? But Cain persecuted his brother Abel for the sake of the sacrifice and Esau, Jacob. And so it is yet today, etc.

Butzer: That the wicked persecute the good, we admit; but that the pious also have driven the wicked, all Scripture shows. What did Christ do in the Temple, what did Peter do with Ananias (Acts 5)?

On the Following Friday

Leonhard: Yesterday, I put questions, as you have heard. Now I can't criticize your talk; and if they also are ready to apply it in practice, then it pleases him indeed; but it isn't sufficient until they set to work to build the Temple, for he and his cobelievers want to help with it. And they have given proper cause to have separated from us and they pray that patience may be shown them; let the light shine and don't chop down the tree because it stands in blood.

(Butzer) One should understand how Christ, the apostles, and prophets managed—at the beginning had enough to do in witness, in love waited upon the work; if they weren't initiated, they treated them according to the ordinance of Christ. Note: As Peter did the first preaching he took into the church those who made public confession. Because they will take from us the practice and the doctrine, they are indebted [for them]. He must also realize that the church has many members; but the preacher should give diligent attention to his office, heal what is hurt, strengthen what is weak. That some are a bad sort among them mustn't be counted against the good sheep. He says, the tree shouldn't be chopped down, etc. Said Butzer: Our prince is of the intention that his people should not be distracted and the Anabaptists not burned. But when he sees that the word is despised and especially by them, the Anabaptists, it is his duty to deal with it, and to see that the best is done with them that they improve themselves. He must hold the church dearer than his father, brother, and mother, 5th Book of Moses 13:7.

(Leonhard) When he was cited for punishment, in that he and his brethren were represented as guilty, he said "No" to it; for he had done his best to build the Temple of God and he wished to demonstrate it with his brethren. Since they now saw that ours were joined to false doctrine and sins, they have best turned away from us. And where we now recognize that, they wish to treat us well also as obedient children of God. They hoped, too, that no one had cause from them to punish them as evil-doers. What they see bad in their neighbor they would judge and defer to no one, according to the Scripture (Matt. 10:32): "Whoever therefore shall confess me," etc. Specifically, the Scripture is in all respects on their side. For Paul says (II Cor. 6:17): One shall come out from among the evil ones. But that they should show evil for good to us, that he wished not to do and rather suffer for it what he should. Specifically, one cannot belong simultaneously to the table of the Lord and of the devil. And we should look about us as to where we stand in order that we don't stand where we should not stand. We should leave the ungodly and follow the godly. If they had sensed that in us they would have remained with us. And now their separation should not be misunderstood; hoped that the prince and the audience would reflect that they have suffered with patience as welldoers and not as evildoers, so that we might see what they have at heart.

(Butzer) Prayed that it would be taken for true what he brings up, that evil must be abandoned, that one could not serve both the table of Christ and of the devil. Now our elders lead in no other way than this. The Bible is against the Anabaptists, for they are joined to works, in the sense Paul said to the Galatians (1:8): Heresy. The Christian doctrine which we confessed before the emperor we know to be grounded in the divine word; and all the children of God owe it to have fellowship with us in such doctrine, regardless if at the same time some are found of evil life. And as long as the doctrine is proclaimed and the sacrament is used, all men owe it to stay by us. Now they have not only broken this same teaching but also defamed it (he hoped however through lack of understanding) and thereby many people pass away ruined into eternity. And if they had a faith to remove mountains and to give their body to be burned, as Paul announces in I Corinthians 13:2 ff., but have not love and throw us out of the kingdom of Christ, they are without Christ and in the worst wickedness. Galatians 6. There is the work of the flesh, not alone the rough outer but also the spiritual inner factions and sects. Now if they had fled all vice, all worldly gain, but each one taught and kindly improved his neighbor and nearest and in the meantime with the true believers kept the holy fellowship of doctrine, sacraments, prayer, and giving of alms, then they would have rightly followed the teaching of Christ and the apostles. But now, since they have shattered the good because of the bad and fled the holy service in his church, defamed it, and—among many of them—cast it down, they have done nothing else but corrupt many souls inwardly, despised the word of Christ, thereby introduced among the common herd a crazy godless life. What could they have undertaken that would have been more disturbing and damaging to the Christian church? No one may represent our confession to be unrighteous or blasphemous. Now we still teach it (the confession) and maintain the sacred rites and yet these people blame us as if all the horror of the Antichrist ruled in all the doctrine and practices of our church. Besides we admit, too, that there are unfortunately all too few true Christians; Paul commonly complained of that, too, in all his Epistles about his churches. If one is overpowered by vice then those who are spiritual should rebuild with the spirit of gentleness and each bear the other's burden (Gal. 6:2). Now when I have done my [duty], then I am excused before God and God will perhaps give his grace. And we do not admit in your case either that you have suffered as innocents, but as those who have the greatest guilt and have done the worst things. Wishes to bring it to an end. You say you have not found the work of the Spirit among us and therefore you have justly separated from us. That we do not concede.

(Leonhard) Requested that he be given the confession which was given to the emperor so that they might reflect for a day or two upon it.

Butzer: That will be done.

Peter Losse said: Since the prince and lords have written them and all their brethren who lay prisoners with them in Wolckstorff, as soon as his brethren were at hand they would talk with them and then give answers.

Hermann Bastian

Desired also to read the confession and would then give answer about it; and said he wished to give his opinion, although he was unprepared to speak before Mr. Butzer. First, he understood that our prince and gentlemen were deeply concerned with this case and therefore have had them sent here. Now the government well knew how things remained. And said, since they had dealt with usury and the ban, he had spoken with our gentlemen about them also in Cassel. Now he had read in the Bible how church discipline (ban) was to be held according to Scripture. That he should now say that there was no Christian church among us because there is no ban, that he couldn't say. But also the church couldn't be without discipline and without faith.

(Butzer) It is true that when there is no discipline and ban there also is no community; for there are two kinds of people, good and bad, and the good must always unite in the fellowship of the Lord and also improve the bad with daily doctrine and discipline. But Christ himself preached a long time but had no properly ordered ban. Now from that Hermann had sufficient evidence to conclude that he should go to church with a good conscience and hear the word of God. There are two fruits of expulsion, the one that he who is expelled may become mortified and convert, and the other that he not mislead the others.

(Hermann) Already a year ago it was said that the ban would be introduced; but that hasn't happened. And the church can't be without the ban. He hasn't separated because of a bad will [toward us]; and cited the text I Corinthians 5:11 as to how the ban should be.

(Butzer) "Do not eat with such," etc. (I Cor. 5:11). Said that if we shouldn't eat with them then indeed someone would die of hunger. St. Paul meant to have eating understood as though one gladly and deliberately had to do with prostitutes and rough sects. And now if there are such people one should point them out to the pastor, if it be obvious. He will rebuke them. If it isn't public then rebuke them between thee and him, etc.

Hermann cited further I Thessalonians 3.

(Butzer) Paul spoke of those who cheat the people and don't work. Now when one has fallen into vice, one should attempt in all manner of friendliness to bring him again to the right course. Just as in a true friendship, when one has a boor among them, then one sends —when the father, mother, brother, or another can't help—a cousin, brother-in-law, or other friend to them, in order to bring the uncouth one to the right course.

(Hermann) When Leonhard said we have no word, for it is dead, brings forth no fruit, Mr. Butzer showed that honor should be directed to God. Christ, the apostles, and the prophets also preached and were but little fruitful. By this he could judge that Mr. Butzer was right. He wished to give honor to God. According to his understanding it couldn't be justified that the unbelievers should be judged by the sword.

(Butzer) God commanded in the Old Testament that the government should also punish adultery, etc., and remove blasphemy, as Paul says in Romans 1:32. In the 5th Book of Moses 13:2 ff.: "If there arise among you a prophet, thou shalt not hearken unto him, for God tempts you to know whether you love him. That prophet shall die," etc. Now to be sure we Gentiles (Heiden) are not bound by the law of Moses. But if a government will act according to the ordinances of God, it will punish adultery more severely than theft, the corruption of religion more severely than finite [matters].

Hermann cited the text (Eph. 4:5): "One faith, one baptism, one God," etc., and said: We confess the same God as you."

Butzer: We confess all that you have read there. But some people won't have one body and one baptism with us.

(Hermann) As [to the point] that the government shall punish false faith. Now God says: Thou shalt love thine enemy, "The son of man is not come to condemn."

Butzer: With that Christ forbade to the government unusual wrath and extraordinary punishment, [punishment] which one can and should exercise with love even to those he kills. When the government punishes a wrongdoer it does it out of love; thus a father, when he punishes his child, doesn't hate it but shows fatherly love for him. Butzer queried whether God had established a good order in the 5th Book of Moses, 13th chapter.

(Hermann) Yes, all things according to God's ordinance. And in this article Hermann is content with us, to punish the false teachers with the sword. He considers that the right doctrine, for faith which is active in love; for without works faith is dead. Said further, he has been blamed because he was in the Anabaptist sect. Now St. Paul was also blamed. But he has sought nothing else but the honor of God and his neighbor.

(Butzer) Hermann belonged to a special sect which has damned us; that was a bad, corrupt sect. If, however, he wants to hold to the articles which we confess we will also hold to them. We baptize the children according to God's ordinance; and when we baptize them, then they share everything with us that we have. If he will believe that with us, then we are one with him in the situation.

(Hermann) God wills it that his unity may come. But up to now he had understood the last of Matthew: "to me is given all power," and cited also the last of Mark: "Go into all the world, preach and baptize," etc. Now the teaching is first, thereafter faith, and then baptism following; that this was originally said for adults, he conceded. Now there is a text, where Stephen baptized, the word was preached to them (I Cor. 1:16). And that the government has the articles and we understand them rightly, that he will let stand. But then he stands caught between two walls; for he can't yet comprehend that children are to be baptized and he can't yet comprehend that they shouldn't be baptized, and he begged that they have patience with him. He won't damn infant baptism nor teach against it, will take the lead with his neighbor in the love that comes from the faith, go with us to the preaching, take the supper of the Lord with us, pray with us and give alms.

(Butzer) Asked if Christ hadn't given the grace to us which he previously had given the Jews.

Hermann: Yes.

(Butzer) Whether he didn't now believe that the God of the former children in the former covenant was truly God.

Hermann's answer: Yes.

(Butzer) Why shouldn't he then be also the God of our children? Now we have in place of circumcision the rebirth, the baptism. At the time of Cyprian there was an error, that the children shouldn't be baptized before eight days. At that time the council concluded against it, that baptism shouldn't be tied to any time; but there was no doubt at that time that the children should be baptized; and Origen, who wrote about the year that was counted 232 after Christ's birth, wrote on the 6th chapter of Romans that the apostles decreed that the children be baptized.

After this debate Butzer had a private discussion with Hermann on the next day (Nov. 2) and Hermann abandoned his doubts as to Infant Baptism; also on Sunday (Nov. 3) Mr. Butzer stated publicly in the preaching service that Hermann had rejoined our church with request for forgiveness and that they pray God for him, etc.

Then Peter Losse was also permitted to speak. He then gave Mr. Butzer such flippant and light-hearted answers that the audience laughed loudly; and therefore, since he answered so contemptuously and despicably, nothing special was discussed with him.[6]

Reason and Conversion
in the Thought of Melanchthon

Clyde L. Manschreck

What happens to man's reason when he is converted? This is a key question for understanding Melanchthon's attitude toward reason in the Christian life. Melanchthon emphasized science and philosophy in such disciplines as education and law, yet denied that he was a "rationalist"; he gave a place to human will in the process of conversion and insisted that he was not a "synergist." Why? Was Melanchthon inconsistent, or was there a core of belief which resolved the apparent incongruities?

In the early years of his association with Luther, Melanchthon disparaged philosophy and ridiculed reason as inferior to the "foolishness of preaching." He called on Christians to abandon commentaries and to look only to Scripture for inspiration; he declared that theologians laboring under the "base hallucinations" of reason have handed to us "the subtle pratings of Aristotle instead of the doctrine of Christ."[1] Everywhere the Scriptures oppose rational judgment, he wrote, and those who have tried to interpret Scripture so as to satisfy the judgment of human reason have attributed to human powers more than is proper.[2] "The impious dogma of Free Will has been received and the beneficence of Christ has been obscured by that profane and animal wisdom of human reason."[3] He pointed to Greek rationalism as "especially pernicious," and said the fusion of Christian doctrine with Platonic and Aristotelean philosophy had weakened the church.[4]

> We must pray that God may transfer our minds from the judgment of human reason and philosophy, to Spiritual judgment. For the blindness of human reason is such that, without the light of the Spirit, we cannot know the absolute nature of sin or righteousness. The whole notion of human reason is darkness. The Spirit of Christ is light, he alone teaches all truth.[5]

In Melanchthon's later writings, however, he praised man's rational powers. "Humanistic learning is that wonderful gift of God . . . noblest and most honorable of the pursuits of man . . . a part of

God's image." [6] He insisted that his students learn philosophy, law, mathematics, and other rational disciplines, and cheerfully commended the "righteousness of reason." [7] Logic is essential if one is not to be a blockhead,[8] and there can be no progress without mathematics. "I often wonder over the absurdity of certain people who fancy that what is right and fair may be known without knowledge and learning." [10] Rational training is greatly needed if we are to avoid the disasters of ignorance.[11] Philosophy in particular contributes to rational judgments. "One can master skillful method only to the extent that he is proficient in philosophy. . . . Almost everything comes forth from natural philosophy as from a spring." [12] Without the logical rules of philosophy, man will join together things that should be separated, and sunder things that should be joined, thus producing "unforeseen mistaken ideas and endless violent rupture. . . . It is necessary to borrow many things from natural philosophy, and put with Christian doctrine many things from moral philosophy." [13]

These and similar statements prompted many observers to say that Melanchthon had departed from the Lutheran principle of justification by faith and had embraced alien principles.[14] Some interpreters have fostered the enigma of Melanchthon by choosing to ignore one of these grouped statements and to expand the other as if it were the essential core of Melanchthon's thought. Melanchthon often modified his statements in an effort "to state things more clearly," but there remains a consistent core in his views despite these modifications. The tirades against reason represent a defense of justification by faith and are an attempt to salvage faith from the wreckage of work righteousness. Later statements praising reason represent a recognition of the goodness of God's creation and the need of man to use reason in bringing about the good life. Melanchthon realized that man might misuse his reason, but berating this faculty as evil *per se* is the same as berating the body or any other part of God's creation as evil. Melanchthon saw justification by faith as the answer to the corruption of work righteousness, and a *redirection* of reason, brought about by conversion, as the answer to the notion that reason should be abandoned.

What happens to reason when a man is converted? Is there any essential difference between the reasoning of a Christian and of a heathen? Could Isaiah or Paul have said anything more fitting about God than did Plato in defining God as eternal intelligence and the ground of all goodness in nature?

> Then what distinction is there between our men and the heathen? Between Plato and Paul? The Gospel makes the difference. Although

Plato knew that there was a God, that He was the ground for the good in nature, he was still in doubt whether God cared for him.[15]

Melanchthon came gradually to realize that there is no difference between the reasoning of the Christian and the heathen, for the change that takes place in conversion is in the nature of a fundamental presupposition or orientation. Conversion does not mean that man is infused with facts and knowledge unavailable to other men, nor does it mean that a secret power is given man so that he is more alert than before. But the realization that God cares for man engenders a trust in God with the dramatic consequence that man turns from himself to God and neighbor. Melanchthon, therefore, condemned reason only in its self-centered pretense of effecting reconciliation with God; he used it as a gift of God in education, politics, ethics, and other pursuits of man. This view was outlined in the *Loci* of 1521, but Melanchthon did not fully explore its implications until years later.

An understanding of Melanchthon's position requires a recognition that for him the very heart of sin was self-centeredness. Melanchthon was keenly aware that death forces man to admit his dependent status, and yet this is the one thing that he is afraid to admit. Unable through reason to go beyond death, unable through reason to assure himself that death is not annihilation, man despairs, and turns to exploit for himself the little time that he possesses. In effect he acts as if he were the center of all things and as if there were no God. Overwhelmed by death, man attempts to live to the fullest here and now. All of life becomes self-centered. This is man's natural propensity which Melanchthon called original sin. As a result of this, the soul "most ardently loves itself, seeks its own desires and wishes nothing but carnal things and despises God."[16] A creature who knows not the love of God,

> loves itself in the highest degree . . . And so the first and chief affection of human nature is self-love, by which it is drawn away to wish for and desire only what seems to its nature good, sweet, pleasant and glorious.[17]

The self, faced with "eternal death," seeks its own ends. Man in this state cannot love God; he lives a lie, acting as if he were the center of all things.[18] "There are some who in outward appearance live right honorable lives" but they are full of disguised, wretched affections,[19] for this condition is deepseated and inscrutable.[20] Human beings marvel at the outer mask of virtue, but philosophers in general teach nothing but reliance on self and self-love.[21] This dungeon of self-love makes mere shadows of such virtues as constancy in Socrates, chastity in Zenocrates, and temperance in Zeno.[22] "Since in all our works we seek our own personal gains, our works are necessarily true sins."[23] We seek God thinking he will be useful to us, but in this we really love self, and the specter of death looms in the background.[24]

This state prevails before justification by faith. Self-centeredness is the presupposition of man, because he fears that all ends in death. The miracle of conversion is that God's concern breaks forth on man's inmost being so that trust in God replaces fear of death. In the cross and resurrection, God reveals his ultimate love by showing man that death is not the final victor. Melanchthon knew that all men encounter death, but he believed that death is under the dominion of a sovereign God who cares for man. Like the language between two lovers which conveys the message of love with a kind of "wisdom" that is neither rational nor irrational, the language of the Bible conveys the message of God's love. This is the "revelation," or conviction, or presupposition, that comes to man in conversion. Convinced that the void of death is not final, convinced by a wisdom beyond rational substantiation that he is in the hands of a God who unfailingly cares,[25] man may not think any more accurately about mathematics, and he may not outwardly act any differently,[26] but the motive for his actions changes from self-aggrandizement to joyous and thankful acceptance of creaturehood under God who holds all things in his hands, even death. Not love of self, but love of God and neighbor results.[27] Man "would be completely subdued," wrote Melanchthon, "if the heart [could] but conceive the magnitude of God's goodness and the fulness of his grace."[28]

Thus in conversion, man is given a trust, a confidence, that God is ultimately benevolent toward him. This is the gift of the Holy Spirit "who regenerates and sanctifies the heart."[29] Man receives or accepts this gift; he does not originate it. "Faith is the *constant assent* to every word of God; a thing that cannot be done except the Holy Spirit of God renews and illuminates our hearts."[30] In this faith man *relies,* even unto death, upon the divine mercy promised in Christ.[31] This is a presupposition beyond rational judgment;[32] it is the "nonsense," "absurdity," "foolishness," and "wisdom of God" of which Paul spoke (I Cor. 1). Man accepts and relies on the divine gift, he cannot offer it to himself, but he can at any time say "no." Man continues, therefore, to need the signs of baptism and Eucharist to establish continual confidence.[33] All things come to pass according to divine purpose, for the God who loves man is sovereign, the final Orderer,[34] said Melanchthon, but man is unable to convince himself of this rationally, and equally unable to convince himself that death is not annihilation.[35] Self-cen-

teredness, sin, therefore, continues in man, for doubt always lingers
about the conquest of death.[36]

No special knowledge is given in conversion; if man could not
work a mathematical equation before conversion, then the trust that
Melanchthon speaks about would not enable him to solve it. The
ethical works that one does in this trust may remain just as imperfect
as before, but the motivating center from which they are done does
change, so that the ethical works done in trust, however imperfect,
are not glorifications of self but thankful responses to God for his
benevolence toward man.[37] Incorrect though they may be, such acts
are not accounted sinful. When self is at the center, good works are
deceit and mendacity, for man serves only himself.[38] But when man
has tasted the mercy of God, wrote Melanchthon, man seeks to serve
others.

> The soul cannot but love God in return and be joyful, and express
> its gratitude by some mutual kindness as it were for such great mercy.
> . . . Therefore it imparts itself to all its neighbors and serves them,
> placing itself at their disposal, considering their wants as its own,
> doing all things with everyone candidly, sincerely, without self-
> seeking and with no malice. Such is the efficacy of faith as it appears
> from the works of those whose hearts are possessed by true faith.[39]

And this faith which motivates man to serve others is nothing more
than a sure reliance on God's ultimate love for us.[40]

Reason, therefore, is not to be abandoned. Man is to use all his
natural endowments in a love of God and neighbor. On this basis
Melanchthon developed his "rationalism." It was not a perverted
means of bypassing justification by faith in order to glorify man.
Though Melanchthon did not fully develop this position in the *Loci*
of 1521, he did indicate the direction. He accepted Paul's statement
that there is within us a natural law, or conscience, which God has
inscribed upon the soul of each man, adapted to form and shape
character.[41] He said that natural reason is also endowed with certain principles (such as, the whole is greater than its parts), and with
certain natural laws pertaining to the social life of man, which are
paralleled by divine laws in Scripture, and that man is to use these
to govern his life.[42] Although man cannot truly love God without
the Spirit's revealing God's love,[43] nevertheless, human laws are to
be honored, and papal laws are to be borne as one would injury or
tyranny,[44] because reason, regardless of the inner motive of man, is a
part of God's created order.[45] To the extent that reason can know
natural law, reason should order human life. Therefore, let man cul-

tivate all the products of reason in government, education, ethics, and philosophy, but let him not think or pretend that a part of creation, even the noblest, reason, is divine.[46] The revelation of God's benevolence does not add to man's factual store, but it turns about the entire perspective and purpose of man. This was Melanchthon's view, obscured by orthodox language but nevertheless present, in the first systematic statement of Protestant theology.

As Melanchthon advanced in his theological thinking, the place of reason in relation to salvation became clearer. In the *Loci* of 1521 his view of the relation of grace to the sinner was confused with the relation of God to the creature; he expressed views on predestination and affections that bordered on determinism. Later, as he reflected on what happens in conversion, the notion that reason is unchanged but redirected became clearer. Cochlaeus' attack on Melanchthon's views in 1524 and Erasmus' *De Libero Arbitrio* of the same year helped bring Melanchthon's thoughts into sharper focus.[47] When Melanchthon formally entered the Wittenberg theological faculty in 1526, he determined to lecture on the Ethics of Aristotle, despite the fact that he had unmercifully criticized Aristotle in 1521 as a gross falsifier. After 1526 Melanchthon adopted the method and, to some extent, the content of Aristotle and regarded him as the best introduction to philosophy, with fewer errors and fancies than the other philosophers.[48] Having reappraised the event of justification as it relates to reason, he had concluded that rational philosophy could and should, as a gift of God, serve the Christian expression of love. As early as 1527, commenting on Colossians 1:15, he wrote: "We must distinguish between the natural life and the relation of the human will to that which is good before God."[49] He maintained that the will has a natural or essential freedom which man must use.[50] "God moves trees in one way, cattle in another way, men in another way; on man he has bestowed reason. *That power of choice he does not remove*, but imparts life and motion, while we choose and act. . . ."[51] He had departed from the hint of metaphysical determinism.[52] Melanchthon's emphasis on law in the *Visitation Articles* of 1528 further showed this turn in his thinking. Still later, Melanchthon emphatically rejected the notion that "God snatches you by some violent rupture, so that you must believe whether you will or not."[53] Melanchthon called Luther's attention to the changes he had introduced,[54] and Luther apparently did not object and continued to praise and recommend Melanchthon's works.[55]

As a result of this pondering, Melanchthon's *Apology* of 1531, his

second monumental work in theology, made clearer the place of reason in the Christian life. Melanchthon did not modify the basic
doctrine, justification by faith alone, "lest any man should boast."[56]
Man can by nature have no true fear of God; by nature man is concerned always to promote himself.[57] "God, therefore, is not loved until
we apprehend mercy by faith."[58] Man, who in his self-centeredness acts
as a god unto himself, cannot in the final analysis be sovereign, for man
faces death, which begets in his despair from which he cannot escape.[59]
As long as this despair beclouds his mind, man's self-centeredness remains, no matter how clever the rational concealment may be.[60]

Only faith can free man from the despair of death and give consolation to the heart.[61] Through faith we "have a sure and firm consolation against the terrors of sin, and against eternal death, and
against all the gates of hell."[62] Faith is not idle talk. It means "a new
and spiritual life," it is "that which liberates from death and produces a new life in hearts, and this is the work of the Holy Ghost. . . .
As long as it is present, it produces good fruits."[63] The faith that
comforts and justifies is more than a mere knowledge of history; it
is a new "reality."[64]

> It is assent to the promise of God that in Christ remission of sins and
> justification are freely offered. Faith is that my whole heart takes
> to itself this treasure. It is not my doing, not my presenting or giving,
> not my work or preparation, but that a heart comforts itself, and is
> perfectly confident that God makes a present and a gift to us, and
> not we to him, that he sheds upon us every treasure of grace in
> Christ.[65]

Melanchthon is careful to note repeatedly that faith which justifies
is not *ex opere operato,* to be infused into an individual by some
mechanical taking of the sacraments.[66] It is not a material substance, nor is it some supernatural message or knowledge. It is simply
a conclusion "in the heart that God has forgiven my sins, and that
he is now gracious to me."[67] Reason remains the same, but the heart
is comforted with confidence in the mercy promised for Christ's sake.[68]
Before man is thus comforted, a presupposition in which man falsely
regards himself as the center of the universe prevails; it "inheres by
nature in men's minds, neither can it be expelled unless we are divinely *taught.*"[69] This love of self blocks love of God and others.[70]
Man can do outward civil works but cannot truly love God, or even
expect aid from God in death, for he himself has displaced God.[71] This
is the miracle: In the process of conversion, an abiding trust in the
love of God comes to prevail in man.

Melanchthon does not use the term "presupposition"; he speaks rather of the inner and outer man and of something that happens to the inner man which takes self-interest from man's acts, even though outwardly the acts may not have changed.[72] "Christian perfection consists in dispositions of the heart."[73] Human wisdom looks only on the external; "we preach a foolishness of the Gospel," revealing another righteousness. This is distinct from reason, "but we are not ashamed of the foolishness of the Gospel."[74]

Melanchthon, therefore no longer disparaged reason *per se.* Christ cannot be compared to Socrates and Zeno, said Melanchthon, as if to say Christ brought a superior philisophical system which the reason of man is expected to evaluate. He did not! He brought something more fundamental—an assurance that death is not final, an assurance which affects reason so as to turn it away from itself to God.[75] The church is a congregation of saints who so believe. The visible church may also have wicked hypocrites, "but the Church is not only the fellowship of outward objects and rites, as other governments, but it is *in principle* a fellowship of faith and the Holy Ghost *in hearts.*"[76] The distinguishing mark is an *invisible,* inward regeneration of the Holy Ghost.[77] The insights of philosophy are not without their limited usefulness in promoting the welfare of man, for reason is a natural endowment from God. Aristotle wrote learnedly on civil life, Melanchthon declared, and to the righteousness of reason which maintains civil discipline Melanchthon cheerfully assigned praises.[78] In external matters, the "eloquence and virtue of reason are great goods," but reason cannot justify us before God, or love God, because without the Spirit reason seeks to promote itself.[79] The first table of the law demanding love of God is beyond reason without the gift of the Spirit, but the second table, which pertains to civil righteousness, reason understands and should keep for the sake of tranquility and discipline.[80]

Because righteousness of the church is a "righteousness that binds and quickens the heart,"[81] outward rites and political ordinances may vary with time and circumstances according to the dictates of reason.[82] Melanchthon, therefore, did not insist that Moses be followed; he maintained that Roman law has many advantages. As a Christian uses air, light, food, and drink, so may he use reason. As there are fixed movements in nature which are God's ordinances, so lawful governments are truly God's ordinances.[83]

> It is our greatest wish to maintain Church polity and the grades in the Church, even though they have been made by human authority.

> . . . With a grateful mind, we embrace the profitable and ancient
> ordinances, especially since they contain a discipline.[84]

Errors and inconveniences are to be expected because human reason
is not infallible, and reason goes astray fundamentally when it imag-
ines the end of these works to be justifying services.[85] But for love's
sake many things can be observed so long as they do not give offense
to conscience.[86] The spiritual and inward Kingdom of Christ "permits us outwardly to use legitimate political ordinances of every nation in which we live, just as it permits us to use medicine or the
art of building, or food, drink, and air."[87]

Julian the Apostate and Celsus charged that Christianity would
destroy the state and prohibit legal redress.[88] Melanchthon answered,

> The Gospel does not bring new laws concerning the civil state, but
> commands that we obey present laws, whether they have been framed
> by heathen or by others, and that in this obedience we should exer-
> cise love . . . The Gospel does not destroy the church, the family,
> civil regulations, but much rather approves them, and bids us obey
> them as a Divine Ordinance, not only on account of punishment but
> also on account of conscience.[89]

Not to see that the Gospel brings righteousness to hearts and outwardly approves various forms of government is a great mistake.[90]

Man has an innate endowment from God, a freedom, for the governing of this life. "The human will has liberty in the choice of works
and things which reason comprehends by itself." Reason comprehends obedience to parents and magistrates and also ways in which
to restrain the hands from murder, adultery, and theft. "Since there
is left in human nature reason and judgment concerning objects subjected to the senses, choice between these things, and the liberty and
power to render civil righteousness, are also left."[91] This "righteousness" reason can render by itself, for civil righteousness is outward
discipline and subject to free will or reason. Spiritual righteousness
is inward and is due to the governing of the Holy Spirit.[92] From this
one must not conclude that man is utterly passive in the reception of
the love of God. Faith is *constant assent* to the Word of God; man
relies upon divine mercy; he *freely accepts* the gift of God.[93] In such
statements Melanchthon acknowledged, even in the early *Loci* and
the *Apology*, that there always remains in man an irreducable element
of free choice. "The remission of sins is alike and equal to all, just
as Christ is one, and is offered freely to all."[94] Man, and man alone,
is responsible for saying "yes" or "no" to God, even though man is
powerless to initiate that to which he gives a yea or nay.

This basic orientation which centered in conversion is the clue to the "changes," the "rationalism," the "synergism," that came into the thought of Melanchthon. They were not really changes, but rather keener apprehensions of the place of reason in the Christian life. The endowment with which man regulates external life is also that which responds to God's gift in conversion. *The Catechism for Youth* of 1532 asserted that the promise of God is made to all and is ours if we only believe, no matter what may be said about pre-destination.[95] *The Commentary on Romans* in the same year placed greater emphasis on man's acceptance of faith. "In conceiving faith there is a struggle in us . . . and there is some cause in the accepter in that he does not reject the promise extended." But Melanchthon denied that this meant man is the author of salvation.[96]

Bugenhagen's notes on Melanchthon's lectures in 1533 show that Melanchthon divided the mind into cognition *(vis cognoscendi)* and affections *(vis appentendi)*, but maintained that the will is able to command and do an external work even contrary to the affections.[97] In the section on the cause of evil and contingence, Melanchthon denied that God is the author of sin. If the cause of evil is in man or the devil, there must be contingent events. But, if God controls and governs the world, how can there be contingent events? Melanchthon asserted that God's providence embraces both freedom and contin-gency, and spoke of it as a mystery beyond rational substantiation.[98]

In the 1535 *Loci* Melanchthon wrote that the will stands between reason and the senses. The will thus is subject to their influences but is nevertheless free to choose; God allows man to act, but sets ulti-mate limits, such as death. This is man's freedom. He is free to ac-cept, free to reject. The Word, Spirit, and Will must combine to fight the "infirmity of man." "God enables us, calls, moves, assists; but we have to see that we do not oppose."[99] The Spirit of God does not act dictatorially on a passive subject. In conversion, the very liberty which man previously exercised in sin is employed to respond to God.[100] By 1535 Melanchthon clearly rejected extreme predestina-tion as inconsistent with religious experience and morality. The bibli-cal demand for repentance implies that the hearer does something. The hearer does not initiate, or in any sense merit his salvation, but he does at least choose to accept rather than reject the gift of God. Not to admit this would be to render evangelical preaching mean-ingless and place responsibility for unethical behavior on God. Man is in some sense an active agent in conversion; if not, he is a beast or a stone without any free will or responsibility. Melanchthon said

God helps man as one would help an invalid into bed, not as one would place a stone in a wall.

> Three causes are conjoined: The Word, the Holy Spirit, and the Will not wholly inactive, but resisting its own weakness. . . God draws but draws him who is willing. . . The Will is not a statue, and that spiritual emotion is not impressed upon it as though it were a statue.[101]

In *De Anima,* 1540, Melanchthon commented on the attempt of Potiphar's wife to seduce Joseph. If Joseph had yielded, he, not God, would have been responsible.

> The Son of God by his own light illumines the mind so that Joseph knows the Eternal Father, and knows that he is and will be cared for by him, and at the same time the Son by the Holy Spirit moves the will and heart of Joseph, so that he wills to obey God, and he increases the fear of God, and the Will assisted assents to the Holy Spirit, restrains the external members, and does not admit enticement. In this contest he perceives that the will is not inactive. Therefore, the Holy Spirit does not destroy the freedom of the Will, but corrects it and turns it to God, according to the saying: He who draws, draws him who is willing. The Will of Joseph might have shaken off the Holy Spirit.[102]

Man is not a block or a stone. "Man can by using his will submit to God in his Word."[103] Melanchthon was striving to eliminate compulsion and vindicate the ethical character of conversion.

In the 1543 *Loci,* Melanchthon placed more emphasis on man's ability to choose or reject grace. He asked: Why is Saul rejected and David accepted by God? And he answered by saying that God's promise is universal and that Saul and David were themselves responsible.[104] The destiny of man depends on accepting or rejecting the available, universal grace of God. This is not to place human will on a par with divine will in conversion; it is a recognition of what really happens in conversion. Melanchthon did not retreat from this position. In the *Confessio Saxonica,* 1551, he declared, "In conversion the will of man, when the Holy Spirit has been accepted, is not inactive." Salvation is offered to all; the cause for rejection is in man.[105] God finally controls, because even death is under his sovereignty, but God does not take away man's freedom. In conversion, man accepts the offer of God's love; it is not forced upon him, for a gift ceases to be a gift if the recipient is forced to take it. And man must keep on making that decision. He cannot rest smugly in some certainty of election or wrap a mantle of security about him saying, "once saved, always saved." With his free will man applies himself to grace, hears the promise, endeavors to assent, and casts off sins against conscience.

> Since the promise is universal, and there are no contradictory wills in God, the cause must be in man that Saul is cast away and David is accepted. This, rightly understood, is true, and its benefit in the exercise of faith, when the heart rests in the Son of God revealed through the promise, will make clear this joining of causes: The Holy Spirit, the Word of God, and the Will. . . .

> Pharaoh and Saul were not coerced, but of their own wills opposed God. . . . David was not converted as if he were a stone. . . . The free will of David worked something when he heard the threats and the promises. . . . The Gospel is the power of God to salvation to the one not opposing, that is, to the one not despising the promises, but consenting and believing.[106]

To Calvin, Melanchthon wrote that there is no secret will in God; God's promises are universal. "The only cause for rejection is our striving against God's Word."[107] He did not know how this harmonized with predestination, but stoic, Manichean *"deliria"* he rejected as a lie; the will is active in good and bad actions, for man is a responsible being.[108]

Luther did not object to the "changes"; he continued to recommend Melanchthon's works.[109] Flacius Illyricus and Nicholas von Amsdorf, two professional rivals of Melanchthon, did not criticize Melanchthon's views as heretical until after the death of Luther.[110] Why did Luther not object? Did he believe Melanchthon was clarifying his own contention that a forced will is no will, *Noluntas?*

The necessity of using reason for the more effective expression of Christian love undergirded Melanchthon's outlook on education. He advocated the study of grammar, languages, philosophy, logic, rhetoric, classics, astronomy, mathematics, physics, and music because the love which man expresses may be made more effective through these disciplines of reason.[111] Man is always imperfect and finite, and learning cannot justify us before God, but man can be guided by the lessons of the past and reason can bring benefits of law and order.[112] Terence and Cicero, Aristotle and Plato, may be regarded as good guides.[113] Melanchthon believed that languages, philosophy, and other classical arts should adorn and enrich the church. Ignorance harms religion, creates contentions, and leads to a destruction of the social order.[114] Unenlightened theology was for him a great evil; it led to contradiction, stalemate, and strife.[115]

Far from abandoning reason, Melanchthon praised learning as "the most beautiful gift of God."[116] Without it men are left without the natural guidance which God provided for this life.[117] Used without pretense, it can help purify theology and lend richness to the metaphors of the Scriptures.[118] "You must take up a school vocation in the same spirit that you would take up the service of the Church, for in the school one is also concerned with godly things."[119] Reason is to be used, but reason without the Holy Spirit is curved in upon itself and cannot ultimately bring solace to man, for reason is a gift of God; reason is not God himself.

Melanchthon could not tolerate the anti-rationalism of Carlstadt. He opposed the radicals who pretended that some special message was infused by the Spirit in the process of conversion just as much as he opposed the Roman Catholics who maintained that something is infused through the material sacraments. In conversion, reason remains the same, but an attitude of trust or confidence rules the heart, altering man's motivation and making the goals of reason not self-aggrandizement but expressions of joy and gratitude for what God has given. Melanchthon, therefore, advocated all the disciplines of reason as means of manifesting thanksgiving in service to others.

Melanchthon never argued that man's reason could settle ultimate destiny, for man's reason was for him neither divine nor immortal, but a part of creation like everything else, and no more entitled to sovereign autonomy than any other part of creation. Reason is to be used in gratitude like the other gifts of God for the worship of God and service of man. Reason prepares for the widest possible expression and communication of the converted man's love to others. Although reason cannot know the absolute nature of things, nor can it trace the works of creation back to their Source,

> . . . nevertheless, even amid this our present darkness, every gleam and every hint of the harmony of this fair creation forms a step toward the knowledge of God and toward virtue, whereby we ourselves shall also learn to love and maintain order and moderation in all our acts. Since it is evident that men are endowed by their Creator with faculties fitted for the contemplation of nature, they must, of necessity, take delight in investigating the elements, the laws, the motions, and the qualities or forces of the various bodies by which we are surrounded . . . The uncertainty which obtains with regard to so much in nature should not deter us from our search; it is none the less God's will that we trace out his footsteps in the creation . . . Let us prepare ourselves for admission to that enduring and eternal Academy where all the imperfections of our philosophy shall vanish in the immediate presence of the Master-Builder, who there shall Himself show us His own archetype of the world.[120]

The Strangers' "Model Churches" in Sixteenth-Century England

Frederick A. Norwood

In a letter dated July 4, 1548, Archbishop Thomas Cranmer wrote to Jan Laski (John à Lasco), noted reformer of Polish origin, as follows:

> We are desirous of setting forth in our churches the true doctrine of God, and have no wish to adapt it to all tastes or to deal in ambiguities; but, laying aside all carnal considerations, to transmit to posterity a true and explicit form of doctrine agreeable to the rule of the sacred writings; so that there may not only be set forth among all nations an illustrious testimony respecting our doctrine, delivered by the grave authority of learned and godly men, but that all posterity may have a pattern to imitate.[1]

In pursuance of this desire he extended an invitation to the Polish scholar to come to England as teacher and adviser. Laski accepted with gratitude in view of the impending execution of the Imperial Interim of Leipzig. In 1550 he was appointed superintendent of the churches of foreigners in London under formal letters patent from King Edward VI. The subject of this paper is the history of these refugee churches, and the thesis is that, at least in the time of Edward, they were intended to serve as models of the pure church of apostolic times in comparison with which the church in England might be reformed. Such we may believe was the intention so rudely interrupted by the accession of Mary.

I

The invitation to Laski was part of an ambitious program headed by the primate himself for bringing to England a number of Continental scholars who would give aid and counsel in the work of reformation. This was in turn part of an even larger project for the unification of evangelical movements in an ecumenical fellowship antedating by some centuries the World Council of Churches. Cranmer was no man to dream small dreams. Invitations were sent to and accepted by Peter Martyr and Bernardino Ochino, who had arrived already in 1547, to Jan Utenhove in 1548, and to Martin Bucer, Paul Fagius, and Valérand Poullain in 1549. These and "divers very learned and godly foreigners," to quote John Strype, "forwarded religion not a little."[2]

Of these visitors the key figure, so far as the foreign community was concerned, was Laski.[3] Although the exact degree of his influence over Cranmer is uncertain, it was undoubtedly extensive. The two men became good friends.[4] This was the man who assumed responsibility for all of the refugee congregations in London, and who was largely instrumental in building a model church on apostolic principles, one purpose of which was the edification of Englishmen. He was one of the foreign scholars who felt a spiritual kinship with the many less well endowed brethren in exile who had fled their native lands *nulla alia quam religionis causa*.[5] These, together with a long established commercial colony, largely Dutch and German, comprised a sizable community. Prior to the arrival of Laski some of the Dutch refugees had begun to meet together for worship in private houses, and the French had started an organization. A small group of Italians needed help. Into this situation stepped Laski. Through his efforts and the influence of Cranmer with the Protector, the Duke of Somerset, young King Edward granted as of July 24, 1550, a charter for the establishment of a "Church of the Germans and other foreigners in the city of London."[6] Already the former church of Augustine Friars had been placed at the disposal of the refugees. Now Laski, convincing the Protector "by arguments as well taken from charity as policy,"[7] obtained the legal charter which, in effect, exempted the new group of congregations from control by the English bishops.

II

This important document, almost unique in the annals of the sixteenth century, must be studied carefully if the reasons behind the extraordinary grant are to be understood. Edward, in the introductory paragraph, reminds himself of the obligation laid on Christian princes to take care that "pure and undefiled religion may be spread throughout the whole body of the commonwealth and that a church founded and brought to maturity in truly Christian and apostolic doctrines and rites may be served by holy ministers."[8] In pursuance of this obligation, therefore, but also on account of natural compassion for persecuted refugees, the king sets apart for their use a church in London to be called the "Temple of the Lord Jesus," to the intent and purpose that there may be, by ministers of the church of the Germans and of other foreigners, an incorrupt interpretation of the most Holy Gospel and ministration of the sacraments according to the word of God and apostolic observance.[9]

That this purpose may be achieved he constitutes and incorporates the superintendent and ministers of this church into a *corpus corporatum et politicum,* with right of succession.

As to the rest, in order that no opposition be raised or obstruction put in the way, the superintendent and ministers are granted the full power of increasing their number and of nominating and electing their successors. The original body is named to include Laski as superintendent, with four ministers, two Dutch and two French.[10] Any further nominations are to be submitted for approval to his majesty. And finally,

> We order and, firmly enjoining, command as well the Mayor, Sheriffs and Aldermen of our City of London, the Bishop of London and his successors, with all our other Archbishops, Bishops, Judges, Officers and Ministers whomsoever, that they permit the aforesaid superintendent and ministers and their successors freely and quietly to practise, enjoy, use and exercise their own rites and ceremonies and their own peculiar ecclesiastical discipline, notwithstanding that they do not conform with the rites and ceremonies used in our Kingdom, without impeachment, disturbance or vexation of them or any of them . . .[11]

An old portrait shows a ceremony in which the young king hands the charter to Laski. In the background stand the Duke of Somerset and Archbishop Cranmer, together with Latimer and Hooper. On the other side are two other figures, perhaps Micronius and Delaenus, the two ministers of the Dutch congregation.[12] The former wrote to Henry Bullinger that the king had granted the right to "have the pure ministry of the word and sacraments, according to the apostolic form."[13] He rejoiced that the new church was exempted completely from the jurisdiction of the bishops, and that the Archbishop had been the chief supporter of the project, "to the great astonishment of some." Utenhove, one of the elders, reported to Calvin that they had obtained more than they had asked for.[14] He gave the reformer of Geneva a complete analysis of the new institution, and was obviously well pleased.

Before turning to the actual organization based on the Letters Patent, it is well to inquire as to the motives for granting so unusual an instrument of toleration in so intolerant an age. In the first place may be listed the reason given by the King, that of compassion for

Christians suffering under persecution and exile. The second motive was not spelled out in the charter because it concerned a more sensitive problem—that of heresy. Edward in his diary noted as of June 29: "It was appointed that the Germans should have the Austin Friars for their church to have their services in, for avoiding all sects of Anabaptists and such like."[15] That this concern was, at least in six-teenth-century minds, well founded is attested by the later history of the foreign churches in England. This concern would help explain the willingness to give responsible organization to the community. But it would not explain the willingness to exempt these congregations from the control of the episcopacy. The amazing degree of autonomy cannot be justified either on grounds of sympathy for refugees under oppression or on grounds of protection against heresy. Another factor must have entered into the thinking of the king and his advisers, a factor that would justify the special status of the foreigners' church, a situation certain to draw the ire and opposition of the bishops, some of whom stood close to the throne and provided much-needed support for the Tudor dynasty as it threaded its tortuous way among the perils of power politics charged with religious tension.

This factor was spelled out explicitly by Laski himself in a work prepared to describe the doctrine, order, and discipline of the London Dutch church but published in Frankfurt after the accession of Mary.[16] In his extended dedication to the king of Poland he explained that the strangers' church had been established in London with complete autonomy in order that it might preach the pure Word of God and administer the sacraments according to apostolic precedents. "We thought in effect that, encouraged by this example, the English churches themselves would be aroused to return to the apostolic worship in all its purity."[17] According to his testimony the plan was carefully worked out. Since many English laws prevented immediate reformation and permitted some remnants of popery to survive (although the King wished to correct this as soon as feasible), and since Laski insisted particularly on new standards for the refugee churches, "it was decided finally that public worship in the English churches should be reformed gradually and only to the degree permitted by the laws." On the other hand the strangers' church, less restrained by law and custom, should be completely free to organize "in perfect conformity with the apostolic doctrine and custom." The King himself became the most ardent champion of the project, aided and abetted by the Archbishop.[18]

Again we encounter the emphasis on reformation in terms of the pure Word of God and apostolic precedent, both in preaching and sacrament, unlimited by statute or ulterior ecclesiastical authority. Such should be the happy condition of the strangers' church, unique in the land. On the other hand the English church could, under the circumstances, be reformed only gradually. It was beset with legal restrictions difficult to remove; it lived under a firmly fixed system of episcopal authority; it was sunk in deep and ancient tradition. Bucer had already recognized the problem in a letter to the ministers of Strasbourg, in which he said that changes would necessarily come slowly, "lest the people, not having yet learned Christ, should be deterred by too extensive innovations."[19] Peter Martyr wrote to Bullinger, "All things cannot be done in a moment, and there must be labour and time for this misshapen embryo to attain its proper symmetry and shape."[20]

Even the refugees moved circumspectly in the area of church order and liturgical reform, and avoided ostentatious parades advertising their differences too blatantly. This may help to explain why the more detailed specifications of order and worship used already in the Edwardian period appeared in print only later.[21] Most of the regulations of Laski's *Forma ac Ratio* were already in effect. But, because of the uncertainty of life and particularly of religion in England, the exiles must move slowly and carefully. They needed time. And who could know how little time was left?

That too much should not be attempted too fast was made clear from the early and persistent opposition from some of the bishops. The key figure was Nicholas Ridley, Bishop of London, at this time a reformer of cautious moderation, who felt a double responsibility to maintain proper order in his diocese and control over the foreigners. At the very outset an intentional delay was encountered in the repair of Austin Friars on the excuse that it must be made appropriate to the honor of the King, its donor. This was, as Van Schelven puts it, the first *kink in den kabel*—kink in the cable.[22] Micronius told Bullinger that the obstacles, set up by the Lord Treasurer, had been originated by the Bishop of London. In spite of the clear admonition in the Letters Patent against interference, the foreigners were for long prevented from free observance of the Lord's Supper.[23] Another attempt at control came in 1552 in connection with a statute requiring regular attendance at the parish church by all Englishmen. When some of the refugees were arrested under this law, Laski appealed directly to the royal authority through Cecil.[24] This resulted in an order in Council directing the Bishop of London to find means of making peace according to the provisions of the charter.

The existence of this opposition on the part of leaders who were not desirous of full reformation indicates their awareness of the danger occasioned by the presence, in the very heart of English life, of a model church supposedly based on the pure gospel. This opposition may be taken as circumstantial evidence further supporting the thesis that the strangers' church was intended to influence the direction of the English Reformation.

III

At any rate the project for a church in Austin Friars was rapidly accomplished. Micronius began preaching in September, 1550. Four elders were installed early in October and four deacons a few days later. Soon the size of the general congregation was so large that provision was made for separate worship by the French in the church of St. Anthony's Hospital in Threadneedle Street, where they were established permanently in the autumn of 1550.[25] Little is known of the Italian congregation, led by Michel Angelo Florio.[26] As already noted the two main congregations, Dutch and French, were served by four ministers, two for each. By 1552 this ecclesiastical community had become so prestigious that all aliens in London were required to join this church by confession of faith before they could qualify for any form of citizenship.[27] The membership is uncertain at this time, but it ran into the hundreds. Later, in the time of Elizabeth, it reached two thousand.[28]

For three years, then, the church of the refugees was a going concern. It survived the opposition of the traditionalists and continued to witness in favor of full reformation on apostolic precedents. From the beginning the intention was that it should serve not only as a means of worship for the foreigners residing in London but also as a model of pure reformed faith showing the way for the slower process of purification of the English church. As such it needed a clear definition of the faith it held, a systematic organization, and a firm discipline. These Laski and his associated ministers proceeded to provide. If this was indeed a "model" for the whole nation, the exact nature of this miniature reformation takes on great significance. Its collapse in the time of Mary becomes by the same taken a major catastrophe.

The main sources for study of the operation of the London Dutch Church, and the French as well, are the writings of Micronius and Laski, especially the latter. The actual archives for the years of Edward have been lost. Micronius' treatise, which appeared in Emden in 1554, is entitled, *De Christlicke Ordinanciën der Nederlandschen Ghemeynten Christi . . . te Londen.*[29] Its exact relation to the longer and more famous *Forma ac Ratio* is difficult to determine. The author used Laski's work in manuscript, and in many respects the works are parallel. The one is best described as a short practical adaptation of the other.

The works of Laski are available in a two-volume edition under the title, *Joannis a Lasco Opera tam Edita quam Inedita.*[30] The first volume contains dogmatic and polemic works as well as a full introduction in Latin. The second, more important for our study, contains liturgical and creedal works. The major piece is entitled, *Forma ac Ratio tota Ecclesiastici Ministerij, in Peregrinorum, Potissimum verò Germanorum Ecclesia Instituta Londini in Anglia . . .* and was published in Frankfurt in 1555.[31] The rest of the volume is devoted to a lengthy confession of faith, catechisms, and letters.[32] A French translation of *Forma ac Ratio,* which this writer has not seen, appeared at Emden in 1556 under the title, *Toute la forme et manière du ministere écclesiastique en l'Église des estrangers dressée à Londres en Angleterre. . . .*[33]

For doctrinal definition the most complete document is the *Compendium Doctrinae de Vera unicaque Dei et Christi Ecclesia . . .* published in London in 1551. A Dutch edition prepared by Utenhove carries the title, *Een kort Begrijp der Leeringhe van de warachtige ende eenighe Ghemeynte Gods end Christi.* In addition there are two catechisms for the London church and another for that of Emden. The London confession of faith is not a true creedal statement, although it was an official standard for all language groups in the church and subscription was required of all members.[34] It is rather a treatise on the nature of the church, and thus begins with a full discussion of the meaning of the word *ecclesia.* It is an apology for the kind of church embodied in the strangers' community in London, which must be the true church, a veritable model for all Christians.[35] It is this emphasis on the church that puts the London Confession in the center of our theme. In the introduction, addressed to Edward VI, Laski explains that this confession is presented in order that his majesty and all men may know what the strangers' church truly stands for and that calumiators may be answered.[36] The church is then defined as *coetus eorum qui voce Dei ex universa toto orbe hominum multitudine in populum illi peculiarem evocantur.*[37] It is a congregation of those who are called out by the voice of God from the multitude of men in all the world to be his peculiar people. There are four marks by which this true church may be distinguished from all other "churches." It is called forth by no human voice but solely by the voice of God.[38] This word has been given to men through angels, prophets, and Christ himself. The Holy Spirit guides the people of God through the word of the apostles and the evangelists. Hence,

> And this will be that true Church of God, which is composed of those called by the voice of God through the angels, the prophets, and Christ the Lord, as the ruler of all the Fathers, and his Apostles, into one congregation and his own peculiar people.[39]

This definition is reaffirmed, in association with elements from the Apostles' Creed, further on.[40] The church is that fellowship of men, past, present, and future *(coetus eorum hominum cum ipsorum semine—de vergaderinghe der menschen met haren zade),* from our first father Adam to the end of the world, who have been called or shall be called from the world to testify and witness their faith in Christ. Great emphasis is placed, in Calvinistic fashion, on Christ the head of the church, as King, Prophet, and High Priest. That this reformed church is not intended to be a new church, separated from other churches, but rather one, catholic, apostolic, is made clear. *Una est igitur atque eadem semper Dei Ecclesia.*[41] False churches, however, such as those of the Turks, the papacy, the Anabaptists, and the Davidists, are no part of this true church. The unity of the church is found in Christ her head. Christ is "the eternal and abiding King of the people of God."[42]

This and other emphases illustrate the strong Calvinistic trend of the thought of Laski. Although Zwinglian influences were also strong among the refugees, especially through relations with Bullinger, both Dutch and French congregations were deeply under the spell of the Genevan reformer. The possible impact of this form of Calvinism in England on the later development of Scottish and Independent thought would be difficult to measure, in view of the more direct connection through English refugees on the Continent. Laski, however, by no means slavishly followed Calvin. He thought his doctrine of predestination too strongly expressed.[43]

Curiously, there is nothing about the sacraments as such in the London Confession. In 1552, however, Laski published in London a *Brevis et dilucida de Sacramentis Ecclesiae Christi Tractatio.*[44] Here the author rejoiced that the Calvinists and Zwinglians had come to a consensus in 1549 according to which they found common ground for the understanding of the sacraments. He rejoiced especially, no doubt, because the Calvinist interpretation came out on top. There would seem to be little original in Laski's own presentation, which follows the common distinction between the outward sign and the inward "mystery."[45] The distinctiveness is not to be discerned so much in doctrine as in the place, described below, given the Lord's Supper in the church order of London. Laski was accused by both Strype and Burnet of interfering in the controversy over the sacraments in the English church—one of the services for which he had been called.[46]

The ordering of the church centered around the ministry. Laski himself tells us in the *Forma ac Ratio* that his models were Geneva and Strasbourg.[47] Van Schelven suggests several other sources, including Zürich, Emden, Cologne, Poullain's liturgy, and the English state church itself.[48] But Laski probably knew best whence came his ideas. Beyond these, however, stood the explicit affirmation that the real source was the pure church of the apostles, the golden age of the primitive church. There Laski professed to find two essential orders, elders and deacons. The former, however, consisted of two kinds, ministers of the Word and administrators of discipline.[49] Differences at this point from Bucer and Calvin are real but not radical. In theory all the elders had the same responsibilities and shared the same ordination. This marks a significant and characteristic emphasis in Laski, who at this point approaches the doctrine of the essential ministry of all Christians. In practice those set apart as ministers of the Word administered the sacraments and were assisted by the other elders. On the other hand the lay elders carried special responsibility for the maintenance of discipline. In the *Forma ac Ratio* he writes of four types of ministry: *ministerium verbi, sacramentarum, mensarum seu eleemosynarum, usus ecclesiasticae disciplinae.*[50] In the *Compendium Doctrinae* he had three offices: *Verbi, gladii, mensarum.*[51] The duties assigned the ministers of the Word and of the "Sword" (elders) differ in emphasis rather than in character. The elders specially guard discipline.[52]

On this basis a complete ministerial organization was raised. Four ministers were elected, as named in the Letters Patent, and then four elders, "according to the apostolic ordinance, to assist the minister, not indeed in the ministry of the word, but in the conservation of doctrine and morals in the church."[53] After these were elected four deacons. Over all was established, of course, Laski as superintendent. There was really no place for such an office according to apostolic precedent. His office was different in authority but not in ministerial character.[54] Once a week the ministers and elders of each congregation met, and with them once a month the deacons. On the first Monday of each month was set the *coetus,* in which the officers of all three congregations met together. This institution, which may be compared with a modern presbytery, continued in operation until the end of the nineteenth century.[55] The French church was probably organized on a more thoroughly Calvinistic basis than the Dutch.[56]

One of the more interesting aspects was the mode of election for church office, alike of ministers, elders, and deacons. In this the London church differed from the practice followed either in Geneva or Strasbourg, and was more democratic than either. Laski was aware of the tradition of universal suffrage in the early church,[57] but was not prepared to go quite so far in his sixteenth-century fellowship. After a period of fasting, communion, and two sermons, the members of the congregation were invited to nominate, in writing, those whom they considered worthy of election. From this list the officers elected by voice vote persons to fill the various vacancies. A week was allowed for any objections to be brought forward. Then followed the service of ordination, which included the examination of the candidates and the laying on of hands for all orders.[58] This method of election was unusually democratic for the times, in that the whole congregation participated in the first act of nomination, and had in the week-long waiting period a further check on any authoritarian tendencies.

Under this form of church government the membership was carefully controlled. Foreigners in London were not at all automatically members. A specific act of commitment, either from infant baptism and strict training or from confession of faith and examination, was required of all. In addition to the linguistically distinguished congregations the members were divided into three geographical groups according to their place of residence in the city.

On Sunday morning at nine o'clock the faithful gathered for worship, either at Austin Friars for the Dutch or Threadneedle Street for the French. The order was carefully worked out on evangelical principles.[59] It began with a short prayer followed by the Lord's Prayer. A Psalm was chanted without accompaniment. Then the minister read out the text from the lectern. This was a high point, tying together the services week after week, because the reading of the Word followed a definite program of procedure through an entire book of the Bible, passage by passage, enough for exposition during an hour's sermon each week.[60] The sermon followed, always in exposition of the portion of Holy Writ falling to that particular Sunday. After the sermon came a prayer that the Word preached might bear the fruits of the Spirit, recitation of the Ten Commandments, prayer of confession and absolution, the confession of faith in the form of the Apostles' Creed; and then a long prayer of intercession for the King, his family, the city, magistrates, England, the refugee churches, all churches, all kings and rulers not subject to Rome, the persecuted, the sick and bereaved, ending with the Lord's Prayer.

This service reflects many elements common to Reformed worship, as already practiced in Strasbourg and Geneva. One of the most distinctive elements was the insistence on progressive exposition of the Bible in consecutive passages, a practice early followed by Zwingli in Zürich. Another point of emphasis was the rather extended worship in prayer and recitation following the sermon.

The morning service was frequently followed by special observances, such as baptisms, marriages, and the Lord's Supper. The latter of course played a central part in the spiritual life of the community. After the service of worship, when the table of the Lord had been prepared, the faithful, who had been very carefully prepared in the two weeks prior to the observance as part of the administration of pastoral discipline, remained to hear a meditation on communion. They were warned against unauthorized participation and engaged in prayer. Then, as the ministers and elders sat on one side of the table, the congregation gathered around the other three sides, all seated. According to the words of St. Paul they were invited to share the bread and wine. One of the ministers administered the elements, breaking the bread and passing the cup. During this time another minister read selected passages from the Gospel of John. This service concluded with a prayer, a psalm, and a final admonition.

A second Sunday service in the afternoon was similar to the morning worship, except for the omission of the portions after the sermon. A main feature was a discussion of the Catechism, either Utenhove's Dutch translation of Laski's, or the French of Geneva. Another service, belonging as much to the area of discipline as of worship, took place on weekdays, the so-called prophecy, or collation, which is discussed later. Jan Utenhove, elder of the Dutch church, prepared a rhymed version of twenty-five Psalms, each to be sung in a dignified musical setting without accompaniment.[61] Although this work had some influence on later Dutch Reformed worship, its place was presently usurped by the fuller versions of Datheen, who set his Psalms to tunes from Geneva.

From the earliest age, children were brought under the guidance of the religious community. At about five they were taught the Small Catechism, the Lord's Prayer, the Apostles' Creed, and the Ten Commandments.[62] At eleven they began study of the Large Catechism, which was a formidable document indeed. At fourteen, upon a Sunday before their first communion, after a public examination of their faith, they were received into membership. Recalcitrant young people fell under excommunication if they reached eighteen or twenty without commitment. Adults were received into membership after a searching examination based on the Large Catechism. This emphasis on confirmation of youth into membership upon confession of faith, already in effect in the London church in the middle of the sixteenth century, is a remarkable development in Reformed practice.

Such was the strict foundation on which were laid the provisions for discipline of the community. This discipline was intended not only for the punishment of sin but also for the remedy of weakness and the strengthening of faith *(non equidem in condemnationem, sed in remedium potius infirmitatis nostrae onmium)*.[63] It should apply equally over the whole "body" of the Christian community and over all its members, without exception. Lines of discipline in the church are like nerves in the structure of the human body *(quod sunt nervi in compage ipsa corporis humani)*, an analogy reminiscent of Calvin in the fourth book of the *Institutes*.[64] Discipline was conceived not as a series of narrow rules for conduct but rather as the complete control of the whole life by the light of Christ. It does not consist, wrote Laski, of control imposed from above by ecclesiastical power, but rather in brotherly admonition by one's peers.[65] Nevertheless, this system would prove helpful in controlling heretical tendencies both within and without the strangers' church.[66]

The procedure was similar to that of Calvin for Geneva, except that great care was taken not to exclude anyone until every effort had been made to reclaim him. The elements of patience and mercy are of central importance for the disciplinary system of Laski, who in this respect improved on Bucer's *Gemeinschaften* in Strasbourg.[67] Private and public warnings would precede charges, and throughout opportunity would be given to mend. If the sinner proved repentant, he appeared before the congregation on Sunday after service, when the members prayed for his forgiveness, he confessed and asked pardon, and finally was readmitted by the Consistory. This service would conclude with the kiss of peace and a psalm of joy. Unrepentant sinners, after two public notices, were excommunicated, but then only by the assembly of all the ministers of both churches and after opportunity for final objections. If nothing availed, then, with the whole congregation on their knees, the sentence of excommunication was read. This was a purely spiritual act, and included no suggestion of a ban or of social ostracism.

A regular method of checking on the condition of individuals was offered by the celebration of the Lord's Supper. No one was allowed at the table of the Lord who had not proved his faith.[68] Two weeks before the event, at a service of preparation, solemn announcement was made of the conditions for admission. During the ensuing days the membership list was made up anew—each time. New members were received after examination, and delinquents were visited in their homes. No name went on the list without the consent of the elders. Those to be excluded from the table were specifically named on the eve of the great day. In this way the regular celebration of the Supper ensured the regular purging of the membership.

But discipline was applied to all alike, including the superintendent. One of the most interesting features of church life was the weekly "prophecy," an institution deriving from precedents in Zürich but not in Geneva, where Calvin would have nothing to do with it. The Dutch met one day, the French another. The purpose was to strengthen the faith of the members by answering questions raised by the sermons, to challenge the ministers to defend their messages, and to provide all an exercise in Bible study.[69] In order that all might be done decently and in good order (*ut omnia ordine ac decenter citraque ullam confusionem gerentur*—compare I Corinthians 14:40), the elders were appointed to receive the questions in advance and choose those for discussion which would be most edifying.[70] In this way the members could have their doubts and misunderstandings cleared up, the ministers could be held to the Word of God in the Bible, and Christian discipline could be maintained and advanced. In some of these discussions English citizens participated.[71] In the French congregation the discussions took on more the aspect of Bible study groups.

And finally, to complete the circle of discipline, every three months, at the *Censures,* in each of the congregations, individual members were permitted to bring forward any complaint, provided they could furnish two witnesses, against any minister, elder, or deacon. Only the superintendent was in this case exempt from inquisition. The democratic influence of these practices in terms of lay participation in theological interpretation and pastoral guidance can scarcely be exaggerated. They were also, and for the same reason, fraught with certain perils as the door was opened to extremists, heretics, and malcontents. That this was no idle peril is proved by the later history of the Dutch church in the time of Elizabeth, when the community was torn by controversies involving some leading ministers.

IV

This, then, was the kind of church that was intended to serve as a model for the English to follow in gradual reformation. For three years this young sapling flourished and began to spread living branches in English life. Did winter come too soon? The accession of Mary brought the whole experiment to an abrupt halt. When the refugee church was re-established under Elizabeth, the Letters Patent of Edward were not confirmed, although the community was granted the use of Austin Friars and most of the old privileges were recognized *de facto*—with one notable exception: The superintendent was henceforth the Bishop of London. There is not much suggestive of a "model church" in this later period. Refugees were more concerned about maintenance of their minimal rights than about spreading the image of the true church.

Did the model church of Edward's time last long enough to bear influence? The evidence suggests that it did. Certainly the London Dutch Church made great contributions to the development of the Reformed Church in the Netherlands.[72] And the French church shared in the building of the Reformed Church of France. But these relations go beyond the scope of this paper. In England one cannot distinguish between the influence of individual refugees like Laski and that of the church as a community. On the other hand men like Bucer and Peter Martyr pursued independent courses not directly related to the foreign community and occasionally in opposition. Laski's significance is crucial. Micronius, writing to Bullinger in 1551, said,

> Master à Lasco, our superintendent, a man (to speak it in one word) almost divine, is not only of the greatest use to the foreigners' churches, but also to the English, by teaching, exhorting, counselling, and writing.[73]

Although Albert Pollard was of the opinion that the influence of foreigners in general was less than that of Englishmen who had had contact with the Continental movements (like Hooper),[74] he specifically defended the influence of Laski over Cranmer, especially in the matter of the real presence.[75] Cecil also had a high regard for the Polish reformer. Strype in many passages illustrates the influence of both Laski and his refugee church.[76] His work on the Lord's Supper, dedicated to Edward VI in 1552, was intended to enlighten the English. In his preface to the King he compared the work of reformation to the rescue of an erring daughter from prostitution. For one must remember that it is not enough for them, thus to have brought this daughter out of the Papist stews home, into their own care and keeping, unless they also put off from her all that dressing which they know to be whorish in the stews. That no such thing may be seen with them, which may be accounted whorish; especially in that city where there is a great variety of judgments; and overruling whereof by man's authority is not to be expected, and where there are so many hucksters for the stews remaining.[77]

Undoubtedly Laski, along with Peter Martyr, took an active part in the work of the Royal Commission for the revision of the canon law, the results of whose efforts bore fruit in print only later in the time of Elizabeth.[78] If this publication did not itself play a large part, the men who worked on it had ample opportunity to share ideas. The connection of Laski with the revision of the Book of Common Prayer is less clear; but the general opinion is that at least indirectly his influence was felt.[79]

The most exciting episode that reveals the involvement of Laski with the English church is the vestarian conflict raised by the consecration of Hooper as Bishop of Gloucester. It seems that the Pole was the only notable foreigner to side openly with Hooper, as against the willingness of Bucer and Martyr to temporize.[80] To him the vestments *sunt pulchra et ornamenta tyrannidis Antichristi*. Bucer believed they were bad, but that foreigners should not interfere. Hooper throughout was most friendly to the Dutch church, and sometimes spent many hours in discussions with his friends in that church.

This association with Hooper suggests a line of influence reaching from the foreigners' churches down to the more decisive Puritan Reformation in England in the seventeenth century. Clear definition of this connection goes beyond the scope of this paper; but it seems to have some validity. The problem would be to distinguish between direct and indirect relations.

It would seem, then, in conclusion, that from their very inception the strangers' churches were planned to serve as models of the pure church of Christ fashioned in the image of the apostolic church, which, established in the midst of the Anglican environment, would be observed by English Christians less favored with freedom. Gradually, as opportunity and the laws permitted, the English church itself would be reformed after this model. A good start was made in the fulfillment of the plan, aided by two of the most influential figures of the realm, the young King and the Archbishop of Canterbury. No wonder that Calvin, observing this great experiment from his fastness in Geneva, addressed Edward VI as a latter day Josiah who sought piously to

root out all the superstitions in the New Jerusalem. He expressed appreciation for the grant of the generous charter to the refugees. Like
Josiah of old the new Josiah should

> aim at the mark which is set before you in the example of this holy
> king, so that it may be testified of you that you have not only de-
> stroyed impieties which were repugnant to the honour and service of
> God, but also that you have abolished and rased to the foundations
> everything that tends only to the nourishment of superstition.[81]

What a pity that, in this new version of scriptural history, Josiah was
followed by Jezebel!

ESSAYS ON THE LEFT WING OF THE REFORMATION

Sectarianism and Skepticism:
The Strange Allies of Religious Liberty

Waldo Beach

From the very beginning of his scholarly career, a major preoccupation of Roland Bainton has been with the history of religious liberty.[1] With sustained passion and assiduous care he has unearthed for Western scholarship the tangled roots of the flower of freedom of conscience, deep in the soil of continental and English history of the sixteenth and seventeenth centuries. With his instinctive feel for the crucial and the dramatic, his research and writing have served to enlighten for the contemporary Christian the perennial issues involved in the dialectic between religious truth and civil peace. He has made it plain that religious liberty is a precarious good, never to be assumed or guaranteed, but freshly championed. Nor is it the goal towards which church history itself moves, as the liberal historians who are children of the Enlightenment might see it, where the grand movement of history is from medieval authoritarian dogma and prejudice to irenic reason and domestic tranquillity.[2] Bainton has perceived, more wisely, how ambiguous are the goods of history and morally mixed are the ways of men. In his "Reflections" which close *The Travail of Religious Liberty*, he notes how "when one problem is solved, another will undoubtedly replace it," and that "every solution, however wise and necessary, carries within itself the possibility of some new abuse,"[3] so that religious liberty becomes both an accomplishment and a perennial problem. He remarks in this connection that "the most serious problem is as to the certitude of truth in the field of religion."[4]

His reflection prompts the exploration of the present essay: to show how the question of epistemology, the uncertainty or certainty of religious knowledge, is at the heart of the case for religious freedom. The thesis is here advanced that in the history of religious freedom there is a curious perennial alliance of groups radically opposite in their view of religious truth, who yet make common cause for religious liberty: on the one hand, the sectarian mind, which rests its case for freedom of conscience on certainty, and the skeptical mind, which rests its case on uncertainty. It is this odd conspiracy of sectarian dogmatism and rationalistic skepticism which can be shown, at crucial points in modern Western history, to have championed the cause of conscience against the confinement or persecution of church and state.

This is not to say, of course, that the question of certitude is the only ground or source of religious liberty. In the dense interconnection of historical causation, many cultural and ideological factors are certainly present, which Bainton has often pointed out.

For one, religious toleration is the product of the gradual domestication of the view of man's destiny. When salvation in the life beyond was the assumed goal of the human pilgrimage, and *extra ecclesiam nulla salus*, persecution for the eternal good of souls was not at all strange. When men's eyes were turned from heaven to earth, civil peace and the economic blessings of mutual forbearance of opposing consciences were extolled. The economic argument for religious liberty, incidentally, emerges strongly in the latter part of the seventeenth century in England, in the writings of William Penn, Robert Barclay, Henry Robinson, and John Locke, though it appears also in the sixteenth century.[5] There is some truth in Voltaire's wry comment that the source of religious freedom lay in the fact that men ceased to speculate about free grace and began to speculate on the price of grain.

Another obvious factor influencing any writer's position on the question of persecution or tolerance is the political one, i.e., where he stands in the church-state power structure. There have been many who while in a minority status have claimed freedom of conscience for their own group, but who on religious grounds have denied that freedom when they were in a position of majority control. The Puritans, persecuted in England, became the persecutors in New England. But the shift of terrain and status does not represent a shift of logic: freedom of *right* conscience, not any conscience, is the constant norm in both instances. So the political question of power is interlocked with the doctrinal question of truth.

Still another factor influencing the course of religious liberty is the theory of the nature of the church. Troeltsch's familiar distinction between the church-type church, as coterminous with a geographical locale or parish and spiritually inclusive in some sense of all in the community, living in memory of and hope for a single *corpus Chris-*

tianum, and the sect-type church, gathered out of the community by distinctive convictions, provides a useful clue in explaining differing responses to the question of religious liberty. The evidence quickly controverts any claim that the church-type church is *per se* conducive to persecution, the sect-type to freedom, for friends and foes of liberty of conscience appear in church and in sect. But there is some ground for maintaining that the case for religious liberty among churchmen is a genial latitudinarian concession which grants privileges for dissenters as long as they do no harm to the body politic, whereas among sectarians it is a right claimed out of a rigid and exclusive view of the church as a community called out of the world to doctrinal and moral purity.[6] By temperament, latitudinarians would prefer peace to truth, if the choice must be made; sectarians, truth to peace.

No one of these factors, economic, political, ecclesiastical, can itself "explain" religious liberty. Each one is linked with the ideological issue of religious truth. In all of these relationships the same two opposite schools of thought of fanatics and skeptics make their appearance, made strange bedfellows by the misery of persecution. Several studies in particular chapters of religious history have pointed to this meeting of opposites.[7] The present essay attempts to deal with four of them.

II

In the sixteenth-century Continental Reformation, the alliance of the skeptic and sectarian minds in defense of religious liberty is fairly elusive because of the limited character of the liberty proposed, in an age where the assumed premise of European culture was Christian dogma. The contemporary view that religious liberty includes the right of irreligion as much as religion would have been completely abhorrent. The vast majority of Protestant and Catholic leadership alike contended for the protection of Christian truth by the sword of the magistrate, and for the privileges of right conscience only. Even the few champions of liberty, like Erasmus and Castellio, drew limits to freedom; against atheists and blasphemous heretics Erasmus acknowledged the right of the state to use the sword,[8] and Castellio allowed that if Servetus had declared God to be a devil, he would have supported his punishment.[9]

Yet the rare minority voices raised in protest against religious persecution rested their case either on the skeptical ground of the uncertainty of truth or on the sectarian ground of the absolute inwardness, certainty, and inviolability of conscience. In some instances, curiously, the opposing motifs are found in a single thinker.

Erasmus of Rotterdam represents fairly clearly the tolerance of rationalistic skepticism, and the spirit of the Renaissance.[10] His stance in an age of bitter controversy was that of the charitable and irenic pacifist, the intellectual who could always see the other side of the argument.[11] His preference for civil peace over religious truth, where these are at odds, roots from his ethical zeal for "the philosophy of Christ" rather than doctrinal niceties. Heresy he defined in moral rather than theological terms; Anabaptists should be excluded for their civil sedition, not their doctrinal error.[12] "The sum of our religion is peace and unanimity and these can scarcely stand unless we define as little as possible and in many things leave each one free to follow his own judgment."[13]

To instance the sectarian case for liberty of conscience in the sixteenth century one might look best to a mystic like David Joris, though others like Menno Simons embody comparable themes. Joris does not fit any nice category: "mystic," "sectarian," "spiritualist," "Schwärmer" are all proper if carefully defined, but classification is not important. The significant thing to note here is how opposite from an Erasmus he stands: fiery, intense, passionate, with the ardor of a zealot and the dogmatic assurance of a visionary.

Bainton is quite correct in noting his "mystical" base for the claim for religious liberty.[14] The argument is not from the uncertainty of religious truth which should allow latitude for error and the tares to remain with the wheat, but rather from the nature of faith itself. The authority of the Spirit is final, transcending any external creed or church, "the faith of Jesus Christ is in no word spoken with the tongue, but in the eternal, true, pure, and divine work and spiritual nature of God against all flesh and is intelligible only to him who has received it."[15] The possession of the Spirit is the one thing needful. With typical sectarian assurance, he affirms that the churches of Christendom, in their contentions over dogma and their persecution of dissenters, lack the spirit, and are not true churches. "They do not have the true faith and love, but a bad spirit."[16] The true church is in the persecuted sect, or—as with Joris himself—in the persecuted prophet.

Joris is not the philosopher dealing with the epistemological problems of truth and error, reason and faith, authority and doubt, that lie behind the question of religious liberty. But the philosophic position implicit in his writing appears to be that which claims freedom

for right conscience by virtue of the assurance itself, inward, invio-
lable, incontrovertible, to which he and his followers alone, in these
latter days, give authentic witness in their suffering.

In his case for religious liberty, Sebastian Castellio represents a
sophisticated and complex mixture of motifs.[17] If anything, he illustrates the confluence of the rationalistic and sectarian principles,
the former preponderant, in a manner remarkably prophetic of the
briefs of later centuries for the rights of conscience. He is still, to be
sure, of the sixteenth century in his assumption of essential Christian
dogma prevailing in Christendom; it is for the variety of Christian
consciences that he pleads freedom, not just any conscience. Yet the
philosophic problem of religious knowledge at the heart of religious
liberty he addresses himself to directly, in the treatise "concerning
Doubt and Belief, Ignorance and Knowledge."[18]

His stance, in this polemical tract, is that of a rationalist, who pro-
tests authoritarian fideism,[19] who acknowledges the inevitable uncer-
tainties of mortal knowledge and the illusions of sense experience,
like the stick which in water appears broken.[20] He knows well the
controls of passion over reason, and the ways in which judgment is
beclouded by "self-love and carnal affection of the mind by which
each looks to his own rights and does not consider the others."[21] Presumably, only by a transcendence of emotion and self-interest can the
mind's sight be cleared and objective knowledge be restored. Such a
position Bainton rightly calls rationalism, but not skepticism.[22] Castellio distinguishes between indubitable doctrines essential to salvation and nonessentials over which men debate; it is the latter in which
suspended judgment is needed for religious peace, since no one really
knows for sure.

The "sectarian" motifs in Castellio are not as readily apparent as
the rationalist, and are subordinate. He does not have the sectarian's
passionate conviction for his particular truth, exclusive of all others.
But he does share with the sectarian spirit the stress on the inwardness of religious faith, which makes it untouchable by any external
constraint, and the inviolability of conscience, even when it is in
error. The respect due the integrity of conscience, right or wrong, is
an argument dear to the sectarian plea in the seventeenth century.
Castellio, writing in the sixteenth, appears ahead of season.

III

Seventeenth-century England is the century and locale of the great
debate on the terms of religious liberty. In the turbulent stretch of

years between the end of the reign of Elizabeth and the Restoration of 1688, beneath the power-conflicts, the church-state problem turned on the question of how to reconcile the common peace of England with plural persuasions of Christian truth. It took the polemical skill of the best minds of England, and a civil war as well, to find the answer.

The many religious groups involved in this debate range themselves roughly along a spectrum from right to left, from "church" to "sect": (1) the small Roman Catholic party, a feared and hated minority, (2) the Anglican party, by far the dominant majority, (3) the Presbyterian Puritan group, (4) the Congregationalists, or Independents, some separatists, some nonseparatists, (5) the Baptists and Quakers, and (6) the plethora of tiny sect groups, such as Seekers and Diggers. These positions are not always clearly delineated, and individual thinkers sometimes move back and forth along the line, as, for example, Roger Williams, who moves from Anglican through several stages to Seeker, while some thinkers like Milton and Locke combine ideas from left and right.

Out of this great variety of religious groups, the two groups most vocal and influential in bringing about the spirit of religious liberty embodied in the Edict of Toleration were the Anglican latitudinarians on the right and the radical sectarians on the left. Making common cause from frequently opposite sides, these two groups illustrate well our thesis that behind freedom of conscience is a curious compound of certitude and incertitude, of faith and doubt.[23]

It is difficult to single out from among the many "men of latitude" in the seventeenth century a single representative who exactly typifies the logic. William Chillingworth, Jeremy Taylor, John Hales, and the Cambridge Platonists stand for a tolerance based on Christian theological grounds and commitment, while the more secular or "lay" latitudinarians, like Francis Bacon, Lord Herbert of Cherbury, or Thomas Browne stand on more skeptical premises. But clerical or lay, they share certain fundamental premises about the way to unite religious truth and civil peace, premises quite opposite to those of sectarianism.

For one thing, they are heirs of the Renaissance and Erasmus in their trust in Reason as an ultimate authority, in whose court all religious controversy can be arbitrated and passions abated. For another, they accept a pluralism of religious interpretations, within a common subscription to fundamentals, as suitable for the life of a broad inclusive church. The way of salvation is open to pilgrims of many garbs and persuasions. "For my desire," says Chillingworth, "is to go the right way to eternal happiness. But whether this way lie on the right hand, or the left, or straight forward; whether it be by following a living guide, or by seeking my direction in a book, or by hearkening to the secret whisper of some private spirit, to me it is indifferent."[24]

The theoretical ground for such charity of differences within the church is an uncertainty about proximate and relative truths. All see through a glass darkly. As Thomas Browne wrote, "Every man is not a proper Champion for Truth, nor fit to take up the Gauntlet in the cause of Verity: many, from the ignorance of these Maxims, and an inconsiderate Zeal unto Truth, have too rashly charged the troops of Error, and remained as trophies unto the enemies of Truth."[25] Jeremy Taylor's *Liberty of Prophesying* (1647), a classic statement of the latitudinarian position, rests much of its argument on the folly of a factious spirit, which insists on its own way in the midst of plural convictions. Certain essentials are fixed, to be sure. But the dissensions that arise over *adiaphora* can be dispelled by mutual forbearance and a gentle diffidence. "If men would not call all opinions by the name of religion, and superstructures by the name of fundamental articles, and all fancies by the glorious appellation of faith,"[26] peace might prevail.

Clearly such a position betokens a kind of philosophic detachment, and a charity toward differences, which mark suspended judgment. At the same time, and paradoxically, it is clear that the latitudinarians have no love for sectarians such as the Quakers, whose "enthusiasm" and arrogant exclusivism are more likely to arise from feverish imagination and self-will than from the spirit of God.

The sectarian case for religious liberty, on the other side, is the extension of the Calvinistic-Puritan zeal for a particular religious truth, whose freedom should enjoy the protection of the state. One of the most striking features of the sectarian tracts on liberty of conscience[27] is their exclusivistic theory of religious truth, or what might be called epistemological intolerance. According to J. W. Allen, the plea of the proletariat sectarians for protection for consciences was in reality a plea for their own rights, based on intransigent conviction, not a recognition that consciences other than their own might be correct.[28] Political expediency rather than religious charity lay behind their polemic. One must not push this conclusion too far. It needs to be qualified, especially in the instance of the Quakers of the Restoration period. But at least it remains true of such fugitive tractarians as Leonard Busher, Henry Jacob, and Samuel Richardson. Busher, for example, contends that a "reason why so many good people are now deceived is because we that have most truth are most persecuted, and therefore most poor. Whereby we are unable to write and print, as we would, against the adversaries of truth."[29]

The sectarian's positive ground, then, for withholding the magistrate's sword is the inviolability of conscience, the separation of the temporal and spiritual jurisdictions, and the folly and cruelty of persecution.

Now for a brief look at the more famous champions of freedom in this period: Milton, Williams, and Locke, whose theories of religious liberty have been thoroughly explicated at other places,[30] and whose positions represent a sophisticated and profound combination and synthesis of ideas drawn from both sectarian and latitudinarian sources.

In Milton the Calvinistic heritage and the Renaissance are conjoined. The Puritan revolutionary and the secular humanist both speak in his eloquence.[31] The epistemological significance of the *Areopagitica* lies in Milton's trust in the power of truth to emerge "in free and open encounter" with error. It is not through the licensing and suppression of error, but through permissive freedom, that truth will out. Here is the rationalist's trust in an order of reason to make its way, at least with reasonable Englishmen, against superstition and folly, combined with the sectarian's first principle of the sacredness of conscience.

Both in temperament and theory, Roger Williams is more the sectarian than the rationalist, though his movement to the left along the spectrum makes any category for him unsuitable. For the most part, however, as his debate with John Cotton illustrates, his argument rests on the separation of temporal and spiritual spheres, and the inviolability of conscience even in error from political control. "It is the will and command of God that . . . a permission of the most Paganish, Jewish, Turkish, or Antichristian consciences and worships be granted to *all* men."[32] Note, however, that this is not because all of these consciences are equally correct or equally uncertain, or equally plausible roads to salvation, but because only by spiritual means can men be converted to the right way. Conviction for Christian truth, not indifference, guided all his seeking.

John Locke, on the other hand, represents a synthesis where the latitudinarian spirit predominates. Locke is thoroughly the rationalist Christian, a precursor of the deism of the eighteenth century. As Bainton points out, he and Castellio were the "only two men in the course of the struggle for religious liberty [who] have written treatises alike on the problem of liberty and the problem of knowledge."[33] His *Reasonableness of Christianity* is a tract calling for the sufficiency for salvation of religious beliefs plain to the simple and untutored.

Locke's *Letters on Toleration* are a summation of the standard arguments for religious freedom. The sectarian threads are: (1) a voluntary theory of the nature of the church, as a gathered society of believers "joined together in order to the public worshipping of God, in such a manner as they judge acceptable to Him, and effectual to the salvation of their souls,"[34] (2) the distinct separation of civil and spiritual spheres, and (3) the sacredness of private conscience from political jurisdiction. The latitudinarian elements are evident in his trust in the finality of reason against all "enthusiasms" of the extreme sectarian,[35] in his attempt to reduce Christianity to its simple essentials, and in his incipient skepticism concerning the accessibility of truth, based on his recognition of the relativity of judgments. "Mankind is so divided that he acts according to reason and sound judgment in Augsburg who would be judged to do the quite contrary at Edinburgh."[36] His skepticism is only incipient, however; essential Christian truths stand as the foundation of his tolerance. It is significant that he would not extend toleration to Roman Catholics, on political grounds, or to atheists, on the religious ground that God is the basis of moral community. "The taking away of God, though but even in thought, dissolves all."[37] He champions, then, freedom for Christian consciences, not any conscience; in this regard he belongs more to the medieval and Reformation than to the modern period.

IV

It is only a short way to our third instance of the alliance of skepticism and sectarianism, across the Atlantic to the General Assembly of Virginia and its "Bill for Establishing Religious Freedom." The actors in this drama again represent opposite persuasions, though they are not as far apart as in the earlier epochs.

The text of the Bill for Establishing Religious Freedom, enacting "that no man shall be compelled to frequent or support any religious worship, place or ministry whatsoever . . . but that all men shall be free to profess, and by argument to maintain, their opinions in matters of religion,"[38] authored by Thomas Jefferson, could elicit the support of sectarians whose theology was very different from his own.

Much has been written on Jefferson's "theology" and on whether he is to be classified as Theist, Deist, Unitarian, Christian, or atheist. The consensus, as A. P. Stokes notes, points toward a rationalistic theism, with many of the latitudinarian and Lockean elements we have noted above.[39] Jefferson believed himself a devout Christian, in the liberal tradition of returning to the simple moral principles of the teachings of Jesus. He follows Locke, and shares with the sectarians, a strict separation of the spiritual and civil spheres, inner conviction and outer action. Yet he belongs essentially in the Erasmian line of rationalism. He is impatient with the particular doctrinal wrangles of sectarian groups, and sees no relation between doctrinal commitment and the jurisdiction of the state. "The legitimate powers of government extend to such acts only as are injurious to others. But it does me no injury for my neighbor to say there are twenty gods, or no God."[40] This divorce of theological conviction from moral and therefore political jurisdiction indicates how much further even than Locke he has moved from Calvinism toward the modern secular mind.

He is the rationalist, too, rather than the fideist or "enthusiast," in his glad acceptance of religious differences and the plural roads to truth. Nothing is to be feared from the differences of religious sects enjoying the equal protection of the laws of the state, since "truth is great and will prevail if left to herself." It is not plural faiths that have caused the prolonged misery of persecution but "the impious presumption of legislators and rulers, civil as well as ecclesiastical, who, being themselves but fallible and uninspired men, have assumed dominion over the faith of others, setting up their own opinions and modes of thinking as the only true and infallible and as such endeavoring to impose them on others."[41] The epistemology implicit here is the recognition of the uncertainty and relativity of all finite grasps of religious truth.

The correspondence of Jefferson, especially his famous letter to the Danbury Baptists, indicates the extent of his cordial goodwill to those with whom he found little in common religiously and who castigated him for his impiety. He feared the sectarians, however, for their crude arrogance and their dogmatic zeal, and fought their intrusions in public policy. His plan for the University of Virginia illustrates his position. He anticipated a chair of ethics and religion, and planned a special room in the rotunda "for religious worship." But denominational schools he would keep at the edge of the campus, independent of the university. At the same time he hoped that by having liberal Christianity on campus and the sects just off campus, "by bringing the sects together, we shall soften their asperities, liberalize and neutralize their prejudices, and make the general religion a religion of peace, reason, and morality."[42]

The Baptists in Virginia, largely of the religious proletariat, having suffered much abuse and discrimination from the established Anglicans, were among the first in that colony to petition for religious liberty. Their case, as of yore, was made not on the ground of the uncertainty of religious truths but on the simple claim to the right of religious conscience, if peaceable, to remain unmolested by the state. Their repeated petitions to the Assembly, protesting establishment, ring with phrases familiar in sectarian history: "that the gospel wants not the feeble arm of man for its support; that it has made, and will again, through divine power, make, its way against all opposition,"[43] and that the two spheres of spiritual and temporal are radically different in purpose and should be carefully discrete in jurisdiction. "New Testament Churches, we humbly conceive, are, or should be, established by the Legislature of Heaven, and not earthly power; by the law of God and not the Law of the State; by the acts of the Apostles, and not by the Acts of an Assembly."[44]

There is no theory of religious knowledge articulated in the Baptist tracts of the times, but it is safe to surmise that ardor for their own religious persuasion, rather than uncertainty as to the truth-claims of the churches of the times, prompted their appeals. Jefferson's deism would seem as heretical to a Baptist preacher as to the Presbyterian and Anglican divines who railed against the unbeliever in the Presidency. But as Jefferson himself noted in writing to the Danbury Baptists, he and they could make common cause in the belief "that religion is a matter which lies solely between man and his God, that he owes account to none other for his faith or his worship, that the legislative powers of government reach actions only."[45] Belief and skepticism thus joined from opposite sides in building "a wall of separation between Church and State,"[46] into the American tradition.

V

In mid-twentieth century, the dynamics of history have altered the character of the church-state problem in America sharply. Since the era of Jefferson, when a Christian nation protected itself against any nationally established church but assumed the "free exercise" of religion in American life, the "wall" of separation has now become a firmly established symbol in the American consciousness, so much so that even Roman Catholic political candidates pledge allegiance to the principle of separation of church and state. Freedom of religion itself, construed as a prohibition against any interference of government into church life, or vice versa, has become itself a kind of absolute, rather than a means to the end of the infusion into public life, through plural forms, of religious norms and values, such as was the ideal in earlier centuries. In the mind of the contemporary American, freedom of religion means that irreligion should have the same political rights as the various forms of religion. "Each in his own way, or not at all." The secularization of the state may prove the too-heavy price paid for the absolutization of religious liberty itself.[47]

The most recent development is well illustrated in the reappearance of the alliance of skepticism and sectarianism in the POAU (Protestant and Other Americans United for Separation of Church and State). Among its stated objectives are:

(1) to enlighten and mobilize public opinion in support of religious liberty as this monumental principle of democracy has been embodied in the Constitution by the separation of church and state;

(2) to resist every attempt by law or the administration of law further to widen the breach in the wall of separation of church and state.[48]

We are here concerned only to point out how, by the ironic logic of history, such an alliance as the POAU, so apparently single-minded in its objective of guarding the wall of separation (especially against Roman Catholic "breaches"), is in reality double-minded in its premises, a mixture not only of opposites but of contradictory ultimate loyalties. The "Others" in the POAU are now the secular humanists, in whom the Erasmian tradition has been extended out to an arrogant or wistful humanism.[49] The "Protestants" are likely to be those of the evangelical sectarian tradition, especially Baptists, who view the threat of Rome as so sinister that they find themselves in the odd position of fighting to keep Christian instruction out of public education,[50] and— if they be Southern Baptists—committing the political heresy of voting Republican to keep a Catholic out of the White House. In the political realm, the direction of sectarian zeal seems to have turned from the positive goal of the spreading of the gospel to the protection of freedom of religion read now in the negative sense.

VI

When one looks back synoptically over the development of four centuries here sketched, it is possible to discern a general family resemblance, shared on the one hand by sectarians from Joris to a Southern Baptist, and by rationalists and skeptics, from Castellio and Erasmus to a Mrs. McCollum or Paul Blanshard. At the same time, it is possible to detect certain crucial drifts of thought over these centuries which make the issue of religious liberty different in character in twentieth-century America from what it was in the Continental Reformation. The most marked drift is from a religiously based theory of freedom of worship, claiming or allowing a variety of Christian consciences to worship God in whatever way seemed true, to a secular theory of religious freedom, which allows *any* conscience, Christian or atheist, equal protection of the laws. To the liberal this trend may constitute progress, but to the Christian there are serious moral ambiguities.

There may be clear gain in the achievement of a humane and secular state of mind which no longer countenances the persecution of any citizen for his religious faith or lack of it. Yet if indeed Christian faith and piety are in some sense necessary to the health of the body politic, then a secular tolerance of indifference which recognizes no greater worth to faith than unfaith may prove to have conceded too much from the cause of truth to the cause of peace, and betrayed true liberty of conscience. As a matter of fact, if one may for the moment use the term "religion" in its deeper sense as "commitment to the ultimate," then it becomes impossible for any state to remain religiously neutral or faithless. In public education, for example, an arrogant secularism may and often does discriminate against if not directly persecute a Christian conscience, the new persecution being no less vicious for being psychological rather than physical in its exercise of power.

In sum, the long story of the travail of religious liberty prompts the sober reflection that our culture may in a misplaced ardor for freedom itself, have shifted to a freedom *from* religion which imperils freedom *for* religion. Perhaps what is needed is a recovery of the ardor of the Christian sectarian tempered with the caution and humility of a Christian skeptic, who at least is of a mind in grounding religious liberty in an objective order of God's truth.

Augsburg and the Early Anabaptists

Paul J. Schwab

The city of Augsburg proudly traces its founding to Caesar Augustus, after whom it is named. During the Middle Ages it became an episcopal seat and by 1276 an imperial city. Augsburg's location encouraged growth in wealth and culture which resulted in its being called "Pearl of the German Renaissance."

With the coming of the Reformation, Augsburg's readiness to accept new ideas prepared its people to welcome the new teachings, for in hardly any other city did the Lutheran doctrines receive so ready a hearing. Despite the aid of Bavaria and the Swabian League, both staunchly Catholic, the Bishop of Augsburg was unable to prevent the domination of the city by the Lutherans under the leadership of Conrad Peutinger, outstanding lawyer and humanist, and Pastor Urban Rhegius, a onetime monk. By 1525 this Catholic-Lutheran rivalry was further complicated by the coming of strong Zwinglian influences under Michael Keller. In fact, by the beginning of 1527 Augsburg had become a Zwinglian city although Catholic and Lutheran services were permitted.

However, the three-way struggle was to become still more confused, for with the first approach of Anabaptism in 1525 and its growth during the next years, the problems of the city multiplied. Closely associated with this new movement in Augsburg were such men as Ludwig Hätzer, Balthasar Hübmaier, Hans Denck, and Hans Hut, none of whom was a citizen or even longtime resident of the city, but they had one thing in common—the loss of their lives within a very short period because of their religious work. A representative product of their labors was a prominent citizen convert, Eitelhans Langenmantel. The overthrow of their new structure took but a pathetically few months. An account of these personalities and developments depicts largely the course of Anabaptism not only in Augsburg but also in several other cities and districts.

Although Ludwig Hätzer was never an acknowledged Anabaptist and never accepted adult baptism, yet he should be considered one of the early forerunners of the movement in Augsburg. He was born about 1500 near St. Gall, Switzerland, and by 1520 or 1521 was consecrated a priest near Zürich. By 1523, however, he went into Zürich and became an active supporter of Zwingli. But at the same time his associations with such men as Conrad Grebel and Felix Manz show that he was coming under the influence of Anabaptist teachings. In June 1524 he was sent to Augsburg to oversee the publication of some Zwinglian writings and there first won the friendship of the leading Lutheran pastor, Urban Rhegius. He also maintained fellowship with some Anabaptist friends there. In October of that year he returned to Zürich and, interestingly enough, spoke against Zwingli's views on infant baptism.

The spring and summer of 1525 found Hätzer in Augsburg again working for the publisher, Otmar. He participated with Protestant-minded workers in small discussion groups called conventicles. During the struggle over the Supper he spoke against the Lutheran as well as Zwinglian doctrines and thus estranged Rhegius.[1] When the latter challenged him to a disputation, Hätzer failed to appear and was thereupon expelled from the city. "Hätzer did not advocate Anabaptist teachings in Augsburg, even though the later Anabaptist congregation here had its origin in these conventicles."[2] In November 1525 he became reconciled with Zwingli for a period, but soon he was traveling to Basel, Baden, Strasbourg, Worms, and other cities of Germany. He returned to Augsburg in August 1527 in time to attend the "Martyr Synod," but he did not participate in it.[3] Leaving Augsburg before the *Rat* started its arrests, Hätzer performed his only known baptisms, these being in Regensburg in October 1527.[4] There is reason to believe he lived in Augsburg from November 1527 to April 1528. In November 1528 he was arrested in Constance, tried on a charge of immoral conduct, and beheaded on February 4, 1529, at the site of Hus' burning. Although Hätzer was not a baptized member, he is counted among the martyrs of historical Anabaptism. Goeters suggests that he might be considered a "marginal Anabaptist," a spiritualist who in his latter years sought refuge in that fellowship because he was in disagreement with the regular ecclesiastical parties.[5]

Although Anabaptism in some form was present in Augsburg in 1525 during Hätzer's stay there, historical Anabaptism came into the city in the spring of 1526 with the arrival of Balthasar Hübmaier, and the rivalry of the three leading religious groups made conditions most favorable for the growth of the new movement.[6] Hübmaier was born about 1480 in Friedberg, a few miles east of Augsburg. He received his baccalaureate degree and his ordination in 1510, later the degree of Doctor of Theology from the University of Ingolstadt where he also taught. After some preaching experience in the Cathedral of Regensburg, Hübmaier was installed as priest in Waldshut, Switzerland, in 1522. By the summer of that year he began to assume a Lutheran position, then gradually moved toward Zwinglianism, carrying his people with him. In 1524 he completed the reform of religion in Waldshut, still adhering to Zwingli's views; but the next year found him holding an Anabaptist theological position, and he received its baptism near Easter 1525.[7]

Escaping from Waldshut during an Austrian attack in December 1525, Hübmaier fled to Zürich where with a troubled conscience he recanted his Anabaptist views. He left the city secretly and made his way to Constance, then to Augsburg where he arrived in April 1526. There he associated with zealous Anabaptists and about May 1 baptized Hans Denck and others.[8] However, he did not remain long, for in July he was in Nickolsburg, Moravia, then went into Austria by way of Ingolstadt and Regensburg.[9] The date of Hübmaier's arrest by order of Ferdinand I is not known, but by January 3, 1528, he and his wife were prisoners in Kreuzenstein. Later they were taken to Vienna where Hübmaier was racked, and when this torture did not produce recantation he was sentenced and burned at the stake on March 10, 1528. A few days later his wife, with a stone tied to her neck, was thrown from the large bridge over the Danube.[10]

Hübmaier's leadership in Augsburg was followed by that of Hans Denck who really gave to Augsburg's Anabaptism its identifying stamp.[11] Born about 1500 in Heybach, Upper Bavaria, Denck like Hübmaier attended the University of Ingolstadt. The autumn of 1519 found him among the humanists of Augsburg writing at least eight booklets against Luther; but by the end of 1522 he was a Lutheran. Kiwiet believes that Denck was won to Lutheranism by Hübmaier in December of 1522 while they both were in Regensburg.[12] Denck returned next to Augsburg in 1525 as a teacher and there was later attracted, won, and baptized by Hübmaier who by that time was an Anabaptist.

In spite of Denck's discipleship of Hübmaier, he was not one of the Swiss Brethren but became the originator of a new group, the South German Anabaptists.[13] He was their leader in Augsburg and although no congregation was founded there before 1527 he baptized numbers of converts including Hans Hut.

While Denck was in Augsburg in 1526 he came into conflict with that ardent pastor and defender of Lutheran orthodoxy, Urban Rhegius. This learned and personable man was in his early thirties when he first came to Augsburg as a priest. Graduate of the Universities of Basel, Freiburg, and Ingolstadt, Rhegius was a devoted disciple of John Eck. He had already received many honors, even to exercising the office of vicar bishop in Constance. It is not known who or what changed him into a Lutheran, but because of his change he had to leave the city in 1521. In 1524 he was permanently installed as a pastor in Augsburg and became the outstanding Lutheran preacher and theologian among the city clergy.[14] Learned, polished, fluent, fearless, he was an opponent to be respected or feared. It is not too surprising that after Rhegius arranged for a public disputation, the uncontentious Denck preferred to leave Augsburg privately, which he did in October 1526.

Working with Hätzer and Jacob Kautz, Denck spread his doctrines very quickly along the Rhine, ministering in the vicinity of Basel and, in August 1527, in the Canton of Zurich. He attended the famous Martyr Synod after which he made his way again to Basel, petitioned Oecolampadius for permission to stay there, and was granted this request upon promising he would never baptize anyone again. There he returned to his original mysticism, even abandoning objection to oaths and infant baptism. He died of the plague on November 15, 1527.[15] Called a beginner of undogmatic Christianity, he was "one of the few personalities of the 16th century who never indulged in controversy except with a heavy heart; not a trace of abusiveness or unfairness is to be found in his writings."[16]

By the side of Denck stood Hans Hut, another builder of the Augsburg congregation. Son of Hans Hut, Sr.,[17] he was born in Haina, near Römhild in Thuringia. He became a bookbinder and traveled widely for a number of years, repeatedly visiting Wittenberg. He is described as "rather tall, a peasant with light brown cropped hair and a blond mustache . . . dressed in a gray, sometimes a black, ridingcoat, a broad gray hat, and gray pants."[18] Upon the outbreak of the Peasants' War, Hut almost participated but "because the shooting was too thick," he hastened from the field. He sheltered the fleeing Müntzer in his home for a day and a night and became an advocate of the ideas of "that firebrand . . . the first Protestant theocrat" with whom "religious and social revolution coincided."[19]

Hut first entered Augsburg about Pentecost 1526 after the complete defeat of the peasants. While there, he joined Denck and Hätzer who, along with Caspar Färber, persuaded him to join the Anabaptists. He was baptized by Denck May 26, 1526, in Denck's small house near the Holy Cross Gate.[20] Although Hut lived with Denck for but three or four days before receiving baptism, and left almost at once, the relationship between these men became of the utmost importance, for through Hut Augsburg became the central point of South German Anabaptism.[21] Goeters gives Hut credit for really establishing and nurturing Augsburg's Anabaptism, and traces back through him to Müntzer's union of economic rebellion and religious enthusiasm as a Germanic beginning of what developed in Augsburg.[22] It was Denck's influence, however, which kept Hut "aloof from any political or revolutionary tendency."[23] Hut's significance was felt in regions much larger than that of Augsburg for "a large percentage of those Anabaptists called up by the authorities in central Germany attributed their conversion and baptism to Hut."[24]

Kiwiet upholds Goeters' point, stating that South German Anabaptism, because of Denck and Hut, did not develop, as is commonly assumed, from the preaching of Swiss Anabaptists. By the side of, and for a time distinct from, Swiss biblical Anabaptism there developed in South Germany a different form of the movement. The spiritual bent of the latter was set in it by both of its great leaders, Denck and Hut, or perhaps more accurately by the spirit of the *Theologia Deutsch*, which was Denck's favorite book as it was Luther's in his earlier years; also by eschatological preaching so characteristic of Hut. Although the Swiss and German streams met in Strasbourg in the fall of 1526 with Michael Sattler, father of Swiss Anabaptism, and Denck, the differences soon were clarified on February 24, 1527, by the Schleitheim Conference over which Sattler presided and of whose Seven Articles he was the author.[25] In these articles the Swiss Brethren, as they were called thereafter, declared that the scriptural word is sufficient for guidance, and that baptism is only for the penitent, thus excluding all infant baptism, "the highest and chief abomination of the pope."[26] Only the baptized could be admitted to the Supper and the fellowship; reading, preaching, and discipline might be exercised only by the pastors *(Hirten)* of the fellowship; pacifism must be practiced in all circumstances; and oaths were never to be taken.

The South German Anabaptists, on the other hand, were freer in their interpretations. They held to faith and love as their criteria; fellowship was maintained with many unbaptized persons; unbaptized but believing persons were admitted to the Supper; and not only the pastor but anyone who felt himself called to it might preach. Some did not refuse to take oaths, and the sword was not uniformly forbidden.[27] Although immersion was established as the rite by Grebel,

the Swiss Anabaptist, on or near Palm Sunday, 1525, Hübmaier baptized some 300 from a milkpail in Waldshut in that same year, and it
does not appear that he ever changed his method.[28] Two Göggingen
converts who were arrested and executed with Langenmantel in 1528
stated under cross-examination that they had been baptized by af-
fusion.[29] It seems that by continual travel and exchange of ideas these
differences gradually faded out and, as Littell says, "It is now clear
that the South Germans, at least, did not significantly differ from the
Swiss."[30] Certainly Wolfgang Musculus, an Augsburg Bucerian pastor
after 1531, criticized the Anabaptists for holding some of the beliefs
which were contained in the Swiss-slanted Schleitheim Articles of 1527.[31]

Leaving Augsburg shortly after his baptism, Hut carried on a preaching ministry in Bavaria, Swabia, Franconia, and Austria. His work was
very effective as he emphasized eschatology, however without his former
dangerous and iconoclastic interpretations.[32] He now held government
to be instituted by God and to be implicitly obeyed. There should be
no community of goods, but he who had a superfluity should help the
poor.

When Hut at the peak of his effectiveness returned to Augsburg in
February 1527, he found a group of earnest and prominent citizens who
had been won to the fellowship although they had not yet received
adult baptism. Among these were Eitelhans Langenmantel, Jacob
Dachser, and Sigmund Salminger. "All [these] were baptized by Hut
in February 1527," and there must have been others. Hut proceeded
with the organization of the congregation although he left the city
after a stay of but nine or ten days.[33] Again Hut preached in various
cities, meeting Hübmaier in Nikolsburg. Escaping from the Nikolsburg
prison, Hut continued preaching in Upper Austria, Freistadt, Gallneu-
kirchen, Linz, Passau, Schärding, Braunau, Laufen, and Salzburg. He
returned to Augsburg in time to participate in the Martyr Synod.[34]

Hut's part in this great synod, which met in August of 1527, was pre-
dominant; whereas that of Hätzer, who was present though not a baptized member, was very minor. Following the synod, Hut was arrested
on September 15 and never got out of prison alive. Dr. Peutinger had
all kinds of torture applied to him, examining him at least a dozen
times on September 16 and following days. It would be interesting to
know if Hut's ten-year-old son still visited his father, for when Langenmantel was arrested in the spring of 1527 he had in his possession a
copy of Hut's *Rathsbüchlein*. Hermann Anwaldt, Langenmantel's servant, testified in his cross-examination of May 13, 1527, that Hut's son
had carried books about for his father.[35]

Among other mysteries of Hut's life are the circumstances of his death in the Augsburg prison. One account says he set the straw of his cell and cot afire hoping to maneuver his escape when the jailer came to free his shackles. However, he was so badly affected by the smoke that he died eight days later, December 6. A second account, told by his son Philip, holds that Hut had been racked in the tower and then taken to his cell where he lay unconscious. A candle left in his cell ignited the straw on the floor, and he was found dead when the guards finally arrived. His body was tied to a chair, taken to court, condemned to death, and then burned at the stake on December 7, 1527.[36] This was the first of two Anabaptist deaths for which the Augsburg *Rat* was directly responsible.

When the writer was making a special report in one of Professor Bainton's Reformation seminars, mention was made of Eitelhans Langenmantel. Professor Bainton, with his characteristic humor, commented, "A man with a name like that must have played quite an important role in Augsburg's struggle." There is, therefore, both sentiment and interest in a closer look at this man with the long name, for he combines the Augsburg patrician and the "Gartenbruder"—the struggle, tragedy, and moral victory of the sixteenth-century Anabaptists.

Eitelhans Langenmantel, son of Eitelhans Langenmantel, Sr., belonged to one of the oldest, most distinguished and influential families of Augsburg. His father, who was a member of the *Rat* for a decade and served as head tax collector, died by 1525.[37]

Little is known of the younger Langenmantel's youth. He married Katharina Wieland in 1501, but she died July 24, 1507, leaving a daughter who survived until 1589. As a result of his marriage, Langenmantel found himself in easy financial circumstances, and the tax record shows he lived in his native city until 1527 without any prolonged absences.[38] It seems that he led a life of privileged ease and lax moral standards. A portrait by Albrecht Dürer shows him in 1515 as a man in his forties with a small moustache, chin beard, and closely cropped hair.[39] Roth cites an interesting and pertinent incident:

> Langenmantel was a rich man who from his youth up frequented prostitutes. As he followed the road of improvement, he became first a Lutheran, then a follower of Karlstadt, then an Anabaptist. By his money as well as his persuasiveness he won many to this sect. While being led to prison he called out to those who were following him: "So long as you knew me as a whore-chaser, I was not despised by any of you, and you all respected me because you knew I was rich. Now that I have become a follower of the Gospel and am in trouble, I am become scandalous and a laughing stock to you. However, this will always be the lot of those who follow Christ."[40]

Langenmantel was baptized by Hut on March 5, 1527,[41] and from then on was one of the fellowship's most active and loyal members. He was a persuasive preacher and generous with his means. "Indeed, the earliest Anabaptist sermon which has been preserved (1527) is that of Eitelhans Langenmantel on Jeremiah 7:3, 4 and 9:8, a sermon which sounded a call for repentance and reformation of life."[42] A small number of his writings survive—three published by him and two or three in manuscript.[43]

The zeal shown by such men as Langenmantel combined with the rapid growth in numbers could not long be ignored by the *Rat*. Although Langenmantel was arrested and warned because of his participation in the brotherhood, and on March 11, 1527, took an oath to keep the peace *(Urfehde);*[44] he returned to his home and permitted its continued use as a meeting place. He also continued his religious activities, apparently not considering all these to be violating the peace.

Langenmantel's next crisis accompanied the meeting of the Martyr Synod in August. Following its close, the *Rat's* officers busied themselves with numerous arrests, incarcerating Langenmantel about September 18. He was often handicapped by gout and on this occasion had to be carried into prison by the police. As a prisoner, he was visited by Rhegius and other ministers on September 23 and 25. Finally he admitted that the Anabaptists were unjustified in their stand and that baptism as practiced by the church was right. Even this did not free him, for on October 14 he was exiled from the city until such time as the *Rat* would permit his return, this penalty being exacted because he had accepted baptism, had opened his home for meetings, and had remained disobedient after having been warned.[45]

Langenmantel made his way to nearby Göggingen, finding shelter in the home of Laux Lang, brother of Cardinal Matthäus Lang who was also Archbishop of Salzburg. Here he worked arduously although in constant danger of further molestation. He was visited by his brother Bernhard, friends, and other Anabaptist exiles who had been present at the August Synod. Roth says these leaders never left Langenmantel out of their sight, so highly did they esteem his membership in their group.[46] In view of his retraction, one wonders if it was not because they also wished to fortify their wavering brother against ministerial blandishments as well as magisterial banishments.

It is apparent that Langenmantel made furtive visits to Augsburg in spite of the city's ban.[47] Hermann, his rebaptized servant, also made numerous trips into the forbidden precincts in order to secure supplies for his master's necessities. Shortly thereafter, and likely fearing he might be arrested because of his continued forbidden contacts, Langenmantel left Göggingen and went to Langenneufnach where he lived in the inn of Matthew Ehem, a maternal relative. Subsequently he went on to Leitershofen, east of Donauwörth, and later slipped into Augsburg where he felt safer than in the open country. Here he stayed three weeks with his brother Bernhard and then left for Leitershofen because of danger from the city authorities. There Langenmantel, his servant, his wife, and Bernhard Zirgkendorffer and Hans Pfefferlin, two Göggingen peasant Anabaptists, were arrested on April 24, 1528, by the Swabian League captain, Diepold von Stein, and taken to prison in Weissenhorn.[48]

The rest of Langenmantel's story is pathetically brief. Those arrested with him were soon ready to submit to the Catholic demands of their captors, but he held out steadfastly until May 7 when he admitted he had erred in accepting rebaptism and confessed the correctness of the rite as practiced by "the church which cannot err."[49] Some records of the Weissenhorn cross-examinations are extant.[50] The prisoners were asked many questions, some of which show the abiding conviction of the authorities that Anabaptists were plotting against established order and were building up a secret force for surprise attack on the magistrates. On April 30 Langenmantel witnessed that Hut had baptized him along with others; that he himself had never baptized anyone as he did not have the authority to do so, and that he had never plotted with anyone to cause trouble.[51] Later he testified that the Anabaptists had no secret recognition signals or passwords other than the salutation, "God greet you, brother in the Lord," and the response, "God bless you, my brother in the Lord." Then they would converse about the evangel and the Word of God.[52] Hermann Anwaldt testified that when he was baptized the only obligation laid on him was to forsake his sins, follow Christ, love God, and love his neighbor as himself.[53] Signals of recognition included the greeting, "God be with you," and the reply, "Peace be with us."[54] Pfefferlin's testimony agreed with Anwaldt's. Poor Margareta Anwaldt, Hermann's young wife who witnessed that she did not go to services with her husband and never attended any Anabaptist meeting, requested mercy of her judges.[55]

The ruthless way in which these prisoners were disposed of, especially the prominent Langenmantel, causes wonder as to what efforts if any were made on his behalf. Roth's researches made before 1900 in the Augsburg Stadtarchiv found no official document indicating that any of Langenmantel's relatives tried to save him.[56]

But there is a letter by the prisoner dated April 28 which expresses appreciation for efforts made on his behalf by some friends and relatives.[57] Their futility is shown by the fact that in view of the recantations, death by fire was not imposed on the men; instead they were given the "mercy" of the sword on May 11, 1528, by an executioner brought from Memmingen. Because of Langenmantel's rather chronic foot trouble, he was carried to the scaffold in a chair and beheaded while seated therein. Margareta Anwaldt, despite her plea for mercy, was executed the same day by drowning.

Back in Augsburg, the small persecution which the *Rat* had carried on in the spring of 1527 had caused scarcely a stir among the majority of the members of the new movement. The brotherhood was growing partly because of the refugees from other cities and territories who came to Augsburg, some to remain, but others, as pilgrims, to "tarry but a night." Of course, as with Langenmantel, numbers of Augsburg citizens were won to the movement. Even Johann Schneid, pastor of the Holy Cross Church, was wholly on the Anabaptist side but conformed outwardly to the regular practices in order to keep his position.[58]

A survey of the work and influence of the founders and builders of Augsburg Anabaptism—Ludwig Hätzer, Balthasar Hübmaier, Hans Denck, Hans Hut—along with the assistance and discipleship of such men as Eitelhans Langenmantel shows that they had given dedicated service and had won a loyal following which might become outstanding. Frequent mention has been made of the Martyr Synod of August 1527, and as it precipitated the next step in the Augsburg struggle it would be well to take a closer look at it and its meaning for the city's Anabaptists. An excellent statement concerning the character and scope of this memorable gathering is given by C. Hege:[59]

> Some scholars have doubted that the meeting known as the Martyrs' Synod ever took place, and J. J. Kiwiet goes so far as to call it a fiction of Ludwig Keller. Walter Fellmann (*Hans Denck Schriften*, 17f.) gives probably the best analysis of what actually happened, based on the latest research. Several meetings were held, the chief one on Aug. 24, 1527, in the house of Mathias Finder, a butcher. It was at this meeting that the missioners were delegated. One meeting had been held two or three days before this at the house of Gall Fischer, a weaver, one of the deacons of the Augsburg Anabaptist congregation. In these two meetings both Denck and Hut were present, with about 60 others. A third meeting was held at the house of Konrad Huber, also a deacon of the Augsburg congregation, where Hut was present, but Denck absent. Hut calls this latter meeting a "council." Although none of the sessions was a synod in the formal sense that a body of delegates deliberated and adopted binding resolutions, yet there was a consideration of certain points at issue and at least a sort of agreement, in addition to the appointment of

missioners. In this sense the term conference would be justifiable.

Fellmann holds that the conference consisted largely of representatives from the areas where Hut had been preaching, i.e., mostly south and east of Augsburg. Denck was not the presiding officer, as Keller supposed. The major theological point at issue was Hut's chiliastic teaching. He had, among other things, prophesied the second coming of Christ to take place in the spring of 1528. The conference decided, with Hut's agreement, to drop certain of the concrete details of the Hut prophecy, but approved the central idea of the return in 1528. Fellmann holds that the urge to send out missioners was based on the concept of the near return of Christ and the urgency of strengthening the congregations and inaugurating a vigorous evangelistic campaign before the end.

Hut's influence on the gathering was very strong. When the missioners left on their evangelistic travels each took with him a copy of Hut's letter in which he admonished those who were initiated into the apocalyptic secrets of the Kingdom not to take offense at those children of God who proclaimed only a life according to Christ. Hege[60] names eleven of those sent out who were executed by 1529, another in 1535. Others in attendance met persecution deaths soon though not delegated as missioners. Littell gives a more macabre estimate: "Only two or three of the Martyr Synod lived to see the fifth year of the movement."[61] He must mean the missioners, not all of those in attendance.

One could wonder that the *Rat* seemed so indifferent to the Anabaptists if they were numerous. But it is likely that their number has been greatly overestimated. One frequently meets the figure 1,100; but Kiwiet points out that it was a Catholic author who first mentioned that total and that this writer lived a century after the time and scarcely knew the difference between Lutherans and Anabaptists. The chronicler Sender later accepted the above number, only to have Keller become still more specific by saying there were that many *members* in "the Anabaptist congregation in Augsburg in the year 1527."[62] Others estimate that by that time they numbered "eight hundred souls."[63] The evidence Kiwiet offers for discounting the larger numbers is that when Hut said he knew a thousand Anabaptists, he added, "but *in Augsburg* not many"; that when a certain Anabaptist prisoner spoke of many being present at a gathering he meant a total of thirty; that after the Martyr Synod only five were banished from the city; and that after the Easter 1528 arrests, when the congregation was at its largest, only 51 from outside the city and 43 from Augsburg had to appear before the *Rat*. Only one statement mentions a larger number and that was when Marx Mayr testified "they often came together by the hundreds," to which Kiwiet answered that "from the minutes of the Council we know that many citizens went to see these 'Gartenbrüder,' which was the reason the Anabaptists were discovered."[64] Even the August 24 main meeting of the Synod consisted of a relatively small gathering in which about 60 took part. But as in the case of later Quakers, a small group of ardent persons can produce results out of proportion to its size.

In the biographical sketches of the five leaders given earlier in this study, some items concerning the persecution of the Augsburg Anabaptists were given in order to complete the individual histories. A few of these names will appear again in the following accounts only for purposes of continuity.

On August 28[65] the first wave of arrests occurred, catching Jacob Dachser, whose earlier defense of Anabaptism had alarmed the clergy to such an extent that on September 6 Rhegius published *Wider den neuen Tauforden notwendige Warnung an alle Christgläubigen,* uniting the city in the purpose of stern repression. Denck and Hätzer left Augsburg before the arrests started or upon receiving news of Dachser's arrest on September 5. New offenders were discovered and imprisoned upon examination of those previously arrested. Sigmund Salminger was not taken until the eighteenth. Just how many were incarcerated does not appear, but the *Rat* handled them with comparative gentleness. On September 16 a number of prisoners were ordered on oath to avoid all Anabaptist gatherings on penalty. On the seventeenth still more were told the same thing although two or three might gather to read and discuss the Bible—but no assemblies. When some refused to swear, they were counseled, but a few still abstained. As the city pastors worked with them, more consented. Finally only six remained obdurate, among them Frau Salminger, and were led out of the city by the bailiff. Eight others were forever forbidden the city. On September 19, Laux Kreler and wife, six other women, and one man had to take the *Rat's* oath; but two other women who refused were sent out. Pastors Rhegius, Frosch, Agricola, and Keller visited, argued with, and preached to the prisoners but without much effect.[66] On September 23, 26, and 30 a number took the required oath, among them Margareta Anwaldt, wife of Langenmantel's servant. On October 1 those who had taken the oath were called before that body and told to recant. Further sermons followed with a talk by the mayor, Ulrich Rehlinger, but all to little effect, for only two men and two women acceded to the demand. Nine others, among them the tailor, Hans Leupold, upon saying they would cling to their Lord, were immediately led out of the city. The others asked for a three-day period, at the end of which time 44 consented to the demand for recantation, one of them Langenmantel's servant, Anwaldt.

On October 11, the *Rat* published, with trumpet call, a decree forbidding anyone, upon pain of corporal, vital, or financial penalty, to embrace any new teachings, to keep children from baptism, to feed or shelter the "Winkelprediger," or to take part in any gathering. Then for some months the *Rat* left off further harassment of the congregation, perhaps to see how similar problems were handled elsewhere. Public quiet lasted until February 1528.[67]

But what of the leaders still in prison from the fall arrests—Langenmantel, Endres Widholz, Gall Fischer, Hans Kissling, Peter Scheppach, and Hans Hut? These men, except Hut, having proven themselves stubborn and disobedient, were exiled and forbidden to return until the *Rat* gave permission. As has been seen, in the case of Langenmantel at least, this order was disobeyed.[68] Hut's tragic fate prevented his ever getting out of prison alive.

Despite the 1527 arrests, refugee Anabaptists still continued to flock through Augsburg's gates, fleeing mainly from Bavaria, Salzburg, Franconia, and the Austrian territories. If ten were driven out, declared a prisoner, thirty others came in, changing their abodes almost daily and finding shelter in appointed lodgings.[69] Their main power, however, seems to have been broken by the persecution of the fall of 1527,[70] although Kiwiet thinks the 1528 number larger than that of 1527,[71] as does Roth also.[72]

Having branded the Anabaptists in its October 11, 1527, decree as *"wider Gott, christenlich ordnung, guot sitten, erber pollicey"* and as tending toward *"zwayung, spaltung, widerwillen, aufruor, zuo abfallung der oberkait,"*[73] terms which might well have been supplied by Peutinger or Rhegius, the *Rat* could not long continue indifferent or compliant. The continuation of Anabaptist growth and activity, with some members violating their oaths, further shortened the temper of the city rulers. Renewed awareness was also stirred by certain communications. On January 4, 1528, an imperial rescript arrived urging that strong measures be taken against the Anabaptists. Another came from King Ferdinand, the emperor's brother, on February 20 ordering that the *Rat* investigate the still imprisoned baptizers, particularly as to their secret signals, greetings, and scheming. He also sent an unusual deposition by a certain Zuberhans in Stuttgart that there was a growing conspiracy of the Anabaptists, including those in Augsburg, to go 700 strong through the country killing all rulers, monks, and papists, also destroying their churches and convents. Enough believed this accusation to stir the *Rat* to strike a telling blow.[74]

The 1527 harassment had already rid the city of the earlier leaders, but in January 1528, the *Rat* was still clearing its prison of a few of the most determined holdouts; or, as with Jacob Dachser, Jacob Gross, and Sigmund Salminger, burying them in the dungeon where they remained until their recantation—Salminger a few days before Christmas, 1530; Dachser on May 16, 1531, and Gross on June 22, 1531, the last two influenced to this step by two new Augsburg ministers, Wolfgang Musculus and Bonifacius Wolfart.[75]

But even as the old were disappearing, new leaders took their places in the still sizable congregation. The two most outstanding were Leonhard Dorfbrunner and George Nespitzer (Jörg von Passau). Dorfbrunner, ordained to the Catholic priesthood in Bamberg in 1524, joined the Anabaptists in the spring of 1527 upon baptism by Hut. By the Martyr Synod he was sent to Linz, Austria, but he was back in Augsburg by November 10. When he finally left the city, he had baptized about 100 persons there. In January, apparently on his way to Linz, he was arrested in Passau and was burned at the stake. He is said to have baptized about 3,000 persons during his short ministry.[76]

George Nespitzer arrived in Augsburg near Easter 1527, having come from Hut in Passau with the authority to baptize others. He took part in the Martyr Synod and baptized there. Having left the city in time to avoid the September arrests, he returned the week before Lent in 1528. In a gravel pit meeting he was chosen superintendent, partly because of his stirring preaching of God's judgment on the persecutors. He worked arduously to organize circles in the city and the neighboring communities, to bring them into closer union, and to furnish shelters for refugees from other areas.[77]

The decree of October 11, 1527, had not been enforced; consequently the Anabaptists again became numerous, both from refugees and from citizen converts. On April 4, 1528, the Saturday before Palm Sunday, 50 to 60 men and women gathered in a cellar and celebrated the Supper with nine or ten loaves and two tankards of wine. Following this meeting, the superintendents formed a sort of council set up to make sure the truth was taught. Another memorable meeting was held at daybreak on Saturday, April 11, in the home of Gall Fischer who had recently left the city. Nespitzer read, baptized, and preached, the service lasting three hours.[78]

Easter Sunday morning, April 12, there was a gathering held in

Susanna Adolf Doucher's home which was located on a side street. About 100 people—men, women, boys, girls, citizens, and strangers— were there to celebrate the Resurrection. Nespitzer and Hans Leupold were the leaders. Noticing guards nearby, the alarm was given and some in the house were able to escape by way of a side door, but 88 were seized and led away in irons. This number included Nespitzer and his wife, Hans Leupold, and some others who in 1527 had sworn to leave the city or had been banished.

In keeping with prevailing custom, the citizens were separated from those known as strangers, most of whom had spent but a few days in Augsburg. The latter were to swear to leave the city for six years, earlier return to be heavily penalized. Of the 22 men and 22 women, 40 took the oath and left on April 13. So hurriedly was this action taken that Nespitzer was not recognized as the superintendent and was permitted to leave with the others. The man and three women who refused the oath were whipped at the post and the next day beaten out of the city.

It was soon clear that the *Rat* would be more severe with the citizens and those who had lived there for a long time. On April 15, 16, and 20, a total of 16 men and 17 women were either scourged or led out of the city. Four who had just happened to be present at the Easter meeting were fined. Subjected to especially severe punishment were one man and four women who had opened their houses either for shelter or meetings. They were pilloried, branded on their cheeks, then led out of the city. Frau Doucher escaped this severity only because of her pregnancy. A certain Elizabeth Hegenmüller who added ridicule of the sacraments to her other offenses had her tongue cut out and, after recovery, was exiled. Frau Salminger who had broken earlier banishment and those who had refused to swear were scourged out of the city on April 30. Many others were also whipped out.[79]

The most severe penalty of all was reserved for the tailor, Hans Leupold. On October 1, 1527, he had been sentenced to lifelong exile from Augsburg, but he had re-entered the city on March 26, 1528.[80] He had been chosen a superintendent, had served as a messenger, and had won many followers. Having violated his previous sentence and refusing to recant after his Easter arrest, he was beheaded on April 25, the only person other than Hut executed by the Augsburg authorities in all their dealings with the baptizers.[81] However, the *Rat* must share the guilt for the deaths of those who, like Langenmantel, were driven out of the city where they fell victims to the forces of the emperor and the Swabian League.

The Augsburg fellowship had received a serious blow which was so consistently followed up that the conventicles rapidly declined. In addition to the severe punishments, rewards were given to informers who would betray the members and patrons. Many who were sincere believers were thus forced to remain silent and inactive. The number of refugees seeking shelter in the newly harsh city understandably decreased greatly. As no one dared to open homes for their assemblies, some gatherings were held in the open; but soon it was generally accepted that the time for open preaching was past and that each person was to wait for God's leading. Some fled; some swore with mental reservations; others hid their lights. The spirit of bold public witnessing was quenched. The last superintendent in Augsburg was George Schachner of Munich who, with Philip Jäger from the Rhine, lived in Augsburg in July and August 1528. But since they felt themselves checkmated in meetings and observances, both of these men left before the close of August. A few later attempts to rekindle the zeal of Anabaptism in Augsburg were easily suppressed by the authorities.[82] "The last recantations were made in April 1535." "There is no evidence of existing Anabaptist congregations in Augsburg after 1535 although there must have been individual Anabaptists resident in the city at various times."[83] Among these was one of whom special recognition must be made.

Pilgrim Marpeck was "the greatest of the South German and Swiss Anabaptist leaders."[84] Not much is known of his early history; even his birth date is unknown. He was a layman, an engineer, and a mine judge in the Tirol. On January 28, 1528, he lost this position because he would not aid in catching Anabaptists as ordered by the Innsbruck authorities. He thereupon made his way to Augsburg where it is possible he received his "re-baptism."[85] In October 1528 he arrived in Strasbourg where he soon became a leader of the Anabaptists, at the same time managing the wood supply of the city.[86] When he was banished from Strasbourg following a dispute with Bucer in December 1531 he made Augsburg his headquarters for his labors among the South German Brethren.[87] "In late 1544 he moved permanently to Augsburg," and secured employment as an engineer. His Anabaptist activities caused him to be warned a number of times that he should desist, but for some unknown reason the city continued him in his position until his death in 1556.[88] It was during his Augsburg residence that Marpeck wrote a number of letters and books, some of them in his controversy with Schwenckfeld. Two outstanding books were his *Verantwortung* (c. 1543-1546) and his *Testamentserläuterung* (c. 1544), a book of more than 800 pages.[89]

Although Augsburg was early considered a city of refuge for persecuted Anabaptists and was so used by Hübmaier, Denck, Hut, and other less well-known workers and refugees, yet the city stands convicted of a vacillating policy toward them before 1528. In that year, however, its attitude became consistent enough. In the light of that day Augsburg was not cruel, yet it outdid Strasbourg, where enforcement of laws did not result in any executions of Anabaptists. Augsburg, by whatever groups or pressures motivated, succeeded in extinguishing within its bounds "the creative tension, the eager expectancy, the catalytic effect upon church and society which was the original genius of Anabaptism."[90] It was a victorious conclusion—but for whom?

Bernhard Rothmann's Views
on the Early Church

Frank J. Wray

The question of the nature of the early church and its place in the whole span of history played an important part in the religious controversy which swept over Western Europe in the sixteenth century. Far from being a matter of mere academic interest, it was intimately related to the issues of the day and to proposals as to what should be done. The Roman party identified itself with the apostolic church and claimed that its episcopacy had succeeded to the place, power, and authority of the apostles.[1] For Luther, Zwingli, Calvin, and their followers the remnant of the true church had remained within the great church, which they wished to free from the control of the papal Antichrist and from which they aimed to remove the abominations that had been introduced. Theirs was a program of reformation designed to restore an ailing and corrupted church to the health and purity of its early centuries. Anabaptists in general called for a separation from the fallen church and the rebuilding of the church upon its ancient foundations. They in particular stressed the pattern of the church of the New Testament, and in contrast especially to the Reformed party they emphasized the distinction between the Old Testament and the New, between the Israelite community and the Christian church.[2] A noteworthy exception appears to have been the Anabaptist revolutionaries at Münster, among whom the Old Testament pattern was followed. The chief Münsterite spokesman, Bernhard Rothmann, had, however, emphasized the New Testament in the first of his major writings, *Bekentnisse van beyden Sacramenten, Doepe und Nachtmaele* (1533).[3] To what extent, then, did his later writings repudiate his earlier view and to what extent did he accommodate his views of the early church to his new frame of reference? This is the question to which the present essay is directed in attempting to analyze Rothmann's references to the apostles and the early church.

In the *Bekentnisse,* Rothmann defined the church as "an assembly of believing children of God."[4] It is composed of believers only, and its indispensable marks are the true preaching of the gospel, true baptism, and the true Lord's Supper.[5] The proper understanding and practice of the two sacraments must, Rothmann insisted, be based upon the words of Christ and the practice of the apostles.[6] At various points in the tract, Rothmann does refer to nonscriptural sources such as Origen, Tertullian, the Roman missal, Ambrose, Augustine, Pliny the Younger, Cyprian, Heinrich Bullinger, and Sebastian Franck;[7] but his use of them is confined to strengthening his arguments with respect to apostolic usage.

According to Rothmann, true baptism is the entrance to the church and "there is no other gate to eternal life."[8] Yet the essence of the sacrament is not the administration of the rite but the commitment of the believer. "Paul and the other Apostles did not regard highly the elements."[9] Drawing upon I Peter 3:20f., Rothmann argued that baptism saves not because one has been immersed in water but because of "the covenant of a good conscience with God."[10] Repentance, faith, and commitment on the part of the candidate are prerequisites for Christian baptism. In support of this position Rothmann quoted Romans 6:3f., Colossians 2:10-12, Galatians 3:27, and Acts 2:37f., as well as from Origen, *Commentary on the Epistle to the Romans,* V, 8, Tertullian, *On Penance,* VI, and an old collect from a service used after Easter.[11] Baptism on this basis conforms to the institution and command of Christ, "and the Apostles also did not otherwise than their Lord and Master had commanded."[12]

Rothmann denied that there is any evidence that the apostles practiced infant baptism. The fact that they were said to have baptized whole households does not necessarily imply that infants were included any more than in the instances where "all Judea" went out to hear John the Baptist (Matthew 3:5) or when "all Jerusalem" shared King Herod's concern over the news of Christ's birth (Matthew 2:3).[13]

Those who follow any meaning and practice other than that which Christ has commanded and the apostles have used do not engage in Christian baptism but commit a sin and an abuse, for which God shall punish them.[14]

With respect to the Lord's Supper, Rothmann believed that John the Evangelist, Paul, and the "ancient teachers" understood the Supper to be "a meeting in love and an eating and drinking together of believers in Christ, which was commanded by Christ to his memory."[15]

Rothmann held that the original church in Jerusalem had practiced it on this basis.[16] He also quoted at length from Sebastian Franck's *Chronicle*[17] a description of early practices of the church in which the Supper appears to have been accompanied by prayer, reading from and interpreting the Scriptures, the correction of deficiencies or errors within the church, the excommunication of those who were evil and unholy, and provision for the material support of those in need.[18] It is worth noting that this particular quotation places a strong emphasis upon community of goods as a characteristic of the early church.

Rothmann believed that corruption and abuses entered the church very early. The apostles themselves recognized the need for continued teaching after baptism to prevent the members of the church from returning to the old sinful life.[19] He saw evidence of abuses in the time of the apostles themselves. One was the attributing of salvation to the act of baptism instead of the commitment it signifies, as seen in Paul's reference to baptism for the dead (I Corinthians 15:29). Rothmann suggested that here we may find the origin of infant baptism, which follows logically from such a point of view.[20] Infant baptism he regarded as the background for monasticism[21] and the major cause of the fall of the church.[22] Among other abuses he mentioned were the misuse of common property by bishops,[23] the hypocrisy of Ananias and Sapphira (Acts 5:1-10),[24] and the abuse of the Lord's Supper by the church at Corinth (I Corinthians 11:20ff.).[25] Still, the fall of the church as it appeared in Rothmann's *Bekentnisse* was a gradual process, for true baptism was in evidence until the ninth century,[26] and the proper use of the Supper and community of goods lasted until the end of the fourth.[27]

The emphasis upon the New Testament and the apostolic pattern is also revealed in Rothmann's refusal to regard the church as essentially one with the pre-Christian Israelite community. In rejecting the argument in favor of infant baptism by analogy with circumcision, Rothmann declared that the covenant with Abraham applied only to Abraham and his descendants, not to Christians. Those who would enter the covenant of the New Testament must believe for themselves. "We are not now under the Old Testament but under the New. . . . Abraham is not here a figure of Christian parents, but a representation of God the father; likewise, the children of Abraham are no images of the children of Christians but of the believing and reborn children of God."[28]

Thus for Rothmann, Christ and his apostles mark a new departure in the history of salvation characterized by true preaching of the gospel, personal repentance, faith and commitment, believer's baptism, love for one another symbolized in the Lord's Supper and demonstrated in community of goods, and excommunication of the unworthy. Rothmann regarded these characteristics as still valid; hence, the apostolic church was the model for a practical program through which the true church was to be restored.

In October 1534, eleven months after the appearance of the *Bekentnisse,* Rothmann issued his second major work, *Eyne Restitution, edder Eine wedderstellinge rechter unnde gesunder Christliker leer, gelouens unde leuens uth Gades gnaden durch de gemeinte Christi tho Munster an den dach gegeuenn.*[29] This tract may properly be regarded as an apology for the revolution through which the so-called New Israel had been established at Münster earlier in the year.

This time Rothmann defined the church as "an assembly, large or small, which with a true confession of Christ is thus founded upon Christ, that they may keep his words along and fulfill all his will and commandments."[30] Although it appears that the Münsterite policy of expelling those who did not join them violated the voluntary principle and moved in the direction of an exclusive state church, as John Horsch has pointed out,[31] the theory of a church of believers was still maintained both with respect to Münster and the early church. Rothmann summarized the gospel which Christ commanded the apostles to preach as follows: "Repent, and be sorry for your sins. Believe the Gospel that Christ died for your sins and let yourselves be baptized in his name, to the washing away of your sins; so shall you receive the gift of the Holy Spirit, that you may have the desire to keep God's commandment."[32] This is the message which Peter preached at Pentecost,[33] and the apostles were afraid, according to Rothmann, to baptize anyone without a previous indication of faith. Thus Philip baptized the Ethiopian treasurer only upon confession of faith, and Peter would never have been so bold as to order that Cornelius and those with him be baptized had they not already received the Holy Spirit.[34]

In the *Restitution,* as in his earlier work, Rothmann held community of goods to be a characteristic of the early church. This time, however, he equated the practice to the fellowship of the saints and made it indispensable. One cannot be a Christian, Rothmann declared, unless he is in such a fellowship or at least desires to be so.[35]

With respect to the Lord's Supper, Rothmann made no reference to the apostolic practice beyond its original institution by Christ. He did, however, claim that at Münster they assembled at a stated place and examined themselves so that they might worthily enter upon it, show forth the death of the Lord with true faith, and break bread together in true love. They also prayed for all kinds of needful things, especially for the brothers and sisters who were still subject to "the dragon." Then they remedied any deficiency in the church.[36] Although Rothmann did not say so, it appears that he may have had in mind the practice which he attributed to the early church in his *Bekentnisse*.

As in the *Bekentnisse,* Rothmann held that the fall of the church began in the time of the apostles, but the reason assigned and the scriptural references are different. For evidence he cited Philippians 3, I John 2, and II Peter 2, and the reason given was not the introduction of infant baptism but human reason, wisdom, and pleasure. The fall was also much more rapid, for within a century after the ascension of Christ falsehood held sway.[37]

A definite increase in Rothmann's anti-intellectualism is to be seen not only in the new reasons for the fall of the church, but also in an additional characteristic he attributed to the apostolic church. Christ's gospel had been delivered to "innocent, poor, simple, unlearned fishermen and ill-bred people."[38] In the *Bekentnisse,* it is true, Rothmann had rejected human wisdom and hairsplitting and had found the "rational theologians and scholars" among the supporters of error;[39] but, as we have seen, he did not hesitate to refer to nonscriptural sources. In the *Restitution,* however, Clement, Tertullian, and other ancient writers appear not as witnesses to apostolic usage but as examples of learned writers through whom the devil has obscured the truth.[40] The restitution of the true church, like the founding of the apostolic one, is to be accomplished not by the intellectuals but through the most unlearned men, such as Melchior Hoffmann, Jan Matthys, and Jan of Leyden, "who is entirely unlearned in the opinion of the world."[41]

Most significant, however, is Rothmann's change in his theology of history and the place of the early church therein. In the *Restitution* Rothmann viewed history as a series of attempts on the part of the devil to overthrow the word of God. These attempts have resulted in a series of "falls" on the part of man, but each time God has restored what has fallen. Thus the original fall of Adam was restored when Adam and his descendents were taught by the Spirit of God and commanded to do his will and to await his promises. The result of a fall from this restitution was the Flood and another restitution in Noah. The same process was repeated with respect to Abraham,

Moses, the prophets, and finally Christ, in whom the most nearly complete restitution was made. Even so, the restoration in Christ and the early church was only a beginning, for it was followed by a fall deeper than any previous one. The next restitution is to be an eternal one and a completion of what was begun in Christ.[42]

This view of the place of the early church in the history of salvation robs it of some of its uniqueness and hence also of some of its value as a model. Furthermore, if the restitution in the first coming of Christ was only a beginning, we might expect the full restitution to be something other than an exact replica of the early church. Indeed, this was the case in Rothmann's thinking. Not all of the prophecies were fulfilled in the New Testament.[43] Rothmann now wrote in terms of the "Kingdom of Christ," which he viewed as a literal one in which Christ will actually rule as king.[44] In the time of restitution, which Rothmann believed was at hand, Christians, unlike the apostles, may use force. There was a time of the Cross and "Babylonian captivity." There is also a time of release, in which the godless shall be repaid in double measure through the same means they have used against God and his people.[45] In setting forth these views, Rothmann claimed that his eschatology was the same as that of the apostles, but that it had not been rightly understood since their time.[46]

The uniqueness and importance of the early church was also diminished by Rothmann's new view of the relationship between the Old and New Testaments. In the *Restitution* his position on this point is almost the reverse of what it had been in the *Bekentnisse*. The Old Testament is not obsolete. Certain practices, such as sacrifices, fire, washings, dietary laws, and the ark of the covenant, are indeed no longer binding upon Christians, for the spirit and truth symbolized by these have been fulfilled in Christ. This is true also of the Sabbath, since Christians regard every day as holy and are to cease from their own works and will to do that of God. Yet the law has not been superceded but restored. Christ came not to abrogate the law and the prophets but to fulfill them. Christ and the apostles had no other scripture than the Old Testament, which Paul and the other apostles cited. The Old Testament contains not only promises to the faithful which have been fulfilled in Christ but also unfulfilled matters relating to the Kingdom of Christ. The New Testament does indeed "testify of Christ and his testament, but it does not stand alone." Its foundation and truth has been determined by Moses and the prophets.[47]

Rothmann's argument for polygamy rests upon this conception of the relationship between the Old and New Testaments. It is clear, he held, that polygamy was permissible in the Old Testament and is nowhere forbidden in the New.[48] In fact, I Timothy 3, according to Rothmann's opinion, indicates that polygamy was permissible in the time of the apostles.[49]

In December 1534, two months after the *Restitution*, Rothmann issued *Eyn gantz troestlick bericht van der Wrake unde straffe des Babilonischen gruwels*,[50] which was a call to all "true Israelites and covenanters in Christ" to join in the destruction of the "Babylonian power." Here he stresses particularly the difference between the time of the apostles and the time of the restitution. The former is the period for proclaiming, embracing, and spreading the Kingdom of Christ. The apostles, however, did not have the power to enforce it. Men did not want Christ to rule them, and they scorned and killed all who worked for the Kingdom of Christ. God waited with patience until the godless had fulfilled the measure of their evil. Now, however, the time of wrath and recompense is at hand.[51]

Rothmann's conception of the relationship between the Old and New Testaments in this pamphlet appears to be essentially the same as in the *Restitution*. He claims that both the prophets and the apostles have foreseen the events which are taking place, and he cites references to both Testaments: Deuteronomy, Isaiah, Jeremiah, Daniel, Ezekiel, Joel, Micah, Zechariah, Malachi, Matthew, Luke, Acts, Romans, and II Thessalonians.[52] The captivity of the historic Israel by Babylon prefigures the history of the church,[53] and the new David (i.e., Jan of Leyden) is preparing the way for the new Solomon.[54] At the end of the pamphlet he called upon the brethren to arm themselves for battle, "not only with the humble weapons of the Apostles for suffering, but also with the glorious armor of David for vengeance."[55] His reference to apostolic weapons here seems, however, to contradict a previous statement, for early in the pamphlet he had advised the brethren to "let fall the apostolic weapons and take up the armor of David."[56] From the general context of the pamphlet and the circumstances under which it was produced, perhaps one might venture to construe Rothmann's meaning in the following manner. The latter statement is evidently aimed at those Anabaptists who practiced non-violence and defenselessness on the ground that they should follow the example of the apostles. The other statement probably means that in addition to using force the brethren should retain the steadfast endurance and boldness of the apostles in the face of all kinds of hardship and opposition. Marginal references to II Corinthians 6 and 10 appear to confirm this interpretation.

In February 1535, Rothmann published another tract under the title *Von Verborgenheitt der Schrifft des Rickes Christi und von dem dage des Herrn durch die gemeinde Christi zu Münster*.[57] Here Rothmann unequivocally adopted the Old Testament as the standard by which all else is to be measured. "The principal true Scripture," he declared, "is Moses and the Prophets." These contain what is sufficient for salvation. There are other praiseworthy books which may be called Holy Scripture, but these have their basis in Moses and the Prophets and must be judged according to them. Especially is this true of the New Testament, in which we find statements such as, "This happened in order that the Scripture may be fulfilled," and, "Thus it is written." Thus the New Testament is an indication that the principal part is actually fulfilled in Christ.[58]

Rothmann's periodization of world history also suggests that the apostolic age does not constitute a sharp break with ancient Israel. History is divided into three principal periods, or "worlds." The first extends from Adam to Noah. The second covers the period from Noah to the time of the restitution, that is, to Rothmann's own time. The third age will usher in the Kingdom of God.[59] Yet within this framework Rothmann did not make the church identical with the pre-Christian Israelite community, a distinction which apparently enabled Rothmann to appropriate certain elements of the Old Testament without taking the ceremonial law or embracing Judaism wholesale. A new period *(newtit)* and a new divine service did begin in Christ, and "the physical descendants of Abraham together with all figurative outward ceremonies, also the outward physical Jerusalem and the Temple were entirely overturned and devastated. For God's word and action which was carried on with Abraham and his descendants was simply a prefiguration."[60]

Rothmann further divided the period between the Incarnation and the second coming of Christ into two parts, as he had done previously in the *Restitution* and in his *Van der Wrake*. The first part is the time of suffering, in which the swords that the apostles purchased[61] were kept sheathed until the godless and Antichrist have increased the measure of their evil and the number of saints has been fulfilled. The second part is that of the restitution (that is, the present) when Christians shall make use of the sword.[62] As before, Rothmann claimed that the Apostles had shared his eschatological views.[63]

In his concept of the church, Rothmann still retained personal faith as an indispensable ingredient. An active commitment to Christ and the fulfilling of the commands and will of God were essential to being a Christian. Baptism signifies such a commitment, and the Lutherans were condemned by Rothmann because they would not enter the "right way to all righteousness" through baptism. Paul and the other apostles preached nothing else than a faith in which men surrendered themselves to Christ that they might become "conformed to Him in all righteousness and holiness."[64]

Rothmann's treatment of the fall of the church was much like that in his *Restitution*. Corruption was evident in the time of the apostles themselves, and the truth of Christ remained undefiled for less than a century.[65] The cause is to be found in men's preference for human opinion over obedience to God.[66] Here one of the opinions which he specifically denounces as a source of corruption is the doctrine of the Trinity.[67] This apparent anti-Trinitarianism is not, however, based on a rationalistic or humanistic approach and is really not a denial of the Trinity as such. It is instead a reflection of Rothmann's anti-intellectual and anti-speculative attitude.

In his essay *Van erdisschen unnde tytliker gewalt. Bericht uith Gotlyker schryfft*,[68] dated in 1535 but probably unfinished, Rothmann reveals much the same view with respect to the place of the early church in the history of salvation as he did in the *Restitution*. Christians were the successors of Israel, which had violated the law and had therefore been rejected by God.[69]

In conclusion, it appears that Rothmann specifically repudiated the apostolic church on one point only: the use of force. Even in this case, the rejection was not complete, for Rothmann claimed to have remained true to the eschatological vision of the apostles. The non-resistance of the apostles was right for their time, but, according to Rothmann, that time had passed.

Throughout the writings considered here Rothmann conceived of both the apostolic church and the church of the restitution as one made up of committed believers. Baptism was administered only on the basis of such faith and commitment in the time of the apostles and in the restored church. Community of goods was regarded as an apostolic practice essential to the church, and the communion service at Münster as described by Rothmann appears to bear considerable resemblance to what he believed the procedure of the early church had been. In the later writings another characteristic common to both the apostolic and the restored churches was that the truth is apprehended by the unlearned.

Perhaps the greatest change in Rothmann's thinking was the role of the early church in his theology of history. Rothmann's *Restitu-*

tion was in fact a repudiation of this part of his *Bekentnisse*. In November 1533, the New Testament, not the Old, and the early church, not ancient Israel, furnished the norm and the pattern, as Rothmann conceived them, for the rebuilding of the true church of Christ. A year later he regarded the two Testaments as more or less a unit; and while the church was not identical with the Israelite community, the New Testament and the apostolic church were viewed in the light of the Old Testament. The apostles were seen as the bearers of and witnesses to an ancient truth which had been partially fulfilled in Christ and part of which was still to be fulfilled. The apostles were not repudiated outright, but their role was fitted into a new frame of reference whereby they could appear to support the new regime at Münster. In the later tracts Rothmann kept essentially the same position except that the normative value of the Old Testament received greater emphasis, with the early church becoming progressively less significant in this respect.

Fecund Problems of Eschatological Hope, Election Proof, and Social Revolt in Thomas Müntzer

Lowell H. Zuck

Thomas Müntzer has been a problem child of Reformation study to all who have heard of him since 1520. He has been rejected by Lutherans from the time of his first conflict with Luther, but Baptists of German origin are equally reluctant to claim him as their father though it would be logical to do so. Heinrich Boehmer, a Lutheran, described him as the "founder of the great Baptist movement,"[1] while Mennonite scholars, from the standpoint of their pioneer Baptist fellowship, regard him as always having remained a Lutheran.[2]

Müntzer does enjoy the dubious honor at the present time, though no Christian denomination honors him, of being promoted as the first modern European to anticipate the utopia of communist faith. Even in that Marxist haven of dogmatic security, however, the latest on Müntzer is that Russian scholars are no longer in agreement that he was truly revolutionary.[3] One may quietly rejoice, perhaps, that even the Russians cannot agree about Müntzer.

Yet this latest disagreement leaves Müntzer's reputation and significance still very much at the mercy of unsettled historic and theological arguments. We here cannot pretend to settle deep-seated differences in interpretation of Müntzer. Our purpose is merely to consider, on the basis of his life, the importance of the problems which he raised so vividly but answered so unconvincingly. The most notable of these problems are: Does eschatological hope result in responsible life; can election be proved; and is revolution in church and society a Christian imperative?

A review of the details of Müntzer's brief life is necessary in order to describe the significance he placed upon religious hopes, election, and social revolt. His life parallels Luther's and since Müntzer's major conflict was with Luther, comparisons and contrasts are in order. About six years younger than Luther, Müntzer grew up in the Harz mountain area of Thuringia, at Stolberg and Quedlinburg, slightly northwest of Luther's boyhood home. The little we know of Müntzer's parents and education indicates a similar background to that of Luther, removed from extreme poverty yet close to peasant stock. Like Luther, Müntzer was a bright student and took advantage of the best German education of the day as it was emerging from scholastic doldrums. He matriculated at Leipzig University in 1506, attended the University of Frankfurt on the Oder, showed facility in biblical languages, may have taken a doctor's degree, became a secular priest, served as provost of a monastery near Halle around 1514, and developed his medieval spiritual sensibilities as confessor to a Thuringian convent around 1519.[4] Müntzer met Luther at this time, either in person or through reputation and correspondence, and allied himself immediately with his equally fiery but greater colleague from the regular clergy. Müntzer's choice to become a secular cleric, rather than an otherworldly regular monk like Luther, may be evidence for Müntzer's greater radicalism from the beginning. Seidemann maintains that Müntzer was present and supported Luther in the debate with Eck at Leipzig in 1519.[5] Luther seems also to have encouraged Müntzer when he came into conflict with the Franciscans in Leipzig. Müntzer may have attended lectures by Luther at this time. Luther was the prime mover, at any rate, in securing for Müntzer a position as substitute pastor in 1520 at Zwickau, the "pearl of Saxony," then in the midst of religious and economic unrest among the miners. The cool Erasmian pastor, Egranus, had had little control over his church nearing revolution in Zwickau. It was at Zwickau that Müntzer's excited religious hopes based upon assurance of election first resulted in radical upheaval.

In a significant article on "Luther and the Fanatics," Karl Holl claimed that Müntzer showed himself to be an original genius when he worked out a theology of election based upon a mysticism of the cross, which brought assurance of election through inward religious experience and resulted in dynamic religious and social action.[6] Roland Bainton developed Holl's view of Müntzer further when he gave Müntzer credit for beginning a new variety of theocracy, the Protestant type based on piety, which flowered late among New England Puritans who strove mightily to supplant the older theocratic methods of Hebrew tribalism and Catholic sacramentalism.[7] Bainton like Holl emphasized that Müntzer was the pioneer reformer to identify the elect by means of feeling, conversion, or piety. When one adds to this the driving spiritual power of Müntzer's eschatological hope and the Marxist insight that Müntzer was the first religious reformer to anticipate a fundamental reformation of society, the fecund nature of his inspiration becomes apparent. Yet the problem of Müntzer looms large also. In spite of all of this originality, Müntzer was thwarted in practice by his lamentable fanaticism, self-delusion, and irresponsibility. Already at Zwickau the fatal flaws in Müntzer appeared.

Müntzer was a born demagogue who impressed his hearers as breath-takingly eloquent and marvelously self-possessed, although his sombre piety tended to conceal the fact that his spiritual development had been marked by inward doubt and turmoil. In Zwickau he found responsive followers when he showed his colors immediately upon arrival. Müntzer's first sermon launched a blistering attack upon the wealthy and influential Franciscans of the town. As a result of the charges and countercharges, Müntzer gained the support of the Town Council, and when Luther heard of his boldness he approved. Zwickau had a tradition of radicalism associated with the Waldenses and the revolutionary Taborite Bohemian brethren. Moreover, economic unrest had resulted from the rich silver mines nearby, and the jealous guild of weavers began to demand justice for the lower classes. Müntzer's religious life was stimulated by a master weaver and biblical prophet from the lower classes, Nicholas Storch of Zwickau.

Storch and his Zwickau prophets, Marcus Stübner and Thomas Drechsel, had created a sensation by their visit to Wittenberg in December of 1521. Evidently Müntzer did not accompany them on that mission, although in his "Letter to the Princes of Saxony Concerning the Rebellious Spirit," Luther stated that "he (Müntzer) has been once or twice in my cloister at Wittenberg and had his nose punched."[8] One scarcely knows how literally this should be taken. The excited dreams, visions, and immediate revelations of the Zwickau prophets had intimidated Melanchthon and Amsdorf during Luther's absence. Storch's vivid eschatological hope impressed his hearers greatly. He claimed that with his gift of prophecy he could forsee that God was about to wipe out the present spiritual and earthly authorities in the church, and that the divine Kingdom would be inaugurated by God's own pious, bold people.[9] When Luther heard of what was going on in Wittenberg, he felt it necessary to return immediately from exile at Wartburg in spite of personal danger to himself. Back home in Wittenberg, Luther brusquely rejected the prophets and restored order through a famous series of gentle but exceedingly firm sermons. Luther proved by his acts on this occasion that he had little confidence in visionaries deriving from the common people. He did not regard himself as one of them. The paradox of Luther is evident here. He was strong enough to reject the prejudices of his own background, yet he thereby lost something vital and relevant to the faith of common men. Müntzer, on the contrary, adopted as his own the increasingly spiritualistic and revolutionary views of Storch. But in so doing Müntzer showed less self-confidence than Luther. The active and emotional master weaver, Storch, had become dominant over the early Müntzer who until then had been scholarly, pastoral, and Lutherlike.[10]

Müntzer did not remain in Zwickau longer than April of 1521. He preferred to begin rather than to complete radical religious reforms, and we find him next traveling to the city of Prague, perhaps in imitation of Storch's pilgrimage there the year previously. At Prague, Müntzer made known his eager eschatological hopes. His purpose in entering the city was to proclaim the immediate fulfillment of the divine rule in that Bohemian center of Hussite reform and revolution, and he made bold claims for his own prophetic mission. Müntzer prepared four different versions of his "Prague Manifesto," two in German, one in Czech, and one in Latin.[11] The different versions betray some calculation in Müntzer's message, since his message of divine judgment whispered more softly to the upper classes and scholars in Latin while it bristled with fanaticism in the vernacular. He not only spoke of general fulfillment of eschatological hope to come but also outlined a program for the inauguration of a "new church," the church of the spirit, composed of the elect friends of God. Müntzer here referred to the familiar radical teaching that Christianity had been falling since the time of the apostles, but he assured his followers that the true church was about to be restored in the latter days when God would bring his elect to victory and complete the overthrow of the ungodly. But the Bohemians had had enough revolution for the present. They were little disposed to dream of the promised era of the church of the spirit or the world of complete social equality; nor were they intimidated by Müntzer's threats of the judgment of God upon them through a disastrous Turkish invasion, if they should fail to repent and take positive steps in preparation for the coming of the Messianic Kingdom. Müntzer left Bohemia in disgust and, after a period of restless wandering, returned to a new ministerial post at Allstedt in the mining area of Saxony, where his ideas were more warmly received.

In Allstedt Müntzer found the kind of unsettled, lawless community which responded readily to his appeals for active religious demagoguery. His enthusiasm brought followers. The townspeople heard him gladly, but the peasants and miners around Allstedt were even more in agreement with his urgent calls for reform. While he was at Allstedt, Müntzer married a former nun who bore him a son, and his sensitive liturgical reform in the church was another fruit of this balanced period of his life. Indeed, his work in writing a German Mass, fully choral, and in preparing beautiful congregational matins and vespers, made him the pioneer liturgical reformer of the sixteenth century and one of the most gifted of them all, perhaps more liturgically inspired than Butzer, Luther, or Thomas Cranmer.[12]

More than before, Müntzer now felt himself called to a rigorous divine mission. All of the extant Allstedt sermons and tracts drive home Müntzer's insistence that "inexperienced faith" on the part of theologians, pastors, and people would not be enough, that only those who possessed inward, emotional proofs of their election could aid in achieving the spiritual victory which Müntzer felt was sure to come. In his "Fuerstenpredigt," Müntzer warned the princes of Saxony that only those who had experienced inner proof of their election would be saved: ". . . none may be saved unless the . . . Holy Spirit have previously assured one of salvation."[13] "Such learned divines . . . wish to instruct the whole world ... And yet [they] are not even assured of their own salvation."[14] Müntzer said of both Catholics and Lutherans that "they mix up nature and grace without any distinction."[15] "The more nature gropes after God, the further the operation of the Holy Spirit withdraws itself."[16] Thus, Müntzer claimed, the "learned divines" "impede the progress of the Word . . . which comes forth from the deeps of the soul . . . you may ask, How does it then come into the heart? Answer: It comes down from God above in exalted and terrifying astonishment." Müntzer had come to distrust the Catholic concern with perfection of nature through grace as well as the Lutheran interpretation of justification with its lack of concern about the way in which the divine Spirit might overcome the natural man. He accused both faiths of externality and shallowness: "He [who has not the Spirit] does not know how to say anything deeply about God, even if he had eaten through a hundred Bibles!"[17] Quotations from Müntzer about the testimony of God from the deeps of the soul ("von Abgrund der Seelen herkoemmt") can be further substantiated in each of his six major works, including the "Protestation odder Empiettung" and "Ausgedrückte Entblössung des Falschen Glaubens."[18] The origin of this terminology seems to have been from the medieval mystical tradition which Müntzer had absorbed from Suso and Tauler, though its connection with mysticism centering in the Cross of Christ was related to Luther's view also. Luther retained less of mystical experience, however, when as an evangelical reformer he spoke of his trust in Christ and the Cross. It was this inward test for election, more than anything else, which bolstered the confidence of Thomas Müntzer and assured his followers of the genuineness of their own election, releasing energies for further radical acts in state and church.

Müntzer's preaching now grew even more excited and radical. He allowed no criticism of his ideas. When his patron, the Count of Mansfield, condemned his preaching and liturgical reform at Allstedt as heretical, Müntzer struck back from the pulpit against his employer and superior with unexpected fury. From this time on, Müntzer signed his letters with an emphatic "Thomas Müntzer, Destroyer of the Unfaithful."[19] It was not meant as a metaphor. But what further action could he take against the orders of his patron? Müntzer turned again to the Bible for illumination, and was rewarded with a further discovery. From the pages of the Old Testament the answer came this time. Here was the proposal of God himself. Self-disgust may have overwhelmed him as he recognized that he had depended too much upon his own efforts to accomplish the designs of God. Could the Lord of heaven and earth forgive impious self-delusion? Could it be that his dependence on the "living Spirit" had been reliance upon his own spirit, that his efforts to follow the "bitter Christ" had been only a veiled attempt to set up himself as a bitter Christ to be followed? Suddenly the answer had come from Scripture, in the midst of his meditation. In inner ecstasy, Müntzer received the demand of God that his people at Allstedt swear a solemn *covenant* with the Lord of heaven and earth and with each other, to fulfill his commands completely. Something more than ecclesiastical correctness of the preached Word and rightly performed sacraments was needed in this situation. Why had he omitted the covenant earlier? Müntzer now realized that this was to be the means by which God elects and disciplines his holy people. The covenant was the answer, in Germany as well as among the Israelites of old. With suppressed excitement Müntzer wrote his friend, the mayor Hans Zeiss, in July 1524 that he had just preached from II Chronicles 34:31 about finding the book of the law and making a covenant between God and his people. Just as Hilkiah had found the book of the law, and as the high priest had made a covenant with God and the whole people within the Temple, so Müntzer saw that it was his divine mission to covenant with God and all the faithful of Allstedt, that they would inquire into the law and keep it with their whole heart and soul.[20]

Müntzer felt that he had to have a precise object of attack in order that zealous followers could feel the literal necessity of swearing to the covenant and slaying the godless. He already had the allegiance of most of the masses. His bold attack upon the Count of Mansfield had attracted two thousand of the curious and discontented miners of Mansfield and the surrounding area to Müntzer's preaching, while at home the artisans and peasants idolized the fiery prophet. Now was the time to attack. Outside Allstedt was a beautiful pilgrimage chapel venerating the Virgin Mary. Müntzer demanded its violent destruction by fire. "The chapel is a cave of vice," he ranted; "the worship of the Virgin is nothing but idolatry."[21] His hearers were persuaded not only by the appeal to iconoclasm, always present among Reformation radicals, but also because the rich chapel symbolized the pretension and wealth of the Roman church in the unsympathetic eyes of the lower classes. Within a few days, Müntzer successfully swore the masses into his covenant of the elect, and the Mallerbach chapel was burned to the ground. His confederates covenanted to "stand up for the Gospel, to pay no more tithes, and to help wipe out monks and nuns."[22] Müntzer's covenant of the elect was self-conscious religious revolt in the name of the common people, demanding the allegiance of the magistrate for their program, and boldly claiming Reformation leadership for Allstedt instead of Wittenberg.

The purpose of Müntzer's covenant of the elect was quite clear. Those who had sworn the covenant of the elect aimed at control of the church and society. But what attitude would the magistrates and Müntzer's rivals for the leadership of the church take? Undoubtedly Luther would never tolerate Müntzer's announcement that he was appointed to take the place of Luther as leader of the Reformation movement. Luther had not hesitated an instant in rebuffing the covenant proposals of the Zwickau prophets. Müntzer was already identified with fanatical Zwickau enthusiasm, but, in addition, his open appeals to revolution and violence frightened Luther, a realistic conservative who depended on the magistrate and the state to restrain evil, never dreaming that saints could aspire to domination of worldly society. For all his strength and self-possession in the service of the gospel, Martin Luther shuddered before the audacity and presumption of Thomas Müntzer. For the conservative Luther, only anarchy and worse would result if the two kingdoms were to be confounded, as Müntzer was proposing.

Luther advised the princes to smite the religious fanatics, if they should draw the sword. The princes wavered, waiting uneasily to see which of the religious leaders could command the loyalties of dissatisfied common people and peasants. They knew that Müntzer's covenant was more than incitement to revolt and violence in the name of the underprivileged. The more positive program of the covenant probably envisaged restoration of apostolic sharing of goods and establishment of a brotherhood of love. The privileges of the nobility were to be restricted when the new covenant was put into effect. Müntzer specified that community of goods need not mean complete abandonment of rank. For instance, distribution of horses to the nobility was to follow a schedule: the princes were to be allowed eight, the counts four, and noblemen two horses.[23] Here was no dishonoring of authority, but it was evident that the nobles were to be subordinate, not dominating, in the covenant of the elect.

The authorities debated whether Müntzer or Luther was advocating true evangelical doctrine. At first, some of the princes leaned toward the truth of Müntzer's position. During Müntzer's earlier conflict with the Count of Mansfield, Hans Zeiss, the Allstedt mayor, in uncertainty about the truth of conflicting religious positions, advocated the traditional method of settling religious disputes, an open disputation at Wittenberg between Müntzer and Luther. But careful avoidance of a disputation, cultivated by other magistrates, only increased the uncertainty. The princes frequently suspected Luther's intentions, and Luther always distrusted the political motivation of the princes. Luther went so far as to refer to the cool young politician, Prince Frederick of Saxony, with the biting epithet "princeps dissimulans et ferians." On the other hand, Duke John of Saxony was half convinced that Müntzer's position might be the true one, because his chief preacher at Weimar, Wolfgang Stein, influenced by Karlstadt and Jacob Strauss, was complaining that the revival of imperial law was unjust and unchristian, and that Mosaic law should be restored within society.[24] Frederick the Wise, like his brother Duke John, was unwilling to move rapidly against Müntzer. Young Prince Frederick exhibited the most eagerness to stand with Luther, but the radical preaching of Strauss and Stein made him hesitate to condemn similar appeals for social reform and revolution by Müntzer. In response to their requests, Luther preached twice on worldly authority at the Weimar court in 1522, and he dedicated his "Von Weltlicher Obrigkeit" to Duke John. Luther insisted that the princes must restrain evil by means of the sword, according to Romans 13. They must remember, he insisted, that *no* Kingdom of God is possible in this world.

The princes traveled to Allstedt to hear personally how Müntzer regarded the office of the magistrate. Characteristically, Müntzer aimed his sermon directly at them, demanding that they submit themselves to his authority as administrator of the divine covenant. Not to be outdone by Luther, Müntzer had his own interpretation of Romans 13. He maintained that one must not allow such great weight to the first verse, "Let every soul be subject to the authorities, for they are ordained of God." Rather, Luther should have emphasized verse four, "The authorities are a *minister* of God for good; but if you do evil, be afraid, for they bear the sword to avenge evil." Müntzer went on to show that Romans 13 did not mean meek subordination of the people to the magistrate, as Luther taught. Rather, the people are the authority; they are good. The magistrates are their ministers. Moreover, the task of the people is destruction of the godless, through the covenant of the elect. Müntzer turned Luther's text for obedience to the magistrate into a revolutionary demand that the princes minister to the elect by wiping out the ungodly.

In a letter of October 1523 to Prince Frederick the Wise, Müntzer reminded him of his duty to support the elect, and made clear to Frederick that Müntzer, not Luther, had correctly identified the elect.[25] But in his sermon to the princes, Müntzer was not content with finding revolution in St. Paul. He used a more inflammatory text, the second chapter of Daniel, to prove that the Lord would complete the history of salvation by means of the divine covenant, and that he had elected a new Daniel (Müntzer) to lead the faltering princes into actual realization of the eschatological Kingdom on earth, the long awaited Fifth Monarchy. What should the princes do? "Wipe out the godless," said Müntzer,

> You are a holy people. Do not spare the ungodly! Break their images, smash their altars, and burn them completely. Wipe out the ungodly with the sword! If you refuse, the sword will be taken from you. Priests and monks who deny the Holy Gospel shall die! Remember that Nebuchadnezzar wisely appointed Daniel to judge what the Holy Spirit has spoken. Only the elect know the future. The godless have no right to live.[26]

Curiously, Müntzer's bold proposal to lead the princes into destruction of the ungodly did not disturb them very much, and they did not think it necessary to act against him immediately. July 13, 1524 ended with Müntzer in safety, and the princes seemed only mildly irritated by his abusive sermon. As long as Müntzer appealed for their support in his program, the princes felt no great apprehension, though understandably they were hesitant in yielding to a bloodthirsty Daniel. But on July 24, Müntzer preached a covenant-sermon which stirred the princes into action against him. They recognized a threat in the secret covenant organization. In his covenant-sermon, Müntzer made it clear that the deafness of the princes toward his program did not eliminate his agency for revolutionary action, which was the secretly sworn covenant of the elect. He was preparing the Allstedt covenanters to inaugurate the revolution, whether or not the princes paid attention to his program. Hans Zeiss continued to be troubled about his duty as a magistrate in Allstedt and reported Müntzer's covenant-sermon to Duke George on July 28, asking whether this preaching was from God, since one ought not resist it if it was.[27] At this point the princes realized that Müntzer's control over a secret revolutionary organization might be dangerous to the state. They summoned him to a hearing at Weimar on August 1.

Müntzer and his Allstedt companions could not conceal their aims from the princes at Weimar nor did they intend to do so. The contradictions in his program were evident. On the one hand, Müntzer recommended willingness to suffer, a mysticism of the cross, without any attention to material goods. On the other hand, he was prepared to lead a social revolution of the peasants and common people, aimed toward community of goods and substitution of the authority of the people for that of the princes. But contradictions in Müntzer did not prevent the princes from recognizing that their fears of a revolutionary covenant organization had some justification. Duke John stiffened, and as a result of the Weimar hearings Müntzer was ordered to disband his covenant organization and to print no more inflammatory writings.

The decisive order from the princes against Müntzer's covenant of the elect checked his influence very quickly. The revolutionaries were quite ineffectual when it came to a showdown. Outwardly Müntzer did not seem to be cowed. He resumed fiery preaching about the covenant on his return to Allstedt, but most of the leaders among his confederates hesitated to defy their princes. Müntzer now addressed his former friend, Nickel Rueckert, as "Judas Iscariot." The Town Council remained steadfast in its new decision to follow the lead of the princes, who were insistent that Müntzer must be kept under control.

Realizing that he could no longer work effectively in Saxony, Müntzer fled about a week later from Allstedt. Muhlhausen in Thuringia was Müntzer's destination, where seething economic unrest aided his revolutionary intentions. Here also he found another revolutionary pastor, Heinrich Pfeiffer, who had already located a base for agitation against the Town Council in the lower-class tradesmen. By his flight from Saxony, Müntzer was assured of a hearing for his covenant-preaching, and the Saxon princes could not block his publishing activities after he had entered Thuringia. Before going to Muhlhausen, Müntzer sought out a radical colporteur in Thuringia, Hans Hut, and entrusted him with publication of another revolutionary tract, "Ausgedrückte Entblössung des Falschen Glaubens" ("Open Denial of False Belief"). Hut, who became one of the important early leaders in South German Anabaptism, printed it with the aid of employees of a Nürnberg printer.[28] Pfeiffer and Müntzer were able to win a quick victory over the Town Council in Muhlhausen, but their triumph was short-lived, and the fleeing Müntzer spent two months in South Germany and Switzerland fanning the flames of the Peasants' War, in the areas where that revolt had begun.[29] By early 1525 Pfeiffer and Müntzer were back again in Muhlhausen, and Müntzer now became the preacher of the peasants and the most notorious leader of the Peasants' War, where his quixotic enthusiasm resulted in one of the tragic massacres of history, though his faith in the realization of the covenant of the elect continued until the end. At the battle of Frankenhausen, Müntzer's fanaticism goaded the peasants into the climactic tragedy of the Peasants' War, where the armies of the Protestant Prince Philip of Hesse and the Catholic Prince George of Saxony massacred half of the 10,000 sheeplike peasants without opposition on May 15, 1525. Müntzer, attempting to escape, was caught, imprisoned, tortured, made a good confession, and calmly accepted his execution by beheading on May 27. Only the legend of Thomas Müntzer now remained for nonconformists to ponder and as a basis for repression of radical groups by the leaders of church and state.[30]

The conclusion of the matter brings us back again to the peculiar mixture of self-centered folly and spiritual wisdom which was in Thomas Müntzer. All men struggle with his problems. Few act on them so rashly as did Müntzer. Yet every Christian who knows that he is part of the world, called to minister to and overcome the world, must deal somehow with the problems of Thomas Müntzer. And, as in the case of Müntzer, excessive confidence in eschatological hope and anxious seeking for proofs of election may lead us astray, though the Christian message does give us unconquerable hope and divine election provides us with our really significant opportunities to do the will of God. In addition, each Christian, and the church as well, is called to a revolutionary task in church and society, as problematic in details today as it was in Müntzer's time, but no less imperative for us also. In spite of his irresponsibility, Müntzer came to grips with reality when he recognized that faith has to do with men's political, economic, and social concerns as well as with their souls.

Gordon Rupp, in a broadcast to the Russian zone of Germany, summarized well when he said of Müntzer that "it was not Luther who in 1525 let the peasants down, but Thomas Müntzer with his utopian pipe dreams and his dialectical thinking which led only to terrible disillusionment and disaster . . . And yet in him . . . we come near to that smothered medieval undercurrent of injustice, resentment, and pain, now defeated once more, now driven dangerously underground—a tradition lost to the church but one day to return to the gates of Christendom—aggressive, heretical, anticlerical, yet a witness somewhere to a Christian failure of practical compassion. Thomas Müntzer, like the Iron Curtain, should give us an uneasy conscience."[31]

A Bibliography of Professor Bainton's Writings on the Reformation Period

Compiled by Raymond P. Morris

MONOGRAPHS

The Age of the Reformation (Princeton, N. J.: Van Nostrand, 1956), pp. 192. Paperback.

Bernardino Ochino, Esule e Riformatore Senese del Cinquecento, 1487-1563. Versione dal Manoscritto Inglese di Elio Gianturco (Firenze: G. C. Sansoni, 1940), pp. x, 213. (Biblioteca Storica Sansoni. Nuova Serie, IV).

Bibliography of the Continental Reformation: Materials Available in English (Chicago: The American Society of Church History, 1935), pp. 54. (Monographs in Church History, No. 1).

David Joris, Wiedertäufer und Kämpfer für Toleranz im 16. Jahrhundert (Leipzig: M. Heinsius Nachfolger, 1937), pp. vi, 229 (Archiv für Reformationsgeschichte, Texte und Untersuchungen. Ergänzungsband, VI).

Here I Stand; a Life of Martin Luther (Nashville: Abingdon-Cokesbury Press, 1950), pp. 422. Reprinted (New York: New American Library of World Literature, 1955), pp. 336. Paperback.
> Translated into German, Greek, Spanish, and Japanese. Portions of this book have been delivered as the Nathaniel Taylor lectures at the Yale Divinity School, 1946-47, the Carew Lectures at the Hartford Seminary Foundation, 1949, and the Hein Lectures at the Wartburg Seminary and Capital University.

Hunted Heretic; the Life and Death of Michael Servetus, 1511-1553 (Boston: Beacon Press, 1953), pp. 270. Reprinted, 1960, pp. xiv, 270. Paperback.

Michel Servet, Hérétique et Martyr, 1553-1953 (Genève: E. Droz, 1953), pp. 148 (Travaux d'Humanisme et Renaissance, 6).

The Reformation of the Sixteenth Century (Boston: Beacon Press, 1952), pp. xi, 276. Reprinted, 1956, pp. 278. Paperback. Translated into Hebrew.

The Travail of Religious Liberty; Nine Biographical Studies (Philadelphia: The Westminster Press, 1951), pp. 272.
> The James Sprunt Lectures, 1950.

PARTS OF BOOKS

"Academic Freedom in the Light of the Struggle for Religious Liberty," in *Proceedings of the Middle States Association of History Teachers*, XXXIII (1935), pp. 37-44.

"The Anabaptist Contribution to History," in *The Recovery of the Anabaptist Vision*, ed., Guy F. Hershberger (Scottdale, Pa.: Herald Press, 1957), pp. 317-326.

"Luther's Simple Faith," in *Luther Today* (Decorah, Iowa: Luther College Press, 1957), pp. 1-33 (Martin Luther Lectures, 1).

"Luther's Struggle for Faith," in *Festschrift für Gerhard Ritter* (Tübingen: J. C. B. Mohr, 1950), pp. 232-243.
> Appeared also in *Church History*, XVII (1948), pp. 193-206.

"Michael Servetus and the Trinitarian Speculation of the Middle Ages," in *Autour de Michel Servet et de Sébastien Castellion; Recueil*, ed., Bruno Becker (Haarlem: H. D. Tjeenk Willink, 1953), pp. 29-46.

"Probleme der Lutherbiographie," in *Lutherforschung Heute*, Hrsg. von Vilmos Vajta (Berlin: Lutherisches Verlagshaus, 1958), pp. 24-31.
> Internationaler Kongress für Lutherforschung, Aarhus, 1956.

"The Puritan Theocracy and the Cambridge Platform," in *The Cambridge Platform of 1648*. Tercentenary Commemoration (Boston: The Beacon Press, 1949), pp. 76-86. Also published in *The Minister's Quarterly*, V (1949), pp. 16-21.
"Sebastian Castellio, Champion of Religious Liberty, 1515-1563," in *Castellioniana: Quatre Études sur Sébastien Castellion et L'Idee de la Tolérance*, par Roland H. Bainton, Bruno Becker, Marius Valkhoff et Sape van der Woude (Leiden: E. J. Brill, 1951), pp. 25-79.
"Sebastian Castellio and the Toleration Controversy of the Sixteenth Century," in *Persecution and Liberty; Essays in Honor of George Lincoln Burr* (New York: The Century Co., 1931), pp. 183-209.

TRANSLATIONS

Châteillon, Sébastien. *Concerning Heretics* . . . Now First Done into English, by Roland H. Bainton (New York: Columbia University Press, 1935), pp. xiv, 342 (Records of Civilization).
Holborn, Hajo. *Ulrich von Hutten and the German Reformation*. Translated by Roland H. Bainton (New Haven: Yale University Press; London: H. Milford, Oxford University Press, 1937), pp. viii, 214 (Yale Historical Publications Studies XI).
The Martin Luther Christmas Book, with Celebrated Woodcuts by His Contemporaries; translated and arranged by Roland H. Bainton (Philadelphia: Westminster Press, 1948), pp. 74.

ARTICLES

"Augsburg," in *The Mennonite Encyclopedia*, I, p. 185.
"Burned Heretic: Michael Servetus," in *Christian Century*, LXX (1953), pp. 1230-1231.
"Changing Ideas and Ideals in the Sixteenth Century," in *Journal of Modern History*, VIII (1936), pp. 417-443.
"The Church of the Restoration," in *Mennonite Life*, VIII (1953), pp. 136-143. Menno Simons Lecture, 1952.
"Congregationalism: From the Just War to the Crusade in the Puritan Revolution," in *Andover Newton Theological School Bulletin*, XXXV (1943), pp. 1-20. Southworth Lectures, 1942.
"The Development and Consistency of Luther's Attitude to Religious Liberty," in *Harvard Theological Review*, XXII (1929), pp. 107-149.
"Documenta Servetiana," in *Archiv für Reformationsgeschichte*, XLIV (1953), pp. 223-234; XLV (1954), pp. 99-108.
"Dürer and Luther as the Man of Sorrows," in *The Art Bulletin*, XXIX (1947), pp. 269-272.
"Eyn Wunderliche Weyssagung," Osiander-Sachs-Luther, in *Germanic Review*, XXI (1946), pp. 161-164.
"Forschungsberichte und Besprechungen," in *Archiv für Reformationsgeschichte*, XLIII (1952), pp. 88-106.
"The Immoralities of the Patriarchs According to the Exegesis of the Late Middle Ages and of the Reformation," in *Harvard Theological Review*, XXIII (1930), pp. 40-49.
"The Left Wing of the Reformation," in *Journal of Religion*, XXI (1941), pp. 124-134.
"Let's Agree on the Reformation," in *Christian Century*, LXIV (1947), pp. 237-239.
"Luther and the Via Media at the Marburg Colloquy," in *The Lutheran Quarterly*, I (1949), pp. 394-398.
"Luther in a Capsule," in *Bulletin of the American Congregational Association*, III (May, 1952), pp. 1-9.
"Man, God and the Church in the Age of the Renaissance," in *Journal of Religious Thought*, XI (1953-1954), pp. 119-133.
    Issued also in mimeographed form in The Renaissance, A Symposium. New York: Metropolitan Museum of Art, 1953, pp. 51-62a.
"Marpeck (Marbeck), Pilgram," in *The Mennonite Encyclopedia*, III, p. 492.
"Michael Servetus and the Pulmonary Transit of the Blood," in *Bulletin of the History of Medicine*, XXV (1951), pp. 1-7 (The Fielding H. Garrison Lecture).
"New Documents on Early Protestant Rationalism," in *Church History*, VII (1938), pp. 179-187.

Review of Per la Storia Degli Eretici Italiani del Secolo XVI in Europa, Testi Raccolti da D. Cantimori e E. Feist, 1937.

"Our Debt to Luther," in *Christian Century*, LXIII (1946), pp. 1276-1278.

"The Parable of the Tares As the Proof Text for Religious Liberty to the End of the Sixteenth Century," in *Church History*, I (1932), pp. 3-24.

"The Present State of Servetus Studies," in *Journal of Modern History*, IV (1932), pp. 72-92.

"The Querela Pacis of Erasmus, Classical and Christian Sources," in *Archiv für Reformationsgeschichte*, XLII (1951), pp. 32-48.

"Sebastian Castellio and the British American Tradition," in *Het Boek*, XXX (1952), pp. 347-349.

"Servet et les Libertins de Genève," in *Bulletin Société de L'Histoire du Protestantisme Français*, LXXXVII (1938), pp. 261-269.

"Servetus and the Genevan Libertines," in *Church History*, V (1936), pp. 141-149.

"The Smaller Circulation: Servetus and Colombo," in *Sudhoffs Archiv für Geschichte der Medizin und der Naturwissenschaften*, XXIV (1931), pp. 371-374.

"The Struggle for Religious Liberty," in *Church History*, X (1941), pp. 95-124.

"What is Calvinism?," in *Christian Century*, XLII (1925), pp. 351-352.

"William Postell and the Netherlands," in *Nederlandsch Archief voor Kerkgeschiedenis*, XXIV (1931), pp. 161-172.

Notes and Acknowledgments

ROLAND H. BAINTON: A BIOGRAPHICAL APPRECIATION
(Harkness)

1. *Heroes and Hero Worship*, "The Hero as Divinity" (London: Chapman and Hall, 1870), 34.
2. *Culture and Anarchy* (New York: The Macmillan Co., 1896), 15.
3. Roland H. Bainton, *Pilgrim Parson* (New York: Thomas Nelson & Sons, 1958), 53.
4. Roland H. Bainton, *The Church of Our Fathers* (New York: Charles Scribner's Sons, 1953), 72-73.

FAITH AND KNOWLEDGE IN LUTHER'S THEOLOGY
(Bendtz)

1. Luther's Works, Weimar edition (hereafter *WA*), 45, 905; 24, 7.
2. *WA* 4, 278.
3. *WA* 40:1, 607.
4. *WA* 42, 397.
5. *WA* 56, 11-13.
6. *WA* 19, 206.
7. *WA* 21, 170.
8. *WA* 16, 4.
9. *WA* 56, 12.
10. *WA* 45, 90.
11. *WA* 42, 292.
12. *WA* 56, 666f.
13. Adolf von Harnack, *Lehrbuch der Dogmengeschichte* (Freiburg: J. C. B. Mohr, 1894-1897), III, 813.
14. *WA* 10:1, 152.
15. *WA* 40:1, 609.
16. *WA* 40:1, 73.
17. *WA* 40:1, 365.
18. Luther, *Den Trälbundna Viljan*, trans. by Gunnar Rudberg (Stockholm: Svenska Kyrkans Diakonistyrelses förlag, 1925), 238.
19. *WA* 39:1, 97-98.
20. *WA* 24, 17.
21. St. Louis ed. (St. Louis: Concordia Publishing House, 1894), Bk. 3, 660-661; Bk. 13, 1532-1533.
22. *WA* 18, 143.
23. *WA* 14, 607.
24. *WA* 50, 273.
25. *WA* 33, 118.
26. *WA* 42, 116.
27. *WA* 39:2, 5.
28. *WA* 38, 608ff.
29. *WA* 39:1, 288.
30. Anton C. Pegis, ed., *Basic Writings of Saint Thomas Aquinas* (New York: Random House, 1945), 316.
31. *WA* 42, 397.
32. *WA* 39:2, 3-5.

A REASONABLE LUTHER (Fischer)

1. "Marburg Colloquy" (1529), in Hermann Sasse, *This Is My Body* (Minneapolis: Augsburg Publishing House, 1959), 237.
2. Douglas C. Macintosh, *The Problem of Religious Knowledge* (New York: Harper & Brothers, 1940), ch. 19, 342.
3. Quoted by Philip S. Watson in his edition of Luther's *Commentary on St. Paul's Epistle to the Galatians* (Westwood, N. J.: Fleming H. Revell, 1953), 13.
4. A. C. McGiffert, *Protestant Thought Before Kant* (New York: Charles Scribner's Sons, 1926).
5. Norman Sykes, *Crisis of the Reformation* (London: Geoffrey Bles, 1950), 39f., cf. 41, 28.
6. *Weimar edition* (hereafter *WA*), 7, 838.
7. "Was bedeutet die Formel *Convictus testimoniis scripturarum aut ratione evidente* in Luthers ungehörnter Antwort zu Worms?" *Theologische Studien und Kritiken* 81 (Gotha: Perthes, 1908), 62ff.
8. "Disputation Concerning Man," Theses 4-9 (1536), *Luther's Works* (hereafter *LW*) (American Edition), J. Pelikan and H. T. Lehmann, eds. (St. Louis: Concordia Publishing House and Philadelphia: Muhlenberg Press, 1955-), vol. 34, 137 (slightly altered).
9. "On Keeping Children in School" (1530), *Works of Martin Luther* (Philadelphia Edition), H. E. Jacobs, ed. (Philadelphia: Holman Press, 1915-1932), vol. 4, 163.
10. F. Edward Cranz, *An Essay on the Development of Luther's Thought on Justice, Law, and Society* (Cambridge: Harvard University Press, 1959). *Harvard Theological Studies*, XIX, especially 148, 173ff.
11. "Against the Heavenly Prophets" (1525), *LW* 40, 175.
12. "Commentary on Jonah" (1:5!) (1526), *WA* 19, 206f. Quoted in George W. Forell, *Faith Active in Love* (New York: The American Press, 1954), 118.
13. "Psalms Commentary" (1513-1515), *WA* 3, 382.
14. "Heidelberg Disputation" (1518), *LW* 31, 35ff. Cf. Walther von Loewenich, *Luthers Theologia Crucis* (Munich: Chr. Kaiser Verlag, 1954) and Gordon Rupp, *The Righteousness of God* (New York: Philosophical Library, 1953).
15. Anders Nygren, "Reconciliation as an Act of God" in *Lutheran Church Quarterly* 7 (Gettysburg, Pa.: Times and News Publishing Co., 1934), 1ff. Cf. the masterful chapter (21) on "Luther's Struggle for Faith" in Roland H. Bainton, *Here I Stand* (Nashville: Abingdon-Cokesbury Press, 1950).
16. Cf. Forell, *Faith Active in Love, op. cit.;* Gustaf Wingren, *Luther on Vocation* (Philadelphia: Muhlenberg Press, 1957).
17. Torgau, "Sermon on Jesus Christ" (1533), *WA* 37, 39f.
18. *Martin Luther on the Bondage of the Will*, J. I. Packer and O. A. Johnston, eds. (London: James Clarke & Co., 1957), 312.
19. *Ibid.*, 90, 78.
20. *Ibid.*, 90, 271.
21. *Ibid.*, 251, 137, 232, 191ff.
22. *Ibid.*, 67, 75, etc.
23. *Ibid.*, 215.
24. *Ibid.*, 265.
25. *Ibid.*, 102ff.
26. *Ibid.*, 268.
27. *Ibid.*, cf. 136ff.
28. *Ibid.*, 141, cf. 149, 190, *et passim.*
29. *Ibid.*, 194.
30. *Ibid.*, 203f., 206, 94.
31. *Ibid.*, 170.
32. More accurately, Luther's words reflect Ezekiel 33:11.
33. *Bondage of the Will*, 170f., 216.
34. *Ibid.*, 132.
35. *Ibid.*, 215ff., 82f., 317f., etc.
36. *Ibid.*, 139, 276, cf. 306.

37. *Ibid.*, 232, 200ff., 184.
38. *Ibid.*, 133f.
39. *Ibid.*, 67.
40. *Ibid.*, 201.
41. *Ibid.*, 190ff.
42. *Ibid.*, 70ff., 123ff.
43. *Ibid.*, 71.
44. *Ibid.*, 73f.
45. *Ibid.*, 169f.
46. *Ibid.*, 170f., etc.
47. *Ibid.*, 101.
48. *Ibid.*, 316.
49. *Galatians Commentary, op. cit.*, 3n.
50. *LW* 37, 161-372.
51. *Ibid.*, cf. 206ff.
52. Ulrich Zwingli, "Christian Answer" (1527), *Huldreich Zwinglis Sämtliche Werke,* hrsg. Emil Egli, Georg Finsler, u. a., Bde. 88- of *Corpus Reformatorum* (Leipzig, 1905-). Bd. 92, 880.
53. "Marburg Colloquy" (1529), in Sasse, *This Is My Body, op. cit.*, 241.
54. Luther, "This Is My Body" (1527), *LW* 37, 75.
55. *Ibid.*, 95.
56. *Ibid.*, 34.
57. "Great Confession," *op. cit., LW* 37, 272.
58. *Ibid.*, 212.
59. Disputation on "The Word Was Made Flesh," Theses 18-21 (1539), *WA* 39:2, 4. Cf. Bengt Hägglund, *Theologie und Philosophie bei Luther und in der occamistischen Tradition* (Lund: C. W. K. Gleerup, 1955). (*Lunds Universitets Arsskrift.* N.F. Avd. 1, Bd. 51, Nr. 4), 94ff.
60. "Great Confession," *op. cit.*, 174, cf. 252f.
61. *Ibid.*, 194f., 212, 294ff.
62. *Ibid.*, 295ff. Illustrations under "c" are drawn from Augustine's "On the Trinity."
63. *Ibid.*, 213ff., 276ff.
64. *Ibid.*, 271f.

ANFECHTUNG IN LUTHER'S BIBLICAL EXEGESIS (Hovland)

1. "Tischreden" (hereafter *TR*), 4777 (1530-1540) in Luther's Works, Weimar edition.
2. Roland H. Bainton, *Here I Stand* (Nashville: Abingdon Press, 1950), 42.
3. Jacob Grimm, *Deutsches Wörterbuch* (Leipzig: S. Hirzel, 1854ff.), 1428.
4. Luther's Works, Weimar edition (hereafter *WA*), 2, 122-126. This translation and explanation of the Lord's Prayer was written in 1519.
5. For an excellent treatment of this see John von Rohr's essay in this volume, "Medieval Consolation and the Young Luther's Despair." Cf. also his unpublished Ph.D. dissertation (Yale University, 1947): "A Study of the *Anfechtung* of Martin Luther to the Time of His Evangelical Awakening with Special Reference to the Problem of Salvation," for a review of the literature. Cf. also Roland H. Bainton's article and review of Heinrich Boehmer's "Road to Reformation," in *Church History* XVI (1947), 167ff.
6. *TR* 352.
7. *WA* 54, 185. Cf. also 43, 537 and *TR* 141.
8. "Briefwechsel" (hereafter *BW*) in Luther's Works, Weimar edition, 4, 272.
9. Paul Reiter, *Luthers Umwelt und Persönlichkeit* (Copenhagen: Levin and Munsgaard, 1937-1941), 2 vols. Cf. Roland Bainton's criticism in his article and review of Boehmer, *loc. cit.*, 169.
10. Cf. C. MacLaurin, *De Mortuis* (London: Jonathan Cape, 1930) for a review of Luther's physical health.
11. Erik H. Erikson, *Young Man Luther*, "A Study in Psychoanalysis and History" (New York: W. W. Norton, 1958).
12. *Ibid.*, 255.

4. Cf. also Søren Kierkegaard's
ning was about to strike him at
Luther und den Protestantismus

rch in Luther's pam-
).

in *Fear and Trem-*

ages our generation. Such words
ininglessness," "alienation," and
out man. The terminology is used
stentialism. Cf. Paul Tillich, *The*
Press, 1952). Tillich is especially
ontemporary language.
526).

ang, *Der Angefochtene Christus bei*

Gotthelf Verlag, 1948), 11.
the Social Sciences (New York: The

OUNG

d das 1. Gebot in der Anfechtung bei
heologie, V (1938), 453-477.

was acquainted,
n. For contempo-
o Scheel, *Martin*
I, 442-480. Some
cated in Luther's
o; 45, 153; and

e (Erlangen: Heyden & Zimmer, 1828-1870),

3off.; 31, I, 25off.

Unscientific Postscript to the Philosophical Frag-
niversity Press, 1941), 410.
Prof. Fritz Blanke of the University of Zurich and
t *bei Luther* (Berlin, 1928), for suggestions in this

ade that he
o be noted
of 1531 out
ated. Thus,
rd Schulze,
ickte Kom-
ere can be
inian Rule
sinfulness
ency.

24, 578 and 44, 100; *TR* 6294; *WA* 44, 102 respec-
'Scheinbaren Parallele zwischen Teufel und Gott—
resschrift* (1934), Vol. XVI,

58. *WA* 27, 22.
59. *WA* 27, 23.
60. *WA* 28, 401.
61. *TR* 3669.
62. *WA* 44, 111. Suffering is held to be a mark of the true chu phlet, "The Councils and the Church," *WA* 50, 160ff. (1539
63. *WA* 24, 382.
64. *WA* 24, 381.
65. *TR* 2754B. Cf. Søren Kierkegaard's treatment of this theme *bling* (Princeton: Princeton University Press, 1941).
66. *WA* 17, II, 201.
67. *WA* 21, 112.
68. *WA* 37, 315.
69. *WA* 24, 381.
70. *WA* 21, 118.
71. *WA* 5, 163.
72. *WA* 21, 111; 11, 41.
73. *WA* 21, 111. Cf. *"Ein Feste Burg"* (1528).

MEDIEVAL CONSOLATION AND THE Y
LUTHER'S DESPAIR (von Rohr)

1. A major exposition of this system, and one with which Luthe appeared in Gabriel Biel, *Collectorium in quatuor sententiarur* rary analysis of its relation to Luther's early thought see Ott *Luther,* 3rd and 4th editions (Tübingen: J. C. B. Mohr, 1930), of Luther's own recollections of this "modernist" theology are lo Works, Weimar edition (hereafter *WA*), 2, 401; 21, 324; 38, 1 "Tischreden" (hereafter *TR*), IV, 5135.
2. *TR* V, 5897.
3. *WA* 40, I, 368.
4. *WA* 40, II, 15.
5. *WA* 43, 615.
6. *WA* 26, 12.
7. *WA* 54, 185.
8. *WA* 56, 348f.
9. *WA* 1, 67.
10. *WA* 3, 423.
11. *WA* 40, II, 92.
12. *WA* 9, 75.
13. *TR* IV, 4007; II, 1681.
14. *WA* 40, II, 331.
15. *TR* I, 141.
16. *WA* 34, II, 410; 41, 198; 47, 99.
17. *WA* 22, 305.
18. *WA* 47, 590.
19. *WA* 44, 775.
20. *WA* 38, 148.
21. *WA* 1, 557.
22. *WA* 44, 717.
23. In the *Commentary on Galatians,* printed in 1535, the claim is m confessed daily. *WA* 40, II, 92, *confitebar quotidie.* However, it is that these words do not appear in Rörer's notes to Luther's lectures of which the printed commentary, which Luther did not edit, was cre one may suppose that this was not Luther's own claim. See Gerha "Die Vorlesung Luthers über den Galaterbrief von 1531 und den gedr mentar von 1535," *Theologische Studien und Kritiken,* 1926. Yet, th no question as to Luther's general diligence at confession. The August required that one confess at least weekly, and Luther's intense sense of appears to have driven him to the confessional with ever greater frequ

24. *WA* 47, 441.
25. *WA* 22, 305.
26. *WA* 43, 537.
27. *WA* 56, 273.
28. *WA* 41, 198.
29. *WA* 11, 90.
30. *WA* 27, 95f.
31. *WA* 40, II, 15.
32. *TR* I, 582.
33. *WA* 43, 537.
34. *WA* 34, I, 35f.
35. *WA* 43, 537.
36. Gabriel Biel, *Collectorium in quatuor sententiarum,* lib. 3, dist. 27G.
37. For discussions of this question see Emanual Hirsch, "Initium theologiae Lutheri," *Festgabe für D. Dr. Julius Kaften* (Tübingen: J. C. B. Mohr, 1920), 152f., and Karl Holl, *Gesammelte Aufsätze* (Tübingen: J. C. B. Mohr, 1923). Vol. I, 26, n. 38.
38. *WA* 44, 486.
39. *WA* 54, 185.
40. *WA* 40, II, 15.
41. *WA* 44, 717.
42. *WA* 40, II, 411f.
43. *WA* 40, II, 413.
44. See Otto Scheel, "Die Entwicklung Luthers bis zum Abschluss der Vorlesung über den Römerbrief," *Schriften des Vereins für Reformationsgeschichte,* XXVII, 1909, 87, and Heinrich Boehmer, *Der junge Luther* (Gotha: Flamberg Verlag, 1925), 95f.
45. For a statement from Paltz's *Coelifodina,* setting forth this point of view, see A. V. Müller, *Luthers Werdegang bis zum Turmerlebnis* (Gotha: F. A. Perthes, 1920), 102.
46. Heinrich Boehmer, *op. cit.,* 96.
47. Karl Holl, *op. cit.,* 24.
48. *WA* 40, II, 15.
49. *WA* 1, 321.
50. John Gerson, *De remediis contra pusillanimitatem,* III, 585C. Here is a description of despair very similar to that which Luther knew in his experience with the sacrament of penance. See Walter Dress, "Gerson und Luther," *Zeitschrift für Kirchengeschichte,* LII, 1933, 155.
51. *Ibid.,* 153.
52. *WA* 40, II, 412.
53. *TR* IV, 4362.
54. *TR* V, 6017.
55. It is true that the claim is made in the first two of these later reflections that help was derived from this command to hope, and it may indeed be that there was here some element of consolation and even a stepping stone to the later conviction of justification by faith. But it is hazardous to attribute too much to them, for critical study of the passages seems to indicate that at this point they bear the mark of a later Luther-legend. For a discussion of this see Otto Scheel, *Martin Luther,* 3rd and 4th eds. (Tübingen: J. C. B. Mohr, 1930), II, 261f. This legendary element would also seem to be involved in the further incident reported by Melanchthon (*Corpus Reformatorum* VI, 159) where the call to trust was offered with salutary effect to Luther by an "old man" in conjunction with the understanding of the article in the Creed dealing with the forgiveness of sins, the claim being that this even led to Luther's rediscovery of Paul and the Gospel. Again see Otto Scheel, *op. cit.,* II, 258ff.
56. Walter Dress, *loc. cit.,* 155.
57. Helmut Appel, "Anfechtung und Trost im Spätmittelalter und bei Luther," *Schriften des Vereins für Reformationsgeschichte,* LVI, Heft 1, 1938, 110, and Karl Holl, *op. cit.,* 28, n. 2.
58. *TR* V, 6017.
59. John Gerson, *De perfectione cordis,* III, 444C. See Walter Dress, *loc. cit.,* 152.
60. John Gerson, *De remediis contra pusillanimitate,* III, 588D. See Walter Dress, *loc. cit.,* 153.

61. *Ibidem.*
62. *WA* 25, 197.
63. *TR* IV, 4082.
64. *TR* II, 1351.
65. *WA* 1, 35.
66. *WA* 3, 447.
67. *TR* V, 5897.
68. *WA* 40, I, 575.
69. *WA* 45, 681.
70. *WA* 41, 698.
71. *WA* 40, II, 414.
72. *WA* 46, 9.
73. *WA* 11, 44.
74. *WA* 5, 622.
75. *WA* 17, II, 20.
76. For a discussion of the consolation given by Dambach, Nider, and Gerson to those who were disturbed by fears of predestination, see Helmut Appel, *loc. cit.*, 29f., 32ff., 54f., 111f., and 77.
77. For discussions of Staupitz's consolation for predestination-despair see Ernst Wolf, *Staupitz und Luther* (Leipzig: M. Heinsius, 1927), 201ff.; Ernst Wolf, "Johannes von Staupitz und die theologische Angänge Luthers," *Luther-Jahrbuch* (Munich: Chr. Kaiser Verlag, 1929), XI, 64ff.; Erich Vogelsang, *Der angefochtene Christus bei Luther* (Berlin: Walter de Gruyter & Co., 1933), 71ff.; and Helmut Appel, *op. cit.*, 96ff., 108ff.
78. Erich Vogelsang, *op. cit.*, 53ff.
79. Thomas Aquinas, *Summa theologiae*, II, 1, Q. 112, art. 5.
80. A. V. Müller, *op. cit.*, 103. Paltz's statement is made with regard to man's inability to have complete assurance of the sacramental transformation of attrition into contrition.
81. *WA* 6, 88.
82. *WA* 38, 153.
83. *WA* 40, I, 575.
84. *WA* 45, 579.
85. *WA* 40, I, 587.

LUTHER'S FRONTIER IN HUNGARY (Toth)

1. Bunyitay, Rapaics, Karácsonyi, *Egyháztörténelmi Emlékek* (Budapest, 1912), II, 272-274.
2. *Ibid.*, "Cum iam omnibus sit illud in ore: Gratis acceptistis, gratis date."
3. Dec. 10, 1533, *ibid.*, 301-302.
4. *Ibid.*, II, 279-281.
5. Georg Loesche, *Luther, Melanchthon und Calvin* (Tübingen, 1909), 71-88.
6. William Toth, "The Christianization of the Magyars," *Church History*, XI, Mar. 1942, 33-54; cf. Latourette, *A History of the Expansion of Christianity: The Thousand Years of Uncertainty* (New York: Harper & Brothers, 1938), 170-174.
7. Jenö Ábel, *Egyetemeink a középkorban.* Our Universities in the Middle Ages (Budapest, 1881), 4.
8. Alexander Szilágyi, *A magyar nemzet története.* History of the Hungarian Nation (Budapest, 1895-1898), II, 630.
9. Joseph Pokoly, *A protestántizmus hatása a magyar állami életre.* Protestant Influence and the Hungarian State (Budapest, 1910), 33f.
10. Michael Horváth, *Magyarország történelme.* History of Hungary (Pest, 1871), II, 458; Jenö Ábel, *op. cit.*, 22-24.
11. Hóman and Szekfü, *Magyar történet*, Hungarian History (Budapest, 1935), *passim.*
12. Érdulyhelyi, "Magyarországi görög katholikusok a mohácsi vész elött," The Greek Catholics of Hungary Prior to the Catastrophe of Mohacs, *Katholikus Szemle*, 1897, 40f.

13. Anthony Hodinka, *A munkácsi görög-katholikus püspökség története*, History of the Greek Catholic Episcopacy of Munkács (Budapest, 1909), 19.

14. Biró, Bucsay, Toth and Varga, *A magyar református egyház története*, History of the Hungarian Reformed Church (Budapest, 1949), 26.

15. The content of the Batthyány library, the only private collection of books from the end of the fifteenth century known to us, included the sermons and commentaries of Nicolaus de Lyra, the sermons of Geiler Kaiserberg, the complete works of Gerson, and the *De integritate libellus* of Wimpheling. The influence of Lyra upon Luther finds expression in the aphorism, "Si Lyra non lyrasset, Lutherus non saltasset;" Gerson advocated a predominantly episcopalian polity; Geiler was known for his sermons in the vernacular, while Wimpheling claimed that the reform of the church devolved upon the secular authorities in view of the lethargy of the clergy.

16. Dominic Kosáry, *History of Hungary* (Cleveland and New York: B. Franklin Bibliophile Society, 1941), 8of.; Béla Pukánszky, *A magyarországi német irodalom története*, History of German Literature in Hungary (Budapest, 1926), 99f.

17. Biró, *et al., ibid.*, 26; *Sermones Pomerii Pelbarti de Temesvar divi ordinis S. Francisci*. Hagenani.

18. Biró, *op. cit.*, 25; see also Vilmos Frankl, *A hazai és külföldi iskolázás a 16. században*, Sixteenth Century Education At Home and Abroad (Pest, 1873).

19. Lewis W. Spitz, *Conrad Celtis: The German Arch-Humanist* (Cambridge: Harvard University Press, 1957), 55-62.

20. Theodore Thienemann, *Mohács és Erazmus*, Mohács and Erasmus (Budapest, 1924), 1-65.

21. Jenö Zoványi, *Kisebb dolgozatok a Magyar Protestántizmus Történetének köréböl*, Essays on Hungarian Protestant History (Sárospatak, 1910), 13.

22. Jenö Sólyom, *Luther és Magyarország*, Luther and Hungary (Budapest, 1933), 18.

23. Hóman and Szekfü, *op. cit.*, III, 168f.

24. Michael Horváth, *Kisebb Töténelmi Munkái*, Minor Historical Essays (Pest, 1868), 4.

25. Archbishop Thomas Bakács is said to have gathered together no less than forty estates, and as the wealthiest lord of the country he kept the court of Louis II solvent with his loans. See Michael Zsillinszky, *Visszapillantás a hazai evang. egyháznak XVI. századbeli zsinataira*, Synods of the Lutheran Church in the Sixteenth Century (Pozsony, 1915), 5. Of another prelate, John Horváth of Szepes the city register recorded that he was bent upon "pecunia, pecunia, tantum pecunia et non iustititia." Gyözö Brückner, *A Reformáczió és ellenreformáció története a Szepességben*. The Reformation and Counter-reformation in Szepes (Budapest, 1922), 31.

26. In 1514 Bishop John Gosztony of Györ complained that "the church has fallen into deep ignorance. One can scarcely find a priest anywhere who is able to understand what he recites and sings in the mass." Quoted in Joseph S. Szábo, *A magyar reformáció Könyve*, Hungarian Reformation (Debreczen, 1917), 14.

27. Education had so deteriorated that the standards of even the cathedral schools were no higher than those of the elementary schools, as we gather, *passim*, in Vilmos Frankl's book, already cited.

28. Michael Hatvani, *Rajzok a magyar történelemböl*. Sketches from Hungarian History (Pest, 1859), 8-9.

29. *Monumenta Vaticana*, II Series I. Tom., 133.

30. Louis Neustadt, *Georg von Brandenburg in Ungarn* (Breslau: T. Schatzky, 1883).

31. Bunyitay, *et al., op. cit.*, I, 143.

32. Burgio wrote: "This country is in no position to defend itself, but is laid open to the mercy of the enemy. . . . How could it be imagined that it could wage war against the might of all Islam, when the king and the nobles are unable even to pay the skeleton army at the frontiers." Quote in Kosáry, *op. cit.*, 89.

33. Tommaseo, I, 270, and Sanuto, *Diarii*, III, 15-23 quoted in Kosáry, *op. cit.*, 88-89.

34. F. Myconius, *Historia reformationis*, 1517-1542, ed., Cyprian (Leipzig: M. G. Weidman, 1718), 23.

35. W. E. Tentzel, *Historischer Bericht vom Anfang und ersten Fortgang der Refor-*

mation Lutheri (Leipzig: M. G. Weidman, 1718), 374. The propositions were read by Thomas Preisner from his pulpit at Leibicz near Késmárk in 1520.

36. The Transylvanian historian George Haner, *Historia Ecclesiarum Transylvanicarum*, 1694, 147 gives a list of the books imported by the merchants of Szeben. The list as given in Lampe, *Historia Ecclesiae Reformatae in Hungaria et Transylvania* (Trajecti ad Rhenum, 1728), 53 includes the following: *De libertate Christiana, Confessione, Poenitentia, Justitia duplici, Baptismo, Passione Christi, Votis Monasticis, Communione sub utraque specie, Captivitate Baylonica, Expositione Epistolae ad Galatas etc.*

37. Vilmos Fraknói, *Werböczi István életrajza;* biography (Budapest, 1899), 160; Martin Aurél, *II. Lajos magyar követsége a wormsi birodalmi gyüésen.* The Hungarian Delegates of Louis II at the Diet of Worms (Budapest, 1926).

38. Bunyitay, *et al., op. cit.,* I, 41.

39. "Iterum Paulum dixisse, quod haberet magnam copiam librorum lutheranorum, nec propter eos libros possent eum ense excoriare, quum tamen venduntur publice." *Ibid.,* I, 169.

40. *Ibid.,* I, 123.

41. "Dogmata, librosque et traditiones eius tenetat." *Ibid.,* I, 189.

42. Alexander Páyr, *Cordatus Konrád budai pap, Luther jó barátja.* Conrad Cordatus Preacher at Buda and Friend of Luther (Budapest, 1928).

43. Letter of Burgio, Aug. 25, 1524 to the Archbishop of Carputa, Bunyitay, *et al., op. cit.,* I, 148.

44. Imre Molnár, *A cenzura története Magyarországon 1600-ig.* History of Censorship in Hungary to 1600 (Budapest, 1912), *passim.*

45. John Nadányi, *Florus Hungaricus* (Amsterdam, 1663), 207.

46. Schmitth, *Archiepiscopi Strigonienses* (Nagyszombat, 1758), II, 32.

47. Jenö Sólyom, *ibid.,* 29f.

48. Ede Mihalovicz, *A katholikus predikáczio története Magyarországon,* History of Catholic Preaching in Hungary (Budapest, 1900), I, 123f.

49. Bunyitay, *et al., op. cit.,* I, 259.

50. *Ibid.,* 141.

51. *Ibid.,* 261.

52. *Ibid.,* 160, 164, 286.

53. "zu predigen das Wort gottes." *Ibid.,* 416.

54. Emma Bartoniek, *Mohács Magyarországa,* Mohács and Hungary (Budapest, 1926), 30.

55. "Ma in queste citati di confini ove sono Germani, sono Lutherani assai, che e gente invida et si deletta di detrahere, non havendo un solo respetto a la verita." Bunyitay, *et al., op. cit.,* I, 210.

56. *Ibid.,* I, 43, 49, 74, 128.

57. *Ibid.,* I, 141.

58. "Cantilenas quasdam in probrum et contumeliam eiusdem sancte Sedis Apostolice totiusque cleri confingere et ore sacrilego decantare." *Ibid.,* I, 108. One of them:

> Pereant Simones Hypocritae.
> Cauponariis lucris squallentes
> Meretrices pessimas alentes!

in Fabritius, *Pemfflinger Márk Szász Gróf Élete,* Biography of Mark Pemfflinger the Saxon Count (Budapest, 1875), 42.

59. Zoványi, *ibid.,* 88.

60. Bunyitay, *et al., op. cit.,* I, 165.

61. *Ibid.,* I, 286.

62. Béla Obal, *Az egyház és a városok a reformácio elött.* The Church and Towns Before the Reformation (Eperjes, 1914), II, 4.

63. Bunyitay, *et al., op. cit.,* I, 160.

64. *Ibid.,* I, 548-549.

65. Vilmos Frankl, *ibid.,* 288f.

66. Kosáry, *ibid.,* 87.

67. *Luthers Werke,* Weimar edition (hereafter *WA*), XIX, 552.

68. At the Diet of Worms he entertained Luther at dinner and presumably tried to effect a change of mind. Sólyom, *op. cit.,* 53f.

69. Zoványi, *op. cit.,* 24.

70. Fabritius, *op. cit.*, 38.
71. Bartoniek, *op. cit.*, 6.
72. Seckendorf, *Commentarius historicus et apologeticus de Lutheranismo* (Frankfurt and Leipzig, 1692), I, 61 and Fabritius, *ibid.*, 40.
73. "Omnes Lutheranos et illorum fautores, et factioni ipsi adhaerentes, tanquam public haereticos, hostesque sacratissimae virginis Mariae, poena capitis, et ablatione omnium bonorum suorum, Majestas Regia, veluti catholicus princeps, punire digeteur." Imre Révész, *Dévay Bíró Mátyás* (Pest, 1863), 22.
74. Bunyitay, *et al.*, *op. cit.*, I, 204.
75. Burgio records in his diary that a delegation of sixty nobles appeared before the king with a demand to dismiss all Germans in the court because they were all Lutherans. *Ibid.*, I, 202.
76. Zoványi, *op. cit.*, 42.
77. In his work dedicated to the queen Luther reflects: "dass sie—i.e. bishops—auch Etlicher unschuldig Blut haben vergiessen lassen, und graulich wider die Wahrheit Gottes getobet." Quoted in Révész, *op. cit.*, 24.
78. Vilmos Fraknói, *Magyarország a mohácsi vész elött.* Hungary Before Mohács (Budapest, 1884), 206.
79. Zoványi, *op. cit.*, 45.
80. Nicholas Sinay, *A Magyar és Erdélyorszagi Reformáció Története 1564-ig.* The Reformation in Hungary and Transylvania Until 1564 (Debreczen, 1911), 164.
81. *Ibid.*, 165.
82. Zsillinszky, *A magyar országgyülések vallásügyi tárgyalásai.* Religious Affairs and the Diets (Budapest, 1881), I, 91.
83. Fabritius, *op. cit.*, 156f.
84. William Toth, "Highlights of the Hungarian Reformation," *Church History*, IX, July 1940, 141-156.
85. Roland H. Bainton, *The Reformation of the Sixteenth Century* (Boston: The Beacon Press, 1952), 146.
86. Páyr, *op. cit.*, 12.
87. William Toth, *The Contribution of Stephen Kis of Szeged to the Trinitarian Struggle of the Hungarian Reformation*, doctoral dissertation under Roland H. Bainton (Yale University Library, 1941), 311f.
88. Sólyom, *op. cit.*, 108.
89. *WÁ*, 30, II, (198), 205.
90. Sólyom, *op. cit.*, 102f.
91. Bunyitay, *et al.*, *op. cit.*, IV, 277.
92. Páyr, *op. cit.*, 9.
93. He informs Jonas Justus, Feb. 16, 1542, "Hungaricas narrationes editypis curavimus." Quote in Páyr, *op. cit.*, 9.
94. A letter in the Archives of Bártfa reveals that, at the instance of Katharine the university attempted to collect the debt. *Magyar Szó*, Feb. 11, 1904.
95. Many citations from the *Tischreden* in Sólyom, *op. cit.*, 75.
96. Sinay, *op. cit.*, 231
97. *Ibid.*, 222.
98. The most powerful lords, Bálint Török, Peter Perényi, Thomas Nádasdy, Gaspart Drágffy, Elek Thurzó and Gaspard Serédi openly patronized or embraced the new faith.
99. Francis Salamon, *Magyarország a Török hódítás korában.* Hungary and the Turkish Era (Budapest, 1864), 328-395.
100. Joseph Pokoly, *op. cit.*, 88.
101. Text in Brückner, *A Confessio Augustana Magyarországi Variánsai.* Hungarian Variations of the Augustana Confession (Miskolc, 1930), 75f.
102. "Anabaptistas et Sacramentarios, iuxta admonitionem Regiae Maiestatis, qui adhuc in regno supersunt, procul expellendos esse de omnium bonis, Ordines et Status Regni statuerunt, neckamploius illos, aut quempiam illorum intra Regni fines esse recipiendos." Vilmos Fraknói, *Magyarországgyülési emlékek.* Documents of the Hungarian Diets (Budapest, 1876), III, 217.
103. "In coena Dominica docemus et credimus verum corpus et sanguinem Domini, de Virgine natum et in cruce passum, sumi ab Ecclesia." Brückner, *ibid.*, 70.
104. "Ita, ut in externis dumtaxat rebus aliquam habeamus eligendi libertatem . . . Sed verum timorem, fidem ac dilectionem Dei etcaetera praestare: Item Evangelio credere, non est in nostris viribus." *Ibid.*, 72f.

THE RELATION OF GOD'S GRACE TO HIS GLORY
IN JOHN CALVIN (Kuizenga)

1. John Calvin, *Commentaries on the Epistles of Paul the Apostle to the Galatians and Ephesians*, trans., William Pringle (Grand Rapids: William B. Eerdmans Publishing Company, 1948), 206.
2. Calvin, *Romans*, trans., John Owen, 369.
3. John Calvin, *Galatians and Ephesians*, 206.
4. Calvin, *Isaiah*, trans., William Pringle, I, 218.
5. Calvin, *Genesis*, trans., John King, II, 47.
6. Calvin, *Romans*, 417; see also 365, and Calvin, *Acts of the Apostles*, trans., Henry Beveridge, II, 97.
7. Calvin, *Psalms*, trans., James Anderson, II, 56.
8. Calvin, *Harmony of the Evangelists, Matthew, Mark, and Luke*, trans., William Pringle, III, 201.
9. Calvin, *Philippians, Colossians and Thessalonians*, trans., John Pringle, 317.
10. John Calvin, *Institutes of the Christian Religion*, trans., John Allen, 7th American edition (Philadelphia: The Westminster Press, 1936), III, xxiii, 11 (hereafter *Institutes* with numbers of book, chapter, and paragraph).
11. Calvin, *Romans*, 367.
12. *Institutes*, III, xxiii, 8.
13. Calvin, *Gospel According to John*, trans., William Pringle, II, 51.
14. Calvin, *Isaiah*, I, 219.
15. Calvin, *Acts of the Apostles*, I, 61. This is only another instance where Calvin says that we sin voluntarily, yet by an inbred bondage, decreed by God from eternity.
16. Calvin, *Twelve Minor Prophets*, trans., John Owen, Vol. III, 430.
17. John Calvin, *Institutes*, III, xxxiii, 9. This is perhaps an example of Calvin's use of what Bauke (Hermann Bauke, *Die Probleme der Theologie Calvins*, Verlag der J. C. Hendrichs' schen Buchhandlung, Leipzig, 1922) calls the principle of *complexio oppositorum* and of the juxtaposition of what Doumergue (E. Doumergue, *Jean Calvin, les Hommes et les Choses de Son Temps*, ed., George Bridel and Cie., Lausanne, 7 vols., 1899-1927) refers to as Calvin's contrarieties.
18. Joannis Calvini; *Opera Quae Supersunt Omnia*, vols. 1-59 in *Corpus Reformatorum*, eds., Guilielmus Baum, Eduardus Cunitz, Eduardus Reuss, Brunsvigae et Berolinae, Apud C. A. Schwetschke et Filium; vol. 59, col. 766 (hereafter *CR* with numbers of vol. and col.).
19. Calvin, *Philippians, Colossians, and Thessalonians*, 148.
20. Matthew 16:25.
21. Luke 15:7.
22. *CR* 65, 290.
23. *Institutes*, III, xxiii, 8.
24. *Institutes*, III, xxiv, 5.
25. Paul Jacobs, *Prädestination und Verantwortlichkeit bei Calvin*, Beitrage zur Geschichte und Lehre der Reformierten Kirche, herausgeben von W. Goeters, W. Wolfhaus, A. Lang, und O. Weber, Erster Band; (Kassel: Buchhandlung des Erziehungsvereins Neukirchen Kr. Moers, 1937), 24. (He cites O. Ritschl, *Die Ethik Calvins*, 16, "in der Erwahlungslehre ist Christus wesentlich ausgeschaltet.")
26. *Ibid.*, 73-83, *passim*.
27. *Ibid.*, 26-27.
28. *Ibid.*, 140.
29. Karl Barth, *Gottes Gnadenwahl*, nachgedruckt auf Veranlassung der Öcumenischen Kommission für die Pastoration der Kriegsgefangenen (Weltbund der Kirchen) in Verbindung mit der Kriegsgefangenenhilfe des Weltbundes der Christlichen Vereine Junger Männer (Genf, 1936), 17.
30. *Ibid.*, 19.
31. *Ibid.*, 16.
32. Joannis Calvini, *Opera Selecta*, ed., Petrus Barth (München: Chr. Kaiser, 1926), Vol. I, 109.
33. Calvin, *Galatians and Ephesians*, 198.

34. Arthur Savary, *La Prédestination Chex Calvin*, Imprimé par les Sourds-Muet, J. Witschy, 1901, 25.
35. In addition to the earlier citations, to show Calvin's views on this point, there are the following: "There is, perhaps, no passage in the whole Scripture which illustrates in a more striking manner the efficacy of his righteousness; for it shows . . . that the final cause [of salvation] is the glory of the divine justice and goodness." Calvin is referring to Romans 3:24 in his commentary on *Romans*, 141. In his *Psalms*, V, 183, he says, "Paul, in speaking of it [mercy] (in Rom. iii, 23), calls it emphatically by the general term of the glory of God, intimating, that while God should be praised for all his works, it is his mercy principally that we should glorify."
36. *Institutes*, III, ii, 11.

CALVIN'S THEOLOGICAL METHOD AND THE AMBIGUITY IN HIS THEOLOGY (Leith)

1. William Adams Brown, "Calvin's Influence upon Theology," *Three Addresses Delivered by Professors in Union Theological Seminary* (New York, 1909), 20: "It is difficult to say anything original about Calvin. . . . There are certain great thinkers whose systems it is possible to approach in the spirit of the explorer, conscious as one turns each page, of the chance of some new discovery, but with Calvin it is not so. What he believed and what he taught has long been a matter of common knowledge."
2. Karl Barth, *Nein! Antwort an Emil Brunner* ("Theologische Existenz heute"; München: Chr. Kaiser, 1934), Heft XIV.
Peter Barth, *Das Problem der natürlichen Theologie bei Calvin* ("Theologische Existenz heute"; München: Chr. Kaiser, 1935), Heft XVIII.
Günter Gloede, *Theologia naturalis bei Calvin* (Stuttgart: W. Kohlhammer, 1935).
3. D. Kromminga, "And the Barthians," *The Sovereignty of God*, ed., Jacob T. Hoogstra (Grand Rapids: Zondervan, 1940), 79-81.
I use the word "traditional" to designate in particular the Calvinism of B. B. Warfield and of the American Calvinistic Congress. In *God-Centered Religion* (Grand Rapids: Zondervan, 1942), 19-20, Paul T. Fuhrmann uses the word "classical" to designate not only American Calvinism of the above type but also the French Calvinism of Doumergue and Pannier. While these types of Calvinism have many similarities, it is also true that the French interpretation has been more liberal than that of the American Calvinistic Congress.
4. Jacques Pannier, *Recherches sur la Formation Intellectuelle de Calvin* (Paris: Alcan, 1931).
Wilhelm Niesel, "Calvin und Luther," *Reformierte Kirchenzeitung*, LXXXI (1931), 195ff.
5. Reinhold Seeberg, *Lehrbuch der Dogmengeschichte*, IV (Leipzig: A. Deichert, 1920), Heft 2, 613.
Peter Barth, "Calvin," *Die Religion in Geschichte und Gegenwart* (Tübingen: J. C. B. Mohr, 1927).
Also cf. Eugène Choisy, *La Théocratie à Genève au Temps de Calvin* (Genève: C. Eggimann & Cie, 1897), with Wilhelm Niesel, *Die Theologie Calvins* (München: Chr. Kaiser, 1938).
6. Georgia Harkness, *John Calvin, the Man and His Ethics* (New York: Henry Holt and Company, 1931), 66 and 87.
7. Hermann Bauke, *Die Probleme der Theologie Calvins* (Leipzig: J. C. Hinrichs, 1922).
8. Martin Schulze, *Meditatio futurae vitae: ihr Begriff und ihre beherrschende Stellung im System Calvins* (Leipzig: T. Weicher, 1901).
9. D. J. Köstlin, "Calvin's Institutio nach Form und Inhalt," *Theologische Studien und Kritiken*, XLI (1868).
10. Émile Doumergue, *Le caractère de Calvin* (Paris: Éditions de foi et vie, 1921), 47.
11. For example, see *Corpus Reformatorum: Joannis Calvini Opera Quae Supersunt*

Omnia (hereafter *CR*), ed. by Guilielmus Baum, Eduardus Cunitz, and Eduardus Reuss (Brunsvigae: C. A. Schwetschke et Filium, 1863-1897), V, 196; XXIII, 26-27; XLIX, 560; see also *Institutes of the Christian Religion*, III, xxv, 1 (hereafter *Institutes* with numbers of book, chapter, and paragraph).

12. *CR* XLVIII, 415.
13. *CR* XLIII, 428-429.
14. *CR* XXXVI, 89.
15. *CR* XL, 84.
16. *CR* XXXVI, 129.
17. *Institutes*, III, ii, 1; see also *CR* XLIII, 550; XLIV, 160; XLIV, 163; XLVIII, 88; XLIX, 272; LII, 256, 424.
18. *CR* XLIII, 428.
19. *CR* XLVII, 316.
20. *CR* XXVII, 244-245, 250, 434.
21. *CR* VIII, 476.
22. *CR* XXIX, 143.
23. *CR* XIV, 590.
24. *CR* XI, 188ff.
25. *CR* VIII, 306-307, 318.
26. Peter Barth, ed., *Joannis Calvini, Opera Selecta* (München: Chr. Kaiser Verlag, 1926), 1:391.
27. *CR* LI, 269.
28. *CR* VIII, 95; LI, 147; LVIII, 49-50.
29. *Institutes*, III, xxi, 5.
30. *CR* XXIV, 363.
31. Compare Peter Barth: "Was ist reformierte Ethik?" *Zwischen den Zeiten*, Vol. X, 1932 with E. Choisy: *La théocratie à Genève au temps de Calvin* (Genève: C. Eggimann & Cie., 1897).
32. Wilhelm Niesel: *The Theology of Calvin*, trans., Harold Knight (Philadelphia: The Westminster Press, 1956). For an example of a balanced study of a theological problem in which the evidence is diverse see Edward Dowey's discussion of the object of the knowledge of faith, Edward A. Dowey, Jr., *The Knowledge of God in Calvin's Theology* (New York: Columbia University Press, 1952), 161ff.
33. *CR* VIII, 395; XXVIII, 303, 547.
34. *CR* IX, 823.
35. *CR* IX, 815.
36. *CR* XXXVI, 507; *Institutes*, III, xxi, 3.
37. *CR* XLIX, 460-461.
38. *CR* XLVIII, 439.
39. For a tabulation of Calvin's use of Scripture see John T. McNeill: "The Significance of the Word of God For Calvin" in *Church History*, Vol. XXVIII, no. 2, June 1959, 135. Also Henri Clavier *Études sur la Calvinisme* (Paris: Fischbacher, 1936), Appendix 4.
40. *CR* XIV, 382.
41. *CR* XXVII, 253: "Et auiourd'huy quand les Papistes diront qu'il faut punir les heretiques; cela est vray, nous confessons qu'ils le meritent. Mais cependant il falloit venir à cest article qui est ici contenu: c'est assavoir que nous ayons cogneu quel est le Dieu auquel nous servons, que nous soyons bien asseurez que ce n'est point à l'aventure que nostre religion a esté publiee: mais que nous tenons la verité infallible que Dieu nous a envoyée, et qu'on nous l'annonce en son nom, et en son authorité: que c'est en luy que nostre foy est fondée. Il nous falloit (di-ie) là venir. Or les Papistes s'abrutissent là dessus, qu'il leur semble qu'en se fermant les yeux ils pourront executer leur rage, et furie contre les innocens." In assessing the significance of this statement, it must be remembered that much of Calvin's theology proclaims the impotence of force in religious matters.
42. *CR* XXI, 170.
43. Emil Brunner, *The Divine-Human Encounter*, trans., Amandus W. Loos (Philadelphia: The Westminster Press, 1943), 123-126; Gustaf Aulén, *The Faith of the Christian Church*, trans., Eric H. Wahlstrom and G. Everett Arden (Philadelphia: The Muhlenberg Press, 1948), pp. 94-105.

LEFÈVRE d'ÉTAPLES: THREE PHASES OF HIS LIFE AND WORK (Brush)

1. G. V. Jourdan, *The Movement Towards Catholic Reform in the Early Sixteenth Century* (New York: E. P. Dutton and Co., 1914), 79.
2. A. Renaudet, *Humanisme et Renaissance* (Geneve: E. Droz, 1958), 201. On 202, Renaudet helpfully sums up the whole problem of putting Lefèvre together into a consistent whole.
3. C. H. Graf, *Essai sur la Vie et les Écrits de Jacques Lefèvre d'Étaples* (These) (Strasbourg: Schuler, 1842). And later, K. H. Graf, "Jacobus Stapulensis, ein Beitrag zur Geschichte der Reformation in Frankreich," in *Zeitschrift für die historische Theologie* (Hamburg and Gotha: Perthes, 1852), 3-86, 165-237.
4. A. Renaudet, *Préréforme et Humanisme à Paris, 1494-1517* (Paris: E. Champion, 1916).
5. R. R. Bolgar, *The Classical Heritage and Its Beneficiaries* (Cambridge: University Press, 1954), 437.
6. *Dialogues of Alfred North Whitehead*, recorded by Lucien Price (Boston: Little, Brown and Company, 1954), 168.
7. Bertrand Russell, *A History of Western Philosophy* (New York: Simon and Schuster, 1945), 472-474, in brief sheds light on the misinterpretations of Aristotle that made Lefèvre's work so desirable.
8. Renaudet, *Préréforme*, etc., 146.
9. Imbart de la Tour, *L'Église Catholique:* la crise et la renaissance (Paris: Libraire d'Argences, 2nd ed., 1946), 390.
10. Renaudet, *Humanisme*, etc., 203.
11. W. J. Bouwsma, *The Career and Thought of Guillaume Postel* (Cambridge: Harvard University Press, 1957). See Index on Lefèvre.
12. See F. Hahn, "Faber Stapulensis und Luther," in *Zeitschrift für Kirchengeschichte* (Stuttgart: W. Kohlhammer, 1938), vol. 57, 400-404, for detailed study of this quasi-Joachite theme in Lefèvre.
13. J. B. Ross and M. M. McLaughlin, *The Portable Renaissance Reader* (New York: Viking Press, 1958), 84-86, from Lefèvre's *Commentarii initiatorii in iv evangeliis praefatio* (Meaux, 1522); trans., M. M. M.
14. *Ibid.*, 85.
15. Bouelles, *In artem oppositorum introductio* (Paris: W. Hopyl, 24 Dec. 1501), in 4; Bibl. de Schlettstadt. 208 (7). Quoted Renaudet, *op. cit.*, 411-412.
16. See Letters of Ignatius, "To the Ephesians," 192, and "To the Magnesians," 82.
17. See Pseudo-Dionysius: *De Div. Nom.* ch. xi.
18. Gal. 2:20; I Cor. 1:18-25; II Cor. 12:1-4.
19. Pseudo-Dionysius, *op. cit.*, ch. viii, 3.
20. See the striking imagery of Cusa in *Of Learned Ignorance*, trans., Fr. G. Heron (London: Routledge & Kegan Paul, 1954), 161-162. This passage is also quoted on 673 of *The Portable Medieval Reader*, Ross and McLaughlin, eds. (New York: Viking Press, 1949).
21. Faber Stapulensis, *Epistolae Divi Pauli Apostoli* (Paris: Henri Estienne, 1512), 269a.
22. *Commentarii initiatorii in quatuor Evangelia* (Meaux: Colines, 1522), 76b.
23. *Ibid.*, 52b.
24. See recent work: R. J. Lovy, *Les Origines de la Réforme française, Meaux 1518-1546* (Paris: Librairie protestante, 1959).
25. M. Mann, *Érasme et les débuts de la réforme française, 1517-1536* (Paris: H. Champion, É. Champion, 1933), 66.
26. *Ibid.*, 47.
27. A. L. Herminjard, *Correspondance des réformateurs dans les pays de langue française* (Génève: H. Georg, 1866), 1, 132-138, 159-169.
28. "The standard French version of Jacques Lefèvre (1512 to 1523-1527) was revised by Louvain theologians and passed through forty editions down to the year 1700." *Cambridge Modern History* (New York: The Macmillan Co., 902), I, 640.
29. A. Renaudet, *Érasme et l'Italie* (Geneva: E. Droz, 1954), 34.

30. Renaudet, *Humanisme,* etc., 210 and f.n. 4.
31. The phrase comes from W. R. Inge.
32. See the diagram, for example, of interlacing circles illustrative of the theme of center-and-circumference, in Lefèvre's meditation on Psalm 119:63. It is on 175 of my own copy of the *1509 Quincuplex Psalterium,* but the pages hereabouts are badly numbered. Hahn, 362, reproduces the diagram and comments helpfully on it. His reading of the pagination is 184b-185a. May I also here refer the reader to Arthur O. Lovejoy, *The Great Chain of Being* (Cambridge: Harvard University Press, 1936), Ch. III, on "The Chain of Being and Some Internal Conflicts in Medieval Thought." When Lovejoy writes, "God's 'love' . . . in medieval writers consists primarily rather in the creative or generative than in the redemptive or providential office of deity . . ." p. 67, what better support could we find for the basic difference between Lefèvre on God, as over against Luther and Calvin on God?
33. *Quincuplex Psalterium, op. cit.,* 140a.
34. *Ibid.,* 200a.
35. Hahn, *op. cit.,* 358.
36. "amore inebrians." *Commentarii initiatorii,* 128a, 130a.
37. At this point and later, I am in debt to H. Dorries, "Calvin und Lefèvre," in *Zeitschrift für Kirchengeschichte* (Gotha: Verlag Perthes, 1925), vol. xliv, 544-581. On 553, he sees the imitation of Christ as the guiding idea of Lefèvre's ethic.
38. *Commentarii initiatorii,* 21b.
39. S. Hahn, 432, sums up Luther's debt to Lefèvre on Bible interpretation.
40. *Calvini: Opera. Corpus Reformatorum,* Baum, Cunitz, and Reuss, eds. (Strassburg, 1863), 123.
41. John T. McNeill, *The History and Character of Calvinism* (New York: Oxford University Press, Inc., 1954), 113-115.
42. Francois Wendel, *Calvin, Sources et Évolution de sa pensée réligieuse* (Paris: Presses Universitaires de France, 1950), 95.
43. Though only tangential to our study, I have found helpful hints on this in P. Jourda, *Marguerite d'Angoulême* (Paris: H. Champion, 1930).
44. *Calvin: Institutes,* I, xiv (Philadelphia: Presbyterian Board of Christian Education, 1932), Vol. I, 154. Luther's blast against Dionysius, near the end of his "The Babylonian Captivity of the Church," 1520, could also be usefully quoted, but it is doubtless more generally familiar.
45. *Révue d'historie et de philosophie réligieuses* (Strasbourg: Presses Universitaires de France, 1955), no. 4, 444. This article, by Jean-Michel Hornus, may be found useful for a review of over twenty years of Pseudo-Dionysian studies.
46. Imbart de la Tour, *L'Évangelisme, 1521-1538* (Paris: Didot, 1914), 289.

CONTINENTAL PROTESTANTISM AND
ELIZABETHAN ANGLICISM (Krumm)

1. *Zurich Letters* (Cambridge: University Press, 1842), I, 23.
2. Cf. letter to Matthias Flacius Illyricus, July 18, 1566, in *Correspondence of Matthew Parker* (Cambridge: University Press, 1853), 287. Cf. also J. Strype, *The Life and Acts of Matthew Parker* (Oxford: Clarendon Press, 1821), IV, 8, 343-344 and *ibid.,* II, 3, 78.
3. J. Strype, *Life and Acts of John Whitgift* (Oxford: Clarendon Press, 1822), Vol. I, 90, Bk. I, ch. 7, sec. 44.
4. A. F. Scott Pearson, *Thomas Cartwright and Elizabethan Puritanism* (Cambridge: University Press, 1925), 33.
5. *Zurich Letters* (Cambridge: University Press, 1845), II, 154-156.
6. J. Strype, *Parker,* II, 110, Bk. IV, ch. 9, sec. 348.
7. Quoted in F. Schickler, *Les Églises du Refuge en Angleterre* (Paris: Fischbacher, 1892), I, 243.
8. Pearson, *op. cit.,* 54, f.n. 1.
9. Strype, *Whitgift,* Vol. I, 106, Bk. I, ch. 9, sec. 52. Strype cites places where Cartwright contradicts Pellican, Bucer, Bullinger, Illyricus, Musculus, Luther, Martyr, and Gualter.

10. *Ibid.*, II, 79-80, Bk. IV, ch. 5, sec. 65.
11. Richard Bancroft, *A Survey of the Pretended Holy Discipline* (London: R. Hodgkinson, 1663), 14.
12. *Ibid.*, 21.
13. *Ibid.*, 31.
14. Quoted in Strype, *Whitgift*, II, 158, Bk. IV, ch. 10, sec. 405.
15. Bancroft, *op. cit.*, 38.
16. *Ibid.*, 41.
17. Strype, *Whitgift*, II, 208, Bk. IV, ch. 12, sec. 425.
18. *Ibid.*, II, 62, Bk. IV, ch. 4, sec. 356.
19. *Ibid.*, II, 64-65, Bk. IV, ch. 4, sec. 357.
20. *Ibid.*, II, 227, Bk. IV, ch. 14, sec. 434.
21. *Ibid.*, II, 229, Bk. IV, ch. 14, sec. 435.
22. *Ibid.*, II, 233, Bk. IV, ch. 14, sec. 441.
23. Cf. H. C. Porter, *Reformation and Reaction in Tudor Cambridge* (Cambridge: University Press, 1958), 347-349. Porter sees nothing conspiratorial in the avoidance of Whitgift's authority, for he writes, "The heads had assumed that Whitgift's judgment on the theological points at issue would be firmly against Barret and in favour of the Calvinist interpretation, as expounded by Some and Whitaker" (page 350). Porter gives no evidence, however, for the judgment that the Calvinist party anticipated Whitgift's support. In view of his role in the Cartwright discussions, Whitgift could scarcely be counted as a strong supporter of any kind of strict Calvinist line.
24. Strype, *Whitgift*, II, 240, Bk. IV, ch. 14, sec. 441.
25. *Ibid.*, II, 241, Bk. IV, ch. 14, sec. 441.
26. *Ibid.*, II, 264, Bk. IV, ch. 16, sec. 453.
27. *Ibid.*, II, 271, Bk. IV, ch. 16, sec. 456.
28. Cf. Porter, *op. cit.*, 358-359. Whitgift plainly believed that much of the Barret controversy was in the realm of theological *Adiaphora*. One of his letters to Burleigh expressed Whitgift's tolerance in clear terms, "Some of the points wherewith they charged him [Barret] and which they had caused him to recant (without either your Lordship's knowledge or mine) were such as the best learned protestants now living varied in judgment upon them." J. Whitgift, *Works*, I, 436. Quoted Porter, *op. cit.*, 350.
29. Cf. P. M. Dawley, *John Whitgift and the English Reformation* (New York: Charles Scribner's Sons, 1954), 220-221. Professor Dawley, representing an effort to paint Elizabethan Anglicanism in a predominantly Catholic light, claims "The controversy bewildered Whitgift. He did not understand the theological cleavage between the churchmen with whom he surrounded himself and the Cambridge Heads" (p. 220). A complete reading of Whitgift's references to Continental Protestantism, however, suggests that it was not so much bewilderment as a genuine appreciation of many of the theological positions both of Luther and Calvin that led Whitgift to the kind of mediating position which we have been noticing.
30. Strype, *op. cit.*, II, 228, lists the following as strongly favoring Calvin, and implying that the others were more of Barret and Baro's point of view: Whitaker of St. John's College; Goad, Provost of Kings; Tyndal, Master of Queens; Duport of Jesus; Barwel of Christ's; Some of Peter-house; and Chaderton of Emanuel. After this listing Strype says, "For among the rest that liked not Calvin's scheme, William Barret etc."
31. Pearson, *op. cit.*, 416.
32. Cf. W. H. Frere, *The English Church in the Reigns of Elizabeth and James I* (New York: The Macmillan Co., 1904), 79. "The Lambeth Articles, though they now seem to be an extreme statement, were, in fact, a compromise."
33. Strype, *Whitgift*, II, 282, Bk. IV, ch. 17, sec. 462.
34. *Ibid.*, II, 286, Bk. IV, ch. 17, sec. 464.
35. *Ibid.*, II, 287, Bk. IV, ch. 17, sec. 464.
36. Strype, *Whitgift*, II, 290, Bk. IV, ch. 17, sec. 466. The word "generally" is to be understood as meaning "universally" as opposed to just the elect.
37. *Ibid.*, II, 287, Bk. IV, ch. 17, sec. 465.
38. *Ibid.*, II, 296, Bk. IV, ch. 17, sec. 469.
39. *Ibid.*, II, 309, Bk. IV, ch. 18, sec. 476.

40. For a detailed description of Baro's manuscript cf. Porter, *op. cit.*, 386-389.
41. Strype, *Whitgift*, I, 126, Bk. I, ch. 2, sec. 62.
42. *Ibid.*, I, 490, Bk. III, ch. 17, sec. 257.
43. *Ibid.*, II, 173, Bk. IV, ch. 10, sec. 408.
44. Bancroft, *op. cit.*, 141.
45. *Ibid.*, 65.
46. *Ibid.*, 356.
47. T. Bilson, *The Perpetual Government etc.* (London: Christopher Barker, 1593), 281. Calvin's views on episcopacy were treated in an article "Calvin et l'épiscopat. L'épiscopat élément organique de l'église dans le calvinisme intégral," by J. Pannier in *Révue d'histoire et de Philosophie Réligieuses*, July-August 1946, quoted in F. J. Smithen, *Continental Protestantism and the English Reformation* (London: James Clarke & Co., 1927), 145. According to this article all Calvin was contending against was the theory that "... il y a différence d'essence entre l'évêque et les prêtres soumis à son autorité."
48. J. Whitgift, *Works*, I, 266.
49. Strype, *Whitgift*, I, 494-495, Bk. III, ch. 17, sec. 259-260.
50. *Ibid.*, II, 165, Bk. IV, ch. 10, sec. 408. Letter dated 1593.
51. *Ibid.*, II, 168, Bk. IV, ch. 10, sec. 405.
52. Bilson, *op. cit.*, 355.
53. Strype, *Whitgift*, I, 279, Bk. III, ch. 10, sec. 192.
54. University Archives, Registry Guard Books, vol. 6 (i), no. 18. Quoted in Porter, *op. cit.*, 144-145.
55. Quoted in Hensley Henson, *The Relation of the Church of England to the Other Reformed Churches* (Edinburgh: W. Blackwood & Sons, 1911), 15.
56. Whitgift, *Works*, I, 185. Whitgift here is paraphrasing Calvin with entire approval. Pearson says Cartwright was actually not far from this same point of view, holding that Presbyterianism was enjoined in Scripture but holding that it was not of the "esse" of the Church but of the "bene esse." It was on this ground that he withstood the Separatists (cf. A. E. S. Pearson, *Thomas Cartwright etc.*, 218).
57. Quoted in F. Schickler, *Les Églises, etc.*, 243.
58. Strype, *Whitgift*, I, 480, Bk. III, ch. 16, sec. 252. This is simply a note made by Whitgift on Travers' appeal to Burghley. It was intended for Burghley's eyes only.
59. *Ibid.*, I, 480.
60. H. M. Gwatkin, *Church and State in England to the Death of Queen Anne* (New York: Longmans, Green & Co., 1917), 264.
61. Strype, *Whitgift*, I, 559, Bk. III, ch. 21, sec. 292.
62. *Ibid.*, II, 205, Bk. IV, ch. 12, sec. 424.
63. *Ibid.*, II, 207, Bk. IV, ch. 12, sec. 425.
64. *Ibid.*, II, 203, Bk. IV, ch. 12, sec. 422.
65. Y. Brilioth, *The Anglican Revival* (London: Longmans, Green & Co., 1933), 3.
66. *Ibid.*, 4.

NEW LIGHT ON BUTZER'S SIGNIFICANCE (Littell)

1. E. C. Messenger, *The Lutheran Origin of the Anglican Ordinal* (London: Burns, Oates and Washbourne, 1934). The title of this work is misleading, for to refer to Butzer as "a German Lutheran" is to misunderstand his stance in the Reformation and to underestimate his very considerable originality.
2. Friedrich Wilhelm Kantzenbach, *Das Ringen um die Einheit der Kirche im Jahrhundert der Reformation* (Stuttgart: Evang. Verlagswerk, 1957), Ch. IV.
3. Messenger, *op. cit.*, 42-47.
4. Cf. Constantin Hopf, *Martin Bucer and the English Reformation* (Oxford: Basil Blackwell, 1946), Ch. V, on Butzer's differences with Stephen Gardiner.
5. G. J. Van de Poll, *Martin Bucer's Liturgical Ideas* (Assen: Van Gorcum & Comp. N. V., 1954), 78.
6. In Gunther Franz, *et al.*, *Urkundliche Quellen zur hessischen Reformations-*

geschichte, IV: Wiedertäuferakten, 1527-1626 (Marburg: N. G. Elwert'sche Verlagsbuchhandlung, 1951); Veröffentlichungen der Historischen Kommission für Hessen und Waldeck, Vol. XI, no. 77, 213-237.

REASON AND CONVERSION IN THE THOUGHT
OF MELANCHTHON (Manschreck)

1. Charles L. Hill, trans., *The Loci Communes of Philip Melanchthon* (Boston: Meador Publishing Company, 1944), 64 (hereafter *Loci*).
2. *Loci*, 64-65.
3. *Loci*, 70.
4. *Loci*, 70-71.
5. *Loci*, 107.
6. *Corpus Reformatorum, Melanchthon Opera*, eds., Bretschneider and Bindseil, 28 vols., 1834-1860; vol. 11:398, 55 (hereafter *CR*).
7. *Apology of the Augsburg Confession*, trans. by Henry E. Jacobs in *The Book of Concord* (Philadelphia: United Lutheran Publishing House, 1883), I, 67 (hereafter *Apology*).
8. *CR* 2:507.
9. *CR* 1:105, 398.
10. *Philipp Melanchthon's Werke*, F. A. Keothe, ed. (Leipzig: F. A. Brockhaus, 1829), V, *Uses of Philosophy*.
11. *CR* 11:278ff.
12. *Uses of Philosophy*.
13. *Ibidem*.
14. Cf. Franz Hildebrandt, *Melanchthon: Alien or Ally?* (Cambridge: University Press, 1946); Karl Hartfelder, *Philipp Melanchthon als Praeceptor Germaniae* (Berlin: A. Hoffman & Co., 1889); K. Steiff, *Der erste Buchdruck in Tübingen* (Tübingen, 1881).
15. *Uses of Philosophy*.
16. *Loci*, 82-85, 95, 101.
17. *Loci*, 83.
18. *Loci*, 216.
19. *Loci*, 86, 196.
20. *Loci*, 86.
21. *Loci*, 87.
22. *Loci*, 86.
23. *Loci*, 89.
24. *Loci*, 99-101.
25. *Loci*, 69f.
26. *Loci*, 196f., 208.
27. *Loci*, 261, 202-204.
28. *Loci*, 188.
29. *Loci*, 171.
30. *Loci*, 176.
31. *Loci*, 177, 184.
32. *Loci*, 72ff.
33. *Loci*, 234, 259f.
34. *Loci*, 81.
35. *Loci*, 72ff., 160ff.
36. *Loci*, 160ff.
37. *Loci*, 193ff.
38. *Loci*, 197, 235.
39. *Loci*, 202-203. Cf. 261.
40. *Loci*, 208.
41. *Loci*, 112. Cf. Rom. 2:15.
42. *Loci*, 227f.
43. *Loci*, 113-130.

44. *Loci*, 131ff.
45. *Loci*, 74, 154. Cf. *Liber de Anima* and *Erotemata Dialectices*.
46. *Loci*, 154ff., 235ff.
47. Reinhold Seeberg, *Dogmengeschichte*, II, 349. Cf. *Augsburg Confession*, art. 18; J. W. Richard, *Lutheran Quarterly*, XXXVII, 1907, 198.
48. *CR* 13:656.
49. *Commentary on Colossians;* cf. *Lutheran Quarterly*, XXXV, 1905, 77-89.
50. *Ibid.*, Excursus on the Will.
51. Cf. *Lutheran Quarterly*, XXXVII, 1907, 198.
52. Lic. th. Herrlinger, *Die Theologie Melanchthons* (Gotha: Friedrich A. Perthes, 1879), 73.
53. *CR* 24:43.
54. *CR* 1:893; 2:457.
55. *CR* 10:302. W. M. L. de Witte, ed., *Martin Luthers Briefe* (Berlin, 1825-28), 5 vols., 1:305; 2:557; 4:17. *Tischreden, Luthers Werke*, Weimar edition, 3:3589, 3695; 5:5511, 5647, 5781, 5787, 5827, 6439, 6458, etc. Cf. *CR* 1:898; 3:383; 7:356; 9:763f.
56. Cf. *Apology*, 96. Rom. 3:24, 28; Eph. 2:8.
57. *Apology*, 76, 79.
58. *Apology*, 105.
59. *Apology*, 94, 103.
60. *Apology*, 139, 282.
61. *Apology*, 206.
62. *Apology*, 98.
63. *Apology*, 94.
64. *Apology*, 100.
65. *Apology*, 91.
66. *Apology*, 94.
67. *Apology*, 144.
68. *Apology*, 97.
69. *Apology*, 132.
70. *Apology*, 79.
71. *Apology*, 85.
72. *Apology*, 133, 115.
73. *Apology*, 228.
74. *Apology*, 123.
75. *Apology*, 79, 85, 89f., 94, 96, 103, 167, 206.
76. *Apology*, 162ff.
77. *Apology*, 164.
78. *Apology*, 86f.
79. *Apology*, 87, 89, 105.
80. *Apology*, 89, 139.
81. *Apology*, 168.
82. *Apology*, 169.
83. *Apology*, 173, 169.
84. *Apology*, 169.
85. *Apology*, 222-226.
86. *Apology*, 227.
87. *Apology*, 227ff.
88. *Apology*, 228.
89. *Apology*, 227f.
90. *Apology*, 228.
91. *Apology*, 230.
92. *Apology*, 231.
93. *Apology*, 91, 104, 109, 113, 115, 140, 183, 227.
94. *Apology*, 116.
95. *CR* 23:179.
96. F. Galle, *Versuch einer Charakeristik Melanchthons als Theologen* (Halle: Lippert, 1840), 291-294. Cf. Herrlinger, *op. cit.*
97. *CR* 21:253-332.
98. *CR* 21:271ff. Cf. *CR* 25:438; 9:467f.
99. *CR* 21:376.

100. *CR* 21:377.
101. Cf. *Loci* (1533). *CR* 21:330.
102. *CR* 13:162. *Lutheran Quarterly*, XXXV, July 1905, 303-345.
103. Cf. Balthaser, *Andere Sammlung zur Pommerischen Kirchen-Historie*, 116ff. *CR* 9:766; 15:544, 680; 16:198; 21:656, 330, 761, 891.
104. *CR* 21:647; 372. Cf. *Lutheran Quarterly*, XXXVII, 1907, 309ff.
105. Cf. *CR* 15:678ff.
106. *Loci* (1559). *CR* 21. Cf. C. B. Gohdes, *The Lutheran Church Review*, XXVIII, July 1909, 325-337, Oct., 551-64.
107. *CR* 22:417.
108. *CR* 5:109; 7:932; 8:916; 9:467f., 766; 25:438. *Lutheran Quarterly*, XXXV, July 1905, 303-45.
109. *CR* 1:898; 3:383; 7:356; 9:763f. Cf. Mix, *Theologische Studien und Kritiken*, 1901.
110. Cf. *Lutheran Quarterly*, XXXVII, 1907, 309-310.
111. *CR* 9:605.
112. *CR* 11:305.
113. *CR* 1:772; 10:101.
114. *CR* 11:106f., 875.
115. *CR* 11:279f., 489f.
116. *CR* 11:666.
117. *CR* 11:107.
118. *CR* 1:666; 11:130, 605; 20:391.
119. *CR* 11:289ff., 445.
120. *CR* 7:472.

THE STRANGERS' "MODEL CHURCHES"
IN SIXTEENTH-CENTURY ENGLAND (Norwood)

1. *Original Letters Relative to the English Reformation* (Cambridge: University Press, 1846), 17. Cf. Hugh Latimer, *Sermons* (Cambridge: University Press, 1844), 141, the 3rd sermon.
2. John Strype, *Ecclesiastical Memorials* (Oxford: Clarendon Press, 1822), II (1), 321.
3. Two of the best books on Laski are: Hermann Dalton, *John a Lasco* (London: Hodder and Stoughton, 1886); George Pascal, *Jean de Lasco* (Paris, 1894, 304p.). See also Oskar Bartel, *Jan Laski* (Warszawa, 1955—, Wyd. I), in Polish; Karl Hein, *Die Sakramentslehre des Johannes à Lasco* (Berlin, 1904, 188p.); Theodor Wotschke, "Zum Lebensbilde Laskis," *Archiv für Reformationsgeschichte*, XXXI, 1911, 233-45. See below for bibliography of works by Laski (n. 30-32).
4. Pascal, 216.
5. John Strype, *Memorials of Archbishop Cranmer* (Oxford: Ecclesiastical Historical Society, 1848, 3 vols.), III, appendix no. 105.
6. The two most important secondary works dealing with these refugee communities are: A. A. van Schelven, *De Nederduitsche Vluchtelingenkerken der XVIe Eeuw in Engeland en Duitschland* (s'Gravenhage: Martinus Nijhoff, 1909, 455p.); Fernand de Schickler, *Les Églises du Refuge en Angleterre* (Paris: Fischbacher, 1892, 3 vols.). See also Marten Woudstra, *De Hollandsche Vreemdelingen-Gemeente te Londen* (Groningen, 1908, 155p.); John S. Burn, *History of the French, Walloon, Dutch Refugees* (London: Longmans, Green & Co., 1846, 284p.). Much valuable material is to be found in the *Publications* and *Proceedings* of the Huguenot Society of London. For Austin Friars see J. Lindeboom, *Austin Friars; History of the Dutch Reformed Church in London, 1550-1950* (The Hague: Martinus Nijhoff, 1950, 208p.). An early history, useful as near source material, is Symeon Ruytinck, et al., *Geschiedenissen ende Handelingen die vornemelick aengaen de Nederduytsche Natie ende Gemeynten, wonende in Engelant ende int bysonder tot Londen* (Utrecht, 1873, 515p.; Werken der Marnix-Vereeniging, Ser. III, Deel I). Prime source material, but not directly useful for this study, is J. H. Hessels, ed., *Ecclesiae Londino-Batavae Archivum* (Cambridge, Eng., 1889 ff., 3 vols. in 4). For economic factors see Frederick A. Norwood, *The Reformation Refugees as an*

Economic Force (Chicago: The American Society of Church History, 1942, 206p.).
7. Strype, *Memorials of Cranmer*, II, 270.
8. Lindeboom gives the full text in Latin and English as an appendix, pp. 198-203. Cf. among others Pascal, 220; Ruytinck, 12ff. The passage reads: "vt per totum rei publice corpus casta sinceraque religio diffundatur et ecclesia in uere christianis et apostolicis opinionibus et ritibus instituta et adulta per sanctos ac carni et mundo mortuos ministros conseruetur."
9. ". . . eo intencione et proposito vt a ministris ecclesie Germanorum aliorumque peregrinorum Sacrosancti Euangelij incorrupta interpretacio sacramentorum iuxta verbum Dei et apostolicam observacionem administracio fiat . . ."
10. Martin Flandrus (Micronius), Walter Loenus (Delaenus), Francis Riverius (Rivius), Richard Gallus (Vauville).
11. Lindeboom, 202.
12. George B. Beeman, "The Early History of the Strangers' Church, 1550 to 1561," Huguenot Society of London, *Proceedings*, XV, 1933-1937, 267.
13. *Original Letters,* 567-568.
14. Utenhove to Calvin, Aug. 23, 1550. *Corpus Reformatorum*, XLI (Calvini Opera, XIII), 627, "imo plura nobis hic esse permissa quam ipsi postulaverimus." And further: "In quo verbum pure populo proponere ac sacramenta ex institutione Christi Domini sine superstitione aliqua administrare licet. Disciplina quoque ecclesiastica ex verbo Dei nobis est permissa."
15. Quoted in Burn, 186. Micronius listed in a letter to Bullinger "Arians, Marcionists, Libertines, Danists, and the like monstrosities, in great number" (*Original Letters,* 560). Cf. also F. Pijper, *Jan Utenhove* (Leiden: A. H. Adrian, 1883, 256, 94p.), 62f.; Schelven, 66.
16. *Forma ac Ratio tota Ecclesiastici Ministerij, in peregrinorum, potissimum uero Germanorum Ecclesia, instituta Londini in Anglia* (Frankfurt, 1555). A modern edition is in Laski's works, edited by A. Kuyper, *Joannis a Lasco Opera tam Edita quam Inedita* (Amstelodami: Fr. Muller, 1866, 2 vols.), II, 1-284.
17. Laski, *Forma ac Ratio,* Dedication to King Sigismund of Poland, in Laski, *Opera*, II, 10, "Huius igitur hortatu eum ego quoque per Regem illum vocatus essem et leges quaedam patriae obstarent, quominus publici potissimum cultus divini ritus, sub Papismo usurpati, pro eo ac Rex ipse cupiebat repurgari protinus possent— ego vero pro Peregrinorum Ecclesiis sedulo instarem—ita demum placuit, ut ritus publici in Anglicis Ecclesiis per gradus quosdam, quantum per leges patriae omnino liceret, repurgarentur: Peregrinis vero hominibus, qui patriis hac alioqui in parte legibus non usque adeo tenerentur, Ecclesiae concederentur, in quibus omnia libere et nulla rituum patriorum habita ratione, iuxta doctrinam duntaxat atque observationem Apostolicam instituerentur; ita enim fore, ut Anglicae quoque Ecclesiae ad puritatem Apostolicam amplectendam unanimi omnium regni ordinum consensu excitarentur."
18. Schelven, 67, writes, ". . . de gadachte om door een modelkerk een voorbeeld te geven voor de reformatie der Engelsche kerk." Cf. Schickler, I, 31.
19. Apr. 26, 1549, *Original Letters,* 535-536.
20. Jan. 28, 1551, *ibid.,* 488.
21. Schelven, 78-79.
22. *Ibid.,* 69. Cf. Pijper, 66ff.
23. Micronius to Bullinger, Aug. 28, 1550, *Original Letters,* 569, given as of 31st. See also 575.
24. Letter to Cecil, in Laski, *Opera*, II, 672.
25. Schickler, I, 24ff.
26. Strype, *Memorials of Cranmer*, II, 280.
27. Micronius to Bullinger, Feb. 18, 1553, *Original Letters,* 581.
28. Lindeboom, 33.
29. Cf. discussion in *ibid.,* 24.
30. A. Kuyper, ed. (Amstelodami, 1866, 2 vols.). The first volume contains an extensive introduction in Latin to the Laski literature, together with the dogmatic and polemic works. The second volume, more important for this study, has the liturgical and symbolic works.
31. A good copy of this rare work is kept in the Rare Book Room of the Newberry Library, Chicago. The title page does not give the place and date. It is small in format, but contains altogether 792 pages in three separate numerations. The

Dedication to Sigismund, King of Poland, occupies 86 pages. This work is to be found in the *Opera*, II, 1-284.

32. *Compendium Doctrinae de Vera unicaque Dei et Christi Ecclesia* (London, 1551), interleaved with *Een kort Begrijp der Leeringhe van de warachtige ende eenighe Ghemeynte Gods ende Christi* (London, 1551; Emden, 1565), 285-339; *De Catechismus, oft Kinder leere* (London, 1551), with Latin translation, 340-475; *Een korte Ondersoeckinge des Gheloofs* (the short catechism, London, 1553; Emden, 1558), with Latin, 476-92; *Catechismus effte Kinderlehre* (Emden catechism, Emden, 1554), with Latin, 495-543; *Epistolae*, 547-766. No French translations of these catechisms were made because the French already had the catechism of Calvin.

33. Copies of this are said to exist at the Bodleian in Oxford and in the French Library of St. Martin in London (Huguenot Society?). Cf. Laski, *Opera*, I, cii ff. of the Introduction.

34. Laski, *Opera*, I, lxxviii. Cf. Lindeboom, 16; Schickler, I, 37.

35. Schelven, 73, "Dit Compendium doctrinae is a. h. w. een apologie, waarin de kerk als geheel, redeneerend vanuit het wezen der Christelijke Kerk, aantoonen wil, dat ze rechtens optreedt zooals ze doet. Meer dan een confessie is het een bewijs, waardoor ze zick legitimeert."

36. Laski, *Opera*, II, 289-90.

37. *Ibid.*, II, 294-295. The Dutch version, "Daerom de Kercke of Ghemeynte Gods, is de vergaderinghe der gener, die wt de gantsche menichte aller menschē, door de stemme Gods, hem tot een eyghen Volck geroepen wert."

38. *Ibid.* "Primum, ut non sane humana ulla, sed ipsius Dei voce atque autoritate, evocetur et colligatur." "Ten eersten, datse niet door eenigher menschen stemme, maar door de stemme ende Autoriteyt Gods, wtgeroepen ende vergadert zy."

39. *Ibid.*, II, 296-97. "Ende dit is de warachtighe Kercke of Ghemeynte Gods, de welcke wtgeroepen is by de stemme Gods, door de Enghelen, de Propheten, ende Christum dē Heere, als der eerster aller Regeerder, ende syne Apostelen, in een Vergaderinge ende Volck, dat hem eyghen is."

40. *Ibid.*, II, 330-333.

41. *Ibid.*, II, 300.

42. *Ibid.*, II, 306.

43. Schickler, I, 55.

44. Laski, *Opera*, I, 97-232.

45. *Ibid.*, I, 128.

46. Pascal, 230.

47. Laski, *Opera*, II, 50.

48. Schelven, 80.

49. Laski, *Opera*, II, 51.

50. *Ibid.*, II, 58.

51. *Ibid.*, II, 328f.

52. *Ibid.*, II, 330-331: "Ut Christi Domini institutiones in tota Ecclesia pure fideliter ac reverenter observari curent, eosque puniant, qui illas, aut temere negligunt, aut adulterant, aut abolere conantur." "Dat sy besorgen, dat alle Instellingen Christi des Heeren, reynlick, getrouwelick en weerdelick onderhouden wesen, ende straffen alle de gene, die deselue verachten, verualschen, of onderstaen te niet brenghen."

53. Micronius to Bullinger, Oct. 13, 1550, *Original Letters*, 570.

54. Laski, *Opera*, II, 52.

55. Schickler, I, 50.

56. Information on the French consistory, mainly from the early Elizabethan period is found in Elsie Johnston, ed., *Actes du consistoire de l'Église française de Threadneedle Street, Londres*, Vol. I, 1560-1565 (London: Huguenot Society of London, 1937), 150.

57. Laski, *Opera*, II, 65, where the mode is described.

58. *Ibid.*, II, 69ff.

59. *Ibid.*, II, 81ff.

60. *Ibid.*, II, 82.

61. Woudstra, 141-147, gives examples in the original Dutch; cf. Pijper, 77ff.

62. Schickler, I, 43.

63. Laski, *Opera*, II, 173.

64. John Calvin, *Institutes of the Christian Religion*, Bk. IV, ch. xii, paragraph 1.
65. Laski, *Opera*, II, 175.
66. *Ibid.*, II, 236ff.
67. *Ibid.*, II, 170, "Disciplina Ecclesiastica est certa quaedam e scripturis petita ratio observandi gradatim Christianas admonitiones ex verbo Dei inter fratres invicem omnes in Ecclesia Christi, ut et corpus universum singulaque illius membra in suo officio, quoad eius fieri, potest, contineantur,—et, si qui in illa deprehendantur obstinati admonitionum istiusmodi contemptores, ut Satanae ad extremum per excommunicationem tradantur, si quo modo per talem pudefactionem e caro in illius interire, quod ad affectus illius attinet et spiritus ita demum revocari ad resipiscentiam a proinde servari etiam possit." On Bucer's *Gemeinschaften* see Werner Bellardi, *Die Geschichte der "Christlichen Gemeinschaften" in Strassburg (1546-1550)* (Leipzig: M. Heinsius Nachf., 1934, 217p., Quellen und Forschungen für Reformationsgeschichte, Bd. 18), especially 113, where he emphasizes Bucer's influence on the London *Freiwilligkeitskirche*.
68. Schelven, 94, quoting Micronius.
69. Laski, *Opera*, II, 101-105.
70. Schelven, 86.
71. Utenhove to Bullinger, Nov. 7, 1551. *Original Letters*, 587.
72. Cf. Woudstra, 98-128; Schelven, 83. Woudstra says the London Dutch church was called "mater et propagatrix omnium Reformatorum Ecclesiarum Belgicarum."
73. Micronius to Bullinger, Nov. 7, 1551, *Original Letters*, 578.
74. Albert Pollard, *Thomas Cranmer* (New York: G. P. Putnam's Sons, 1904, 399p.), 269-270.
75. *Ibid.*, 216.
76. Strype, *Ecclesiastical Memorials*, II (1), 377, 399; II (2), 33; *Memorials of Cranmer*, II, 201-204, 279-280.
77. Strype, *Ecclesiastical Memorials*, II, 35. Micronius' work of 1552, *Van het Nachtmael Christi ende van de Misse*, had slight influence, if any (in Cramer & Pijper, eds., *Bibliotheca Reformatoria Neerlandica* (M. Nijhoff: The Hague, 1905-1914), IX; cf. I, 428).
78. Peter Martyr to Bullinger, Mar. 8, 1552; and Micronius to Bullinger, Mar. 9, 1552, *Original Letters*, 503, 580. Pascal, 231.
79. Strype, *Memorials of Cranmer*, II, 201-204. See also M. M. Knappen, *Tudor Puritanism* (Chicago: University of Chicago Press, 1939, 555 p.), 97.
80. Hooper to Bullinger, Aug. 1, 1551, *Original Letters*, 95; Strype, *Ecclesiastical Memorials*, II (1), 399, II (2), 444ff.; Schickler, I, 54; Pascal, 224-225.
81. Calvin to Edward VI, Jan. 1, 1551, *Original Letters*, p. 709. Utenhove also called him "our Josiah" *(Simplex et Fidelis Narratio de instituta ac demum dissipata Belgarum, aliorumque peregrinorum in Anglia Ecclesia* (Basel, 1560, 6).

SECTARIANISM AND SKEPTICISM: THE STRANGE ALLIES OF RELIGIOUS LIBERTY (Beach)

1. Among his first published monographs are: "The Development and Consistency of Luther's Attitude to Religious Liberty," *The Harvard Theological Review*, XXII, 2 (April, 1929), and "Sebastian Castellio and the Toleration Controversy of the Sixteenth Century," in *Persecution and Liberty, Essays in Honor of George Lincoln Burr* (New York: The Century Co., 1931).
2. Cf., J. B. Bury, *A History of Freedom of Thought* (New York: Henry Holt and Company, 1913); W. E. H. Lecky, *History of the Rise and Influence of the Spirit of Rationalism in Europe* (New York: D. Appleton and Co., 1873).
3. Roland H. Bainton, *The Travail of Religious Liberty* (Philadelphia: The Westminster Press, 1951), 253-254; cf. 13-14.
4. *Ibid.*, 254.
5. Bainton, "The Struggle for Religious Liberty," *Church History*, Vol. X, no. 2, June 1941, 14.
6. *Ibid.*, 19-20. Also *The Travail of Religious Liberty*, *op. cit.*, 258. The accuracy of

Troeltsch's typology is not qualified by the fact that there are frequent mixtures of church-type and sect-type, or churches in migration from one to the other.

7. See especially Thomas Lyon: *The Theory of Religious Liberty in England, 1603-1609* (Cambridge: The University Press, 1937), who delineates two main types of tolerationists, on the one hand, those whose lives are conditioned by the passionate conviction that they are in possession of known and ascertained truth, for whom "toleration is not an end, but a means to a great light" (p.2), and on the other hand, the tolerationists "who are sceptical about human beliefs being efficacious towards salvation *per se*," and for whom "truth is not so absolute, still less so ascertained, that a man should be damned for an error which he sincerely believes to be true" (p. 4). Cf. Francisco Ruffini, *Religious Liberty* (London: Williams & Norgate, 1912).

8. Bainton, *The Travail of Religious Liberty, op. cit.,* 59.

9. Bainton, "Sebastian Castellio and the Toleration Controversy of the Sixteenth Century," in *Persecution and Liberty,* 201.

10. Bainton regards Erasmus as a composite of "humanism" and "mysticism" (*The Travail of Religious Liberty, op. cit.,* 57-59). The case is made more easily for the former than the latter.

11. Wallace Ferguson, "The Attitude of Erasmus Toward Toleration," in *Persecution and Liberty,* 172. See also Joseph LeCler, *Histoire de la Tolérance au Siècle de la Réforme,* Vol. I, 133-149 (Paris: Aubier, 1955).

12. Ferguson, *op. cit.,* 178.

13. Quoted in Bainton, *The Travail of Religious Liberty, op. cit.,* 58.

14. *Ibid.,* 135.

15. *Ibid.* See LeCler, I, 221-226. Also Johannes Kühn, *Toleranz und Offenbarung* (Leipzig: Felix Meiner, 1923).

16. Bainton, *The Travail of Religious Liberty, op. cit.,* 137.

17. See Sebastian Castellio, *Concerning Heretics,* translated and edited by Roland H. Bainton (New York: Columbia University Press, 1935).

18. Sections of the argument of this treatise, Bainton makes available in *ibid.,* 287-307. See also Bainton, "New Documents on Early Protestant Rationalism," *Church History,* VII, 2, June 1938. Also, LeCler, I, 340ff.

19. Castellio, *op. cit.,* 299.

20. *Ibid.*

21. *Ibid.,* 301.

22. Bainton, *The Travail of Religious Liberty, op. cit.,* 116.

23. The literature on the toleration controversy in this period is mountainous. *Tracts on Liberty in the Puritan Revolution,* edited by William Haller, 3 vols. (New York: Columbia University Press, 1934), provides facsimiles of original texts. For synopses of the positions of the many disputants and schools, W. K. Jordan's 4 vols. on *The Development of Religious Toleration in England* (Cambridge: Harvard University Press, 1933-1946) is the most valuable. For interpretation, William Haller, *Liberty and Reformation in the Puritan Revolution* (New York: Columbia University Press, 1955), Geoffrey Nuttall, *The Holy Spirit in Puritan Faith and Experience* (Oxford: Basil Blackwell, 1946), and T. Lyon, *The Theory of Religious Liberty in England, 1603-1639* (Cambridge: The University Press, 1937) are penetrating. Treatments of individual thinkers like Hooker, Chillingworth, Milton, Locke, Penn, Williams, etc., are manifold. Michael Freund, *Die Idee der Toleranz im England der Grossen Revolution* (Halle: M. Niemeyer, 1927), and Johannes Kühn, *op. cit.,* are also useful.

24. W. Chillingworth, *Works* (Philadelphia, 1844 ed.), 18.

25. Thomas Browne, *Religio Medici* (New York: E. P. Dutton & Co., Inc., 1906), 7.

26. Jeremy Taylor, *Liberty of Prophesying; Works,* Heber ed. (London, 1839), vol. vi, preface, ccccvi. Cf. Freund, *op. cit.,* 43.

27. See Haller, *op. cit.; Tracts on Liberty of Conscience* (London: Hansard Knollys Society, 1846); and William L. Lumpkin, *Baptist Confessions of Faith* (Philadelphia: Judson Press, 1959).

28. Allen, J. W., *English Political Thought, 1603-1660,* Vol. I (London, 1938), 200-228. The wording of the Savoy Declaration on liberty of conscience is instructive: "God alone is Lord of the conscience, and hath left it free from the doctrines and commandments of men, which are in anything contrary to his Word, or not

contained in it; so that to believe such doctrines, or to obey such commands out of conscience, is to betray true liberty of conscience." Philip Schaff, *The Creeds of Christendom* (New York: Harper & Brothers, 1877), Vol. III, 719.

29. Leonard Busher, *Religion's Peace, or a Plea for Liberty of Conscience* (in Hansard Knollys Society, *Tracts*), 78.

30. Bainton, *The Travail of Religious Liberty, op. cit.*, Chs. VII, VIII, and IX.

31. Haller, *Liberty and Reformation in the Puritan Revolution*, 185.

32. Roger Williams, *The Bloudy Tenent of Persecution* (London: Hansard Knollys Society, 1848), preface.

33. Bainton, *The Travail of Religious Liberty, op. cit.*, 247.

34. John Locke, *Letters on Toleration* (London: A. Millar, 1765), 38.

35. See John Locke, *Essay Concerning Human Understanding*, Bk. IV, ch. 18.

36. Locke, *Letters on Toleration*, 93. Cf. A. A. Seaton, *The Theory of Toleration under the Later Stuarts* (Cambridge: University Press, 1911), Ch. IV.

37. Locke, *Letters on Toleration*, 60.

38. Anson Phelps Stokes, *Church and State in the United States* (New York: Harper & Brothers, 1950), Vol. I, 334.

39. Stokes, *op. cit.*, I, 333-339. See Norman Cousins, *In God We Trust: the Religious Beliefs and Ideas of the American Founding Fathers* (New York: Harper & Brothers, 1958), ch. 5.

40. Quoted in Stokes, *op. cit.*, 335. He does not always remain consistent on this point, for in another instance he related political resistance to theological foundations. "Resistance to tyranny is obedience to God."

41. *Bill for Establishing Religious Freedom.*

42. Stokes, *op. cit.*, 337-338. See also Cousins, *op. cit.*, 132, 139, 151.

43. Stokes, *op. cit.*, I, 373.

44. *Ibid.*, 374.

45. *Ibid.*, 335.

46. It is in this same letter that Jefferson uses this famous and much controverted phrase.

47. Bainton, *The Travail of Religious Liberty, op. cit.*, 254.

48. J. D. Dawson, *Separate Church and State Now* (New York: Richard R. Smith, 1948). Appendix B, A Manifesto, 209. The current president of POAU is Mr. Louie D. Newton, noted Baptist preacher and one-time president of the Southern Baptist Convention.

49. The writings of Paul Blanshard, *Communism, Democracy, and Catholic Power* (Boston: The Beacon Press, 1951); *American Freedom and Catholic Power* (rev. ed., Boston: The Beacon Press, 1958); *God and Man in Washington* (Boston: The Beacon Press, 1960) are typical, as is Horace M. Kallen, *Secularism is the Will of God* (New York: Twayne Publishers, Inc., 1954).

50. Among those supporting the case of Mrs. Vashti McCollum, who protested religious instruction for her son in Champaign, Illinois, were the American Unitarian Association, the American Ethical Union, the Ethical Culture Society, the Southern Baptist Convention. Vashti McCollum: *One Woman's Fight* (New York, 1951), 165. See also Waldo Beach, "A Protestant Position on the Church-State Issue," *Religion in Life*, XXIII, 2, Spring 1954.

AUGSBURG AND THE EARLY ANABAPTISTS (Schwab)

1. Friedrich Roth, *Augsburgs Reformationsgeschichte, 1517-1530*, I (Munich: Thdr. Ackermann, 1901), 219-221, *passim*. "He was a disciple of Karlstadt in the Supper." J. F. Gerhard Goeters, *Ludwig Hätzer (ca. 1500-1529) Spiritualist und Antitrinitarier. Eine Randfigur der frühen Täuferbewegung* (Karlsruhe: Heinrich Schneider, 1957), 66.

2. Goeters, *op. cit.*, 60-66, *passim*, "Hätzer hat allerdings in den Konventikeln den Grundstein zur späteren Augsburger Täufergemeinde gelegt."

3. Gerhard Goeters, "Haetzer, Ludwig," *Mennonite Encyclopedia*, II (Scottdale: Herald Press, 1956), 623.

4. This act seems anomalous; at least it was not customary practice. There is no

record that Hätzer ever administered it except on this occasion in Regensburg. *Ibid.*, 624.

5. Gerhard Goeters, "Ludwig Haetzer, A Marginal Anabaptist," *The Mennonite Quarterly Review*, XXIX, no. 4, Oct. 1955, 259. Goeters, "Haetzer, Ludwig," *Mennonite Encyclopedia*, II, 624-625.

6. R. J. Smithson, *The Anabaptists: Their Contribution to Our Protestant Heritage* (London: James Clarke & Co., 1935), 57.

7. Johann Loserth, "Hubmaier, Balthasar," *The Mennonite Encyclopedia*, II (Scottdale, 1956), 827.

8. Walter Fellmann, *Das Leben Dencks* (Gütersloh: C. Bertelsmann Verlag, 1956), *Quellen und Forschungen zur Reformationsgeschichte*, XXIV, pt. 2, 8-19, 12.

9. Loserth, *loc. cit.*, 828.

10. *Ibid.*, 833.

11. Goeters, "Ludwig Hätzer (ca. 1500-1529) Spiritualist und Antitrinitarier," *Mennonite Encyclopedia*, II, 111.

12. Jan J. Kiwiet, "The Life of Hans Denck (ca. 1500-1527)," *The Mennonite Quarterly Review*, XXXI, no. 4, Oct. 1957, 233.

13. *Ibid.*, 245. Denck was a follower of Thomas Münzer theologically but not in radical social reforms; Hans Hut was essentially eschatological and not lastingly sympathetic with Münzer's revolutionary social reforms. Jan J. Kiwiet, *Pilgram Marbeck, Ein Führer in der Täuferbewegung der Reformationszeit* (Kassel: J. G. Oncken Verlag, 1957), 43.

14. Roth, *op. cit.*, I, 57-175, *passim.*

15. Kiwiet, "The Life of Hans Denck," 243-253, *loc. cit.*

16. W. F. Neff, "Denk (Denck), Hans," *The Mennonite Encyclopedia*, II, 35.

17. Christian Meyer, "Die Anfänge des Wiedertäuferthums in Augsburg," *Zeitschrift des Historischen Vereins für Schwaben und Neuberg* (Augsburg, 1874), I, 229; cross-examination of Oct. 5, 1527.

18. R. F. Loserth, "Hut (Hutt, Huth, Huet), Hans," *The Mennonite Encyclopedia*, II, 846, citing a Council of Nürnberg poster of Nov. 26, 1527.

19. Roland H. Bainton, *The Travail of Religious Liberty* (Philadelphia: The Westminster Press, 1951), 62-63.

20. Loserth, "Hut, Hans," 849; Meyer, *op. cit.*, 211-212.

21. Meyer, *op. cit.*, 212.

22. Goeters, *Ludwig Hätzer (ca. 1500-1529) Spiritualist und Antitrinitarier*, 112.

23. Loserth, "Hut, Hans," 847.

24. Franklin Hamlin Littell, *The Anabaptist View of the Church* (Boston: Beacon Press, 1958), 124.

25. John Christian Wenger, *Glimpses of Mennonite History and Doctrine* (Scottdale: Herald Press, 1947), 33.

26. Harry Emerson Fosdick, ed., "The Schleitheim Confession of Faith" art. 1, *Great Voices of the Reformation, An Anthology* (New York: Random House, 1952), 288.

27. Kiwiet, *Pilgram Marbeck*, 43-45, cites Sebastian Franck's description of the Strasbourg Anabaptists. After having described the small group of Sattler Swiss Anabaptists, Franck says: "Die andern und fast all/ halten man mög die warheyt wol mit eyd bezeugen / so es die lieb erfordert oder den Glauben betrifft /. Ziehen hier auff vil leren und exempel beyder Testament /. Der meynung ist auch Joannes Denck gewesen. Dise lassen auch die Oberkeyt Christen seyn / so sy nach dem bevelch Gottes handlen / und billiche auch die notwöhr und Krieg / so man nit freventlich / sunder auss not und gehorsam für sich nemen musz." *Chronica, Zeitbuch, und Geschichtsbibell*, 1536, 2 aufl., Bd. 3, 197.

28. Henry C. Vedder, *Balthasar Hübmaier, The Leader of the Anabaptists* (New York: G. P. Putnam's Sons, 1905), 142.

29. "hab tauffer geredt: 'so knie nider!', und hab im auss ainem hillzin geschirr ain wasser mit der handt auff den kopf gossen im namen des vattern, des suns und des hailligen gaists." Friedrich Roth, "Zur Lebensgeschichte Eitelhans Langenmantels von Augsburg," *Zeitschrift des Historischen Vereins für Schwaben und Neuburg* (Augsburg, 1900), 26; "Er, tauffer, gesagt: 'so nem buess und lass dich tauffen.' darauf er im ain wasser auff den kopf gossen und getaufft." *Ibid*, 27.

30. Littell, *op. cit.*, 159.

31. Paul Josiah Schwab, *The Attitude of Wolfgang Musculus Toward Religious Tolerance* (Scottdale: Mennonite Press, 1933), 44-46.
32. Loserth, "Hut, Hans," 847. Meyer, *loc. cit.*, 218, says that from now on Hut gave his most constructive messages. Kiwiet, *Pilgram Marbeck*, 43, says "Für Hut war die eschatologische Botschaft das Zentrum seiner Predigt; die sozialen und revolutionären Reformen eines Thomas Münzers lehnte er aber ab."
33. Christian Hege, "Augsburg," *The Mennonite Encyclopedia*, I, 183.
34. Loserth, "Hut, Hans," 848.
35. This "Büchlein" contained a catechism, a prayer before meals, and a concordance with 78 items. It is published in Roth, "Zur Lebens," 39ff.
36. Loserth, "Hut, Hans," 849, quoting *Geschichtsbuch;* Roth, *Aug. Ref.* I, 239; Hege, "Augsburg."
37. Roth, *Aug. Ref.* I, 225. Meyer, *op. cit.*, 213, is followed by Loserth and others in mistakenly identifying Langenmantel's father as Hansen Langenmantel who was 14 times elected mayor of Augsburg and was a *Hauptmann* in the Swabian League. Roth frequently refers to Meyer's history but intentionally differs from the latter's statements about the parentage.
38. Roth, "Zur Lebens," 3-4.
39. Roth, *Aug. Ref.* I, 260, n. 26.
40. *Ibid.*, 264, n. 90, citing Kiliam Lieb's *Annalen* as printed in John Jos. Ignaz von Döllinger *Beiträge zur politischen, kirchlichen und Cultur-Geschicht des sechs letzten Jahrhunderte;* Bd. II, *Materialen zur Geschichte des fünfzehnten und sechszehnten Jahrhunderts* (Regensburg, 1863), G. J. Manz, 517.
41. Hege, "Augsburg," 185, says he was baptized in February. Langenmantel after his 1528 arrest testified in cross-examination that he was baptized by Hut the same night as his servant Hermann Anwaldt, Roth, "Zur Lebens," 11. Anwaldt in his testimony said he was baptized by Hut on Shrove Tuesday. As Easter Sunday in 1527 fell on Apr. 21, the baptism took place Mar. 5.
42. John C. Wenger, "The Biblicism of the Anabaptists," *The Recovery of the Anabaptist Vision*, Guy F. Hershberger, ed. (Scottdale: Herald Press, 1957), 167.
43. Johann Loserth, "Langenmantel, Eitelhans (Hans)," *The Mennonite Encyclopedia*, III, 289-290.
44. Roth, *Aug. Ref.* I, 230-231.
45. Roth, "Zur Lebens," 5.
46. *Ibid.*, 7.
47. Other exiled Augsburg leaders did this also, but especially the "Capitanier der Ketzer" Langenmantel, Widholz, Gall Fischer, Scheppach, and Kissling. Friedrich Roth, "Der Höhepunkt der Wiedertäuferischen Bewegung in Augsburg und ihr Niedergang im Jahre 1528," *Zeitschrift des Historischen Vereins für Schwaben und Neuberg* (Augsburg, 1901), 4.
48. Meyer, *op. cit.*, 214-215; Roth, "Zur Lebens," 8-9.
49. Roth, *op. cit.*, 16.
50. *Ibid.*, 9-29.
51. *Ibid.*, 15.
52. *Ibid.*, 21.
53. *Ibid.*, 21.
54. *Ibid.*, 23.
55. *Ibid.*, 12.
56. *Ibid.*, 9.
57. Roth, *Aug. Ref.* I, 270-271. He names Jorigen Wieland, his brother-in-law, and Matheus Langenmantel, son of Hansen Langenmantel, famous Augsburg mayor.
58. Roth, "Zur Lebens," 42-44.
59. Christian Hege and Harold S. Bender, "Martyrs' Synod," *The Mennonite Encyclopedia*, III, 530-531.
60. *Ibid.*, 530.
61. Littell, *op. cit.*, 122.
62. Kiwiet, "The Life of Hans Denck," 254-256, *passim.*
63. Friedrich Hermann Schubert, "Die Reformation in Augsburg," *Augusta 955-1955* (Augsburg: Hermann Rinn, 1955), 290; Roth, *Aug. Ref.* I, 231, cites Sender in giving the number as "achthundert Seelen."
64. Kiwiet, *op. cit.*, 254-256.

65. Roth, *Aug. Ref.* I, 234, and Meyer, 213, say it was Aug. 25.
66. The ministers received 4 guilders per sermon; Conrad Peutinger was paid 100 guilders for conducting the examinations. Hege, "Augsburg," 184.
67. Roth, *Aug. Ref.* I, 231-237, *passim.*
68. *Ibid.,* 237-239, *passim.*
69. Roth, "Der Höhepunkt," 3.
70. Schubert, *op. cit.,* 291.
71. "At Easter 1528, when the congregation was at its largest." "The Life of Hans Denck," 255.
72. Roth, "Der Höhepunkt," 8.
73. Meyer, 251.
74. Roth, *Aug. Ref.* I, 247-248, *passim.*
75. *Ibid.,* 256; Hege, "Augsburg," 185.
76. Christian Hege, "Dorfbrunner, Leonhard," *The Mennonite Encyclopedia*, II, 93, says he started his work in Sept., but in his "Augsburg," I, 184, Hege has him returning Nov. 10, 1527. Roth, *Aug. Ref.* I, 244, uses the Nov. date.
77. Roth, "Der Höhepunkt," 7-8; Christian Hege, "Nespitzer (Nospitzer), Georg," *The Mennonite Encyclopedia*, III (Scottdale, 1957), 824.
78. Roth, *Aug. Ref.* I, 245-247, *passim.*
79. *Ibid.,* 247-250, *passim.*
80. Roth, "Der Höhepunkt," 5.
81. Roth, *Aug. Ref.* I, 251, specifically says that any talk of twelve or more involves those executed by imperial order in 1530 and by other authorities in Augsburg's vicinity.
82. Roth, "Der Höhepunkt," 11.
83. Hege, "Augsburg," 185.
84. Littell, *op. cit.,* 24, also note 119, 172 citing John C. Wenger *et al.*
85. H. W. Bender, "Marpeck (Marbeck), Pilgram," *The Mennonite Encyclopedia*, III, 492.
86. Littell, *op. cit.,* 24.
87. *Ibidem.*
88. Bender, 500. Henry Hege, "Augsburg," *The Mennonite Encyclopedia*, I, 185, suggests some possible reasons for this patience: (1) The *Rat* may have relaxed its proscription of the Anabaptists; (2) Marpeck may have refrained from preaching and promoting within the city; (3) Marpeck's services as an engineer may have been so valuable that the authorities winked at his activities.
89. Wenger, *op. cit.,* 173, 177.
90. Littell, *op. cit.,* 137.

BERNHARD ROTHMANN'S VIEWS ON
THE EARLY CHURCH (Wray)

1. Cf. *Canons and Decrees of the Council of Trent, 23rd Session, July 15, 1563*, in P. Schaff, *Creeds of Christendom*, II (New York: Harper and Brothers, 1919), 186ff.
2. Cf. Franklin H. Littell, *The Anabaptist View of the Church*, 2nd ed. (Boston: Beacon Press, 1958); Frank J. Wray, "The Anabaptist Doctrine of the Restitution of the Church," *Mennonite Quarterly Review*, XXVIII, no. 3, July 1954, 186ff. and "The 'Vermanung' of 1542 and Rothmann's 'Bekentnisse,'" *Archiv für Reformationsgeschichte*, 1956, Jahrg. 47, Heft 2, 248f.
3. Heinrich Detmer and Robert Krumbholtz, eds., *Zwei Schriften des Münsterischen Wiedertäufers Bernhard Rothmann* (Dortmund: Fr. Wilhelm Ruhfus, 1904), 1-84.
4. *Ibid.,* 81.
5. *Ibid.,* 80-81.
6. *Ibid.,* 10-11, 17, 59.
7. *Ibid.,* 24, 26-27, 50, 70-72.
8. *Ibid.,* 28.
9. *Ibid.,* 4.
10. *Ibid.,* 17.

11. *Ibid.*, 21-27, 33.
12. *Ibid.*, 36.
13. *Ibid.*, 52.
14. *Ibid.*, 5, 30.
15. *Ibid.*, 59.
16. *Ibid.*, 62.
17. *Chronica, Zeytbuch und Geschychtbibel* (Strassburg: Balthassar Beck, 1531), fol. 495.
18. Detmer and Krumbholtz, *op. cit.*, 70-72.
19. *Ibid.*, 13-14.
20. *Ibid.*, 51-52.
21. *Ibid.*, 39.
22. *Ibid.*, 28-29.
23. *Ibid.*, 72.
24. *Ibid.*, 30.
25. *Ibid.*, 61.
26. *Ibid.*, 51.
27. *Ibid.*, 72.
28. *Ibid.*, 43-44.
29. Andreas Knaake, ed., *Flugschriften aus der Reformationszeit,* VII (Neudrucke deutscher Litteraturwerke des XVI und XVII Jahrhunderts, no. 77 u. 78) (Halle, 1888).
30. *Ibid.*, 49.
31. "The Rise and Fall of the Anabaptists of Münster," *Mennonite Quarterly Review,* IX, no. 3, July 1935, 132-133.
32. Knaake, *op. cit.*, 41.
33. *Ibidem.*
34. *Ibid.*, 44.
35. *Ibid.*, 70-71.
36. *Ibid.*, 74-75.
37. *Ibid.*, 12-13.
38. *Ibid.*, 13.
39. Detmer and Krumbholtz, *op. cit.*, 2, 41.
40. Knaake, *op. cit.*, 14.
41. *Ibid.*, 17.
42. *Ibid.*, 6-11.
43. *Ibid.*, 26, 92, 100.
44. *Ibid.*, 18, 95-96.
45. *Ibid.*, 109-110.
46. *Ibid.*, 15, 92.
47. *Ibid.*, 9, 21-25.
48. *Ibid.*, 86-87.
49. *Ibid.*, 84.
50. K. W. Bouterwek, ed., in *Zeitschrift des Bergischen Geschichtsvereins,* I (Bonn, 1863), 345-359.
51. *Ibid.*, 349.
52. *Ibid.*, 347-348.
53. *Ibid.*, 351-352.
54. *Ibid.*, 347.
55. *Ibid.*, 359.
56. *Ibid.*, 347.
57. K. W. H. Hochhuth, ed., *Bernhard Rothmanns Schriften,* I (Gotha, 1857).
58. *Ibid.*, 7, 16.
59. *Ibid.*, 47-48.
60. *Ibid.*, 49.
61. Probably a reference to Luke 22:36.
62. Hochhuth, *op. cit.*, 73-74.
63. *Ibid.*, 50, 57.
64. *Ibid.*, 10.
65. *Ibid.*, 76.
66. *Ibid.*, 10.
67. *Ibid.*, 43.

68. Detmer and Krumbholtz, *op. cit.*, 86-129.
69. *Ibid.*, 110.

FECUND PROBLEMS OF ESCHATOLOGICAL HOPE, ELECTION PROOF, AND SOCIAL REVOLT IN THOMAS MÜNTZER (Zuck)

1. Heinrich Boehmer, in "Thomas Müntzer und das jüngste Deutschland" in *Gesammelte Aufsätze* (Gotha: F. A. Perthes A.G., 1927), 221.
2. Robert Friedmann, in "Thomas Müntzer's Relation to Anabaptism," in *Mennonite Quarterly Review*, XXXI, no. 2, Apr. 1957, 85, notes that Müntzer remained to the end of his life a priest-preacher both in Allstedt and in Muhlhausen city churches, and hence never actually opposed an institution of that kind. Another article in this school is by Harold Bender, "The Zwickau Prophets, Thomas Müntzer, and the Anabaptists," in *Theologische Zeitschrift*, VIII, July-Aug. 1952, 262, and *Mennonite Quarterly Review*, XXVII, no. 1, Jan. 1953, 3.
3. The Soviet historian M. M. Smirin has had his Marxist interpretation of Müntzer, first published in Moscow, translated and published in East Germany as *Die Volksreformation des Thomas Münzer und der grosse Bauernkrieg* (Berlin: Dietz Verlag, 1956). Smirin based his work largely on Frederick Engels' work of 1850, translated as *The Peasant War in Germany* (Moscow: Foreign Languages Publishing House, 1956). A similar work is by Alfred Meusel, *Thomas Müntzer und seine Zeit mit einer Auswahl der Dokumente des grossen deutschen Bauernkrieges* (Berlin: Aufbau-Verlag, 1952), while Smirin's Russian colleague, O. G. Tschaikowskaja, denies the revolutionary character of the peasant movement, in "Vaprosy istorii," 12/1956, 129-143. Another Russian, A. D. Epstejn, attempts to mediate between Smirin and Tschaikowskaja by calling the Peasants' War in Germany the "first bourgeois revolution," in "Vaprosy istorii," 8/1957, 118-142. See references to this discussion in Gerhard Zschaebitz, *Zur mitteldeutschen Wiedertäuferbewegung nach dem grossen Bauernkrieg* (Berlin: Rütten & Loening, 1958), 166, a well-balanced East German work.
4. Müntzer's first biography, published at Hagenau in 1526, was by a bitter opponent (Melanchthon?) and not altogether reliable: "Historie Thomae Muentzers, des Anfengers der Doeringischen Uffruhr, sehr nutzlich zu lesen," reprinted in Otto Brandt, *Thomas Müntzer. Sein Leben und seine Schriften* (Jena: Eugen Diedrichs Verlag, 1933), 38-50. J. R. Seidemann published the first of the modern lives of Müntzer: *Thomas Muenzer* (Dresden: Arnoldsche Buchh., 1842).
5. Seidemann, 4-5.
6. Karl Holl, "Luther und die Schwärmer," in *Gesammelte Aufsätze zur Kirchengeschichte* (Tübingen: J. C. B. Mohr, 1923), I, 420-467. For an interpretation of Müntzer as an enthusiast, consult K. G. Steck, *Luther und die Schwärmer* (Zurich: Evangelischer Verlag-Zollikon, 1955). A more recent consideration of Müntzer's pedigree is "Luther and Thomas Müntzer," by E. Gordon Rupp, in *Luther Today*, by R. H. Bainton, W. A. Quanbeck, E. G. Rupp (Decorah, Iowa: Luther College Press, 1957), 129-146. Annemarie Lohmann, of Boehmer's school, published a fine genetic study of Müntzer's development, *Zur geistigen Entwicklung Thomas Müntzer's* (Leipzig: B. G. Teubner, 1932). Other relevant works are by H. Kamnitzer, *Zur Vorgeschichte des deutschen Bauernkrieges* (Berlin: Rütten & Loening, 1953), K. Kupisch, *Feinde Luthers* (Berlin: Lettner-Verlag, 1951), and H. Gerdes, "Der Weg des Glaubens bei Müntzer und Luther," in *Mitteilungen der Luther Gesellschaft* (Berlin: Lutherisches Verlagshaus, 1955).
7. Roland H. Bainton, *The Reformation of the Sixteenth Century* (Boston: The Beacon Press, 1952), 66-67.
8. Martin Luther, "Letter to the Princes of Saxony Concerning the Rebellious Spirit," in *Luther's Works* (Philadelphia: Muhlenberg Press, 1958), XL, 52.
9. Marcus Wagner, *Einfeltigen Bericht Wie durch Nicolaum Storcken die Auffruhr in Thuringen angefangen sey worden* (Erfurt, 1597), 23a. See references to Storch

in Paul Wappler, "Thomas Münzer in Zwickau und die Zwickauer Propheten" (*Wissenschaftliche Beilage zu dem Jahresberichte des Realgymnasiums mit Realschule zu Zwickau,* Zwickau, 1908), 30.

10. See Lohmann, 16. Consult also E. Sommer, *Die Sendung Thomas Münzers, Taboritentum und Bauernkrieg in Deutschland* (Berlin: Aufbau Verlag, 1948).

11. The four versions are included in Heinrich Boehmer and Paul Kirn, *Thomas Müntzers Briefwechsel* (Leipzig: B. G. Teubner, 1931).

12. Müntzer's liturgical works include: *Deutsch Kirchenamt* (Allstedt, 1523), and *Deutsch evangelisch Messe* (Allstedt, 1524). See Oskar J. Mehl's summary, "Thomas Müntzer als Liturgiker," in *Theologische Literaturzeitung,* Feb. 1951, 76, and, in more detail, Mehl, *Thomas Müntzers Deutsche Messen und Kirchenämter,* 1939. Also, R. Herrmann, *Thomas Müntzers 'Deutsch-evangelische Messe'* (Allstedt, 1524), verglichen mit Luthers drei liturgischen Schriften 1523-1526 (*Zeitschrift des Vereins für Kirchengeschichte in der Provinz Sachsen, 1912,* Bd. 9, 57ff.), K. Schulz, "Thomas Muentzers liturgische Bestrebungen," in *Zeitschrift für Kirchengeschichte* (Gotha: Druck von F. A. Perthes, 1928), and E. Jammers, "Thomas Müntzers deutsche evangelische Messen," in *Archiv für Reformationsgeschichte,* 1934, vol. 31 (ARG).

13. "Sermon Before the Princes," in George H. Williams, ed., *Spiritual and Anabaptist Writers* (Philadelphia: The Westminster Press, 1957), 51.

14. *Ibid.,* 56.

15. *Ibid.,* 58.

16. *Ibid.,* 57.

17. *Ibid.,* 58.

18. *Protestation odder Empiettung* (Allstedt, 1524). *Ausgedrückte Entblössung des Falschen Glaubens, der ungetreuen Welt durchs Gezeugnis des Evangelions Lucae vorgetragen, der elenden erbaemlichen Christenheit zur Innerung ihres Irrsals* (Muhlhausen, 1524). (Open Denial of the False Belief of the Godless World on the Testimony of the Gospel of Luke, Presented to Miserable and Pitiful Christendom in Memory of its Error). Müntzer's other works include: *Gezeugnis des ersten Capitels des Evangelions Lucae,* 1524, *Vom Gedichteten Glauben* (Allstedt, 1524) and his reply to Luther's letter to the princes of Saxony, *Hochverursachte Schutzrede und Antwort wider das geistlose, sanftlebende Fleisch zu Wittenberg, welches mit verkehrter Weise durch den Diebstahl der Heiligen Schrift die erbaermliche Christenheit also ganz jaemmerlichen besudelt hat* (Nürnberg, 1524). (A Well-Grounded Defense and Reply to the Godless, Easy-living Flesh of Wittenberg, which Has Pitifully Sullied Unhappy Christianity through Shameless Distortions of the Holy Scripture.)

19. Boehmer and Kirn, 48.

20. *Ibid.,* 74. A significant recent interpretation of Müntzer's reform as theocentric rather than social is by Walter Elliger, *Thomas Müntzer* (Berlin: Wichern Verlag, 1960).

21. *Ibid.,* 163 (from Müntzer's Confession of May 16, 1525). See the discussion in Carl Hinrichs, *Luther und Müntzer, Ihre Auseinandersetzung über Obrigkeit und Widerstandsrecht* (Berlin: Walter De Gruyter & Co., 1952), 11.

22. C. D. Foerstemann, *Zur Geschichte des Bauernkriegs,* Neue Mitteilungen aus dem Gebiet historische-antiquarischer Forschungen, 1869, XII, 215.

23. Boehmer and Kirn, 162.

24. G. Mentz, *Johann Friedrich der Grossmütige,* I, 36, quoted by Hinrichs, 30. See J. Rogge, *Der Beitrag des Predigers Strauss zur frühen Reformationsgeschichte* (Berlin: Evangelische Verlagsanstalt, 1957).

25. Boehmer and Kirn, 50.

26. Brandt, 161, 162.

27. Foerstemann, 181.

28. Brandt, 164. For Muentzer's minimum influence on Hut see Jan J. Kiwiet, *Pilgram Marbeck* (Kassel: J. G. Oncken Verlag, 1957), 43, and Herbert Klassen, "The Life and Teachings of Hans Hut," *Mennonite Quarterly Review,* XXXIII, nos. 3 & 4, July-Oct. 1959, 172, 267-280. For Müntzer's maximum influence on Hut see Grete Mecenseffy, "Die Herkunft des oberösterreichischen Täufertums," in *Archiv für Reformationsgeschichte,* 1956, vol. 47, 252-258. Walter Fellmann cites twenty-four passages from Müntzer in the writings of the other leader of

South German Anabaptism, Hans Denck, thus claiming Müntzer's influence on the literary beginnings of Anabaptism. In *Hans Denck Schriften. 2. Teil* (Gütersloh: C. Bertelsmann Verlag, 1956), 6.

29. For the history of the Peasants' War, consult Günther Franz, *Der deutsche Bauernkrieg* (München: R. Oldenburg, 1943). The letters of Conrad Grebel and his friends in Zurich to Müntzer appear in Williams, *op. cit.*, 73-85.

30. M. Steinmetz, "Zur Entstehung der Müntzer-Legende" *(Beiträge zum neuen Geschichtsbild. Alfred Meusel zum 60. Geburtstag,* 1956).

31. Rupp, *op. cit.*, 145.